NEW PERSPECTIVES ON DEVIANCE

The Construction of Deviance in Everyday Life

Edited by Lori G. Beaman
University of Lethbridge

Prentice Hall Allyn and Bacon Canada
Scarborough, Ontario

Canadian Cataloguing in Publication Data

Main entry under title:

New perspectives on deviance : the construction of deviance in everyday life

Includes index.
ISBN 0-13-083161-1

1. Deviant behavior. I. Beaman, Lori G. (Lori Gail), 1963– .

HM291.P476 2000   302.5'42   C99-930112-8

Prentice-Hall, Inc., Upper Saddle River, New Jersey
Prentice-Hall International (UK) Limited, London
Prentice-Hall of Australia, Pty. Limited, Sydney
Prentice-Hall Hispanoamericana, S.A., Mexico City
Prentice-Hall of India Private Limited, New Delhi
Prentice-Hall of Japan, Inc., Tokyo
Simon & Schuster Southeast Asia Private Limited, Singapore
Editora Prentice-Hall do Brasil, Ltda., Rio de Janeiro

ISBN 0-13-083161-1

Vice President, Editorial Director: Laura Pearson
Acquisitions Editor: Nicole Lukach
Marketing Manager: Christine Cozens
Developmental Editor: Lisa Phillips
Production Editor: Andrew Winton
Copy Editor: Mary de Souza
Production Coordinator: Peggy Brown
Art Director: Mary Opper
Cover Design: David Cheung
Cover Image: Photodisc
Page Layout: Carol Magee

1 2 3 4 5   04 03 02 01 00

Printed and bound in Canada.

Visit the Prentice Hall Canada web site! Send us your comments, browse our catalogues, and more at
www.phcanada.com. Or reach us through e-mail at **phabinfo_pubcanada@prenhall.com.**

Contents

Preface

This edited collection focuses on the construction of notions of deviance in everyday life. The book is concerned both with images of what constitutes the "normal," as well as how deviations from norms are constructed as deviant behaviour. The first section considers topics which are traditionally found in deviance text books: prostitution, drug abuse, alcoholism and mental illness. In the second section of the book, and in contrast to more traditional approaches to the study of deviance, assumptions about what constitutes "normal" families, bodies, and cultural practices are highlighted. Discussions of traditional theories are included to provide students with a well-rounded overview of theoretical approaches to deviance. However, the guiding theoretical framework of the book is a focus on the social construction of deviance, both at the macro and micro levels.

The inspiration for this book arose out of the editor's frustration in choosing a book for a deviance course. Most deviance readers and texts focus on very narrow conceptualizations of what constitutes deviant behaviour. In particular, there is an over-representation of the "nuts, sluts, and perverts" type of approach to deviance, with little attention paid to "everyday" constructions of deviance related to poverty, body image, and family values.

In addition, there seems to be a trend toward collapsing criminal behaviour and deviant behaviour in recent books, which results in an inaccurate and narrow conceptualization of deviant behaviour as criminal behaviour. While the book includes discussions of some criminal behaviours, it focuses on non-criminal, everyday aspects of the construction of deviance, and on the implications of those constructions for those who live outside of the "normal."

Key features include:

- Canadian authorship and Canadian focus
- a critical approach to the study of deviance and social control
- a review of traditional theories of deviance
- exploration of recent theoretical developments such as feminism and postmodernism
- examples of the practical application of theories
- a focus on the social construction of deviance in everyday life
- inclusion of issues such as poverty and the media

Although primarily intended for a mid- to upper-level course in deviance or social control, this book is also well-suited for courses that examine the practical application of critical theories as well as courses that explore issues in social inequality.

ACKNOWLEDGMENTS

Edited collections are notoriously difficult to compile, as one works with multiple authors, multiple perspectives, and tight deadlines. I would like to thank each of the contributors for her/his quality work, patience, and willingness to graciously accept and follow suggestions for change. Lisa Phillips at Prentice Hall is also owed a special thank you for her helpful comments and guidance. My research assistant on this project, Kristine A. Peace, was invaluable. Her organizational talents and her keen eye made my work much easier. Thank you also to the following reviewers: Kelly Hannah-Moffat, Brock University; Leslie Miller, University of Calgary; Bill Stuebing, Red Deer College; and Edyta Kuey, Grant MacEwan Community College. Finally, thanks to Nancy Carpenter for her listening ear.

L.G.B.

Introduction

It is May 23, 1657 and Mary is about to be burned alive. The birthmark discovered on her arm has been deemed by church officials to be the mark of the devil. She denies the accusation while being bound to a stake in the village square. She pleads with the people who were her neighbours and, she thought, her friends. She feels the searing pain of flames as they begin to devour her body. She looks through the smoke, smelling the burning of her own flesh, at the host of villagers watching. As a single woman who was present at a stillbirth three weeks ago, she has no hope of persuading the crowd that she is not a witch.

James and Brian briefly hold hands on their way home from a movie in their suburban Toronto neighbourhood. Suddenly they are surrounded by a group of six young men who start taunting them with obscenities and name calling. They are forced to the ground where they are kicked in the head and the genitals. Brian survives the attack, James lies in a coma for three weeks and he dies from brain injuries. It is January 12, 1999, and as a gay couple they have suffered the result of living in a homophobic society—a society which defines people as abnormal based on their sexual orientation.

In this book we are primarily concerned with how deviance, or behaviour which is seen to stray from the "norm," is constructed as such. How was it that Mary's behaviour came to be designated as deviant? What was the process by which she was labelled a witch, and what were the social factors that created the situation in which people, mostly women, were designated as deviant and punished as witches? Why does sexual orientation prompt such horrible informal social punishments, and what are the formal social structures which act to facilitate gay bashing? How do definitions of deviance and social constructions of the normal differ from culture to culture? What are the cultural boundaries of the social construction of definitions of deviance?

What does it mean to talk about the social construction of deviance? In this book we are combining macro and micro approaches, which means that we are looking at both the structural factors which contribute to the shaping of definitions of norm violation, as well as the process by which individuals or groups are actually constructed as deviant. So, for example, in the case of poverty, we will explore the social factors that contribute to the maintenance of a class of impoverished people, as well as to their experiences of stigmatization based on their lack of economic well-being. Such a social constructionist view includes a number of assumptions, including the most basic premise that there is no underlying agreement or consensus in society about what constitutes normal behaviour. No behaviour is inherently deviant; rather, deviance must be situated in its social and historical context. As we have already seen with the example of Mary in the opening paragraphs, definitions of deviance vary across time. In other words, what in one time period constitutes a violation of a social norm will not necessarily constitute deviance in another period in history. What is constructed as deviance also shifts between social groups. For example, the Amish in

Pennsylvania do not drive cars, and consider the use of them by their group members to be a violation of a norm which is subject to serious sanctions. What gets identified as deviant behaviour, and the process by which it is sanctioned or socially controlled shifts in multiple ways. We no longer burn or drown witches, but people who belong to the wiccan faith are viewed by some as deviant. While we try to socially control gay bashing through criminal sanctions, gays and lesbians do not feel free to express their sexuality in the same way that heterosexual couples do.

Definitions of deviance also vary depending on one's gender. Social expectations for men and women are different no matter how much we might like to believe we are moving toward equality. Men who cry in public are still seen as deviant, women are viewed as simply being women. Women who are assertive are viewed as bitches, men are seen as fulfilling their role. In using a social constructionist approach we explore the ways in which social structure, such as legal institutions, reify gender role expectations and norms. We also explore how women and men are sanctioned when they deviate from these norms. Another factor in norm construction is age—norms vary depending on a person's age. What is deemed as appropriate and "normal" for one age category may not be classified as such for another. A temper tantrum at age three is viewed differently than a temper tantrum at age twenty-eight.

Needless to say, these factors which cause definitions of deviance to shift do not exist in neat packages. There is often an intersection of a number of factors which link to the naming of a behaviour as deviant. Mary was labelled a witch because of her gender and the social context in which she was situated. Categories of deviance are fluid, and it is this shifting nature which makes the study of deviance particularly challenging. The dynamic process by which these boundaries change is linked to the ways in which various groups exercise power, another key site of exploration for social constructionists.

However, power in this context is not simply the exercise of power by one group over another, but the process through which power is negotiated. Power relations shift and are as transitory as definitions of deviance. They may differ from one site to the next—for example, while James and Brian are brutally attacked on the streets, in the courts they may be successful in having their sexual orientation recognized as a protected basis for equality under the Charter of Rights and Freedoms. To talk about power in terms of a simple dichotomy of powerful/powerless is not always a helpful way to explore power dynamics and relations. The study of deviance from this perspective is a complicated undertaking.

A recent trend in the study of deviance is to collapse the study of crime and the study of deviance. While we do discuss criminal behaviour and criminal sanctions in this book, it is important to realize that deviance and crime are not identical. Deviance can range from eating spaghetti with your fingers to killing another human being. Obviously, the Criminal Code does not sanction the former behaviour, but does punish the latter in many instances (an exception is killing in the context of war). We are examining the ways in which norms, or rules of conduct, are created. Deconstructing how norms are established and examining the sanctions they attract is an important exercise in the process of critically examining why some behaviour is deemed to be deviant. In the following chapters, the ways in which boundaries of the normal are established and maintained are explored through a variety of issues. In the first section of the book, we take issues which have traditionally been the focus of the study of deviant behaviour and re-examine them from a social constructionist point of view. Chapter one sets out both traditional and new theoretical directions in the study of deviance. From there, we look at prostitution, addictions, mental illness, and sexual orientation, each representing an area which has preoccupied social scientists who study deviant behaviour. However, these chapters challenge us to use new theoretical perspectives where the old ones have failed to offer a comprehensive or satisfactory explanation of how and why certain behaviours are seen to be abnormal or deviant.

In chapter three, Nick Larsen examines prostitution, which is an area that has been a traditional focus of studies of deviance. Larsen presents the dichotomous views of prostitution as a legitimate form of sexual diversity and prostitution as immoral behaviour. He looks at how the voice of the prostitute has been excluded from debates over the social control of selling sex. He also explores the ways in which the activities of prostitutes have been constructed as deviant. In his analysis, Larsen also presents the positions of feminist groups and prostitutes'-rights activists. Since social controls over prostitution have been relatively ineffective, Larsen proposes to decriminalize prostitution, an approach which also serves to lessen the stigma attached to earning a living by selling one's body for sexual pleasure.

In their chapter on addictions, Jennifer Butters and Patricia Erickson look at how moral, medical, and criminal models of deviance have influenced our perception of "the drug user." By dealing with addiction in the context of deviant behaviour, the authors highlight the means by which the definition of drugs and what is defined as acceptable for use has changed. They argue that the stigmas and negative connotations associated with drug use (including alcohol and tobacco) serve to socially construct both "the addict" and "the addict as deviant." This chapter offers a challenge to the medical model of substance use which constructs the addict/deviant as someone to be cured. The authors propose the harm-reduction model as an effective method for dealing with "addicts," reframing the moral, medical and legal biases that these individuals face.

Similarly, the medical model dominates the social construction of mental illness. In "The Criminalization of Mental Illness," Danielle Laberge discusses the process by which social acts are transformed into designations of mental illness and sometimes criminal behaviour. She argues that we categorize situations and people according to what is "normal and acceptable," and that anything outside of this boundary is open to being constructed as deviant, often as mental illness. Laberge provides us with an examination of the differing characteristics of men's and women's deviance and the corresponding social controls which regulate mental illness.

Sandra Kirby grapples with a little-explored issue: the needs of older gays and lesbians. This chapter highlights the life-long impact of being a member of a marginalized group. It also illustrates the frustrations in translating the legal protection of equality based on sexual orientation into practice. Conflicting and competing interests in society means that law does not have the ability to eliminate socially constructed categories of deviance. Another contribution of this chapter is its illumination of the voices of gays and lesbians as they explain the impact of negative labelling.

The second section of the book introduces some new issues for consideration: the impact of the media on the social construction of deviance, poverty as deviance, the deviant family, and gender and deviance. William Ramp's discussion of the role of the media in the social construction of deviance is a critical piece of any analysis of the process by which some behaviours come to be defined as deviant. Ramp argues that the use of the "crime story" to dramatize deviance has influenced the way we see, read, talk, and think about deviance. By using both current and historical examples, Ramp identifies the influence of the media in reinforcing notions of what is good/normal versus what is bad/deviant.

In "The Social Construction of Welfare Recipients as 'Lazy'," Jason Doherty draws on theoretical insights on the social construction of knowledge to examine the ways in which poverty is constructed as deviance in our society. Doherty argues that it is important to use a combination of macro and micro perspectives in order to gain an understanding of poverty in Canadian society. This chapter highlights the creation of an ideology around poverty which works to oppress the poor and to ensure that the social safety net provides only minimal support. Despite the nearly one in five people who live in poverty in Canada, being poor is constructed as being abnormal.

In her chapter, Lori Beaman argues that ideal images of women work to minimize support payment awards from courts when women deviate from those ideals. The difficulty is not only the ideals, but their shifting nature, as women are alternatively supposed to be good mothers and "liberated" women. Each of these norms or standards for women carry with them rigid standards about who fits and who doesn't. Most women can meet neither ideal, and so the courts have used women's deviance from the norm as a way to deny them economic stability on marriage breakdown.

In Chapter 7, Ted Schrecker gives us some specific examples of the ways in which poverty is defined as deviant and the poor are socially controlled through criminalization. Schrecker recognizes the unique vulnerability of those who live in poverty and highlights some of the state strategies that exacerbate their poverty. He called to our attention the "class-biased character of the institutions of criminal justice" (123) and the limitations of existing research that bind our ability to map the nuances of these biases. Using the examples of the "war on drugs," Schrecker argues that the social construction of behaviours as deviant (and in this instance criminal) expands the state's opportunities for surveillance of the poor.

Three chapters deal with the social construction of the normal family and explore some of the ways in which people deviate from the norm. Each of these chapters deconstructs our notions of the normal and examines the sanctions against people who do not conform. In "The Good Mother," Sandra Wachholz discusses similar issues specifically as they relate to mothering. She focuses on the ways in which mothering becomes constructed as heterosexual mothering, thus leaving lesbians in a double deviance bind. They are often constructed as deviant based on their sexual orientation apart from mothering, and when they are mothers they are not seen to fit into the category of the "normal" mother. Being a mother and being a lesbian are constructed as choices which cannot be embodied in the same person, an idea which Wachholz challenges. She also points out that motherhood is expected to occur within the context of the heterosexual family unit which itself exists in a patriarchal society. Wachholz examines both structural factors as well as the experiences of individual women to complete her analysis of the social construction of the good mother.

Rebecca Johnson provides us with a deconstruction of typical portrayals of the normal family. She uses the movie *Leaving Normal*, as well as cases from the Supreme Court of Canada, to highlight the narrow ways in which family has been constructed, in contrast to the variety of forms families take in our society. For those who are designated to be "abnormal," the result can be alienation, exclusion, and practical consequences such as economic disadvantages. Johnson explores the ways in which laws works to maintain symbolic boundaries of the "normal" in our society.

Nob Doran combines a discussion of labelling theory and Foucauldian postmodernism in his discussion of the modern approach to the policing of families and the development of the category "delinquent." Doran explores the silencing of the voices of youth even in sociological research which focuses on them. He compares this to the ways in which women's voices have been largely absent from "scientific" research.

A central theme in the exploration of the "normal" woman is women's bodies, and social norms about how women should look, behave sexually, and the roles they should take. Gayle MacDonald focuses on the ways in which women's sexuality is constructed as deviant.

The standard, argues MacDonald, is set by men, and constructs women as the "other." Women are either conformists, non-conformists, or they transcend boundaries completely. MacDonald explores the ways in which women are sanctioned and socially controlled within and between these categories. The methods used to create boundaries and construct categories of sexuality are the central focus of MacDonald's work. She demonstrates the narrow limits placed on women in terms of sexual expectations.

In her chapter "The Body Beautiful: Adolescent Girls and Images of Beauty," Beverly Matthews argues that women are under a great deal of pressure to conform to the standard of a "beautiful body." She points out how women's choices in relation to eating and appearance are constrained by socially created ideals. Matthews uses a tri-level model of the construction of gender identity to discuss appearance in terms of individual role orientations, and micro and macro structures. She also examines the ways in which bodies outside of the "norm" are constructed as deviant. Research presented in this chapter looks at the perceptions of adolescent girls about status and appearance, providing us with valuable insight into the world of adolescent girls and how exclusion for not "looking right" impacts their lives.

Jo-Anne Fiske's postmodern analysis of two historical female figures—the Roman Catholic nun and the Aboriginal school student—provides insight into the importance of considering the intersection of multiple identities in the construction of "the deviant." Her chapter portrays the female body, both the virgin nun and the "wild" Aboriginal girl, as a site upon which power, control, and domination are exercised for the purpose of shaping them into ideals of the "normal." Fiske documents the impact of the historical treatment of Aboriginal peoples as deviants and illuminates the peculiarity of the designation of the nun as normal and the Aboriginal girl as deviant.

The second section of the book also explores the "abnormal" male. Leonard Green's discussion of Attention Deficit Hyperactivity Disorder is both a timely and important contribution to our understanding of the ways in which norms around male behaviour are created and maintained. The use of medical intervention as a sanction against "abnormal" behaviour is nothing new, but the overwhelming use of ADHD as a diagnostic category warrants a closer examination of the process by which young men come to be defined as deviant, or in this case "sick." Green demonstrates the rather arbitrary nature of the diagnostic process and bluntly challenges us to consider the likelihood that ADHD is a from of social control masquerading as a disorder.

The deviant male is examined from another perspective in Deborah Harrison's chapter, "Violence in the Military Community." She reveals the ways in which the military defines the normal man and the normal woman. In her research, Harrison uses a unique feminist methodology which highlights the importance of women's voices and the standpoint of the military wife. The culture of violence within the military means that definitions of the normal are constructed in unique ways. Harrison gives us a rare glimpse into the social construction of the normal military wife.

Each of the chapters in this book contributes to our overall understanding of what it means to talk about deviance as being socially constructed. Definitions of deviance vary across time, gender, age, and social group. The ways in which deviants are socially controlled also varies from criminal sanctions to economic control. People who are constructed as "the other" in our society suffer for their positions in so-called marginal categories. However, the discussions in this book should demonstrate that each of us, whether because of gender, sexual orientation, or socio-economic status, has the potential to be constructed as deviant. It is through this process of deconstruction that we can begin to challenge the borders between normal and deviant.

I

OLD THEORIES, NEW DIRECTIONS

THEORETICAL APPROACHES TO THE STUDY OF DEVIANCE

Kristine A. Peace

Lori G. Beaman

Krista Sneddon

INTRODUCTION

In this book we are focusing on what might be considered to be an amalgam of critical theories that make up what we are calling a social constructionist approach. However, it is also important to be aware of the major theoretical perspectives that have guided the study of deviance in sociology. Theories shape what we define as deviant behaviour, who we study, and how we study them. Theories also guide public policy; for example, labelling theory cautions us about the stigma of labelling someone deviant. We see the practical application of labelling theory in the Young Offenders Act, which protects the identity of youth who violate the Criminal Code. Theories are also reflected in popular discourse — how many times did your parents caution you about hanging out with the wrong crowd? Edwin Sutherland and Donald Cressey recognized the possible influence peers and significant others could have in their theory of differential association. Theories are lenses which both illuminate some aspects of deviant behaviour, and obscure others. They should be approached critically, and with an appreciation of both their strengths and weaknesses.

As with any area of sociology, the study of deviance has been approached by a number of theoretical perspectives, which can be roughly divided into two "camps" — consensus theories and conflict theories. Consensus theories are based on the premise that there is a shared understanding in society about values, norms, what constitutes violations of norms, and how violations should be punished or controlled. Conflict theories are based on the premise that there is no underlying agreement about what constitutes norms or violations of norms, and that deviance is socially constructed based on the interests of those who hold or exercise power in society.

The study of deviance has not only centred around these theories, but it has also focused on a relatively narrow range of subjects: prostitution, mental illness, alcohol and drug abuse, and behaviours related to sex and sexuality have preoccupied social scientists who study deviance. The first section of this book focuses on these traditional areas of study, but with a social constructionist twist.

The following brief overview is intended to be a beginning introduction to a number of theories of deviance. There are many variations of these perspectives which have been used to explain deviant behaviour. It is not our intention to give a comprehensive review of those; rather the following sections will outline the basic features of these theories. Use them as lenses, asking yourself how each one explains any behaviour identified as "abnormal."

HISTORICAL ROOTS

The demonic perspective is perhaps the oldest explanation for deviant behaviour. Its basic tenet is that those who stray from social norms are seen as possessed, or at least tempted, by evil spirits. This explanation was at its peak during the Middle Ages. Hundreds of thousands of women (and thousands of men) were accused of being witches and killed for their alleged deviance. Although we may laugh when we think about explaining deviant behaviour with "the devil made me do it," and it certainly does not have credibility as a sociological theory these days, it has been, and in some measure continues to be, an explanation to which we sometimes turn when there seems to be no other workable explanation. Religious groups still turn to demonic explanations for deviant behaviour, believing that a commitment to God will drive evil away. We might even point to some modern-day treatments of behaviours defined as deviant, such as alcoholism, as being partially rooted in demonic explanations of deviance. The elimination of the deviant behaviour, such as drinking, is seen to rest in the hands of a higher power.

With the dawn of the Enlightenment came a new approach to thinking about human behaviour, which has come to be known as the classical approach or theory. No longer were human beings controlled by supernatural forces; in this new era humans were seen as rational beings who make decisions based on a ratio of pleasure and pain. The shift to this model also brought a shift from the secret trials and confessions of the demonic period towards a move to what we today call due process, which guarantees a fair and public trial. Two of the best known proponents of the classical school are Jeremy Bentham and Cesare Beccaria, both born in the 1700s. While the classical theory does have some application to deviance, it emerged primarily in the context of thinking about crime. Out of this school of thought came the notion that the punishment should fit the crime, and that this punishment should deter repeat offences. This approach was premised on the idea that all offenders should be treated equally, and therefore circumstances should not be taken into account, nor should individual personalities. A person who took bread for her starving children was to be treated in the same way as a person who made his living from stealing.

The harshness of the classical model was eventually tempered by neo-classical theorists, who argued that mitigating factors, such as starvation, should be taken into account, at least in sentencing the deviant for his/her transgressions. Past criminal record and individual capacity for free will were also seen as being relevant. The theory is both difficult to test and simplistic. Even the neo-classical modifications to classical theory are not sufficient to account for the complex nature of crime and deviance.

CONSENSUS THEORIES

Subcultural Theories

Subcultural theories have primarily focused on youth and gangs. Culture is made up of material (clothing, buildings, food) and non-material (beliefs, language, values and norms) aspects. Subcultural theories of deviance argue that particular subcultures are likely to foster or promote behaviour which is different from the values of the mainstream culture. These theories are likely to focus on gangs, but may also target particular ethnic groups as being deviant subcultures. Such groups are portrayed as being in opposition to the norms of society, with different (often defined as deviant) behaviour resulting from values shared by the members of that subculture.

Subcultural theories build on sociological work which emphasizes groups as important mechanisms of socialization and highlights their mediating power between the individual and the world. Each of us identifies with a variety of groups. When the primary group we are involved in is classified as deviant, subcultural theories would argue that we are likely to adopt the values and activities of that group.

Because subcultural theories are consensus theories, they can be challenged on the basis that there is no agreement in society about what constitutes deviant behaviour, and that such assumptions are class-biased to place the majority of blame on those who are socio-economically disadvantaged. These theories also minimize individual agency by emphasizing the impact of belonging to a particular subculture. In other words, there seems to be an underlying assumption that all individuals who are part of a subculture adopt the subcultural norms. One further criticism is that these subcultural values, if they can be said to exist at all, do not necessarily translate into behaviour.

Differential Association

A close cousin of subcultural theories of deviance is differential association, which focuses on the process by which someone becomes deviant. Many of us are familiar with the basic tenet of this theory from hearing a parent warn us about hanging out with the wrong "crowd" or group of people. Edwin Sutherland (1883–1950) and Donald Cressey developed a theory that argued that deviance is learned behaviour.

Sutherland and Cressey essentially argued that an excess of definitions in favour of committing a deviant act resulted in deviant behaviour. This theory argues that deviance is learned through face-to-face interaction with others in small, intimate groups. Also learned are the techniques (how to break into a safe, how to approach a customer as a prostitute) and the motives (I need the money, they don't; selling my body for sex doesn't hurt anyone). One important contribution of this theory is its normalization of deviance — one underlying assumption of differential association is that anyone can learn to be deviant. Learning deviant behaviour is just like any other kind of learning, and the deviant is normal in his or her desires, it is simply the manner in which he or she goes about achieving them that is different from anyone else. Another aspect of this theory is that associations vary in frequency, duration, priority, and intensity, indicating that if we associate with a particular group frequently and for longer periods of time, we are likely to be influenced by their ideas.

Despite the fact that differential association has been a very popular theory, it has been criticized for being vague, complex, and impossible to test. In addition, structural factors which may contribute to a person's engaging in deviant behaviour are not considered, nor is the individual's agency. Not everyone who hangs out with a bad crowd engages in deviant behaviour. This theory fails to consider that an individual's sense of right and wrong may serve to counterbalance the influence of the group. Another criticism of differential association is that it doesn't examine why an individual engages in deviant behaviour, and it is not applicable to all situations (for example, it fails to explain crimes of passion).

Strain Theory

When Robert Merton looked at American society in the 1950s, he saw the dominance of an ideology known as the "American Dream," which essentially perpetuated the myth that anyone, with a little hard work, can succeed. Success here was rooted in material acquisitions and the status attached to them. Merton argued that social structure pushes people to violate norms. He examined the disjuncture between culturally defined goals — those things which are worth striving for — and the legitimate ways in which society sees those goals being achieved. Merton argued that deviance results when there is an overemphasis on goals and not enough support for the reaching of those goals through socially sanctioned means. School, the family and the workplace were identified as the primary agents of socialization for goal formation and maintenance. Failure of these institutions to do their job meant that an individual might not conform to social norms.

Merton identified five modes of adaptation to the goals/means norms of society. The first is *conformity*, in which both cultural goals and means are accepted. The fact that most people are conformists adds to the stability of society. In fact, Merton argued that if too many people did not conform society would become unstable and anomie, or normlessness, would be the result. The second mode of adaptation is *innovation*, in which cultural goals are accepted, but there is little or no emphasis on achieving them through legitimate, or culturally sanctioned, means. In other words, having a house and a nice car may be a cultural goal which is accepted, but the means of acquiring those legitimately through work is replaced with "deviant" means like theft, or earning a living through the sale of drugs. Merton identified an overemphasis on wealth, power and prestige in society as potentially problematic, particularly where the emphasis is not matched by a respect for the achievement of those goals by legitimate means. Too many innovators result in social instability. The third mode of adaptation is *ritualism*, in which cultural goals are not accepted, but the means are. In other words, the means and goals become disconnected, and a person behaves in a culturally acceptable way without accepting the goals that drive the means. The fourth way in which people deal with the tension between means and goals is simply to retreat. *Retreatism* is a denial of both means and goals, and is characterized by escapist behaviour such as drug abuse, dropping out of school, and in its most dramatic form, suicide. The final mode of adaptation is *rebellion*, in which the goals and means of a society come under attack. Here a group may reject both the goals and means and attempt to bring about reform or redefinition.

Merton's work has been criticized for being too sweeping in its generalizations: can we really identify shared cultural goals in our society? Research on generational differences indicates that baby boomers as a group share different cultural values from generation Xers.

And indeed, within these groups there is a diversity of goals which are valued. This criticism is of course applicable to all consensus theories — are there culturally shared norms on which we can base theories of deviance?

One major difficulty with strain theory and other explanations which emphasize the role of families in socializing conformity is that they rely on a particular version of the structure of the family and assume that a particular set of values is transmitted. In other words, these theories assume homogeneous structure and values amongst families. As Doran argues in his chapter, families which do not fit into a narrowly prescribed notion of normal are vulnerable to surveillance and monitoring. Johnson argues that the family norm we are inundated with most often is the middle-class heterosexual couple with children. Although she notes that we do see other kinds of families (single mothers or working class), they are often "treated as humorous, anomalous, as failures, as unfortunate." The reality for many women and children who live/have lived in the halcyon model of the family is violence and abuse. And yet we resist alternative forms of family and label them abnormal.

These notions of the normal are reinforced by law, which, although there is some diversity, favours the "traditional" model and is particularly resistant to families composed of same-sex couples. Johnson uses the Supreme Court of Canada decision in *Mossop v. Canada* to illustrate the law's adherence to the notion of the traditional family and resistance to same-sex families. Although the Supreme Court has read sexual orientation into the Canadian Charter of Rights and Freedoms as an analogous ground to be protected under the equality provisions of s. 15, the law still clings to a narrow definition of the family.

Certainly we see the tendency of law and society to construe families narrowly when we examine the difficulties lesbian mothers face. As Wachholz points out, lesbian mothers depart from the ideals of both the normal woman and the good mother, rendering them especially vulnerable. Lesbian women who mother are seen to violate the most scared of social institutions — the family. One of the dominant assumptions of our society is that mothering can only take place within the confines of the traditional family.

Control Theory

Travis Hirschi is the theorist most often associated with control theory, which, like other consensus theories, is based on the assumption that there is a shared value system among the members of a society. Rooted in Durkheimian notions of group solidarity and cohesion, Hirschi's theory examines the elements of the social bond, and argues that deviance is the result of weak and broken bonds between an individual and society. The theory also proposed that we conform as a result of strong bonds to conventional society. The social bond is made up of the following elements: strong attachments to conventional others; commitment to and involvement in conventional activities; and belief in the conventional social values and the need to follow norms. This theory implies that only deviant individuals do not accept the dominant value system of society. It also assumes that there is a dominant value system in society. As the most recognized contexts for conventional values, the family, school, and church are classified as important social institutions in which the formation of proper social bonds occurs.

As with all consensus theories, this one is vulnerable to the criticism that it is difficult to determine what these conventional values, others, and beliefs are. This theory translates into the popular rhetoric of the New Right which argues that the deterioration of society is caused by the erosion of the family and the diminished role of the church in our culture. Without these purported conventional influences, social bonds do not form, or are broken, and individuals engage in deviant behaviour.

Green explores the emergence of ADHD as a syndrome as being rooted in a control theory interpretation of hyperactivity. Control theory focuses on conformity, and ADHD represents a failure to conform. The solution, which is the pathologization and treatment of the "disorder," is designed to enhance conformity. By identifying ADHD as a medical, rather than as a social, problem, parents and teachers may rest easy knowing that a child's difficulties have nothing to do with them.

Social Disorganization

This theory came out of the Chicago school in the '20s, '30s, and '40s and is based on the premise that rapid social change in communities causes deviance and crime. The focus here, initially at least, is on the place, or geography, rather than the person. As a precursor to social control theory, social disorganization theory connected deviance to fissures in the structure of social organization. Researchers such as Shaw and McKay and Thrasher linked rapid change in neighbourhoods to the existence of delinquency. Change included physical deterioration, such as deserted buildings, shifts in population, and ethnic conflict. Urbanization, migration, immigration, industrialization, and technological change were named as the causes of social disorganization. Such shifts in social organization provided a context in which deviance became more likely. These theorists simultaneously emphasized the failure of institutions such as the family to control deviance. Underlying this research were some obvious biases against those of lower socio-economic status and the areas in which they lived.

Social disorganization theory can give us some insight into the profound impact physical dislocation can have on human beings. Fiske's chapter takes us to the terrain of one of the more recent applications of social disorganization theory — aboriginal communities. However, the limitation of the social disorganization perspective in this context is serious: the causes of social disorganization amongst aboriginal peoples are linked to white colonization, and therefore focusing on physical conditions diverts our attention from the root cause of aboriginal oppression.

Larsen's research on prostitution also highlights the spatial context of deviance. Residents of one Vancouver neighbourhood entered into negotiations with prostitutes to come to an agreement about where prostitutes would work. Such "managed" deviance points to the limitations of the social disorganization theory, which sees deviants as being immobile.

Shaming

In some senses shaming is not really a theory of deviance at all; rather it explains social control, or why people conform to social norms. As a consensus theory, the shaming perspective focuses on underlying shared values in social groups. It assumes that normal behaviour is agreed upon by members of a particular culture. The use of shaming theory to explain human behaviour makes the most sense in small, cohesive societies or groups. In such groups, social sanctions such as shaming are more likely to work. Conformists are interdependent members of a communitarian, or tightly knit, society. Interdependence is an individual characteristic which reflects the degree to which an individual is dependent on others, and the extent to which others are dependent on that individual. This theory draws on the Durkheimian notion of social cohesion — the more a person is interdependent, the more effective the social control. Unlike much of our society today, communitarian cultures do not emphasize the importance of individualism, but rather focus on its members' dependence on each other and the desirability of dependability. A good example of a subculture in which shaming is very effective is among the Amish. Distinctiveness as an individual is discouraged, especially in outward displays of wealth or status. The Amish have formal shaming mechanisms which allow them to exercise maximum social control over group members through shunning. After a period of time the deviant member is reintegrated.

Shaming theory distinguishes between two forms of shaming: reintegrative and disintegrative. The former is a sanction which is followed by the group's reacceptance of the deviant, in which the religiously inspired maxim "love the sinner, hate the sin" epitomizes the approach to deviance. Disintegrative shaming is a sanction which creates a group of people in the community who are outcasts, and who form a deviant subculture. This theory recognizes the family as an important mechanism for social control.

Pathological Approach/Medical Model

One of the most pervasive models in the explanation of deviant behaviour is the medical model or the pathological approach. This approach to understanding and reacting to deviance has a long and interesting history. One of its early proponents (late 1800s), Cesare Lombroso, argued that deviants and criminals were atavists or evolutionary throwbacks. A later variation of this was developed by William Sheldon, who suggested that deviance could be predicted by body type. Further variations looked to chromosomes as an explanation for deviance. It was thought that the existence of an extra chromosome was accountable for deviant behaviour: an extra "x" produced feminine characteristics in males and a likelihood of mental illness; an extra "y" increased aggression. Each of these theories rests on the assumption that the causes of deviance are discoverable through positivism, or the use of scientific method through controlled experimentation. The pathological approach has developed into perhaps the most pervasive framework for understanding deviance in our society.

In his chapter, Ramp points to the gradual shift from the conceptualization of deviants as "fallen citizens" to "cases." This emergence of the deviant as a case is an important part of the gradual dominance of the medical model of deviance. Ramp also identifies the eugenics movement of the late 19th and early 20th centuries as a beginning site of categorization of the "normal," and the "abnormal" citizen through wide-ranging categories such as intelligence, sexual properties, and emotional alienation. The range of behaviours which have been pathologized knows no bounds, and includes homosexuality, prostitution, and promiscuity.

According to the medical model, deviance is essentially viewed as a sickness that can be cured. The medical model both blames the individual and yet takes responsibility away from the deviant. Deviance as sickness diverts attention away from the structural factors that contribute to the behaviour labelled deviant, such as alcoholism, poverty and mental illness, as examples. In this way, this model blames the individual. At the same time, the person who is deemed to be deviant is seen to be suffering from an illness which means, at least to some extent, the deviant behaviour is beyond the individual's control. The medical model sets up a taxonomy, or categories, whether it is signs of alcoholism, or characteristics of a psychopath, that delineate the characteristics of the "illness." Once the individual is diagnosed, a treatment is then implemented that will "cure" the individual deviant.

A variety of professionals and caregivers participate in the diagnostic process, depending on the deviant behaviour. These may include psychologists, probation officers, psychiatrists, and social workers. Deviance as pathology is perhaps the most influential theory in our society. Those who are processed by the criminal justice system often go through a variety of assessments, and almost certainly are screened for appropriate "treatments" prior to entry or upon arrival at a federal correctional institution. But it is not only the criminal justice system that employs the medical model. Many behaviours labelled "deviant," such as excess alcohol use, gambling, or sex "addiction," are subject to social control through treatment.

Butters and Erickson draw on Weitz (1996) to succinctly describe the medical model and its approach to illness, which is defined as "a. a deviation from normal, b. specific and universal, c. caused by unique biological forces, d. paralleled to the breakdown of a machine, e. defined and treated through neutral, scientific processes." This model presents itself as neutral and objective, with no underlying biases as to who is diagnosed with a disease. As we shall see, this neutral façade is an especially problematic aspect of the medical model.

We can criticize the medical model on numerous grounds, the most general being that it fails to consider the broader structural questions about the behaviours it targets as deviant. Issues of inequality, oppression, and power are excluded from the medical approach, that pathologizes the individual rather than the social conditions which facilitate the destruction of human life, or quality of life. Butters and Erickson highlight a number of more specific criticisms: the underlying assumption of the medical model that the "normal" is determinable; the medical approach does not treat people holistically; it ignores the differences between people and their unique response to treatment; it presents as morally neutral when in fact social judgments are part of the identification of "illness," and, finally, there are very few "cures" actually found.

Another impact of the predominance of the medical model is its diffusion of the structural aspects of the social construction of deviance. As Ramp points out, the media play a role in this by focusing on the individual as abnormal. The individual as responsible agent is a powerful rhetoric in our society that has its roots in the classical school. The medical model has become a tool for the diagnosis and treatment of deviance not only for the "professionals," but for anyone who can access the language of sickness. Laberge et al. discuss the ambiguity of those categories, and this, compounded with their rampant use by professionals and non-professionals alike, renders this approach to deviance especially dangerous. Ramp notes the careless use of the medical model by all forms of the media. He discusses how reporters, both historically and presently, often use forensic psychology to discuss the mental capacity of the criminal or the deviant.

A direct response to the medical model was the emergence of the anti-psychiatry movement, which argues that mental illness does not exist as a biological and pathological designation (see Laberge). Those who espouse this critical approach argue that the "psy" professions create and maintain designations of mental illness in order to self-perpetuate. In short, mental illness is fabricated to keep the "psy" professions in business. The "founder" of this school of thought is Thomas Szasz, who does not deny the reality of the problems people suffer, but objects to the categorization of experience of problems as being mental illness (see Green).

Green examines the tenuous nature of medical categories designed to identify the ADHD child. Not only physicians, but teachers and social workers as well have become part of the diagnostic "team" involved in the identification and curing of this new prevalent disorder. Put simply, "ADHD is a form of social control masquerading as a disorder" (Green).

The breadth of "problem" behaviours captured by this model is illustrated by Butters, Laberge, and Green (in this text), who consider the medical model and its limitations. These authors criticize the taxonomies which are used to create the addict, the ADHD child, or the mentally ill person. The move from badness to sickness meant that every individual can be "cured" of his or her deviance. Yet, as the authors of these chapters note, categories are fluid and when deconstructed, too imprecise to warrant the blind faith society seems to have adopted in relation to medical or quasi-medical diagnoses.

CRITICAL THEORIES

Conflict Theory

The "father" of conflict theory is Karl Marx (1818–1883), who argued that society is characterized by class struggle between different groups with varying degrees of power. Marx sparked an inquiry into inequality and power imbalances which still generates lively debate in a variety of disciplines, including sociology, anthropology, political science, and economics. Explanations for deviance which use the conflict approach focus on power as an important explanatory variable. The identification of particular behaviours as normal and others as deviant is one means by which the powerful maintain the status quo and preserve their own interests. For example, the popular belief that people on welfare don't want to work is one way to minimize responsibility to those who are disadvantaged in our society. Another related aspect of conflict theory is the identification of ideology which is used to perpetuate inequality. Conflict theorists argue that those who are most powerful in society create definitions of deviance that are used to control the less powerful. An interesting example of this might be the emphasis in our society on street crimes to the exclusion of corporate or white-collar crimes. There is a relatively low visibility and punishment of crime occurring within the context of corporations (e.g., tax fraud or pollution) and a high visibility of so-called lower-class behaviours such as prostitution and illicit drug use and sale.

In his chapter on the social construction of the poor as deviant, Doherty uses a conflict analysis to illuminate the ways in which the poor are socially constructed as deviant. One aspect Doherty focuses on is the way knowledge is used as ideology to maintain the limited resources of the poor. Common sense, scientific knowledge, and absolute truth are all used to create "facts" about the poor that are in turn used to disempower them. For example, the state and those who perceive their economic status to be threatened by the maintenance of a social safety net perpetuate the "fact" that most people who are on income assistance are "not victims of capitalism and federal mismanagement, but are simply lazy" (Doherty). Hand in hand with this fact often goes the myth of the availability of "lots of jobs." In sum, the poor are constructed as "not normal," despite the fact that they make up nearly one fifth of the population of Canada.

Ted Schrecker explores the links between crime and economic structure of Canadian society. His discussion outlines the impact of poverty on the choices available to individuals in the course of their everyday lives. Schrecker argues that many thefts are crimes of poverty. Further, having a criminal record exacerbates poverty by limiting employment possibilities for the offender. Schrecker provides us with startling examples of the class-biased character of the institutions of criminal justice.

The role of ideology in the preservation of the status quo or hegemony cannot be over-stated. Increasingly the media play a role in the preservation of hegemony, or the creation of a "precarious consensus out of conflicting and unequal social interests" (Ramp). By owning the media, the interests of the powerful are perpetuated and preserved. Choose an industrial city in Canada and ask yourself what it would be like if newspapers reported the number of asthma attacks in the emergency rooms of hospitals as opposed to the number of break and enters or robberies. Because industry frequently controls or influences the media, it is street crime rather than harm resulting from pollution which dominates the news.

As Butters and Erickson point out, the social construction of drug abuse has shifted as the interests of various groups in society are defined. Ideologies about what constitutes an addiction and a "bad" drug are created in the interests of the powerful. Thus middle-class women addicted to prescription drugs are less likely to be named addicts than women in lower socio-economic groups who use illegal drugs to cope with everyday life.

One important aspect of social control is the role of law in identifying and enforcing norms. While the law certainly plays a role in constructing and maintaining boundaries between the normal and the abnormal, the extent to which it is used as an instrument of social control by the powerful remains the subject of considerable debate. For example, Larsen argues that the law has not been an effective mechanism of social control over prostitution. And, as Kirby argues, although sexual orientation has received legal protection under the Charter of Rights and Freedoms, discrimination against gays and lesbians has not been eliminated or even noticeably reduced. The anti-gay impetus in our society is strong, and homophobic ideologies persist.

Labelling Theory

Another theory which does not assume that there is an underlying consensus in society about what constitutes deviant behaviour is labelling theory. This perspective examines the social processes and consequences involved in the labelling or naming of someone as deviant. Whether this label is "drunk," "crazy," or "thief," labelling theorists are interested in how such labels impact those who are so designated. Although the foundations for this theory were laid by other theorists, Howard Becker developed it as a serious theoretical contender in the late 1960s and early 1970s. Labelling theorists see deviance as a social construction which involves the taking on of a deviant identity by a person involved in acts that are deemed to be deviant. This micro theory is also known as an interactionist theory, because it examines the interactions, or relationships, between people.

Central to labelling theory is the notion that the subject of study is both the deviant and those who are defining the deviant behaviour as such. Although labelling is not concerned with social structure, but rather the process of labelling, it does ask questions about who does the labelling and in what circumstances. The social circumstances (i.e., the identification of a particular behaviour as problematic at a given time), the person involved in the "deviant" act, and the person or group who is affected by the behaviour all impact on how and whether a person will be labelled. Using this perspective we ask how and why some people are labelled mentally ill, addicts, or prostitutes and so on. Two key concepts in this theory are primary deviance, or the act which attracts attention and a label in the first place, and secondary deviance, or the internalization of the label by the person to the extent that it becomes part of his/her self-image and impacts on other relationships and interactions.

Labelling theory examines the micro levels of social processes and asks what is the process by which someone is labelled deviant? If we examine poverty as deviance, for example, we ask what are some of the labels associated with poverty? Welfare bum; cheat; lazy; unemployed (between positions); and welfare mother are each categories which convey a negative meaning by implying that the person is deviant or somehow not normal. For example, Beaman examines some of the labels associated with the process of separation and divorce. Women are deemed to be not worthy for legal aid, bad mothers, liberated women, dependent, self-sufficient, with each label impacting on the woman's self-image. In addition, labelling changes a person's public identity to the extent that a person will be seen as deviant or undesirable in other respects. For example, a criminal record affects the likelihood of being hired in a variety of employment positions, the implication being that a person with a criminal record (the "criminal") is generally not trustworthy. The media contribute to this process by the identification of individual criminals, but also by generating categories from which stigmatizing labels are drawn.

It is important to note that labelling theory is not concerned with structural issues like the identification of the "powerful." What we ask when we use a labelling perspective are questions about social context by recognizing that responses to behaviours vary across time, and depend on who commits the act. In sum then, labelling theory focuses on the definition of particular behaviours as deviant, the labels that are used, and the way in which the person who is labelled interprets that label. Also central to a labelling analysis is the use of symbols such as language and material objects.

Butters and Erickson identify the needle as an important symbol in the social construction of the addict. Depending upon the social context, the needle is representative of either "the addict" or "the patient." They also point to language as a powerful tool in the creation of the addict as a problem. Labels such as patient, addict, user, and drug are all important in the sorting process between normal and abnormal behaviour. Butters and Erickson draw on the distinction between tobacco and alcohol and illegal drugs to make this point. They argue that if we do an economic analysis of the costs of tobacco, alcohol, and illegal drug use, the former two are far more costly in many respects than the latter.

Similarly, Laberge et al. examine the process by which a person comes to be labelled mentally ill. They point out a serious difficulty in the analysis of such designations. While the label is stigmatizing and the process socially constructed, the person may be truly suffering. The reaction of the observer of an incident and the ambiguity of a situation are both important factors in the labelling process. Without a reaction, there is no designation of mental illness. Laberge et al. also point out the importance of shifting a label from deviant to criminal. While both are stigmatizing, a criminal label may have profound effects, such as preventing the person so labelled from securing employment, as was noted above.

While Laberge et al. focus on the process of labelling, Kirby documents the impact of a deviant label. She points out that the process of not naming gays and lesbians has rendered them invisible in law. Kirby follows the impact of labelling through the life course of the gays and lesbians who participate in her study. She argues that elderly gays and lesbians are a group of people who "spent their formative years in a society which criminalized their conduct, branded their orientation a psychiatric illness, and pronounced them sinners." Homophobia is, notes Kirby, still a fact of life. Perhaps no other group in society recognizes as well the stigmatizing effect of labels.

The labelling theory does have limitations, including the criticism that it is not a theory at all because it does not really explain the causes of deviance, but simply traces the process by which someone comes to be called deviant. It is also not clear that a deviant label necessarily results in the self-identification of the person labelled as deviant. In other words, not everyone who is named a deviant will take that label on as an identity. Further, labelling theory neglects the structural aspects of the process of categorizing particular behaviours as deviant, and therefore it does not deal adequately with issues of power. Finally, it is too relativistic in that it does not identify any behaviour as wrong or as being inherently deviant.

Doran notes the attempts of labelling theorists to move the study of crime and deviance away from positivist approaches, which argue that deviance can be scientifically measured and explained, to one that focuses on the interactionist aspects of the identification of youth as deviant. Instead, argues Doran, through the use of longitudinal studies we see an increased surveillance of youth and their "criminal careers." Doran notes the usefulness of both the interactionist and structural analyses, but calls for an integration of the two that would allow for a more comprehensive understanding of the social construction of deviance.

In part, the harm reduction model advocated by Butters and Erickson is an attempt to diffuse the negative labels associated with drug use. They argue that by focusing on the adverse consequences of drug use and minimizing those, we can work toward a model that eliminates or reduces stigma.

Postmodernism

Although postmodernism is a term that was initially employed in relation to architecture and other artistic media, it has gradually come to be used in the social sciences as well. Describing what, exactly, postmodernism is presents a challenge. Those who call themselves postmodernists are diverse in their thinking, often defying the identification of a unified stream of thought. Further, postmodernists rarely set out exactly what it is they mean by postmodernism, assuming or hoping that the reader can figure it out for herself or himself. This approach is of limited use to the student who is looking for a beginning place to comprehend this complex body of thought. This being said, we have attempted to identify some of the features of postmodern approaches to social theory.

Postmodernism is a response to the ideals of modernity, the dawn of which was essentially marked by the advent of the Enlightenment. Postmodernism is perhaps best defined and understood in terms of what it rejects: notions of the self, knowledge, and truth are all eliminated in the postmodernist world. Universality and comprehensive or grand theories are shunned. Reason as an objective, reliable, and universal foundation for knowledge is rejected. Postmodernists challenge the neutrality of scientific methods and contents, and thus science itself is rejected as the only legitimate basis for knowledge. Since the social world is heterogeneous, general categories like gender, class, and race are eliminated in the construction of postmodernist social theory. The local and the practical become the explanatory foci of postmodernism (Fraser and Nicholson, 1990: 24–25).

One of the most cited theorists in relation to crime and deviance is Michel Foucault. His work, although he himself might deny this, reflects the postmodern approach described above. His major contribution is a reconfiguration of the concept of power, and its linking to knowledge. For Foucault, power and knowledge are inextricably linked. The collection of information (knowledge) facilitates the creation of categories of deviants, which in turn allows us to name them as such (power). For Foucault, professionals are key players in this process, be they teachers, physicians, or priests.

The two chapters in this collection most explicitly following the postmodern turn are those by Doran and Fiske. Fiske draws out the connections between colonial knowledge about natives and the exercise of power on the site of the aboriginal body. Petty disciplines and technologies of power are designed to create the docile aboriginal. Doran draws explicitly on the work of Michel Foucault to document the creation of the "problem" youth and the abnormal family.

Feminism

The most difficult aspect of talking about "the" feminist theory of deviance is the nature of feminist theory itself. More aptly named feminist **theories**, feminism includes a myriad of approaches that make the development of a singular feminist theory of deviance almost impossible. With this important caveat in mind, we can make a number of general statements about feminist theories and deviance. Until very recently, the vast majority of research on deviance has ignored women and gender differences. Men have been the focus of theoretical and empirical work. When women have been the focus of research, topic areas have been narrow and stereotypically female, e.g., prostitution, shoplifting, and mental illness. Unlike Larsen's approach, past research has focused on prostitution as deviance, rather than the process of defining what constitutes prostitution, and why women, rather than men (the customers), are stigmatized and penalized for exchanging sex for money. Similarly, mental illness has been studied as a problem unique to women. We see a more comprehensive approach by Laberge et al., who note that women's deviance is more likely to be categorized as mental illness, while men are more likely to be processed through the criminal justice system.

Why is gender an important consideration in sociological research on deviance? Women and men are often socially controlled in different ways, and norms for women are often different than they are for men. As Matthews argues, the "beautiful" female body and the beautiful male body are socially constructed in different ways, women's roles are seen differently, as are behaviour norms for women. As is illustrated by MacDonald, women's sexuality is controlled and abused in ways that men's is not. This is not to say that the deviance of women as a social construct is more important to study than that of men, simply that it has been ignored or under-studied in the past, and that it is important to study gender patterns.

Clearly then, feminist approaches to the study of deviance focus on women and the social construction of gendered expectations in relation to what constitutes normal behaviour and appearance. Feminist theories also draw out the fact that women are often the victims of male deviance, whether it is abuse or sexual exploitation, because of the patriarchal structure of our society which privileges and empowers men over women. Like conflict theories generally, many feminist approaches focus on power as the most important site of oppression; however, the power analysis for feminists is integrally linked to a gender analysis.

Another concern for feminist theorists is the intersection of gender and other characteristics such as race, ethnicity, ability, age, and socio-economic position. Feminist theorists focus on the social context in which women are defined as deviant. For example, Wachholz points out how the lesbian mother is dually stigmatized, first as a lesbian (as this deviates from the norm of heterosexuality) and secondly as a lesbian mother (bringing to light the homophobic belief that lesbians should not have kids because this "breeds homosexuals"). Beaman also provides an example of how women's socio-economic status influences their ability to access legal and economic resources during divorce.

The complex nature of feminist theory means that there is no comprehensive "feminist" theory of deviance. The diversity of feminism and of feminist theories means that it is difficult to identify many common themes. While they all share a critique of patriarchal relations, their differences are sometimes as important as their similarities. Nick Larsen's chapter reveals the tension that can emerge when different feminist approaches are applied to the same situation. Larsen points out that all feminist approaches agree that any strategies in relation to prostitution must not increase the oppression of women. However, radical feminists argue that prostitution is simply an extension of patriarchy, and that no woman really chooses to become a prostitute. Liberal feminists, on the other hand, argue that most women do actually choose to become prostitutes and that their oppression can be alleviated by giving them more complete control over their working conditions. In essence, before we consider the feminist response to a behaviour identified as deviant we must ask *which* feminist response we are seeking to understand.

Fiske, Matthews and MacDonald each recognize the body as a central focus in the oppression of women. Fiske compares the body of the Roman Catholic nun with that of the Aboriginal girl. The latter is particularly threatening to notions of the normal woman. The "wildness" of Aboriginal women was a threat to the colonialists' puritanical notions of women's sexuality. They thus become objects to be controlled, tamed, subjugated. In contrast, and yet equally as subjugated, is the religious sister, subordinated to man. Both the sister and the Aboriginal are deviations from the norm, but one is characterized and socially constructed as pure, the other as dangerous. Fiske traces the present-day reaction to the horrors of the residential school experience, which include both denial and minimalization by the church. She concludes "whether the aboriginal woman is denigrated as an ungrateful recipient of Christian charity, as an unfit mother, or as immoral, unmarried mother and pagan, she re-emerges within the imperial precepts as deviant to Christian patriarchal normalcy."

The subjugated body also becomes a theme in women's efforts to meet the norm of a "beautiful" body. Matthews argues that this compliance is not as simplistic as it at first may seem — adolescent girls are not passive in their attention to appearance norms. Rather, they negotiate their compliance within a complex gender structure. This is not to deny that appearance norms exist, but to affirm that women exercise agency. The impact of that may be short-term gain leaving young women feeling isolated and disempowered. Matthews's discussion can be extended to an analysis of patriarchy. At each level of the hierarchy, whether adolescent girls meet the criteria for the socially constructed categories of being "popular" versus being a "loser," patriarchy plays a role in defining these criteria. The expectations and ideals of beauty are defined by men, and form the standard to which adolescents compare themselves.

Feminist scholarship on deviance attempts to identify and challenge conceptualizations of the normal woman. For example, Wachholz examines the myths surrounding women and mothering. Core assumptions include: all women want and should have children; women are primarily responsible for childcare; and mothering should only take place in the context of the "traditional" family. Thus women who do not want or cannot have children are constructed as abnormal. So too does society lay a burden on women who use childcare services.

Women who mother outside of the confines of the traditional family are also constructed as deviant. These assumptions make their way into law, which punishes both the woman who chooses to stay at home with her children (the good mother) and the mother who works in the paid labour force (the liberated woman). The law sets up very narrow categories of the normal women, so narrow in fact that most women do not fit.

The ways in which society constructs gender norms is modelled in its extremes by the military, discussed by Harrison, where men are men and women are expected to serve men. The normal woman in the military context is expected to give up her career and her ambitions in favour of her husband's career. Sanctions that act to socially control women are imposed on their husbands, who will fail to advance if their wives do not conform.

Harrison's article also underscores the importance of feminist methodologies in conducting research about women. She uses Dorothy Smith's institutional ethnography, which focuses on the lived experiences of women in explaining any social phenomenon. Positivistic assumptions about the possibility and the desirablity of objective research are rejected, and the assumptions of the researchers together with the experiences of the woman are highlighted. True to this methodology, Harrison stresses the lived experiences of the military wives she interviewed in reporting her results.

Gender cuts across any discussion of deviance, be it mental illness, drug and alcohol abuse, or the social construction of ADHD. Women are more likely to be labelled "mad" than "bad." Transgressions of gender roles result in women being denied financial support or custody of their children, either because they are lesbian, liberated, or lazy.

CONCLUSIONS

Studying any social phenomenon requires a variety of approaches if we are to capture the complexities of the social world. Although we argue that a critical approach which begins with the premise that deviance is socially constructed is the best way to understand deviance in our society, we also acknowledge that other theories can add to our understanding of how and why behaviours come to be viewed as deviant. Further, as Doherty argues, a dually focused analysis is preferable: we should consider both macro analysis which explores structural factors, as well as a micro approach which examines the negotiation of definitions of deviance at a local, contextualized level.

Finally, it is essential that we not lose sight of the agency of those who are marginalized in our society. To conceptualize some people as having all of the power and others as having none is too simplistic. Those with minimal resources also exercise agency in their day to day lives. Sociological analysis should not portray them as puppets at the mercy of an anonymous group of others who are powerful. As social constructionists, we recognize that definitions of deviance change over time. This is in part due to the agency of those who are marginalized. For example, although change is slow, we can see a gradual shifting in attitudes about same-sex relationships in our society. Recognizing agency is a delicate balancing act though: while we cannot portray the people on the margins of our society as powerless, we must also not go too far in emphasizing their agency. Such an approach can lead to the tendency to blame the victims.

Defining deviance and shifting the boundaries of what we consider to be deviant is a complex task. It is important to ask ourselves why we define some behaviours as deviant and others as normal. While examining the micro processes of the ways in which people are labelled deviant is informative, it is also critical to search for patterns in the social construction of deviance so that we can identify structural factors that contribute to our conceptualizations of the "normal." Exploring mythologies of the normal, such as the "normal family," is an important component of the deconstruction of categories of deviance.

REFERENCES

Becker, Howard
   1963 *Outsiders: Studies in the Sociology of Deviance.* New York: Free Press.

Foucault, Michel
   1977 *Discipline and Punish: The Birth of the Prison.* New York: Vintage Books.

   1978 *The History of Sexuality: An Introduction, volume 1.* New York: Vintage Books.

Fraser, Nancy and Linda J. Nicholson
   1990 "Social Criticism without Philosophy: An Encounter between Feminism and Postmodernism," in *Feminism/Postmodernism*, edited by Linda J. Nicholson. New York: Routledge.

Hirschi, Travis
   1969 *Causes of Delinquency.* Berkley, CA: University of California Press.

Merton, Robert
   1938 "Social Structure and Anomie," *American Sociological Review* 3:672–82.

Shaw, C. and H. McKay
   1942 *Juvenile Delinquency and Urban Areas.* Chicago: University of Chicago Press.

Sutherland, Edwin H. and Donald R. Cressey
   1978 *Criminology* (10th ed.) Philadelphia: Lippencott.

MORAL SPECTACLES Norm and Transgression in the News Media

William Ramp

A CAUTIONARY INTRODUCTION: THE MEANINGS OF "MEDIA"

As the terms "deviance" and "the media" are often loosely defined, let's begin by identifying some of the different meanings attached to these words, starting with "media." This term covers several complex, interrelated social and technological processes, which can be grouped as follows (see Lorimer and McNulty, 1996: 40–52):

a) Technologies for recording, transmitting, and storing information

b) Organizations concerned with the production and dissemination of information, ideas, and images: e.g., corporate, regulatory/policy, legal, and professional bodies

c) Content types or genres (e.g., news, entertainment, advertising) governed by embedded "rules for reading"

Our knowledge of deviance is both direct and mediated: we have personal experience of it, but we are also "familiar" with a wider range of deviant behaviour as represented in media accounts. These representations are the complex products of organizations, technologies, and people: thus while the media may serve as mirrors, reflecting our conduct back to us, they do so in terms of specific organizational circumstances and priorities. These are never simple: the interests of owners, advertisers, and journalists can and often do conflict, and our own response to media messages is likewise affected by our specific social location and our cultural priorities.

I gratefully acknowledge as inspirations for many of the ideas in this chapter Andrew Wernick's course lectures on media and culture, at Trent University in the 1970s, 1980s, and early 1990s. However, I take full responsibility for any misinterpretations and errors contained herein.

CHARACTERIZING DEVIANCE: SCANDAL, SELFHOOD, SCIENCE, AND SPECTACLE

To understand media representations of deviance, we must also look at some of the different ways in which deviance has been defined and characterized. Sociologists commonly distinguish between types of deviance in terms of the types of sanctions invoked or rules transgressed. Actions which break laws and result in official prosecution may be called crimes (or alternatively, criminal deviance); as such, they can be distinguished from actions which, though legal, break moral norms and result in condemnation, social ostracism, or informal correction. Actions which break social customs with little moral force (Weber, 1978: 29) may be seen as mere curiosities, or in the field of contemporary fashion, as creative innovations. All three forms of deviance can excite media attention, but we will be concerned mainly with the first two.

Acts which transgress moral norms or legal statutes excite attention and generate reactions among observers. Through media coverage, we can become observers of deviant acts, even if we are not physically present as they happen. Media messages not only report such acts, they also portray, and focus on, *reactions to* them, inciting further responses both to the particular acts and to "deviance" as a generalized social phenomenon. We will examine the significance of this incitement later; now, let's look at the history of three alternative images of deviance which serve as core cultural resources in the construction of media accounts of it.

Deviance as Transgression of Traditional Prerogative

In *Discipline and Punish*, Michel Foucault describes the public torture and execution of one Damiens, accused of an attempt on the life of the King of France, in 1757. The punishment marked vividly on Damiens's body the power of the monarch whose life he had tried to take. Such public, physical retribution spoke of a regime in which the king's privileges were seen as manifestations or extensions of his *physical* presence. To transgress the king's peace was to insult his extended body: punishment took the form of revenge inflicted visibly and publicly on the body of the offender, in a set of rituals that were also a means of displaying and proving the true significance of the crime (Foucault, 1977: 10–16, 28–29, 43–57). Damiens's family shared in his punishment (through banishment and forced name changes) for no other reason than that they were his relatives.

We can speculate that similar mechanisms were used for non-criminal offences: conduct codes and ritual boundaries which kept respectful distance from lapsing into familiarity helped maintain the traditional prerogatives of the old aristocracy. Offences against etiquette might not have meant torture or the stocks, but informal rituals of humiliation could reinforce *visibly* the distance and barriers crossed by the deviant act, just as did public executions. In both instances, the purpose of punishment was less to affect the offender's behaviour than to make visible a transgression of social boundaries, by making a spectacle of the offender as an example both of and to his class (see, e.g., Goethe, 1958: 85–91, for a literary example of the clash between a traditional aristocratic concern with social boundaries, and a new, bourgeois emphasis on distinction as the result of achievement).

Deviance as Failure of Self-Governance

Foucault contrasts the violent show of public execution to the new "corrective" regime of nineteenth-century penitentiaries. He links the rise of the latter to two longer-term developments in the social order. First, new definitions of sovereignty: in place of king and subjects, self-sovereign and self-subjected citizens maintain their place in democratic society precisely by ruling over, and taking responsibility for, *themselves*. Crime, in this new order, becomes evidence of a failure of self-governance (and a betrayal of "society' from within), and punishment a meticulous, technical exercise in awakening repentance and a renewed sense of self-responsibility in the fallen citizen. This work is internal and hidden: the quiet work of the reformatory on the soul (Foucault, 1977: 80–131). But with the idea of the self-sovereign citizen, there also arose a *practical* concern (ostensibly of and for such citizens), to guarantee two things: the detailed, bodily obedience of reformed *individuals* to social rules, norms, and conventions, and the stability, order, and productivity of *populations*. Fittingly, in the latter case, this new emphasis on benevolent governance, improvement, and correction was called the art and science of *police* (see Foucault, 1991; Pasquino, 1991a). Crime became a "social problem" to be dealt with through the interventions of magistrates and learned men, working within or alongside new social institutions: hospitals, clinics, public health agencies, penitentiaries, orphanages. Their object was to understand and redirect the motivations and passions of individuals, to intervene in personal and family life to root out suspect habits and associations, and to encourage self-responsibility and "healthy" social relations (Valverde, 1991). In this light, the interior drama of self-reformation or "correction" became a theatre open to the interrogation of psychologists, prison administrators, social workers, and others. The psychodrama of the "criminal mind" was born. The new pioneers of "scientific" criminal detection — the fictional Holmes in Britain, the real Bertillon in France — began to employ insights from these disciplines in their work. Detection of patterns in a criminal's behaviour became a way to predict his weaknesses: a predictability ensured by a central weakness of character (see, e.g., Pasquino, 1991b).

Foucault's analysis of the broad "carceral complex" that this benevolent surveillance erected around suspect individuals and groups can be extended to many kinds of deviance, including "potential" deviance in the form of "delinquency" (Foucault, 1977: 257–292; 293–308). Ultimately, violations of any social rule, even of manners, could be reinterpreted, beyond "insubordination," as signs of "degeneracy," or even of incipient madness. By the late Victorian era, non-criminal deviants were attracting their own legions of scientific inspectors, and responses to such deviance often resembled the new penitential forms of criminal correction: the imposition of social isolation combined with surveillance. "Sickly" youths, the poor, or "unladylike" young women might be termed, by doctors or other certified professionals, unsuitable for marriage or likely to reproduce weakness of character. Sexual deviants might find themselves in asylums, subject to the earnest gaze and interrogation of clinicians, or even the corrective knife of surgeons (see Anderson, 1996: 344–346; also Weeks, 1985: 189–192). Here, we can see the beginning of a redefinition of deviants, not as "fallen citizens," but as cases: owners of disabilities that mark them as objects of inquiry, dependent on corrective systems.

Deviance as Abnormality

In the 1830s a Belgian statistician, Quételet, coined the idea of the "normal man" as a way to measure traits in the human population. The "normal man" was a mathematical abstraction; a way to relate the diversity of human characteristics and conduct to a mean. But the concept of normalcy, as adapted and extended by Francis Galton, Karl Pearson, and others, eventually gained life and flesh of its own; taking on a second meaning as an *optimum*;

thus, deviance and criminality could be defined not just as specific transgressive events or signs of *personal* weakness but also as examples of *pathological variance from a norm* (see Durkheim 1982: 85–107; Anderson, 1996: 180–181; Hacking, 1986, 1991). The eugenics movements of the later nineteenth and early twentieth centuries flourished on this rich soil: doctors, social workers, psychologists, and activists formulated exhaustive categories of abnormality — in intelligence, sexual propensities, emotional alienation, and many other categories. Any tendency away from the norm, now defined as a state of health in character and mental fitness, was defined as dangerous and in need of correction or containment, lest it find behavioural expression, spark social contagion, or be reproduced within a "subnormal" population through heredity (see McLaren, 1990). While eugenics fell into disgrace after the Second World War, the concept of the norm as optimum still thrives. "Normal" children are happy, healthy, and likely to be successful; abnormal children and adults are not, and are likely to be clients/consumers of the service agencies which identify and study them. Such clients are no longer "fallen subjects" to be called to self-confession, but are *objects* (and consumers!) of behavioural correction (Lotringer, 1988), and sources of information for corrections experts. The science has changed; definitions of deviance, in this instance as a negative potential signalled by variation from the norm, haven't.

Today, in news, comedy, drama, and documentaries, the media serve up stories using all three of these different images of deviance. Scandal, self-evaluation, and science mix, and the outcome is fertile ground for the reproduction of talk about deviance. A quick example will demonstrate.

In the spring of 1998, news reports in the US and elsewhere began to centre on allegations that US President Bill Clinton had had a sexual *liaison* with a young White House intern, Monica Lewinsky, and that he might have encouraged her to lie about it under oath. These stories fuelled speculation that the affair could be the President's political downfall and even lead to his criminal prosecution. From a legal standpoint, the key allegation was "subornation of perjury": encouraging another to lie under oath. But the central focus of the news coverage was on the alleged sexual relationship and the possibility that its details might be publicly confirmed. "Sex sells," one might say. But there was more to it than this: the news stories built up two different discourses about *two distinct types of scandal*, along with a third discourse that fed interest in the scandals while *representing itself* as *not* scandalous.

First, news coverage focused on the scandalous *social inappropriateness* of an alleged *liaison* between the most powerful man in the world and a junior intern: a man well into middle age and a woman scarcely older than his daughter. While no longer akin to an improper collision of king and peasant, or a violation of the boundaries distinguishing the old "estates" of post-medieval Europe, the Clinton scandal showed three other boundaries to have a firm hold on American life. The President and Lewinsky had, allegedly, violated social barriers placed on sexual relations by *age*, by *position* in a political and employment hierarchy, and by *marriage*.

Second, news stories and talk shows focused on the alleged affair as a sign of scandalous *personal weakness*. Former acquaintances were unearthed to claim that Lewinsky was mercenary, sexually aggressive, or flighty. The President was said to lack self-control, a dangerous feature in a man with his finger on the nuclear button. He was said (like Prince Charles, a few years earlier) to lack the moral strength to represent the nation. Lewinsky and the President were united in *personal failure*; their *failure as responsible, self-governing persons*.

Third, many of the stories also portrayed Clinton and Lewinsky as abnormal: *flawed human beings* in need of professional help. An alleged ex-lover said that she had confronted Clinton concerning his "sexual addiction," and that he had wept listening to her. Talk shows and Web sites, replete with experts, addressed the social prevalence of sexual addiction in light of the Presidential scandal (see Valpy, 1998; *Maclean's*, 1998b: 26–37; Concerned Counseling, Inc., 1998; National Council on Sexual Addiction and Compulsivity, 1998). Lewinsky was said to have been scarred by the breakup of her parents' marriage, to be lacking in self-confidence, and thus vulnerable to the attentions of an older, powerful man. The President and Lewinsky, thus, were incomplete persons, at variance with norms of happiness, fulfillment, and stability.

We see here three striking features of contemporary media coverage of deviance. Deviance is an attractive topic because it is still about *transgression*, and thus dramatically scandalous, socially and personally. But as a tragedy of *self*-failure, deviance can be *imagined* by any of us. And as an *abnormality*, it lies inherent in any variance from the norm of personal integration, *potentially within* any of us, and *potentially threatening the population* as a whole. Thus, even the sober, scientific analysis of deviance gains scandal-cachet, deviance professionals join the talk-show circuit, and the *scientific* discourse of deviance becomes the mechanism by which we are encouraged to *know ourselves*.

THE VISIBILITY OF ORDER: DEVIANCE, PUNISHMENT, AND MORAL SPECTACLE

The scandalous aspect of deviance as transgression is directly related to the ways in which stories about deviance, and ways of dealing with it, involve the creation and manipulation of *spectacles*. For example, Damiens, the man who attempted to kill Louis XV, was sentenced on 2 March 1757 to be taken in a cart to make an *amende honorable* at the main door of the Church of Paris, "wearing nothing but a shirt, holding a torch of burning wax weighing two pounds." From there, he was to be taken to a scaffold at the Place de Grève, where,

> ... the flesh will be torn from his breasts, arms, thighs and calves with red-hot pincers, his right hand, holding the knife with which he committed the said parricide, burnt with sulphur, and, on those places where the flesh will be torn away, poured molten lead, boiling oil, burning resin, wax and sulphur melted together and then his body drawn and quartered by four horses and his limbs and body consumed by fire, reduced to ashes and his ashes thrown to the winds (Foucault, 1977: 3).

Aside from the horrific description, note the slow, stately progression of events, the ritual exactitude of dress, stopping places and poses, and the escalating sequence of acts of torture and destruction. This punishment is *meant to be watched*; it is meant to *transfix* with awe and horror all who watch. These acts arrest us not only because of their brute force but also because of their *symbolic* nature: they constitute a *ritual event,* a pageant. The punishment is also a *story* about the power of royal revenge and the terrible necessity of crushing, visibly, a threat to the king's authority and the king's peace.

Public executions and public punishments offered onlookers a ritual dramatization that brought to public fulfillment a particular narrative, the story of a given crime. Such punishments could take different forms. Proclamations might be read; the condemned might (with audience encouragement) make a speech, sometimes from a prepared text, printed and sold among the crowd by hawkers. The condemned would be watched closely to see how he played his part: with bravery? fear? repentance? defiance? Sometimes the spectacle would threaten to derail if the crowd were caught by a wave of sympathy for the condemned (Foucault, 1977: 58–69). And sometimes, from the seventeenth century on, a spectator's account of the event might be published in a news sheet. Here is an extract from the *Gazette d'Amsterdam* of 1 April, 1757, describing the execution of Damiens, which included a botched and prolonged attempt at drawing and quartering using six horses unaccustomed to the task:

> [T]hey were forced, in order to cut off the wretch's thighs, to sever the sinews and hack at the joints ... [T]hough he was always a great swearer, no blasphemy escaped his lips; but the excessive pain made him utter horrible cries, and he often repeated: 'My God, have pity on me! Jesus, help me!' The spectators were all edified by the solicitude of the parish priest of St. Paul's who despite his great age did not spare himself in offering consolation to the patient (Foucault, 1977: 3).

Here we see a drama of punishment and pain, but also another of consolation, edification, and a kind of redemption. How do we explain such dramatization, and the need for ritual it betrays? And how does it relate to the role of the media *today* in articulating the meaning of deviance, crime, and their punishment? Let's begin with some possible answers to the first question.

Emile Durkheim, a founder of modern sociology and anthropology, made the apparently scandalous remark that "crime" is "normal." What he meant was that, while society exists as a system of limitations defining human actions (Durkheim, 1984: 31–67; also 1982), social limits are, by definition, open to transgression: a rule is a rule inasmuch as it may be violated. Further, if rules are to be noted and obeyed, they must be made *visible*. Such visibility is made possible by two things: violation, and the punishment which necessarily follows. Specifically, it is the *dramatic* nature of violation and its punishment that allows rules to be seen or felt materially; to have *weight* (see, *e.g.*, Durkheim, 1915: 244–245, 255–266, on the force of religious symbols). *What* rules are violated is beside the point: their definition and importance will vary in different social and cultural settings. But all societies are defined by rules of some kind, and in any society these will sometimes be violated, and the violations punished. Thus, in any "normal" society, a certain level of crime (and its punishment) will exist, however defined. The important point here is that deviance and crime embody drama that has the force of social necessity. Transgression of limits stokes the potential for dramatic scandal; its punishment in turn may take the form of ritual drama.

This theory of punishment has been criticized for stressing the social necessity of enforcement *in general*, rather than how the rules thereby enforced benefit *particular* groups or classes at the expense of others. For example, in England from the sixteenth century, economic and social displacement of peasants by private landowners fuelled vagabondage, poaching, theft, and banditry; threats were met by an increase in the number of offences defined as capital crimes. This response protected the rights of property owners against those whose displacement had made the consolidation of landed wealth possible (see Hay et al., 1975). Punishment arguably becomes *hyper-dramatized* precisely when social contradictions make transgression a real possibility: such drama serves both to make the law clear and to instill fear. Durkheim himself suggested that "repressive" punishment was more evident in absolutist regimes, a point that might help explain poor Damiens's treatment by an absolute monarch (Jones and Scull, 1992; Durkheim, 1992b: 45–46).

In this light, neither crime nor punishment should be thought of as givens with fixed meanings. Instead, both are *social constructions: effects* of the words and actions which create them. In this light, "society" and its "rules" are *contingent accomplishments*: the actions or accounts by which we *enact* and *represent* social life and social order to ourselves and to each other. Society "exists" as a set of *objectifications*: the products of acts by which we *represent* it "as if" it existed independently of us. News stories which refer to what "society tells us to do" bring "society" and its constraints *into existence* in *talking about* them (Berger and Luckmann, 1966; see also Foucault, 1978; Garfinkel, 1967). Durkheim tended to refer to the social as if it existed concretely in its own right, but the dramatization of punishment he talked about can be seen as an effective way to "objectify" rules, values, and beliefs, giving them an *apparent concreteness*. Social drama, it could be said, masks a secret terror that the emperor really has no clothes; that rules really don't exist "out there."

Thus, the dramatization of transgression and punishment can be said to serve a *social* requirement (whether or not just or democratic) to *call out* and concretize the power of the social; to illustrate and give emotional weight to the limiting structures of our lives. Dramatization does so in and through *particular instances*, by telling *stories*: drama is *narrative* borne by ritual. Violations of social rules may be inevitable, but the dramatic device of scandal is employed to say otherwise. And scandal provides an occasion — a dramatic break with ordinary conformity — to start a story that must inevitably end with punishment of the offender and restoration of order (Turner, 1969; 1980). Note an interesting reversal of the idea of inevitability here. While crime and deviance — however defined — may be inevitable in any society, and must be redressed at the peril of social breakdown, the ritual drama of scandal and punishment claims the opposite. Transgression is represented as the *unexpected* and thus scandalous act, to be followed, necessarily and *inevitably*, by punishment. The execution of Damiens, in its slow, terrible majesty, narrates the majestic response of the king whose life was threatened. For this singular event, a singular perpetrator was found and made an example of; was made dramatically *other* to observers. But this judicial drama was interwoven with other stories: that of the crime, as told by witnesses and prosecutors; of the punishment-to-come that judgment sets in motion; the various stories of bystanders. And one of these accounts ends up in a newspaper, the *Gazette d'Amsterdam*.

NEWSPAPERS AND THE ORIGINS OF THE CRIME STORY

The Rise of the Newspaper

In order to understand contemporary media treatments of crime and deviance, we should first examine their history; in particular, the history of newspapers. Other forms of print media (detective novels, "true crime" magazines, etc.) are also worthy of study, but newspapers became the primary "factual" chroniclers of crime and deviance on a daily or weekly basis until the age of television, and newspaper accounts of deviance set templates that news magazines and television later followed.

One way to do a potted history of news is to argue that "the public" has always been hungry for it, and that with the invention of printing, newspapers simply displaced town criers. There is an element of truth to this: we have long conversed about our circumstances, and as social life became more complex, we came to rely on specialized organizations to disseminate information. But while we now take the modern daily newspaper for granted as having a standard format and a unitary identity, it is actually a complex composite of several different forms of communication that only slowly came together over a period of 300 years. For much of that time, newspapers struggled financially. And the crime story as we know it today, an even more recent phenomenon, likewise took time to develop.

The first appearance of documents that in any way resemble the newspapers we read today rested on certain key social and technological developments, like the introduction of printing with movable type to Europe in 1458. An explosion in the number of printed books was the most famous result, but printing quickly became an eclectic art. Printers published advertisements for their books, and began to print proclamations, handbills, and charters. These activities subsidized and promoted each other, and printers looked for new opportunities to expand such business (Smith, 1979; Eisenstein, 1983; Benn, 1978; Febvre and Martin, 1976; Boyce et al., 1978).

The first news sheets began to proliferate in the century between 1580 and 1680, specifically to serve the ideological needs of growing urban, literate populations: merchants, civil servants, some early professionals, and gentry (see Gouldner, 1976: 96–106). They typically carried selective mixes of commercial news, parliamentary politics, official proclamations, doings of the royal court, news of wars or expeditions, correspondence on various scientific, legal, and public issues of the day, or various kinds of small advertisements. But the mix was volatile, and none of the apparatus of today's standard newspaper (distinctions between reporters, editors, and publishers; separation of editorial material from reportage and advertising; standard criteria for content; broad-based and regular coverage of standardized news "beats" or themes) had yet appeared. Few of these early journals had begun to resemble the modern newspaper in regularity of output and content by the late 1700s. All suffered to some degree from revenue crises: sales of copies alone could not sustain them, and many came to rely on sponsorship by governments, political parties, and religious organizations.

In this developmental period, newspapers did not treat crime or deviance as categories of regular coverage, and the "crime story" as we now know it did not exist. News of crime typically might appear as it affected the interests of a paper's sponsorship as well as its readership: thus, treason might be discussed in political journals, fraud or piracy in commercial organs, and so on. Damiens's punishment gained attention because of the unique object of his crime. Papers might also print notices of hangings and other punishments, discussions of changes to criminal law, and occasional accounts of theft, murder, and insurrection. But again, no thread called "crime" or "deviance" ties together these accounts: they were printed as they affected a particular constituency's interests in, or curiosity about, peace and order, government, commerce, religion, or political reform.

Between 1800 and 1870, a series of developments in Europe and North America changed this picture completely, so that newspapers in major centres became recognizably familiar in organization and coverage to those of today. In these papers, stories about "crime" and punishment, as well as reports on deviance and eccentricity for their own intrinsic interest, became commonplace. The crime story and the police beat had arrived.

The first half of the nineteenth century saw successful experiments with new printing technologies such as the Hoe Cylinder Press, in which type templates were attached to a spinning drum rather than laid flat on the bed of a press, allowing for much faster, continuous-flow printing. The action of the cylinder press was easy to mechanize by coupling it to a steam engine. In addition, steam transportation made possible the distribution of printed material more quickly, over longer distances. But these developments would have meant nothing without a corresponding expansion of readership, which was supplied by four key developments. The Industrial Revolution fed a reconfiguration of the commercial classes to include industrialists, as well as merchants, financiers, and landowners. These classes, through now-legal political parties, increasingly asserted and debated their political interests. They also sponsored a burgeoning population of literate professionals: lawyers, clerks, scientists and inventors, career politicians, and others. Second, philanthropists, unions, and mutual-aid societies working among the urban working classes, provided educational courses and lending libraries, especially for skilled workers. Third, in North America, the settlement of land by independent farm-owners gave rise to a literate and politically-aware rural constituency which formed the readership of innumerable journals and papers. Finally, from mid-century, most European and North American governments progressively established comprehensive primary and secondary education systems. The regulatory and legislative regimes governing newspapers also began to stabilize and liberalize, especially in Britain and the United States (Smith, 1979; Boyce *et. al.*, 1978; Kesterton, 1967).

None of these developments, in themselves, solved the old problems of a stable source of revenue. The cylinder press and the steam train might make it technically possible to print and distribute large numbers of cheap newspapers, but they also entailed heavy financial commitments to expand operations. Again, the price per copy of a paper did not cover these costs. What set newspapers "free" from religious, political, or government sponsorship was a fundamental revolution in the market. In the course of the nineteenth century, more and more people came to live and work in new industrial cities, becoming increasingly dependent on manufactured consumer goods. Further, a growing segment of the skilled and semi-skilled working class was making enough money not only for necessities, but also for cheap forms of entertainment, recreation, household durables, status items, and books. These developments were accompanied by a mid-century revolution in retailing: the modern department store, no longer mere storage space for unpurchased goods, but a display centre in which customers could stroll past decorated windows and aisles to look at items. Manufacturers, in turn, found it to their advantage to place advertising on the surface of such goods and on packaging, using two more innovations, the brand name and commercial art, to increase the market rather than simply waiting for orders (see Wernick, 1991; Leiss, Kline, and Jhally,1990, chs. 5 and 6).

Manufacturers and retailers, both seeking a broad market for their goods, needed a vehicle for the mass dissemination of advertising messages. This they found in newspapers, which now began to make good, steady money from "display" advertising. In the process, everything about them changed. New mass-market papers, reliant on a heavy investment in new print technology and utilizing cheap pulp paper, developed into large enterprises, in which the roles of publishing, editing, administration and reporting were differentiated, along with their respective staffs. By the end of the century, the first newspaper chains had formed, along with co-operative news-sharing services, utilizing the first electronic communications technology, the telegraph (see Smith, 1979; Rutherford, 1978; Kesterton, 1967). As they came to rely more on advertising revenue, newspapers engaged in circulation wars with rivals, to attract readers most inclined to spend on advertised goods. Around such activities developed organizations like the audit bureau of circulation (to verify circulation figures) and advertising agencies (to design and place increasingly sophisticated display advertisements). A new print medium, the modern consumer magazine also developed to carry pictorial advertising.

But while these newspapers no longer needed to please sponsors, they now had to please two other groups: advertisers and mass-market consumers. The business of commercial newspapers, by the end of the century, was to attract readers for advertisers ... and, incidentally, to print news. This new, commercial orientation had two effects on news content. First, the concept of "general interest" news was born: newspapers catered not to particular religious or political groups, but to a consumer class, or to a mass (cross-class) readership. Second, news became a device with which to attract readers. Reporters and editors continued to promote the idea that they were in business to provide news "in the public interest," as they still do today. But news could be packaged attractively and sold like any other commodity, and journalists could develop new ways of identifying and defining news in terms of consumer interest. These considerations had two consequences. First, attractive news was increasingly seen as spectacular, eye-catching news with large, arresting headlines (and later, photographs): news which aroused shock or emotion first and intellect second. Second, the development of "types" of news was now oriented, not to sectarian or political interests, but to the interests of particular consumer pocketbooks (hence the sectioning of the paper by gender, age, income, and consumer interest: buyers of real estate or personal goods, automobiles or stocks, recreational goods or furnishings), *and also to the universal interests of the reader as "everyman."* Here, we find the birth of the modern crime story, and of the "crime beat," with reporters haunting Police Headquarters around the clock in every major city.

Crime News and the Privatization of Punishment

To look back at crime coverage in turn-of-the century newspapers is an interesting experience: far from being "grey" and "unheroic" (Foucault,1977: 69), even the respectable press featured dramatization that today would be called yellow journalism. Spectacular shootouts, deathbed confessions, daring escapes, and dramatic captures were the stock-in-trade of the crime story, as were such melodramatic stereotypes as wronged wives, ruined girls, sinister foreigners (often connected with vice), or fallen scions of respectable families (see, e.g., "Batch of Small Fry," *Hamilton Herald*, 1903: 1; "Dr. Crippen Gone," "Jealous Old Man," "Fruit Man's Suicide," all in *Hamilton Times*, 1910: 1; see also Rutherford, 1982). Characterizations that today surface only in the most neutral descriptive language, or the judicious addition or omission of a descriptor (as in headlines like "mother of four charged with fraud"), were made much more openly: in urban Ontario, for example, blacks, working-class Catholic Irish, Chinese, southern or eastern Europeans, or Jews, could be characterized in ways that left no doubt about their lower level of civilization or strangeness in the eyes of middle-class Protestant readers. Here is a typical report of a shooting, involving two black men ("Johnson" and "Moore"), one "crazed by drink." Johnson, a barber, had shot Moore and then had tried to shoot himself; note how the news report provides a dramatic reconstruction of the event:

> There was still one chamber loaded in the pistol, but Johnson thought he had emptied them all. He had enough sense to try to hide the weapon, which he threw behind the kitchen door.
> In the meantime, Moore's cries of "I'm shot," brought help to his side.... Constables Barrett and Hasselfelt, drawn by the reports of the revolver, came hurrying up John Street.
> "Hurry, Frank's shot at a man," begged the wife, who met them, wringing her hands.

Now, note the staccato, almost telegraphic reconstruction of the encounter between Johnson and the constables:

> [They] ... drew and cocked their revolvers, and went in through the shop to the kitchen, where the barber sat in a pool of blood.
>   "If I had any more bullets, you wouldn't come in here," Johnson snarled.
>   "What have you been doing, Frank?" demanded P. C. Barrett.
>   "Oh, nothing, nothing," answered that worthy.

And in the *dénouement*, note how the reporter situates the two men for a middle-class, white readership:

> The ambulance was called and the wounded men driven to the hospital. An examination showed the doctors that Moore was in much worse shape than the barber, whose thick African skull had turned the bullet aside....
>   ... Moore, the victim, is not altogether unknown to fame. Several years ago, his marriage to a white woman caused considerable talk.... Three weeks ago, he was in court for a brawl near H. Brazier's barber shop..." ("Shooting Affair Saturday Night," *Hamilton Herald*, 1903: 1)

Of course, moral disruption could surface even in respectable lives. When it did, the events were reported with an odd mixture of salaciousness, obsequiousness, garrulity, curiosity and reservation. (See, e.g., "Princess Shot Actress Rival," and "Murder and Suicide," *Hamilton Herald*, 1903, 1; "Fruit Man's Suicide," *Hamilton Times*, 1910: 1).

Perhaps the most important thing about the burgeoning of crime reporting in the late nineteenth and early twentieth centuries was that it took place in the context of a gradual privatization of punishment. By 1900, public executions and the stocks were memories: the ritual drama of public punishment had been replaced by the grey walls and cells of the penitentiary. Executions took place behind those walls, in the sight only of an invited few, and at an hour guaranteed to ensure few others would be awake. Punishment lost the aura of public spectacle (Foucault, 1977: 15). Even crime underwent a transformation: it did not need to occur as a public and dramatic event before the machinery of justice began to move. With the popularization of scientific detection (and the rise of the detective to folk-hero status, alongside the "brilliant criminal"; see Foucault, 1977: 68–69), justice became successfully proactive, searching out evidence of wrongdoing from apparently innocent surface anomalies. Both the detection of crime *and* its punishment had become increasingly subject to standard procedures: these could still be dramatized, but they were not in themselves dramatic events. But if we accept the Durkheimian hypothesis that the dramatization of crime and punishment is a necessary social dynamic, we are left with a question. In the absence of the public spectacle, what other mechanism of dramatization was available? Here, though the exact historical causality is uncertain, it is tempting to see more than a coincidence in the fact that the abandonment of official public executions, and the rise of the crime beat as a news staple, generally took place, across the United States and Canada, within the same sixty-year period.

The establishment of crime news as a standard category of journalism entailed many changes in the nature of newsmaking, as well as in the ways in which crime was defined and thought about. Crime journalism, like crime detection, became more proactive, and entered into a close if sometimes uneasy alliance with police. Reporters actively sought out news of criminal activity, both actual and possible. They also sought to dramatize all stages of the crime–punishment process, interviewing witnesses, describing the scene as luridly as convention and space might allow, following the activities of investigating detectives, sitting in on trials, commenting on sentences, and gaining interviews with prisoners, guards, and wardens. By doing so, they sought to lift the flat procedures of the authorities, the grim dreariness of the lives of offenders, and the bare factuality of events, into the realm of high drama: violence and adventure, relentless pursuit, tragedy and weakness, repentance and sorrow (see, e.g., Birchall *et al.*, 1890: 59–70). In this way, they mixed together, as the situation warranted, the three different approaches to crime that we noted earlier. A good crime story involved a *scandalous overturning* of the established order of things: not just the legal order, but also those of *privacy*, respectability and propriety. In this light, crimes that were accompanied by evidence of other forms of deviance made good news. But reporters also speculated on the *personal* tragedy of the criminal as a *fallen self*, irresponsible citizen, prodigal son, faithless husband, or uncaring mother. The criminal became an important story element; not merely a human vehicle of transgression and punishment, but a *flawed person* dramatically lacking in responsibility; a moral weakling or defiant reprobate. As such, the criminal could become the focus of more stories after sentencing: stories of repentance, or of continued rebellion. (Best of all was the case of Canadian bank robber and choirboy, Red Ryan; *both* a repentant *and* a reprobate: see Rasky, 1958) Finally, reporters also used, often in the crudest ways, elements of phrenology, eugenics, forensic psychology, and amateur sociology to discuss things like the mental capacity of the criminal (i.e., his "natural" capacity for moral development), the unsavoury nature of his childhood and home life, or associations with disreputable characters which had brought him low.

Of course, not all crimes received an intensive and obsessive treatment from the turn-of-the-century press. Crimes would get more attention depending largely on how they affected two key elements of late-Victorian or Edwardian middle-class society: property and propriety. Thus, crimes involving large amounts of money, dramatic violence, death, or the violation of innocence would receive more press, as would crimes involving apparent social contradictions (an "unlikely criminal," like the convicted murderer Reginald Birchall, the well-born, married son of a clergyman, in 1889: see Birchall, *et al.*, 1890). Crimes involving other forms of deviance or eccentricity as sideshows — a bank robber who was also a bigamist or philanderer — would merit special attention. Categories of people treated as *inherently* deviant would come to public attention through news reports if they committed acts that signified their "nature," or conversely, that crossed social boundaries. Turn-of-the-century reporting also evidenced a lively interest in personal eccentricity; usually tied again to a crossing of status boundaries, to withdrawal from social life (as in stories about hermits and recluses), or to crime. In these characteristics, crime reporting shared much with the developing genre of detective fiction (e.g., Birchall *et al.*, 1890: iii–xxv; Rasky, 1958).

It is important to note that the role of the reader of these accounts had certain parallels to that of the reporter. The task of the reporter was often likened to that of the detective: to ferret out that which was *kept private* (either by the criminal or his associates, or even by the authorities) and to make it *public*. The newspaper reader (and collectively, the reading public), unlike the spectators at public executions, witnessed the events of crime and punishment second-hand and in private: paradoxically, what was "made public" in the newspaper was consumed in *private* by *individual* readers. If crime news can be said to have constituted newspaper readers as a "public," this public was vastly different from a crowd at an execution. Typically, the criminal and judicial process engaged the latter only at the moment of execution or public humiliation (e.g., the stocks). But through the reporter's prose, the privatized *reading* public gained access to the crime scene and its details, peered figuratively over the backs of the investigating officers, attended the trial, heard the sentence, and saw the reaction of the accused (e.g., Birchall *et al.*, 1890). Thus, the account of the *crime* had as much impact as the process of *punishment*; one can argue that a privatized *fear of crime* began to take the place of the intimidation (or vicarious satisfaction) formerly generated by public punishment. Further, the reader's fear of crime, fascination with the criminal, and moral evaluation of the trial, all now took place individually or in the private circles of family or friends. Crime's public now formed, not as a crowd stirred instantly by rumours and collective feelings, but as a replication, across thousands of breakfast or dinner tables, of the individual reader as everyman. As an individual, each reacted to what he read in terms of individual fears for family, property, or propriety. As an individual, he (typically, readers were addressed as male) also reflected on his own sense of self-responsibility and his own status as a citizen and as a normal, moral human being: "could I ever do that?" (see, e.g., the questionnaire, "10 ways to tell if you're addicted to lust," in Valpy, 1998). The news report helped him to do this with vivid descriptions and back-pocket analyses.

At the same time, the reporter's identification with his reader, expressed in what was spoken *and* unspoken in his prose, assured the latter that, as everyman, he represented and was accompanied by a vast unseen mass: the individualized bearers of "public opinion." In the old model of public punishment, the attending crowd was called to respond as a *collective body* by the stately ritual of the event. The grim burlesque of a botched execution, or collective sympathy for an accused, could turn this collective into a mob in minutes. In the new regime, the prisoner isolated in his cell, exhorted by chaplains, and later psychologists, to reflect individually on his character or nature, had his counterpart in the individualized newspaper reader, similarly isolated in his living room, called to reflect, as a "law-abiding citizen," on the deeds and fates of others ... *others who could have been him* in a weak moment — or perhaps his son, caught up by wrong companions, drink or dissipation, or his daughter kidnapped off the street and sold into white slavery. The crowd at the execution of Damiens saw, in the dismemberment of the condemned, the power of their subjection written publicly on his body. The crime story called out and constituted its readers as a different kind of subject: individualized, self-conscious and self-responsible. The reporter's account was transparent, a window from the drawing-room on to the scene: journalists intruded with commentary only to offer themselves to the reader as people "like you": fellow-citizens.

To be sure, the sovereign power of the state still exerted external and official force in this new world, through the police, and through the consultation or employment of new professionals in scientific detection, psychology, eugenics, and crime statistics. But these offered their opinions, *via* the crime story, to a reader who was now (with their help) his own policeman, psychologist, judge and jury; who, reflecting on himself, judged events as they exemplified what he knew of his own personal fears and insecurities, his certainties, pride and self-respect; the safety of his property, and his privacy.

One other thing needs to be noted about the crime story and its readers: the *commercialization of newspapers* (packaging news to attract readers for advertisers) entailed the *consumerization of news* (see Wernick, 1991: 95–102). Readers became vicarious thrill-consumers: the emotional charge generated by the spectacle of crime and punishment became something that could be bought and taken to the office or home every morning or afternoon, and rival papers competed to bring that commodity, suitably polished, to the market. This was not completely new; Roman officialdom had sought revenue from punishment by employing condemned prisoners as gladiators. And as late as the eighteenth and nineteenth centuries, public executions had commercial sideshows; hawkers selling refreshments, foods, or even printed broadsheets containing the condemned's confession. But the publicizing of crime and punishment by news organizations now became a fully integrated commercial operation, undertaken for commercial purposes, and targeting consumers as a resource to be mined and delivered to advertisers.

This model of the mediatization of crime would survive largely intact into the world of television. But before we turn to the portrayal of deviance in the electronic media, a few words of caution must be said about the picture of the newspaper crime story and its reader drawn above. News readers may form groups predictably stable enough for marketing purposes, but they can also react unpredictably to news coverage and they are fully capable of communicating those reactions beyond the confines of the family home, the office, bar, or coffee shop. We must also remember that the newspaper medium is the produced effect of a complex mix of technologies, business and professional practices, political pressures, and forms of administrative organization (Tuchman, 1978; Philo, 1990). These complexities have specific consequences which any general model cannot fully account for. Journalists and editors do their work according to a mix of time pressure, office politics, budget limits, professional concerns, and business priorities. News, including crime news, is produced in terms of a conception of "public interest" informed by professional values, class assumptions, cultural and legal standards of privacy, libel and slander laws, and current ideologies respecting political order, public safety, property rules, and the family (see Tuchman, 1978: 15–103; Lorimer and McNulty, 1996: 242–275; Smith, 1978). The changing technology of newspaper production affects the product too: an emphasis on descriptive detail in news journalism fell off as newspapers gained the ability to print black and white, and later colour, photos. News organizations and their products are also affected by their external relations to state agencies and to the market. As the average rate of profit of newspaper operations has fallen, even the largest have faced pressures to cut back on investigative journalism in favour of readily available pre-produced news from the public relations agencies of governments, police, lobby groups, and corporations. Such reliance can affect the extent to which news organizations turn a critical eye on their sources. Newspapers also report crime differently depending on the consumer market they serve: thus, for example, street and small-property crime will be more a staple for tabloid papers like the *Toronto Sun*, with a readership composed of working- and middle-class people who perceive themselves to be vulnerable to petty theft, burglaries, or assault. Papers with a professional and business readership, like the *Globe and Mail*, will report "major" crimes with less overt emphasis on sensationalism, and will tend to focus coverage more on the kinds of crime likely to affect the business environment in general, or a less-vulnerable upper-middle-class readership in particular.

Still, the basic rules laid down for crime journalism more than a century ago have survived well, as coverage of a 1998 British trial showed. That summer, a Canadian businessman named Albert Walker was tried for the murder of a friend, Ronald Platt. The interest of the Walker trial was that he had disappeared from Canada a few years earlier, taking with him funds from a number of people who had invested in his southern Ontario financial services company. Until 1997, he had lived in England, using the name Platt. Platt himself had disappeared, but was later found to have drowned after being hit over the head and thrown from Walker's yacht. The trial was reported in great detail, and much was made in the Canadian coverage of the fact that the British media, and the rich and famous, were in evidence at the trial. The amount of money Walker actually stole, while large to his investors, was inconsequential in relation to the size of the Canadian financial services industry. Even the manner in which he stole it, or the way in which he eluded detection, were not new. But the case aroused media attention because it was colourful. Walker himself was articulate, handsome, and persuasive; he had a family and had been a churchgoer; he was a "charming sociopath," and thus a wonderful example of the kind of person who "should" be an upstanding citizen but turns out to be the opposite. His efforts to cover his tracks, and of the police to uncover them, complete with the role played in his conviction by the repair records on a Rolex watch worn by the victim, all fit the formulae of detective fiction. This was an eminently saleable story, suited to be read by anyone who had ever fantasized about making off with someone else's money. But another aspect of the Walker story made it even better copy. Walker had left Canada with his teenage daughter. When they were caught, it turned out that she had posed as Walker's wife, and that during their time on the run she had borne two children. The ambiguous parentage of these children was not an issue in the trial, but it — and the possible moral trespass it implied — soon became a focus of the coverage. The Walker trial made news because of this element of scandal — because it was about the moral as well as criminal downfall of a gifted but abnormal man. The coverage encouraged readers to look behind the offence *at this man*, and to judge him on the basis of his moral responsibility, not only to his family and his investors, but also to his lost better self — a self lost to a pathology hiding under an elaborate cloak of normalcy (see, e.g., *Maclean's*, 1998a: 26–33)

TELEVISION DEVIANCE

Unlike newspapers, television is not sold to the public, but distributed free, or for a fee paid to a cable or satellite distributor. Nonetheless, the organization of television news bears a distinct resemblance to that of print news. Television carries advertising, and to attract advertisers, it must maintain ratings: the number of viewers who tune in per day or week. (In Canada, even non-commercial broadcasters face this ratings pressure: the dominance of commercial TV, the growing popularity of satellite transmission, and the onset of digital broadcasting ensure that the offerings of non-commercial broadcasters are increasingly judged by their ratings or sales, and funding is calculated accordingly.) Thus, television programming, including news programming, must sell itself; it must attract viewers. It does so in ways that strongly resemble the protocols of print journalism: television crime news is constructed according to the same basic rules established in newspaper journalism earlier this century, and both must package stories to make them as attractive as possible. In both instances, such packaging tends to blur distinctions between news, entertainment, and advertising (Wernick, 1991: 100–101). Conversely, both also make reference to the public interest as their overriding concern, and both define that interest as the individualized middle-class householder, worker, and taxpayer. Television is watched, as newspapers are read, largely in private, domestic settings (Morley, 1986; see also Morley, 1992; Ang, 1995).

However, there are four differences between television and newspapers that affect the coverage of deviance and crime offered by both. Television, like the newspaper, is a complex mix of different types of information. But television is also a full-fledged entertainment vehicle, carrying a wide range of *non*-news material: comedy, talk shows, and drama, for example. A full discussion of the portrayal of deviance on television must take into account that most television programming genres have deviance, in one form or another, as their subject matter. Situation comedies rely on the laugh value of minor or apparent infractions of manners or morality; drama deals with the tragic consequences of transgression; talk shows and pro wrestling present a carnivalesque feast of transgressive indignity.

Second, television is an audiovisual medium with the power to represent events (as if) "live." The rise of television news coverage has meant both a new kind of news, dependent on immediacy and action sequences, and a change in print journalism, as television and print work out a tacit division of labour. Television images take over the job of emotive description from the inflated prose of turn-of-the-century reporters; newspapers tend more to the presentation of factual detail and background (though this claim does not address the "televisual" effects developed by colour print tabloids, or their characteristically emotive journalistic devices). Above all, television provides immediacy, figuratively putting the viewer in the middle of the action. Where journalistic description had served as a device by which readers could *imagine* the scene brought to them, videotape puts them right *there*: it allows for the illusion that the viewer is transparently present to the scene. This sense is especially pronounced on shows such as *Cops*, a series in which viewers are treated, courtesy of mobile video recording equipment, to rides in police cruisers, foot chases after suspects (camera image bobbing realistically), and close ups of scuffles and handcuffing. Of course, the irony is that the sense of being on-the-spot is a *produced effect*, in which tape editing, camera angles, choice of establishing shots, and the use of visual analogies serve as mediating codes just as much as the reporter's prose once did in newspaper journalism (Knight, 1989; Tuchman, 1978; Fiske, 1987: 21–47; Fiske and Hartley, 1978: 37–67)

Third, television encourages participation on the part of its viewers. Marshall McLuhan dubbed television a "cool" medium because its mixture of audio and visual information allowed the viewer to invest in and respond to the presentation in a number of ways (McLuhan, 1964: chs. 2, 3, 31). Today, many are inclined to treat television viewing as a passive (and thus negative) affair. But the immediacy of its presentation encourages response: television viewers are encouraged to think of themselves as if they are "there" on the scene, just as their ancestors a few hundred years earlier might have been physically present at an execution. Of course, they are not present physically, and they are not present *to each other* as members of a public group. But the illusion of immediacy feeds a wish to respond; thus, docuentertainment shows like *America's Most Wanted* also become law-enforcement devices: people who recognize a face are given an 800 number to call. Local news stations advertise for amateur video of newsworthy events, and interview those who submit worthwhile footage.

Finally, I would suggest that television, much more than print news, encourages the public carnivalization of deviance, and implicitly, the development of multiple viewpoints on crime and deviance. This is not to say that television coverage of crime and deviance lacks standards by which they are to be defined. The signifiers of a sober, self-conscious, middle-class "public" are still there, in the cool demeanour of news anchors, in the talk show host's end-of-show summation, and in the professionalized jargon in terms of which an officer on *Cops* evaluates events at the end of a shift. The unfit, unhealthy, unfashionable, quarrelsome, evasive, belligerent "others" who wreak mayhem on talk shows like the *Jerry Springer Show*, who race away from pursuing officers on *Cops*, or who make obscene gestures to news cameramen, are all chosen to be placed in a harsh middle-class light. But at the same time, the increasing popularity of such "images from the other side" indicates something else: a revelry in transgression of middle-class morality, taste, and especially, privacy codes. In talk-show confessions, deviance becomes externalized display; a development parallelling the behavioural re-externalization of correctional procedures, and the revival of retribution as both a popular cause and a symbolic blood sport (see Lotringer, 1988: 165–177). The consumerized savour of outrageousness stands alongside the moral expression of outrage. The world of US television, especially, appears to be composed of equal parts moral outrage and outrageous spectacle, as the news coverage of President Clinton's purported sex scandals in 1997 and 1998 illustrates. The Clinton scandals were fed by the outrage of the religious right, but they ended up producing a burlesque president — a figure of fun and sexual comedy. The *Jerry Springer Show*, one of the more far-out offerings of late-90s talk TV, marketed a video of events judged "too hot for TV," complete with a disclaimer by the host to the effect that while the behaviour shown was outrageous, its presentation was a matter of free speech. Television feeds a fascination with transgression with dramatic but ambiguous images (Fiske, 1987: 240–264).

Overall, the message of commercial television remains conservative: the portrayal of crime feeds a fear of crime among the more socially vulnerable viewers, and the "bad news" of the nightly newscast is placed in an ideological context in which fundamental social institutions remain unquestioned. (Even revelations concerning the Los Angeles police force which arose from the O.J. Simpson and Rodney King trials in the 1990s led to the usual "bad apples" arguments, rather than to fundamental questioning of the nature and necessity of policing as a social institution.) For transgression to be fascinating, it must continue to be defined as transgression. Still, the constant parade of transgressive images entices a desire for images progressively hotter than those "too hot" for TV, and introduces a note of carnival subversion and grotesquerie that a middle-class frame and middle-class privacy codes cannot quite recover.

THEORIZING THE PORTRAYAL OF DEVIANCE IN MEDIA MESSAGES

A number of theories have been developed to explain the construction, organization, impact, and significance of the products of contemporary mass media organizations. In this section, we will examine a few of these theories in an attempt to come up with a comprehensive view of the construction and communication of media messages about deviance and crime.

Interpellation

Like all forms of human communication, media messages have two aspects. They communicate their contents: they are *about* something. But they also communicate a *frame* for responding to that content. A letter, memo, or e-mail message normally arrives with an address attached so that one knows who it is from and for whom it is meant. More generally, the way in which any message is constructed constitutes a "form of address" that calls out or, to use the technical term, "interpellates" its intended receiver as *a particular kind of subject*. Let's say that you meet someone on the street who calls out a greeting using your first name. The content of the message may be a simple question, "How are you?" or a statement, "Long time, no see!" But the *form* in which the message is put — the use of your first name, the use of stock phrases — signals to you that you are being greeted as a particular kind of person in relation to the greeter — as a *friend*. And you are expected to respond in kind. The French philosopher Louis Althusser used the concept of interpellation to explain how ideology works. He defined ideology not simply as a set of ideas but as a way of being in and orienting to the world; one structured in terms of unreflective responses to others, and to ruling ideas embodied in voices of authority. We are interpellated as subjects when we are addressed, and when we respond, in ways that place us in a shared world of values, judgments, and expectations; for example, as students, workers, employees, crime suspects, prisoners, consumers, men, women, gay, or straight (Althusser, 1971; see also Fiske, 1987: 48–61).

We can use this idea to talk about how media accounts of deviance or crime recommend to their readers not just a particular definition of deviance or a particular set of values, but also a *way of reading* which amounts to a specific *way of being a subject* interested in or concerned about crime or deviance. For example, a typical account of crime in an established newspaper will be written to be read from the standpoint of a middle-class, law-abiding citizen. It will omit or include what such a person typically judges to be important or unimportant about such crime, and it will define crime as a threat in terms of a middle-class view of the world. A news account of a crime, a criminal, or a trial will typically construct the criminal as "other," to the "I" of the reader (see Cohen, 1972: 16–18) unless a similarity to the imagined average reader can be used for dramatic contrast (as in the cases of middle-class murderers Albert Walker and Paul Bernardo), and will rely on official sources staffed by middle-class professionals for most of that construction. Thus, if readers accept the story as authoritative, they also accept a certain subjective way of looking at crime in terms of relations of authority. Successful interpellation means to provide answers to the implicit questions, "Who am I [supposed to be] as I watch this news item or read this article? Who must I be to understand it successfully?" Take, for example, a news story about squeegee kids: young people who dart out from street corners in large cities to wash the windshields of stopped cars for tips. To define them as "unemployed," and to highlight questions about the potential intimidation of drivers or traffic tie-ups, would be to present the story for car drivers, not squeegee kids. More to the point, such a story would address car drivers as ideological subjects — people who believe in the rights of private property (including one's car), in the right of automobiles to dominate streets, and in the legitimacy of ways of making money which occur only off-pavement and in accordance with business licences.

How is this important to discussions of deviance in the media? First, definitions of deviance are always relative to a particular form of accepted order; thus, the definition of deviance is always in some sense political. Most news articles and television shows dealing with deviance assume that their audiences and readers know what deviance is. That is, the politics of decisions about what is and isn't deviance, and who decides, is bracketed and left aside. If you can read a news article about crime without fundamentally questioning what is *defined* as crime, then you share in the ideological universe represented by the article: you accept the recommended reading and thus accept yourself as the kind of subject the article addresses. News about crime daily teaches us who "we" are as law-abiding citizens merely by encouraging us to read or watch crime coverage. This does *not* mean that definitions of deviance are simply imposed by "the media": such definitions are produced within organizations staffed by people whose job it is to, in some sense, "think like us." But the mere fact that media messages are constructed and conveyed by a sophisticated social, economic and cultural apparatus entails that the relation between viewer and producer is unequal; further, the messages conveyed will be so constructed as to defend and legitimate the systemic interests which the apparatus represents and supports.

The "Bardic" Function of Television

John Fiske and John Hartley (1978) argued that television is particularly suited to tell us "who we are" as collective subjects because, as an audiovisual medium, it contains requisites that made ballad singers and storytellers so powerful in traditional societies. Television is immediate: it conveys powerful symbolic images, and does so to the accompaniment of sound: music, the voice, sound effects. In traditional societies, bards tell the community about itself in ways that strengthen its shared sense of itself as a collective subject with one history, one purpose, and one way of being. Bards also tell tales that speak of damage to that collective self-image, and in speaking of it seek to "repair" it and to recover that which is broken, ambiguous, or contradictory in the shared experience of the community. Similarly, Fiske and Hartley argue, television programming constitutes its viewers as a community, celebrates that community, repairs its contradictions, and recovers its ambiguities through forms of narrative (drama, comedy, news) that tell it about itself in terms of symbolically loaded stock characters (Fiske and Hartley, 1978: 85–100). However, we might also note, with Althusser, that television programming, the product of a multibillion dollar worldwide industry, cannot be equated simply with the songs and stories of traditional bards. Television programming may fit the bardic role in a broad sense, but it also reflects the complex organizational circumstances of its production, and the class and institutional interests at work in that production.

In line with this caveat, we can suggest that television also works as an instrument of what Antonio Gramsci called *hegemony*, creating a precarious consensus out of conflicting and unequal social interests. Gramsci argued that some classes benefit more than others from the commercial and institutional organization of capitalist society, and some classes exert more control and influence over social life than others. Those who own newspapers or television broadcasting and production industries, and those who occupy places of authority within such industries, though not necessarily of the same class, tend to share similar outlooks and interests. Television programming may not always directly reflect those interests, but material which directly *contradicts* them will tend to be marginalized if presented at all. Gramsci argued that class rule, in modern societies, is rarely exercised directly or repressively; rather, dominant classes tend to recruit other social groups into a broad ruling consensus by including within that consensus some attention to the concerns of the latter. Thus, for example, the welfare state can be said to have bought social peace for capitalism by recruiting the loyalty of workers through the provision of social services and visions of security and equal opportunity. Neo-liberalism, which argues for the reduction of the welfare state, is an influential ideology not merely because it reflects pro-globalization capitalist interests, but also because it has been made attractive to the middle classes, through appeals to the need for "freedom" — from taxes, red tape, government restrictions on entrepreneurship, and so on (Gramsci, 1971; see also Hall, 1977).

In this light, newspapers and television can be said to be instruments of hegemony. The ideological world that they celebrate and call us to be members of, individually and collectively, benefits the interests of the dominant social classes (owners of capital, professionals, administrators and managers). The "rituals of consensus" (Dayan and Katz, 1988) embedded in television programming recruit us into that world by representing and celebrating it as "ours too." It does so most strongly by recruiting viewers to a *lifestyle* and a set of lifestyle beliefs, and by contrasting these to forms of crime and deviance which threaten that lifestyle. For example, by generating fear (not necessarily intentionally) among ordinary homeowners about home invasion robberies, crime reporting reinforces middle-class beliefs in the value of private property in general. This need not be done consciously or as part of a conspiracy: "the media" are not agents in their own right. The bardic function of television is a *social process* rather than a *conscious purpose*: television *acts as* a bard in modern culture, but television programming need not be consciously *planned* for that purpose.

The "Visualization" of Deviance

The power of television to represent crime and deviance is the power to make deviance more than a set of ideas: television provides powerful *images* of transgression and its consequences. On television, crime and deviance once again become visual spectacles. To return to Fiske and Hartley's conception of television as "bardic," we note that bards told their communities' stories through a highly formulaic language employing powerful verbal and gestural imagery. Similarly, television today evokes emotional responses through the employment of visual images which call us out — which *interpellate* us — as citizens and as "human beings," *emotionally* as well as intellectually. These images tend to be formulaic (a wife, mother, or sister collapsing in grief at the funeral of a murder victim), and often represent archetypal codes that appeal to deep-seated prejudices. Televisual representations of murder scenes, for example, will often focus on traces of blood — something which is far more than a liquid. Blood is an archetypal symbol both of life and also of the [violent] loss of life. Blood evokes fear and fascination in viewers, and its association with a crime scene drives home a powerful emotional message. As Durkheim might have said, an intellectual knowledge of social limits and of the consequences of transgression is not enough: such limits and consequences have to be *seen* and *felt*, and much as we find them disturbing, we also crave vivid representations of them.

Thus, while it may have a powerful emotional punch, television imagery, like newspaper prose, follows a set of conventional formulae constituting a code. Typically, television representations of deviance are set in narrative form: whether we are watching a comedy, a drama, or the evening news, television, like the bards of old, tells us *stories*. These may be fully worked out, or incomplete story-elements, but any media portrayal of deviance will generally take the form of, or borrow from, certain basic narrative conventions. To tell a crime story is to open a tear in the web of cultural conformity: to introduce a contradiction into the calm surface of the ordinary. This sets up a dramatic tension: how will order and legitimacy be re-established? The narrative takes us on a journey toward that end (called, in the structuralist analysis of narrative, "closure"). Closure amounts to the restoration of cultural order and confidence, either by returning matters to a pre-existing *status quo*, or by re-establishing order at a new level or in a different way. Closure involves an ideological repair job on the damage done by deviance. In that repair, various narrative tools may be employed, of which the most common are the employment of contrastive stock figures (competent *versus* incompetent, good *versus* bad, responsible *versus* irresponsible), and the use of contrast between the human actors in a story and the ideals which they flout or defend (see Fiske, 1987: 128–147).

Closure, for a crime story, might appear to come with the arrest and conviction of a criminal. But often, crime stories cannot be ended so neatly. A criminal may be caught, but the damage done (let's say, the murder of a child) may be irreparable. Or a criminal may never be caught, and the crime may go unsolved. In the worst case, the crime may remain unsolved, the criminal at large, *and* the institutions charged with bringing matters to a close may be brought into disrepute. Such was the case in 1995 when an Ontario man, Guy Paul Morin, who had been charged and convicted of the murder of a six-year-old girl, was finally acquitted and then exonerated. Media attention focused once again on the hunt for a killer. But by 1998, hope that the real killer would ever be found was running low. The year previous, a provincial government inquiry into the case had brought to light disturbing evidence of apparent incompetence and prejudice on the part of investigating officers and forensic scientists.

Here, then, was the worst possible example of an "unclosable" story: no killer, irreparable damage to the family of the girl, lost years in the life of Morin, and an untrustworthy criminal investigation system. News reports and media discussion of these events responded to the felt need for closure by raising closure to another level. The damage done by the murder was irreversible, and that could only be acknowledged. But an innocent man had been freed, and thus Justice was shown to have been done, at least in part. The investigating police force, forensic scientists, Crown attorneys, and even Morin's original defence lawyer could be represented as deeply flawed *agents* of that Justice, but the concept of *justice itself*, *embodied* in the law, was not challenged: the implication was that the justice *system* was reparable, and that its ideals remained valid. What was needed was to reveal and eliminate the bad *practices* and incompetent *practitioners* who had brought Justice temporarily into disrepute. To this end, reporting and editorializing on the Morin inquiry now deviantized (as prejudiced and/or clumsy) several of those unquestioningly accepted as official sources during the initial investigation (see, e.g., Laframboise, 1995a). On the other hand, the villain became a hero. In the original coverage of Morin's arrest and trials, news accounts had reported aspects of his and his family's lives which appeared deviant, later reinforced by his defence counsel's apparently ill-advised use of an insanity plea. But at the inquiry, Morin's image was transformed *via* quotes highlighting his magnanimity, and the human drama of his partial reconciliation with some members of the murdered girl's family. In particular, a contrast was drawn between an investigating officer's continued reluctance to admit that Morin was innocent, and Morin's own initial outrage at, and later his forgiveness of, those who had doubted him. Morin himself became a representative of Justice — not an agent of revenge, but a symbol of personal and social redemption: the truth winning out (e.g., Laframboise, 1995b).

Television is particularly suited to rendering transgression, reconciliation, and resolution as dramatic spectacles, even when, as in the Morin case, little or no evidence of the original crime could be shown. Television works best in close up: directly, in the formulaic drama of words, gestures, or facial expressions, or through evocative shots of meaning-laden dramatic props and settings: murder weapons, crime scenes, or (where available) traces of blood. In this capacity, however, television risks becoming "deviant" in its own right. That which we most abhor is also that which fascinates us. And while television programming may serve the social function of bard in our culture, it does so as a *commercial* enterprise: its business is the *selling* of powerful images in return for ratings. Thus, television, film, and video may tend to cross a line to feed a fascination with transgression and its products, death and violence, because such images *sell*. Once again, we must remember that no one general theory captures all dimensions of the media portrayal of crime and deviance.

The Social Construction of the Crime Story

We have seen that media representations of crime and deviance, especially in televisual representations, employ powerful narrative and symbolic devices to tell us things about ourselves and our culture, and to call us out, individually and collectively, as particular kinds of subjective selves. The way in which these messages are *produced* is also complex, embodying a mix of intended and unintended consequences. Deviance is a *social construct*, and the vehicles of that construction, namely stories about crime and deviance carried in the news and entertainment media, are themselves the end products of a complex set of organizational practices. Dorothy Smith (1974) argues that the effect of media representations is to bring into being a world she calls "documentary reality" — a cumulative effect of the production of print and audio-visual documents by human labour employed in complex organizational processes. No document (no crime story, for example) is ever simply a straight reflection of "reality."

To illustrate this point, let's look at the production of a news report about a criminal occurrence. Typically, before a reporter even finds out about the occurrence, it has already been worked up into a number of accounts, all of them involving decisions about the significance and nature of the event. The officer at the scene must decide (on the basis of witnesses' reports, each one an already-constructed story) whether the event warrants further investigation or charges. To proceed further will involve decisions about the stories of the alleged incident: Are those involved making it up? Are bystanders exaggerating? Did the event significantly disrupt public order? Is this kind of event common or rare in this particular area? What else is going on, or likely to go on during the officer's beat? Who is likely to complain if the event is ignored? What sections of the Criminal Code might apply?

To charge someone means to construct a unified account of what they have done (a police report). When the suspect is taken into custody, this account may be augmented by further questioning. The suspect may call a lawyer, who in turn uses the accounts already developed to construct yet another story to defend the accused in court. Working on the basis of police reports, a crown attorney will also construct an account for court, based on a decision that the alleged crime is worth prosecuting. When the occurrence comes to the attention of journalists, they too will have to decide whether it merits attention as "newsworthy": this decision will depend on a number of factors, including what else is going on that day, whether the crime fits certain recognizable patterns that would make a story saleable in terms of popular fears (e.g., "another teen swarming incident") or the "the public interest." Reporters may go on to interview witnesses, neighbours, investigating officers or their superiors, defence or prosecuting counsel, experts on a particular type of crime, and so on. From each, they will get a different story, from which they must construct a version of events to fit the slant of their particular organization, the wishes of editors, news deadlines, and the anticipated perceptions of the readership or audience. Once published or televised, the story will be read or watched not just by ordinary news-consumers, but also by competing news organizations, who will adjust their coverage accordingly.

Note two things about the above example. First, any news story is constructed from several already produced accounts, each of which will typically reflect specific personal and organizational settings. Second, the construction of all of these accounts involves decisions at every step of the way. The definition of a "crime" is not simply the direct function of the existence of a law and an action which contravenes it. The contravention must be *shown to exist* through an account which *names it* and *makes it visible* as such. Justice is interpreted, applied, and reported through human actors working in complex organizational situations, responding to pressures of time, convenience, self-presentation, self-preservation, organizational loyalty, professional ethics, and so on. To their work, they bring a set of working stereotypes, prejudices, and ideals, from their class and gender backgrounds, and from their previous practical and organizational experience. The definition of deviance or crime, then, is always political, not just in the sense that such definitions are culturally relative, but also in the sense that they are constructed through complex processes of account-building, on-the-spot categorizing, and decision-making. In this process, as Smith makes clear, what really happened is only raw material for the production of *accounts* about "what really happened," and it is only through such accounts that we have access to worlds of crime and deviance beyond our personal lives. These accounts are the materials out of which readers and viewers construct visions of reality: "worlds" to inhabit and respond to.

Richard Ericson, Patricia Baranek, and Janet Chan (1987; see also 1991), who studied the various organizational processes through which news accounts of crime and deviance are constructed, found a high degree of reliance by news workers on official accounts generated by police and judicial organizations and by professionals. This reliance signalled that the legitimacy and accuracy of such official accounts was taken for granted in a way that was only rarely shaken (the Morin inquiry was "news" precisely because it did so dramatically). In other words, news organizations and their employees show an organizational bias toward accounts produced professionally within similar organizations. Thus, people with no strong organizational ties, who are clients of organizations (and thus dependent on them, as in the case of welfare recipients), or who are relatively inarticulate and unable to deal with organizations, are easily "deviantized," both in official reports of their actions and in news accounts (Ericson, Baranek, and Chan, 1987: esp. 282–286). Further, both police and news organizations set up regular information-gathering "beats" in which certain groups or areas are defined as more likely sources of crime or deviance, while others may be benignly ignored. As well as proactively fishing for deviance, journalists also exercise a great deal of latitude in their *definitions* of it. Through their dissemination of such definitions, they become influential in articulating visions of order, as well as moral panics. The politics of crime and deviance is thus not simply a reflection of the complexity of organizations and of the process of building accounts and deciding definitions. Stories about crime and deviance are political because they also reflect an *institutionalized inequality in the power to produce accounts and to have those accounts listened to and taken seriously*. Many of those who come into contact with the press and the judicial system without a position of strength find that their power to render their own accounts of their actions is taken away and they become both "defendants" and "dependants," dependent on co-operation with the official machinery of judicial account-producing to make their way through the system (Ericson and Baranek, 1982).

Designating Deviance

So far, we have looked at the process by which media representations of deviance are constructed, largely leaving aside questions about *what* gets represented as deviant or criminal. The definition of what is criminal might seem at first more clear-cut than the broader category of deviance: criminal codes would appear to give the answer. But as we have seen, the law can be *interpreted and applied* differently in different circumstances (which are themselves the results of definitional work), and some kinds of criminal activity receive far more attention, both from police and from the media, than others. Designating deviance involves matching cultural and organizational knowledge of central values, symbols, prejudices, and competencies to one's definitions of given situations. If the types of activity defined and publicized as criminal or deviant in a given society reflect that society's priorities, then a study of what is held most dear in a given social setting will tell us much about what is condemned, and *vice versa*.

For many, when the word "deviance" is mentioned, sexuality easily comes to mind. Indeed, in recent years, crimes of a sexual nature have gained a great deal of media attention. In the popular point of view (reinforced by stories about repeat offenders), sexual criminals are supposed to be particularly incorrigible and a constant threat to the peace and order of domestic life and neighbourhoods. In any society, sexual taboos tend to be among those most powerfully enforced, perhaps because of their symbolic force, or the potential which sexual relations have to disrupt social, economic, and property structures. Michel Foucault has also pointed out that, since the nineteenth century, "sexuality" has come to be taken as a privileged point of entry by which psychologists can understand human persons and their social lives. By virtue of that privileged status, sexuality has become at once a legitimate object of inquiry, and an object of surveillance and control by professionals and state agencies (Foucault, 1978; Lotringer, 1988). However, the importance of sexuality in the definition of deviance often reflects an alliance between fears about sexual matters and deep-seated beliefs about *other* features of social life. For example, the way in which sexual crimes are defined today has much to do with the importance of the concept of the individual person, and the right of the individual to autonomy and self-ownership, expressed through control of the body (Elias, 1978: 169–205). Sexual harassment, sexual assault, and the like tend to be defined as violations of one's personal rights to one's body, one's privacy, and one's sexual autonomy. Durkheim referred to modern individualism as a sort of religious phenomenon (the "cult of the individual"), and today many of the strongest penalties in law are reserved for actions which most directly or dramatically violate the right of the person to his or her own life, autonomy, and body (see, e.g., Durkheim, 1979).

Individualism as a central cultural value (Durkheim, 1992a: 68–71; Abercrombie, Hill, and Turner, 1986) also affects the definition of the criminal. In law and in cultural tradition, we think of a criminal act as the product of a criminal *individual*: individuals commit and are responsible for crimes. As obvious as this may seem, it is not the only way in which criminal responsibility can be assigned or defined. Take, for example, the execution of Damiens. Damiens, individually, was found guilty and executed. But there is a sense in which he was incidental to his own execution. His public dismemberment was less a punishment of *him* personally than a sign to *all others like him* of their status as subjects of an absolute monarch, and of the revenge that awaited them should they trespass upon the royal privileges or person. Today, by contrast, criminals own their crimes, and do so in two senses. First, they are legally *and morally* responsible for them, and are judged as such in the courts of law and of public opinion. Second, they are often treated as incompetent owners of a *disability*, a deviant or criminal personality or propensity which led them to commit the act. Thus, for example, sex offenders are treated as legally guilty and morally reprehensible, but also as possessors of *abnormal behavioural tendencies*, subject to behavioural re-engineering, unless deemed ineradicable (Lotringer, 1988; see also Anderson, 1996: 383–386; Goffman, 1963). In a culture which stresses the centrality of individuals (as moral subjects, as consumers, or as object-units of an aggregate population measured according to statistical/prescriptive norms), the idea that deviance and crime have *social* aspects is sometimes difficult to sustain, because such social dimensions are seen to detract from the moral responsibility of the offender and the individualized "abnormality" of crime (the exception being the identification of suspect or "dysfunctional" *groups*, such as "street people," or "gangs").

While the culture of individualism deeply marks definitions of both crime and punishment, it is modified by the existence of distinctions between different *kinds* of individuals based on race, class, gender, age, and ability. These too generate categories of deviance. Latterly, many of these distinctions have been deemed illegitimate for official purposes: ideas that there is such a thing as "women's work" in any normative sense, or a racial predisposition to crime, are neither as popular — nor as legally enforceable — today as they were seventy years ago. Nonetheless, such distinctions still show up subtly, for example, in television comedies like the popular 1990s series *Friends*, in which women, formally the equals of men, take on *in*formal roles as emotional caregivers within quasi-families of peers, or are comedically penalized for *not* doing so (Martin, 1997: 134–149).

We also live in a society which values the institution of *property*, specifically property held by individuals (even corporations, in law, hold property as "legal individuals"). Thus, *property crime* is of particular importance, especially when a particular type of crime symbolizes a threat to the propertied as a whole. When threats to property are combined with threats to *persons*, a great deal of frantic publicity may result. For example, "home invasion" robberies have a relatively minor impact on society as a whole compared to white-collar or organized crime, but they combine three key elements to make them the foci of public anxiety. First, they are, in the popular imagination, crimes committed by the faceless, propertyless, and place-less (strangers, gang members) against the propertied and settled: those with solid, individualized, material identities. Second, they combine threats to property with the compromising of personal space and safety. Third, they are *dramatic* crimes, involving the potential for violence ranging from broken doors, to beatings, to hostage-taking.

Finally, we live in a society in which buying and selling are fundamentally important and all-pervasive sociocultural activities. Andrew Wernick (1991) relates this phenomenon to what he calls "promotional culture," in which goods are produced first to be marketed and second for use; in which goods embody their own promotional devices, advertising themselves through packaging, design, and so on. Cross-promotional activity and the commercialization of private life (Ewen, 1976) have ensured that large parts of modern culture have become vehicles for selling: we live in a world in which something that does not sell, and does not advance the cause of selling, is deemed useless. University educations become relevant only if saleable to employers; municipal governments take out magazine ads marketing their citizens to multinational corporations, and individuals undertake self-improvement regimes (including fitness and higher education) in order to be able to promote themselves as prospective employees, friends, and mates. Parents buy children computers by the age of three not only to help them get a leg up in academic and later employment competition, but also to ensure that the children grow up into *symbols* of successful parenting. In this world, the "unimproved" person — the person without saleable skills, the right accent, grammar, clothes, body shape, or teeth — becomes a "loser." Such people are defined as deviant not because of what they do, but because of what they *do not do* and because of what they *are*. It is no accident, then, that educational programs for youth at risk of crime include self-promotion as a "life skill," or conversely, that those who do not pay enough attention to the requisites of self-promotion are said to be at risk not only of a lack of success but also of a life of crime.

Therein may lie the attraction of some of the people who appear as guests on the *Jerry Springer Show*, or who come to the attention of the police on *Cops*. They often appear fascinatingly unsuccessful and unsaleable in middle-class terms: their otherness communicated by how they dress, how much they weigh, how they talk, or how they fight. They are portrayed as part of a carnival of the grotesquely unpromotable, providing middle-class viewers with yet another venue for transgressive fascination. But again, such a fascination, and the multiplication of images that it breeds, subverts the official message. Paradoxically, the inarticulate, overweight, and unfashionable gain a certain promotional legitimacy through their popularity in television spectacles (see Fiske, 1987: 240–264).

WHO WATCHES? WHO CARES?

Much of this chapter has focused on ways in which media messages about crime and deviance recommend certain ways of reading or viewing — of visualizing the social world, and of defining oneself as a subject in relation both to authority and to those who transgress it. We have cautioned that such forms of recommendation are functions not only of the institutional *place* of media in the social world, but also of the sometimes unpredictable *effects* of the complex production of media messages. "The media" do not necessarily set out deliberately to propagandize on behalf of a particular vision of the world, though this can happen in specific instances. Neither do they successfully "tell us what to think" about crime and deviance according to some brainwashing model. It certainly can be said, on the other hand, that what the media provide us with may *limit* our ability to understand the worlds of crime and deviance, either by limiting the criteria according to which we are able to judge events or define crime, or by limiting the types and amounts of information we have. For example, news reports on individual crimes tend to leave the cumulative impression that certain types of crime, especially violent or sexual crimes, are on the rise. Statistical information which might give the lie to some of these impressions is often not highlighted: it makes drier news. Further, media reports on crime and its perpetrators often tend to leave the latter strangely "faceless," even when well-described: we get little sense of who the accused are as human beings, rather than as representatives of a threat.

Despite these imposed limitations, however, readers and viewers still take an active part in the process by which the popular meaning of crime and deviance are made, accepting reports which confirm their beliefs and discounting those which do not. Working with Smith's notion of "documentary reality" as the produced effect of multiple layers of accounts, we can say that the final account to be constructed is that made by the *newspaper reader or television viewer*. Readers and viewers may simply accept the story as it is meant to be understood. But often they do not, and they can generate meanings that subvert the intended meanings of news stories (Fiske, 1987: 62–83). No better examples of this can be found than the reactions of blacks and whites to the coverage of the O.J. Simpson trial in the US, and in the response to media coverage of the Clinton scandal. Whites overwhelmingly took the coverage of the Simpson trial to be a convincing exposé of Simpson's guilt. A majority of blacks, watching the same coverage, were convinced of his innocence. In the case of the Clinton scandal, many readers and viewers were so unmoved by the combination of editorial moralizing and salacious coverage in the media that their refusal to buy into the news media "take" on Clinton became a story in its own right (Posner, 1998).

How those who read or watch media accounts of crime and deviance will interpret and respond to what they see or hear depends who they are, and who they talk to. Who we are, as consumers of media content, depends both on our background and on our present circumstances: the patterns of our past and present experience powerfully shape how we see, evaluate, live in, and reproduce the world. "We" inhabit the world differently from others — it can even be said that we inhabit different worlds — depending on our past and present experience of class, gender, race, occupation, region, and religion; whether we grow up in urban or rural environments; what age and stage of life we are at; whether we have or have not spent time in prison; whether or not we are dependent on government aid to live; and what perceived abilities and disabilities we are said to "have." In fact, class in the form of "cultural capital" affects our ability to respond in the first place (Bourdieu, 1987; Martin, 1997: 79–81).

Who we talk to also affects the likelihood that our responses to media messages will be affirmative or subversive, the extent to which and the manner in which they will be so, and whether our responses will be reinforced or undermined. Earlier in the chapter, the point was made that the consumption of media messages was largely privatized — that individuals watch TV or read newspapers in private, domestic settings. This is largely, but not totally true. It also needs to be said that even domestic, family settings can become forums for debate. Beyond family and friends, crime news also gets discussed at work, on public social occasions, and in leisure settings. Most people undertake such discussion, usually with others whose opinions they respect, and they allow such discussions to affect their opinions as much as they do their consumption of media messages. To a limited and controlled extent, letters to the editor also serve as vehicles for response and interpretation of news about crime and deviance.

In the last several years, a new forum for response and reinterpretation has grown to become a major consideration in any evaluation of the mass media and their relations to consumers. The Internet and the World Wide Web have allowed millions the opportunity to respond publicly to media messages with their own evaluations and interpretations, leading some media theorists to suggest that the Internet may provide ways in which audiences can collectively reconstitute themselves as active, critical agents. Major newspapers and television news bureaus all now have proprietary Web sites to which readers and viewers can post messages. As in the case of the Paul Bernardo/Karla Homolka murder trials, Internet discussion of the coverage of the crime or the trial can become news in its own right as users post new information of wildly varying reliability, flout publication bans, or float theories and opinions. The first news of the Clinton/Lewinsky sex scandal came from an Internet newsletter, and thereafter, more conventional news media made it a practice to troll for Internet discussion of the scandal on a regular basis (Rushkoff, 1998). Today, most major stories about crime and deviance generate Internet discussion, and some even boast dedicated Web sites. The quality of the discussion on the Web and the Net can vary from the obsessive and the pornographic to the scholarly. But in general, it can be said that audience response, through the Internet, has become part of the news itself, and a way for audiences to become increasingly active and responsive.

The unpredictability of such responses has, of course, led some to deviantize the Internet itself, and to call for controls on its use, especially in the areas of hate literature and pornography. But perhaps more effective — though still debatable — means of control lie in the *commercialization* of the Net, and its increasingly close tie-ins with more traditional forms of media *via* cable providers and integrated media appliances. These integrative developments will make it ever more easy for the average news consumer, through one media appliance, to read, watch, or listen to news, talk to others electronically about news, and respond to those who produce news. Some might argue that in such developments lies the potential for subversion of the cultural status quo and the opening up of alternative ways of defining, evaluating, and acting in the social world, *via* "horizontal" links between media consumers rather than "vertical" ones between consumers and the producers of mass-marketed messages. But it must also be said that the most effective way to control a mass of people is to *encourage their participation* in the exercise of social control and ideological reproduction. In a small way, television shows like *America's Most Wanted* have done this by listing an 800 number that viewers can call should they see someone resembling the night's featured suspect. If, in the old days of public executions, there was always the danger that a crowd could turn on the officials and loose the prisoner, today, some might argue that the Internet gives the same ability; and certainly good use is being made of it by groups committed to helping the wrongfully convicted. But the parallel forms of individualization undergone by punishment and media consumption, along with the marketing techniques developed by media organizations and public relations agencies, might indicate another set of possible conclusions in which public expression is tamed and reframed as individualized consumer choice or personal opinion, while creative subversion is swept under a blanket definition of criminality encompassing pornographers, hackers, and purveyors of hate literature.

We have attempted to outline some of the cultural patterns and dramatic formulae governing media coverage of crime and deviance, and some of the mechanisms by which it is produced. What remains to be emphasized is that "the media" are not monolithic; nor are the messages they produce simply attributable to some conscious and sinister intent. Media organizations produce messages that are shaped by organizational politics, the economics of media production, personal ambition and office politics, reliance on other bureaucratic organizations, and a host of other considerations, including idealism. Similarly, audiences and readers are neither as passive nor as atomized as a marketer's dream or a paranoid imagination might suggest. In the world of interactive media technology now opening up — a world which is transforming audiences, news production, media organizations, and the shape of corporations and governments — nothing is certain but the fact that the politics of deviance will need to be revisited, and this discussion rewritten, within a very few years.

REFERENCES

Abercrombie, Nicholas, Stephen Hill and Bryan S. Turner
    1986 *Sovereign Individuals of Capitalism*. London: Allen and Unwin.

Althusser, Louis
    1971 "Ideology and Ideological State Apparatuses: Notes Toward an Investigation." In Althusser, *Lenin and Philosophy*. New York: Monthly Review Press.

Anderson, Karen
    1996 *Sociology: a Critical Introduction*. Toronto: Nelson Canada.

Ang, Ien
    1995 *Living Room Wars: Rethinking Media Audiences for a Postmodern World*. London: Routledge.

Benn, Carl
    1978 "The Upper Canadian Press, 1793–1815." *Ontario History* 70 (June): 91–114.

Berger, Peter L. and Thomas Luckmann
    1966 *The Social Construction of Reality*. New York: Doubleday.

Birchall, Reginald *et al.*
    1890 *Birchall: The Story of His Life, Trial and Imprisonment, As Told By Himself.* (6th ed.) Toronto: National Publishing Company.

Bourdieu, Pierre
1987 "What Makes a Social Class?" *Berkeley Journal of Sociology* 22: 1–18

Boyce, George *et al.*, eds.
1978 *Newspaper History*. London: Constable.

Burchell, Graham
1991 "Peculiar Interests: Civil Society and Governing 'The System of Natural Liberty'." In Graham Burchell, Colin Gordon and Peter Miller, eds. *The Foucault Effect: Studies in Governmentality*. Chicago: University of Chicago Press.

Cohen, Stanley
1972 *Folk Devils and Moral Panics: the Creation of the Mods and Rockers*. Oxford: Blackwell.

Concerned Counseling Inc.
1998 "Power: the Greatest Aphrodisiac?" *CCI Journal* http://www.concernedcounselling.com/ccijournal/page2a.htm

Dayan, Daniel and Elihu Katz
1988 "Articulating Consensus: the Ritual and Rhetoric of Media." In J. C. Alexander, ed. *Durkheimian Sociology: Cultural Studies*. Cambridge: Cambridge University Press.

Debord, Guy
1983 *Society as Spectacle*. Detroit: Black and Red.

Donzelot, Jacques
1979 *The Policing of Families*. (tr. Robert Hurley) New York: Pantheon.

1991 "The Mobilization of Society." In Graham Burchell, Colin Gordon and Peter Miller, eds. *The Foucault Effect: Studies in Governmentality*. Chicago: University of Chicago Press.

Durkheim, Emile
1915 *The Elementary Forms of the Religious Life*. New York: Macmillan.

1979 "A Discussion on Sex Education," (tr. H. L. Sutcliffe) in W. S. F. Pickering, ed. *Durkheim: Essays on Morals and Education*. London: Routledge.

1982 *The Rules of Sociological Method and Selected Texts on Sociology and Its Method* (tr. W. D. Halls) New York: Macmillan.

1984 *The Division of Labour in Society*. (tr. W. D. Halls) New York: Free Press.

1992a *Professional Ethics and Civic Morals*. (tr. C. Brookfield, preface B. S. Turner) London: Routledge.

1992b "Two Laws of Penal Evolution." In M. Gane, ed. *The Radical Sociology of Durkheim and Mauss*. Routledge.

Eisenstein, Elizabeth
1983 *The Printing Revolution in Early Modern Europe*. Cambridge: Cambridge University Press.

Elias, Norbert
1978 *The Civilizing Process: the Development of Manners*. (tr. E. Jephcott) New York: Urizen Books.

Ericson, Richard, and Patricia Baranek
1982 *The Ordering of Justice: a Study of Accused Persons as Dependents in the Criminal Process*. Toronto: University of Toronto Press.

Ericson, Richard, Patricia Baranek and Janet Chan
1987 *Visualizing Deviance: a Study of News Organization*. Toronto: University of Toronto Press.

1991 *Representing Order: Crime, Law and Justice in the News Media.* Toronto: University of Toronto Press.

Ewen, Stuart
1976 *Captains of Consciousness: Advertising and the Social Roots of the Consumer Culture.* New York: McGraw-Hill.

Febvre, Lucien and Henri-Jean Martin
1976 *The Coming of the Book.* London: NLB.

Fiske, John
1987 *Television Culture.* London: Methuen.

Fiske, John and John Hartley
1978 *Reading Television.* London: Methuen.

Foucault, Michel
1977 *Discipline and Punish: the Birth of the Prison.* (tr. Alan Sheridan) New York: Pantheon.

1978 *The History of Sexuality, Volume 1: an Introduction.* New York: Pantheon.

1991 "Governmentality." In Graham Burchell, Colin Gordon and Peter Miller, eds. *The Foucault Effect: Studies in Governmentality.* Chicago: University of Chicago Press.

Garfinkel, Harold
1967 *Studies in Ethnomethodology.* Englewood Cliffs, N.J.: Prentice-Hall.

Goethe, Johann Wolfgang von
1958 *The Sufferings of Young Werther.* (tr. B. Q. Morgan) New York: Ungar.

Goffman, Erving
1963 *Stigma: Notes on the Management of Spoiled Identity.* Englewood Cliffs, N.J.: Prentice-Hall.

Gouldner, Alvin W.
1976 *The Dialectic of Ideology and Technology.* New York: Oxford University Press.

Gramsci, Antonio
1971 *Selections From the Prison Notebooks of Antonio Gramsci.* (tr. and ed. Q. Hoare and A. N. Smith) New York: International Publishers.

Hacking, Ian
1986 "Making Up People." In T. C. Heller, M. Sosna and D. E. Wellbery, eds. *Reconstructing Individualism: Autonomy, Individuality, and the Self in Western Thought.* Stanford CA: Stanford University Press.

1991 "How Should We Do the History of Statistics?" In Graham Burchell, Colin Gordon and Peter Miller, eds. *The Foucault Effect: Studies in Governmentality.* Chicago: University of Chicago Press.

Hall, Stuart
1977 "Culture, the Media and the Ideological Effect." In J. Curran *et al.*, *Mass Communication and Society.* London: Edward Arnold.

Hamilton Herald
1903 "Shooting Affair Saturday Night," "Princess Shot Actress Rival," "Batch of Small Fry," "Murder and Suicide," "Daring Thieves." Hamilton, Ontario: December 7, Page 1.

Hamilton Times
1910 "Sensation in the Moir Escape Case," "Dr. Crippen Gone," "Jealous Old Man," "Fruit Man's Suicide." Hamilton, Ontario: August 20, Page 1.

Hay, Douglas, Peter Linebaugh, John G. Rule, Edward. P. Thompson and Cal Winslow
1975 *Albion's Fatal Tree: Crime and Society in Eighteenth-Century England*. London: Allen Lane.

Jones, T. Anthony and Andrew T. Scull
1992 "Durkheim's Two Laws of Penal Evolution: an Introduction." In M. Gane, ed. *The Radical Sociology of Durkheim and Mauss*. London: Routledge.

Kesterton, Wilfred H.
1967 *A History of Journalism in Canada*. Toronto: McClelland and Stewart.

Knight, Graham
1989 "The Reality Effects of Tabloid Television News." In M. Raboy and P. Bruck, eds. *Communication for and Against Democracy*. Montreal: Black Rose.

Laframboise, Donna
1995a "Those Who Ruined Morin's Life Should Be Held Accountable," *Toronto Star*, 24 January, Page A17.

1995b "Morin's Story Both Infuriating and Inspiring," *Toronto Star*, 26 December, Page A31.

Leiss, William, Stephen Kline and Sut Jhally
1990 *Social Communication in Advertising*. Toronto: Nelson Canada.

Lorimer, Rowland and Jean McNulty
1996 *Mass Communication in Canada*. 3rd ed. Toronto: Oxford University Press

Lotringer, Sylvère
1988 *Overexposed: Treating Sexual Perversion in America*. New York: Pantheon.

McLaren, Angus
1990 *Our Own Master Race: Eugenics in Canada, 1885–1945*. Toronto: Oxford.

Maclean's Magazine
1998a "Death and Deceit." (Cover story by Barry Came and related articles) Toronto: Maclean-Hunter (July 6).

1998b "Sex and Lies." (Cover story by Jane O'Hara and related articles) Toronto: Maclean-Hunter (September 28).

Martin, Michèle
1997 *Communication and Mass Media: Culture, Domination and Opposition*. Scarborough: Prentice-Hall Canada.

McLuhan, Marshall
1964 *Understanding Media*. New York: Mentor Books.

Morley, David
1986 *Family Television: Cultural Power and Domestic Leisure*. London: Comedia.

1992 *Television, Audiences, and Cultural Studies*. London: Routledge.

National Council on Sexual Addiction and Compulsivity (NCSAC)
1998 "Public figures and Problem Sexual Behaviours," NCSAC Position Paper, http://www.ncsac.org/article2.htm

Pasquino, Pasquale
1991a "Theatrum Politicum: the Genealogy of Capital - Police and the State of Prosperity." In Graham Burchell, Colin Gordon and Peter Miller, eds. *The Foucault Effect: Studies in Governmentality*. Chicago: University of Chicago Press.

1991b "Criminology: The Birth of a Special Knowledge." In Burchell *et al.*, eds. *The Foucault Effect: Studies in Governmentality.* Chicago: University of Chicago Press.

Philo, Greg
1990 *Seeing & Believing: the Influence of Television.* London: Routledge.

Pickens, Donald K.
1968 *Eugenics and the Progressives.* Nashville: Vanderbilt University Press.

Posner, Michael
1998 "Media at Stake." *The Globe and Mail* Toronto, October 10: C 1, C 3.

Rasky, Frank
1958 *Gay Canadian Rogues.* Winnipeg: Harlequin Books.

Rushkoff, Douglas
1998 "Clinton is a TV President in the age of the Internet" *Globe and Mail*, Toronto, October 10: C-11.

Rutherford, Paul
1978 *The Making of the Canadian Media.* Toronto: McGraw-Hill.

1982 *A Victorian Authority: The Daily Press in Late Nineteenth-Century Canada.* Toronto: University of Toronto Press.

Smith, Anthony
1978 "The Long Road to Objectivity and Back Again: The Kinds of Truth We Get in Journalism." In G. Boyce *et al.*, eds. *Newspaper History.* London: Constable.

1979 *The Newspaper: an International History.* London: Thames and Hudson.

Smith, Dorothy E.
1974 "The Social Construction of Documentary Reality" *Sociological Inquiry* Vol. 44, No. 4, pp. 257–268.

Tuchman, Gaye
1978 *Making News: a Study in the Construction of Reality.* New York: Free Press.

Turner, Victor
1969 *The Ritual Process: Structure and Anti-Structure.* Chicago: Aldine.

1980 "Social Dramas and Stories About Them." *Critical Inquiry* 7: 141–168.

Valpy, Michael
1998 "Is He a Sex Addict?" *The Globe and Mail*, Toronto, September 19: D 1, D 2.

Valverde, Mariana
1991 *The Age of Light, Soap and Water: Moral Reform in English Canada, 1885–1925.* Toronto: McClelland and Stewart.

Weber, Max
1978 *Economy and Society.* (eds. G. Roth and C. Wittich) Berkeley: University of California Press.

Weeks, Jeffrey
1985 "The Population Question in the Early Twentieth Century," in V. Beechey and J. Donald, eds. *Subjectivity and Social Relations.* Milton Keynes: Open University Press.

Wernick, Andrew
1991 *Promotional Culture: Advertising, Ideology and Symbolic Expression.* London: Sage.

PROSTITUTION
Deviant Activity
or Legitimate
Occupation?

Nick Larsen

INTRODUCTION

Prostitution represents one of the most frustrating and contradictory social and political dilemmas facing contemporary Canadian society. The roots of this dilemma stem both from the ambivalent attitudes towards prostitution expressed by the Canadian public and the difficulties inherent in attempting to control prostitution to minimize the negative aspects of the prostitution trade. In this respect, there is little doubt that prostitution is an activity that many members of the public consider deviant and undesirable. At the same time, there is increasing evidence that both the public and many politicians feel that prostitution is impossible to eliminate and that the best course of action would be some form of decriminalization or legalization (Larsen, 1991). This basic dilemma is complicated by the philosophical dichotomy between the liberal argument that prostitution is a legitimate form of sexual diversity and the conservative view that prostitution is immoral. Further, many recent discussions have focused on the feminist position that prostitution is a patriarchal evil that represents the ultimate expression of male domination and oppression. All of these intersecting and frequently contradictory viewpoints contribute to a situation in which most Canadians consider prostitution a deviant activity, many nevertheless feel it should be tolerated in some fashion, and absolutely *nobody* wants it in their neighbourhood. This paradox is complicated by the fact that the prostitutes themselves are becoming increasingly vocal in demanding that their "chosen occupation" be legitimized. Many prostitutes' rights organizations[1] have begun to argue that prostitution is a viable occupation and that it should be regulated like any other legal occupation.

Regardless of the opinion one holds regarding prostitution as a social and moral issue, it is clear from the recent public debate that it cannot continue to remain in its current legal and political quagmire. Although the act of prostitution itself is not, and never has been, illegal in Canada, "communicating in public for the purposes of prostitution" and certain other offences are prohibited by the *Criminal Code of Canada*. Aside from the fact that this legal anomaly effectively criminalizes most attempts to engage in a legal activity, prostitution's uncertain and contradictory legal status also makes it difficult to deal effectively with many of the important issues involved in its practice. The fact that prostitution itself is legal calls into question any attempt to eliminate it through use of criminal sanctions. At the same time, the illegal nature of some prostitution-related activities, combined with the fact that the *Criminal Code* does not explicitly stipulate whether any prostitution-related activities are legal, makes it difficult to regulate prostitution in the same fashion as any other legal activity would be regulated. Many analysts have argued that this situation is untenable and must be resolved by either outlining the specific circumstances under which prostitution is legal or else making it fully criminal (Larsen, 1996; Lowman, 1994).[2] The proponents of the latter approach argue that criminalization would allow the police to control prostitution more effectively and reinforce the public sentiment that prostitution is not acceptable behaviour. On the other hand, the advocates of some form of legalized toleration argue that prohibition will never work and will simply add to the existing problems. Further, many feminists point out that tougher legal controls will simply add to the oppression experienced by female prostitutes without effectively controlling or eliminating prostitution.

Although the feminist movement is badly divided on the best way of dealing with prostitution, all feminists agree that the approach taken towards prostitution must not increase the oppression faced by female prostitutes. At the same time, it is also clear that prostitution, and particularly street prostitution, frequently constitutes a divisive social issue, in which the rights of many different groups are in conflict. Thus, it is imperative that Canadian society resolve the legal, political, and philosophical dilemmas which currently exist regarding prostitution, and adopt a legal and political approach which incorporates the rights and interests of all parties, including the prostitutes. The intent of this chapter is to discuss many of the issues that are considered crucial to understanding why prostitution evokes such a myriad of conflicting attitudes and emotions, as well as why it is so difficult to achieve effective control with our current policy of prohibition. These issues include the stigma associated with prostitution, the historical context of prostitution, the societal factors which motivate the entry into prostitution, and the failure of recent attempts to control prostitution through ever tougher laws. This chapter will conclude by outlining an approach to prostitution that is grounded in an understanding of the nature of prostitution as a sociological phenomenon and which also attempts to respect the rights of all groups involved in the debate, including the prostitutes.

THE LEGAL AND SOCIAL CONTEXTS OF PROSTITUTION

Any discussion of prostitution as a social phenomenon must necessarily be predicated on a clear definition of exactly what types of behaviours constitute prostitution. Interestingly enough, arriving at a consensus regarding the definition of prostitution is not as easy as many people might assume. Legal definitions of prostitution usually define it as engaging in sexual behaviour for financial payment, and although this definition appears satisfactory from an enforcement perspective, it is clearly problematic from a sociological point of view. Sociologists quickly point out that many activities which satisfy the criteria of sexual services in return for financial gain are excluded from the legal definition. For example, numerous types of relationships in which people exchange financial support for sexual favours are not illegal. Thus, mistresses, gigolos, "sugar babies," and people who exchange sex for a night's entertainment are not breaking any laws, even though the basic parameters of the relationship are similar to the commercial exchange that occurs between prostitutes and their customers. In this respect, all of the above listed participants engage in sexual activity primarily because of the financial benefits they receive in return, but only prostitutes are subject to criminal sanctions.

Sociologists have attempted to clarify this anomaly by refining the definition of prostitution to exclude relationships which are longer term and/or in which there is a pretence of an affective relationship. Thus, many sociologists would limit the definition of prostitution to those activities in which sex is exchanged for *immediate financial reward*, and in which there is no ongoing emotional and/or social relationship between the participants. In addition, the sociological definition of prostitution also stipulates that there must be a more or less indiscriminate selection of partners before a woman is considered a prostitute (Gomme, 1993). Although this clarification is useful in defining prostitutes as a sociological group for the purposes of study, it nevertheless fails to address why only some types of financially motivated sexual activity should be considered "prostitution." It also fails to address the even more basic issue of why commercial sex should be illegal at all.

The sociological definition also raises several important issues related to the intense social stigma which is almost universally applied to prostitution but rarely to other financially motivated sexual activity. In this respect, some sociologists distinguish between "overt" prostitution, which is the purely commercial exchange of sex for money, and "covert" prostitution, which usually involves some pretence of an affective relationship (Thio, 1995). Although it can be argued that all forms of sex for financial gain constitute prostitution, the covert variety is much less likely to be stigmatized and is almost never illegal. This situation is central to our discussion of prostitution as a "deviant" activity, since the selective application of a stigma only to commercial prostitution speaks volumes about the values inherent in society. Further, the existence of the stigma itself is also relevant to any discussion of the best way of dealing with prostitution from a legal and political point of view.

THE ORIGINS OF PROSTITUTION AS A SOCIAL INSTITUTION

The stigma associated with prostitution can best be understood by examining the context within which prostitution evolved as a social institution. Although it is unlikely that prostitution is the "world's oldest profession," there is little doubt that it appeared very early in our history. One of the earliest recorded instances of prostitution can be traced to the temple prostitution that existed in Babylon and other ancient civilizations. For example, all unmarried Babylonian women, before being allowed to marry, were required to prostitute themselves to the first man who approached them in certain designated religious temples. Inasmuch as this custom was a universal pre-condition of marriage, it appears that the participants were not stigmatized in any way (Decker, 1979: 30). However, the actual organization of this practice illustrates several interesting points about the role of women in Babylonian society. Although men who wished the services of temple prostitutes had to offer some financial consideration, it did not have to be significant. Further, the fact that temple prostitutes were not permitted to refuse a customer, combined with the fact that it was required of all women, suggests that its primary purpose was to reinforce the notion that women were the property of males. It is also likely that temple prostitution facilitated the double standard which allowed men greater sexual freedom than women.

The existence of a sexual double standard was also a major factor in the development of purely commercial prostitution in larger centres. Unlike temple prostitutes, the participants in these new forms of prostitution were frequently stigmatized, often to the point of being ostracized from the mainstream social life of their societies (Richards, 1982: 89–90). The rise of Christianity in most of Europe added a moral dimension to the stigma, but it is interesting that the Roman Catholic Church and other religions exhibited an ambivalent attitude towards prostitution during the Middle Ages. Indeed, an influential Catholic theologian, Thomas Aquinas, argued that prostitution was a necessary social evil and that "...[p]rostitution in the towns is like the cesspool in the palace: take away the cesspool and the palace will soon be an unclean and evil smelling place" (Decker, 1979: 44). This attitude was widely held during the Catholic era, and although the Protestant reformers did occasionally attempt to repress prostitution, it was generally tolerated as a necessary social evil (Little, 1995: 29). Despite sporadic venereal disease epidemics, which were often used as pretexts for brutal crackdowns on prostitution, prostitution was largely tolerated during the latter part of the Middle Ages. Indeed, high-class "courtesans" even gained significant influence among the nobility and upper classes. During the late 18th and the early part of the 19th centuries, the practice of regulating lower-class streetwalkers was refined to the point that substantial numbers of marginal women were pushed into the occupation. Although this was ostensibly motivated by a desire to protect respectable women from the sexual demands of lower-class men, it also helped ensure the continuance of the double standard (Little, 1995).

Despite the general toleration of prostitution during this period, the working conditions and social position of the prostitutes were nothing short of abysmal. They were almost universally abused and exploited by pimps, madams, and their customers (Bristow, 1977: 55–56). Nevertheless, the generally poor social and economic conditions of women ensured that legions of young women continued to enter the "profession" in order to maintain a subsistence existence (Hollis, 1979). Although public opinion was generally unconcerned with the welfare of the prostitutes, this slowly started to change during the 1830s in response to the lobbying activities of church groups and other reform-minded organizations. Although these initial reform efforts were motivated by conservative and religious views regarding the "immorality" of prostitution, they set the stage for the much more radical attack on prostitution mounted by the early feminists under the guidance of Josephine Butler (Walkowitz, 1983: 115–117). Combined with the increasingly conservative attitudes towards sex which developed during the Victorian Age, the feminist reformers were able to influence public opinion so that female prostitutes were defined as victims, who were exploited and abused by the lustful activities of capricious and immoral males. This shift in public opinion allowed the feminists to exert a major influence on the political and legal approaches to prostitution and resulted in several legislative changes aimed at protecting women involved in the prostitution trade (Walkowitz, 1983).

This shift in public opinion regarding prostitution was relatively short-lived and failed to have much effect in Canada. Although early Canadian approaches to prostitution during the latter part of the 19th and early 20th centuries paralleled the British scene, the Canadian women's movement was much more conservative than its British counterpart. As a result, the concern for the welfare of female prostitutes failed to materialize in Canada to the same extent as occurred in Britain (Larsen, 1991). Thus, prostitutes were frequently harassed and blamed for various social ills, including the spread of venereal disease and mental retardation (Larsen, 1993). It is worth noting that prostitution itself has never been illegal in Canada and prostitution was controlled by using a vagrancy-related offence (referred to as Vag. "C") which barred prostitutes from appearing in public without a legitimate reason (Larsen, 1991). This legislation applied only to female prostitutes and had the effect of criminalizing a woman's status as a prostitute, rather than the activity of engaging in prostitution. It was used very selectively, and the major reason why the government chose not to criminalize the act of engaging in prostitution was likely because such a course of action might have necessitated charging male customers as well.

The vagrancy provisions remained in effect until 1972, when they were replaced by legislation that made it illegal to solicit in public for the purposes of prostitution, but did not criminalize the act of prostitution itself. Although this approach eliminated the focus on the prostitute's status, it still allowed the legislation to selectively target female prostitutes, since male customers could not be convicted of soliciting for the purposes of prostitution (Larsen, 1991).[3] Nevertheless, this law clearly reduced the ability of the police to harass prostitutes because it made it necessary to prove that a prostitute had actually engaged in an overt act, rather than simply being in a public place. Despite their initial unhappiness with the law, the police generally considered the anti-soliciting law satisfactory until a 1978 court decision drastically reduced its application. In the 1978 *Hutt* decision, the Supreme Court of Canada ruled that soliciting had to be "pressing and persistent" before it was illegal. Canadian police considered this decision extremely unsatisfactory, and many politicians and citizens' groups joined the police in lobbying for a stricter prostitution law to circumvent the Supreme Court decision. In 1985, Parliament enacted Bill C-49, which criminalized any public communication for the purposes of prostitution. This law has remained in effect to the present time and its effectiveness will be discussed later in this chapter.

COMPETING PERSPECTIVES ON THE DYNAMICS OF THE PROSTITUTION TRADE

One of the most important issues that must be assessed in any discussion of prostitution centres on the contemporary social and political dynamics of the prostitution trade. Questions relating to the demographic background of the prostitutes, why they enter prostitution, and their experiences while working as prostitutes are central to any consideration of the best way of dealing with prostitution. In this respect, there are several potential social problems associated with prostitution that form the basis for competing theoretical and philosophical approaches to prostitution. It is important to assess the validity of these different approaches, since the degree to which prostitution is associated with serious social problems is clearly important to the legal and political approach taken towards it.

The best place to start any discussion of prostitution is by examining why women enter prostitution. Much of the social-psychological research on prostitution portrays prostitutes as young, poorly educated women who turn to prostitution because of significant personal problems (Shaver, 1993). In this scenario, they are likely to be addicted to drugs and come from backgrounds where they were physically and sexually abused. Thus, they suffer from low self-esteem and are easily manipulated by other participants in prostitution, including customers and pimps (Benjamin and Masters, 1964; Greenwald, 1970). Feminists, and especially radical feminists, accept much of this portrait, but argue that these characteristics can be attributed to a patriarchal society, which views women as sexual property and systematically oppresses them socially and economically. Within this perspective, both prostitution and the social conditions that force women into prostitution are extensions of patriarchy, and thus cannot be ameliorated without eliminating patriarchy. However, liberal feminists and prostitutes' rights groups, who argue that this portrait only applies to the lower echelons of streetwalkers, challenge this interpretation. They argue that the majority of prostitutes work for escort agencies and massage parlours, and that these latter types of prostitutes voluntarily enter the business at an older age and have no history of abuse (Perkins, 1991). Liberal feminists and prostitutes' rights groups would further argue that it is possible to ameliorate the working conditions associated with prostitution by affording prostitutes more control over their working lives.

The question of drug abuse is less clear and much of the evidence is somewhat more equivocal. Shaver (1993) and Gomme (1993) suggest that the use of hard drugs such as heroin and crack cocaine is relatively low. Citing a 1984 study, Shaver argues that it ranged from a low of 7 percent in Montreal to a high of 50 percent in the Maritimes. She also suggests that the prostitutes (both male and female) did not generally use drugs while working. However, the writer's own research, conducted in 1989 and 1992, contradicts this position. Police in Toronto, Winnipeg, and Vancouver were unanimous in arguing that drug use (particularly crack cocaine) was endemic among street prostitutes. This information was supported by interviews with prostitutes and other informants. As well, residents in all three cities argued that the dangers posed by used hypodermic needles was one of the most troubling aspects of living in red-light areas. This latter evidence suggests that street prostitutes were using heroin on the job as well as at other times. What is not clear is whether drug use among off-street prostitutes was lower. Since street prostitutes are a minority of total prostitutes, it is difficult to draw any firm conclusions regarding overall levels of drug use among the total prostitute population.

Another persistent argument regarding prostitution centres on the belief that most prostitutes are coerced into prostitution by pimps, who force them to turn over a large portion of their earnings. This commonly held belief is central to the radical feminist approach to prostitution. However, although pimp control of the prostitution trade is more common in the United States, much of the Canadian research suggests that it is less true in the Canadian context. For example, research conducted by Shaver (1993) found that 50 percent of the prostitutes interviewed in Toronto, and 69 percent interviewed in Montreal, reported that they had entered prostitution voluntarily. Although it is slightly more likely for juveniles to be forced into prostitution, this is still much rarer than the public perception reported in recent surveys. The Badgely Commission (which investigated child abuse and child prostitution) found that at least 50 percent of child prostitutes could not identify any specific person who got them involved in prostitution.[4] On the related topic of pimps controlling the prostitution trade, research indicates that this is much less common than generally believed. Studies conducted in 1984 indicated that the majority of prostitutes were not controlled by a pimp, with the percentage of women working for themselves ranging from 50 percent in Toronto to 69 percent in Montreal. The only exceptions were in the Maritimes where 75 percent of the women were controlled by pimps, and on the Prairies, where most Native women worked for a pimp (Shaver, 1993). More recent data provided by CORP indicated that at least 60 percent of the prostitutes in Toronto worked for themselves (Shaver, 1993).[5]

Two further issues related to the dynamics of the prostitution trade are the violence associated with prostitution and the perceived link between prostitution and venereal disease and AIDS. In dealing with the argument that prostitutes play a significant role in the spread of VD and AIDS, almost all of the available evidence indicates that prostitutes are actually less likely to transmit either disease than other promiscuous people. The writer's own research, as well as the data collected by other researchers, indicates that a majority of prostitutes (90 percent in some cases) use condoms when performing oral or vaginal sex (Gomme, 1993). Although juvenile prostitutes (of both sexes) are more likely to engage in risky sexual practices, there is little solid evidence to suggest that VD and AIDS are prevalent among young prostitutes.

In dealing with the violence issue, almost all of the available evidence suggests that prostitution is an extremely dangerous occupation. In addition to the possibility that pimps use violence to control prostitutes, most prostitutes report that sexual assaults and robbery are almost constant occupational hazards. Indeed, one of the most important services provided by organizations such as POWER and MAGGIES is the maintenance of "bad tricks sheets" which describe the assaults and provide descriptions of the offenders. Further, some researchers have argued that the levels of violence are heightened by the illegal nature of prostitution, and research conducted by Lowman and Fraser (1995) indicates that levels of violence and homicide against Vancouver prostitutes has increased dramatically since Bill C-49 was implemented. Although all feminists and prostitutes' rights groups generally agree on this point, they differ on its causes and their proposed solutions. This issue will be discussed further later in this chapter.

Two remaining aspects of prostitution as a social problem involve the nuisance associated with street prostitution and the feminist contention that prostitution is degrading to all women, both prostitutes and non-prostitutes. With respect to the first issue, it is clear that there are significant amounts of noise and other nuisance associated with street prostitution. It is equally clear that this nuisance is caused because prostitution frequently takes place in residential and business areas where it is incompatible with existing activities. Although some of the political controversy over this issue arises from the refusal of residents and business owners to tolerate even minor amounts of prostitution, there is little doubt that street prostitution constitutes a genuine social problem in this particular respect. The key question is whether the illegal nature of prostitution makes the problem worse. Certainly, its illegality precludes using zoning by-laws to regulate where prostitution will take place and thus prostitutes select the areas based on factors of convenience to themselves. Unfortunately, other users of these areas often refuse to tolerate prostitution and conflict arises.

The argument that prostitution is degrading to all women is a philosophical position which is difficult to verify empirically. Many radical feminists argue that prostitution constitutes the ultimate representation of patriarchy insofar as it consists of males purchasing women for sexual purposes. They also argue that this aspect of prostitution started with the temple prostitution that existed in ancient societies, and was constantly reinforced throughout its history by the manner in which prostitution was regulated to support the double standard. Thus, radical feminists do not consider prostitution a legitimate type of sexual diversity, and argue that its existence denigrates all women by reinforcing chauvinist attitudes regarding women as sexual property. They further argue that there is no legitimate role for prostitution in society and that it is enough of a social evil that it ought to be repressed. Liberal feminists, however, are more likely to view prostitution as a legitimate form of sexual diversity and concentrate their efforts on fair treatment for female prostitutes. Prostitutes' rights groups, such as POWER and COYOTE, go even further and argue that prostitution is a viable service-related occupation, and that it is hypocritical for radical feminists to advocate its elimination (Jenness, 1993; Bell, 1987). In this respect, prostitutes' rights groups argue that many of the oppressive conditions cited by radical feminists are actually made worse by the refusal of radical feminists to recognize the legitimacy of prostitution as an occupation (Shaver, 1994).

AN EVALUATION OF BILL C-49[6]

One of the most important criteria involved in the discussion of the best social and legal approach to prostitution centres on the effectiveness of criminal sanctions in controlling the undesirable aspects of the prostitution trade. In this respect, it can be argued that it is pointless to attempt to repress prostitution if it is not possible to accomplish it. As was noted previously in this chapter, Bill C-49 was enacted in 1985, largely because of a concerted lobbying campaign by police and other groups who felt that prostitution had become an endemic problem in large urban centres. Inasmuch as Bill C-49 is considered one of the toughest prostitution laws currently existing in contemporary western societies, it provides an ideal test case for assessing whether legal sanctions can ever be successfully used to control prostitution.[7] The discussion in this section will focus on the implementation of Bill C-49 in Toronto and Vancouver from 1986 to 1990. This analysis will assess the degree to which the law was effective at reducing levels of prostitution and/or minimizing the levels of nuisance associated with street prostitution. In addition, an assessment will be conducted regarding the degree to which the implementation of Bill C-49 was associated with any negative unintended consequences.

Bill C-49 in Vancouver

The Vancouver police immediately adopted an aggressive approach to the implementation of Bill C-49.[8] During the first few weeks of January, 1986, the Vice Squad conducted several sweeps in all of the prostitution strolls in Vancouver.[9] The new law initially appeared to have exerted the desired effect, as both the number of arrests and the number of visible prostitutes remained low throughout January in all areas (*Vancouver Sun* [*VS*], Jan. 8, 1986: A3). Although this situation prompted several politicians and community leaders to publicly proclaim the law a "success," this optimism was not borne out by subsequent events. According to one source close to the prostitution community, prostitutes had only been staying off the streets until they had a sense of how the Vancouver police would enforce the new law. They quickly returned to the streets and the number of arrests increased as they reappeared in greater numbers. There were also several challenges based on the Canadian Charter of Rights and Freedoms, and a Provincial Court decision overturning the law increased the numbers of prostitutes returning to the streets. The situation was further exacerbated when the Vancouver mayor directed the Vancouver Police to move against several bawdy houses, thus forcing even more prostitutes out on the street (*VS*, Mar. 27, 1986: A3). Considering that the major goal was to keep prostitutes off the street, this action suggests that the Vancouver Police and City Council had failed to develop a coherent strategy for dealing with prostitution.

The above-mentioned constitutional challenges were over-ruled by the BC Supreme Court on May 7, 1986, and the police adopted even tougher measures against prostitutes. Prosecutors began routinely asking that area restrictions be made part of probation orders for convicted prostitutes, even though this tactic was of dubious effectiveness since most prostitutes simply moved to the edge of the restricted area (*VS*, May 9, 1986: A3).[10] In any event, the prostitutes appeared to have overcome their fear of the new law and continued to remain on the streets in enough numbers to constitute a continuing problem from the perspective of many community groups. The fact that the area restrictions did not apply to customers ensured that there was a steady supply of customers, and many commentators argued that prostitutes would remain on the street as long as there was business. The practice was also criticized by prostitutes' spokespersons and some defence lawyers because it contravened the principle of equal enforcement.

The debate over Bill C-49 continued, and by late 1986 it was clear that Bill C-49 was not the definitive solution which many people had expected. Once prostitutes overcame their fear of the law, they quickly developed new strategies to cope with it, including not discussing anything until inside the potential customer's car and waiting for the customer to make the first offer. Although the Vancouver police appeared satisfied with the law, many community groups were arguing that it was clearly a sham. This was particularly true of the Mount Pleasant area, a working-class neighbourhood near the city centre. The Vancouver Police had stopped responding to prostitution-related calls from the area, and many residents became convinced that the Vancouver police were using Mount Pleasant as a "dumping ground" for street prostitution because of its lower social economic status. In response to these criticisms, the Mount Pleasant Task Force was established to co-ordinate police efforts during the summer months of 1986 to 1988. The Task Force experimented with several "harassment" tactics and organized periodic "blitzes" against prospective customers. In addition, they stepped up the frequency of visible uniformed patrols near where prostitutes were working to discourage customers from cruising the area. Although the Task Force was reasonably effective, it is important to note that these tactics were not dependent on Bill C-49, and could have been used before it was implemented. Further, the activities of the Task Force displaced large numbers of prostitutes into the "Downtown Eastside" area, including the respectable working-class area known as Strathcona.[11]

The scenario which developed in Strathcona differed significantly from other areas, largely because the residents and the police both adopted radically different attitudes towards the problem. Instead of adopting confrontational tactics, residents entered into negotiations with the prostitutes in an attempt to reach a solution. The prostitutes responded by agreeing not to work near schools and negotiating a "no go" map outlining areas where prostitutes would not work. This map was distributed to prostitutes working in the area, who were asked to avoid the indicated areas. This approach was reinforced when the police also became involved in negotiations between prostitutes and residents, and even suggested that patrol personnel would tolerate some prostitution if the prostitutes stayed away from schools and residential areas. Patrol officers were directed to steer prostitutes back toward commercial streets if they were found in residential areas (*VS*, Apr. 20, 88: B5). In the event that a prostitute seemed determined to remain in a "no go" area, the police would harass her and in some cases even parked a marked police cruiser near her "until she got the message."[12] These tactics have been continued by the uniformed patrol team responsible for the area, and recent research indicates that the police have extended their liaison work with prostitutes to include regular consultations with the affected groups. Thus although there continues to be significant amounts of prostitution activity in the Strathcona area, there is remarkably little conflict.

In summarizing this discussion of Bill C-49 in Vancouver, it is clear that the new law was not effective in reducing the numbers of street prostitutes in Vancouver.[13] Although it did give the police somewhat greater ability to control the areas where prostitutes worked, and thus helped quiet public controversy, harassment tactics using traffic codes and other non-criminal laws were far more effective. The most effective solution, however, involved the negotiation and other "social work" tactics practised by the police and residents in Strathcona. While these tactics did not appear to reduce the numbers of prostitutes, they did minimize conflict. Unfortunately, this tactic has been limited to the Strathcona area, as residents and patrol teams in other areas have been unwilling to adopt it. As a result, conflict continues in the Mount Pleasant area, and there is an ongoing media debate regarding the best approach to the problem.

Two further points need to be made about Bill C-49 in Vancouver. The first involves the gender imbalance among the people charged with communicating for the purposes of prostitution. Feminist groups and spokespersons for the prostitute community consistently criticized the Vancouver police for concentrating on female prostitutes to the virtual exclusion of male prostitutes and male customers. The second point centres on violence against prostitutes. Unfortunately, the law also appeared to correlate with increased numbers of assaults against prostitutes and several unsolved murders of prostitutes in Vancouver. Marie Arrington and other prostitutes' spokespersons complained that the new law had increased the amount of violence against prostitutes because it forced them to enter cars without carefully screening the occupants. POWER also complained that the practice of seeking area restrictions further contributed to the problem by forcing the prostitutes to work in less safe areas such as poorly lit back lanes and to adopt riskier tactics such as hitchhiking. These were dangerous tactics since prostitutes were unable to screen their customers thoroughly. One spokesperson noted that only one prostitute was murdered between 1978 and 1985, whereas 40 had been murdered between 1986 and 1992. Similarly, other defence lawyers reported an increase in the number of "bad tricks" mentioned by their clients (Lowman and Fraser, 1995). Although this evidence is far from conclusive, it suggests that Vancouver prostitutes have had to pay a high price for a law that is not effective in any case.

Bill C-49 in Toronto

The initial implementation of Bill C-49 in Toronto appeared to involve much more planning and co-ordination than had been evident in Vancouver. After consultation with the prosecutor's office and other groups, the Toronto police announced several enforcement guidelines intended to reassure civil libertarian groups that they intended to enforce the new law with discretion (*Globe and Mail*, Jan. 18, 1986: A1). However, the most important policy directive to emerge from the consultation process involved the decision to concentrate on customers. The Toronto Police adopted a stated policy of attempting to "dry up the supply of customers" and announced that they would co-operate with social service programs designed to help prostitutes change their lifestyles (*Toronto Star* [*TS*], Jan. 26, 1986: A6). The police quickly adopted a pattern of arresting more customers than was occurring in Vancouver. Although prostitutes initially remained on the streets in large numbers, they quickly left once it became clear that the police activity was scaring clients away. In April 1986, the Toronto Police announced that the numbers of prostitutes working the streets had dropped to approximately one third of their pre-Bill C-49 levels (200–300 vs. 600–700)

(*TS*, Apr. 27, 1986: A8). The police claimed that their strategy of going after the customers was effective because middle-class customers (often with families) were much more easily deterred than prostitutes, most of whom already had long criminal records.

The police and residents were happy with the movement of prostitutes off the streets; however, this development was not the complete success that the Toronto police had predicted. Many of the prostitutes who temporarily vacated the streets moved into escort agencies (*TS*, Apr. 27, 1986: A8). Although the police were initially content to watch the transformation of streetwalkers into callgirls without taking immediate action,[14] it quickly became obvious that the movement into escort agencies and massage parlours increased the number of pimps and their ability to dominate the prostitution trade.[15] The police were forced to place increased emphasis on escort agencies, and this precipitated a gradual increase in street prostitution. The prostitutes adopted new tactics to cope with police surveillance, and a Provincial court decision overturning Bill C-49 further increased the numbers of prostitutes and customers returning to the streets. At this point, the police changed their tactics and began concentrating on female prostitutes, but the evidence suggests that their efforts simply displaced many prostitutes to other areas. By August of 1986, street prostitution had again become a major problem and the police conducted a prolonged series of sweeps, in which female prostitutes were the major targets. Although Toronto police adopted many of the tactics being used in Vancouver, the increased police activity failed to significantly affect the prostitution trade (*TS*, Aug. 22, 1986: A1).

The controversy and conflict regarding street prostitution intensified in 1987 despite much more aggressive enforcement of Bill C-49. The Toronto police formed the Police-Community Prostitution Committee to facilitate co-operation and information sharing with residents and business owners, the Crown Attorney's office, and local politicians. The Committee was primarily intended as a forum for citizens to express their concerns, and to explore possible solutions to the increasingly obvious failure of Bill C-49. The one group that was not included was the prostitutes, and this may explain why this Committee was less successful than the one in the Strathcona area of Vancouver. Further, although this Committee likely represented a genuine effort to deal effectively with citizens' concerns, it also was clearly an attempt to appease some of the most vocal groups and to subvert local political activity to serve the interests of the police (Larsen, 1996). In this respect, it was relatively successful at minimizing public criticism of the police, and directing public lobbying efforts against politicians.

Although the police were able to minimize public conflict, they were not able to reduce the numbers of prostitutes. Despite their aggressive enforcement of Bill C-49, the numbers of prostitutes on the streets doubled between January and October of 1987 (*Globe and Mail*, Oct.15, 1987: A3). The fact that most of this increase occurred after the police shifted their emphasis from customers to prostitutes underscored the futility of tougher laws against prostitution. Although the police ultimately returned to their previous concentration on customers, there is little evidence to suggest that it was effective. Although conviction rates remained high, the number of visible prostitutes also remained high (Moyer and Carrington, 1989). Further, public dissatisfaction began to grow and the Police-Community Liaison Committee was no longer able to contain it. In order to appear more effective, Toronto police instituted a practice of moving prostitutes from area to area, never allowing them to stay in one area for lengthy periods of time (Larsen, 1996). These practices have been continued to the present time, and although some prostitution activity has even been displaced into Toronto's outer suburbs, this has simply spread the nuisance problem over a larger area. The Toronto media continue to debate the prostitution issue and there are constant reports of conflict between residents and prostitutes. In this respect, it is instructive that local politicians have started calling for legalized "zones of tolerance" and bawdy houses (*Globe and Mail*, Oct. 26, 1991: A10).

In concluding this discussion of Bill C-49 in Toronto, several additional points need to be addressed. In addition to the general ineffectiveness of the law, it is also evident that Bill C-49 has caused confusion and conflict for the operators of escort agencies and bawdy houses, two types of prostitution which had previously caused few problems for the police. In addition to the problem with pimps controlling escort agencies, there were early reports that organized crime was beginning to move into escort agencies and bawdy houses (*Globe and Mail*, Sept. 28, 1987: A1). There were also persistent reports that pimps were invading the Eaton Centre in a modern day version of "white slavery" to force runaway girls to work in escort agencies and bawdy houses (*TS*, May 12, 1987: A23). These factors underscore the problems which accompany attempts to drive prostitution underground through the use of tough laws.

On the related topic of violence against prostitutes, the evidence is less clear. Although some prostitutes reported that they felt less safe after Bill C-49, others reported that there was no appreciable change (Moyer and Carrington, 1989). However, recent media reports and interviews with spokespersons from the prostitute community indicate that violence is a continuing problem. Unfortunately, there is little pre-Bill C-49 evidence available, so it is difficult to establish whether the violence is due to the law, or simply an occupational hazard associated with prostitution.

DISCUSSION AND CONCLUSIONS

The discussion in this chapter has focused on several inter-related themes. One of the most important strands of the analysis has centred on the general ineffectiveness of most legal controls on prostitution. Both the historical analysis and the assessment of Bill C-49 suggest that legal controls on prostitution have rarely been effective at reducing the numbers of prostitutes or controlling the aspects of the trade which give rise to social problems. This suggests that some other method of dealing with prostitution needs to be considered. Such a discussion must be situated within the context of the previously discussed perspectives regarding the nature and roles of all participants in the prostitution trade. In addition, any discussion of the "best" way of dealing with prostitution must also respect the rights and interests of the people who live and work in prostitution areas.

In terms of the dynamics of the prostitution trade, it seems clear that an almost irreconcilable dichotomy exists between radical feminists, on the one hand, and liberal feminists and prostitutes' rights advocates on the other. Radical feminists argue that prostitutes come from generally oppressive backgrounds and are further oppressed by the male participants in the prostitution trade. They argue that these oppressive conditions, including drug abuse, violence, and the prevalence of pimps, can be directly attributed to patriarchy and that the only viable solution in the long term is to repress prostitution. This, they argue, should be accomplished by much tougher enforcement efforts directed against male customers and pimps, combined with social programs designed to help prostitutes leave the trade and develop legitimate skills. A small number of radical feminists, although they accept this basic position, also argue that it might be necessary to decriminalize some prostitution activities in the short term to reduce the exploitive aspects of prostitution and give prostitutes more control over their working lives. All radical feminists, however, are committed to the eventual elimination of prostitution, and argue that radical change to existing patterns of gender inequality are necessary to accomplish it (Freeman, 1989; Cooper, 1989).

The liberal feminists and prostitutes' rights advocates dispute much of the evidence regarding the oppressive backgrounds of prostitutes and argue that it only applies to a small minority of young, lower-class streetwalkers. They further argue that many of the purported undesirable features of the prostitution trade are either exaggerated or created by its illegality. And although they agree that the dynamics of the prostitution trade currently favour male customers and pimps, they argue that current laws are responsible for this gender bias. They also argue that prostitution does not have to represent patriarchal values, and that eliminating its criminal status would help transform it into a viable service-related occupation (Jenness, 1993). In particular, many prostitutes' rights organizations point out that legal status would afford them greater legal protection from pimps and violent customers. They also suggest that they would be willing co-operate with residents and other groups, as long as they were able to work legally (Larsen, 1992).

On balance, the arguments articulated by liberal feminists and prostitutes' rights groups appear more persuasive than the more extreme radical feminist approach. Although the radical feminists are clearly correct in many of their assertions regarding the basic patriarchal character of prostitution, many of their suggested solutions were actually implemented in Toronto without success. In this respect, the more extreme radical feminist approach fails to give enough consideration to both the abysmal social conditions that prompt many streetwalkers to enter prostitution, and the fact that the suppression of prostitution will ultimately cause greater oppression for many prostitutes. Thus, regardless of whether one supports the more moderate radical-feminist perspective or the prostitutes' rights groups, one must conclude that the best approach to prostitution, at least in the short term, must include some form of decriminalization.

The remainder of this chapter will be concerned with outlining a decriminalized approach to prostitution control, which appears mandated by the discussion in this chapter. The most basic tenet of the approach is that most prostitution-related offences should be decriminalized and regulated though statutes similar to those used to regulate other businesses. In this respect, several Canadian cities, including Montreal, Vancouver, and Calgary, used civil bylaws to control prostitution in the aftermath of the *Hutt* decision. The relative success of these bylaws suggests that such an approach would *work as long as prostitutes are legally allowed to work somewhere.* This latter point is crucial to the success of a decriminalized model, since prostitutes will choose to work where they please if all areas are prohibited to them.

Another crucial aspect of a decriminalized approach to prostitution control involves the ability of prostitutes to work legally in fixed off-street locations as long as they do not contravene other laws that might apply to the area. This was recommended by the Fraser Committee, which studied the prostitution problem in the aftermath of the *Hutt* decision, but was rejected by the Ministry of Justice on the grounds that prostitutes would probably use their apartments to service clients picked up on the street (Larsen, 1991). It was argued that this would not reduce street prostitution and might cause additional problems in apartment buildings. It was also argued that bawdy houses[16] are currently uncommon even though they are rarely prosecuted, and that this indicates that most prostitutes prefer to work on the street. Both of these arguments are invalid because they fail to consider the fact that prostitutes are not currently allowed to advertise the locations of bawdy houses to attract clients. Legalized bawdy houses would likely become much more common and thereby reduce the nuisance associated with street prostitution. They would also increase the safety of prostitutes, who would be able to operate in small groups for mutual protection.

It is also recommended that local governments be empowered to establish legal prostitution areas through the same zoning laws that are used to regulate other forms of land use. Although there is some legitimate concern that this approach would create areas of concentrated "vice," this approach has been used successfully in Europe. Most of the research referred to in this chapter indicated that prostitutes would be willing to adhere to zone restrictions as long as there was a designated area where they could operate legally. In any case, it is further recommended that areas which permit legal prostitution be required to establish prostitution committees composed of residents, business owners, prostitutes, politicians, and police representatives. The function of these committees would be to monitor the prostitution trade and liaise among the various groups to identify and resolve problems before they became serious. In this respect, it is essential that any discussions regarding the control of prostitution include the prostitutes themselves. This would ultimately protect the interests of all affected groups. Not only would prostitutes be afforded a safer, less-stressful working environment, but residents and other groups would be able to influence the activities of prostitutes in a manner that is not possible today. It is only by encouraging a dialogue between all affected groups, that the social and political conflict that so frequently characterizes the issue can be eliminated.

ENDNOTES

1. These organizations include Prostitutes and Other Women for Equal Rights (POWER), the Canadian Organization for the Rights of Prostitutes (Corp), and Call Off Your Tired Old Ethics (COYOTE).

2. The video, *Anywhere But Here*, provides an interesting discussion of this paradox. The interviews portrayed in the video clearly exemplify the degree to which most people consider prostitution undesirable, but few feel that anything can realistically be accomplished. The video's narrator, Dr. John Lowman, argues that prostitution is caught in a legal conundrum in which it is neither criminal nor fully legal. As long as that state of affairs continues, he argues, it will be impossible to resolve the many issues involved in the prostitution debate.

3. It should be noted that it initially excluded male prostitutes as well. However, this was rectified by later amendments of the law.

4. The writer's own research refutes this evidence to some extent. In interviews conducted in 1989, police officers and social workers in Toronto suggested that it was common for the pimps to frequent the areas where runaways congregated. One Juvenile officer stated that it was a constant battle to reach the runaways before the pimps recruited them.

5. Many police officers would dispute this figure. The writer's own research in Vancouver and Toronto also suggests that prostitutes are reluctant to admit that they work for

pimps, and that the actual numbers of prostitutes who work for pimps may be higher than the figures discussed above.

6. The following section is a revised version of a similar analysis published previously. See Larsen (1996) for the full text.

7. Bill C-49, which was incorporated into Section 195.1 of the Canadian Criminal Code, essentially criminalized all public communication for the purposes of prostitution. It included automobiles as "public" places and prohibited any attempt to stop automobiles or impede pedestrians. It also applied to any place open to public view, even if the actual conversations could not be heard by other people.

8. It should be noted that Bill C-49 legally became S. 195.1 of the *Canadian Criminal Code* once it was proclaimed into law. However, the numbering of the section changed during the time period covered by this chapter and the term Bill C-49 will be used throughout to avoid ambiguity or confusion.

9. Responsibility for prostitution control was divided between the Vice Squad and uniformed patrol teams. The Vice Squad utilized a combination of routine undercover work and major sweeps in which entire areas were blanketed for several hours. The uniformed patrol teams were responsible for order maintenance calls and attempting to deter prostitution activity through routine patrols in prostitution areas.

10. In fact, the area restrictions may have exacerbated the problem by expanding the red-light area. Referred to by some as the "creeping red-light district" phenomenon, it spread the problem of street prostitution over a larger area and actually increased the amount of public outcry.

11. This area was located along the Vancouver Harbour and near Chinatown. It encompassed skid row, a large area of public housing, some established working-class residential districts, and the trendy restaurant and shopping area known as "Gastown." Although the area had always contained significant amounts of prostitution, the transient nature of the population, combined with its preponderance of seedy bars and other transient-oriented businesses, minimized conflict.

12. It should be noted that although the majority of the evidence supports the scenario outlined above, there was some disagreement about the effectiveness of the initial police response to the Strathcona situation. A group of Strathcona residents who were unhappy with the levels of street prostitution in the area organized the Strathcona Prostitution Action Committee (SPAC) in May of 1988. The group organized a short lobbying campaign aimed at Vancouver Police and City Hall. This quickly resulted in the formation of a Special Police Liaison Committee for Strathcona, which met with the dissatisfied residents and drew up a plan of increased uniformed patrols. Three area prostitutes also attended the meeting and participated in the discussion and negotiations over the problem (Vancouver City Manager's Report to Council, August 26, 1988). This appeared to resolve the issue, as there was no further indication of trouble in the area.

13. In addition to the qualitative information gathered for this study, the official evaluation conducted by the Department of Justice came to similar conclusions. For example, although the average number of visible prostitutes did decline in 1986, it rebounded to even higher levels in 1987. (The figures were 1985 – 44.0, 1986 – 23.6, 1987 – 54.2.) (Lowman, 1989).

14. They explained their inaction on the grounds that escort agencies were much more difficult to investigate and in many cases were not illegal (S/Insp. Jim Clark, OIC Toronto Police Morality Division). Since telephone lines are not public places, it was not an offence to use them for soliciting as long as the prostitutes did their own soliciting and as long as they did not use the same location more than once to service their clients. If the former qualification was breached, the person doing the soliciting on behalf of the prostitutes could be charged with "living on the avails" of prostitution. If the same location was used more than once, common bawdy house charges could be laid.

15. This was because pimps now found it easier to control their girls than when they were on the streets. While a prostitute working the streets could "turn tricks" without giving her pimp his share, this would be more difficult in an agency where the pimp could monitor all calls without leaving the office. The police were virtually powerless to intervene since they lacked an effective way of monitoring the activities of the pimps (*SS*, Apr. 27, 1986: A8).

16. Under the *Criminal Code*, brothels, massage parlours, and other-off street venues where prostitution occurs are defined as "bawdy houses," and are illegal if prostitution occurs more than once in the same location. This provision prevents prostitutes from working out of their homes, which is legally permitted in Great Britain, for example.

REFERENCES

Bell, L. (1987) *Good Girls/Bad Girls: Sex Trade Workers and Feminists Face to Face.* Toronto: The Women's Press.

Benjamin, Harry and R.E.L. Masters (1964) *Prostitution and Morality.* New York: Julian Publishers.

Bristow, B. (1977) *Vice and Vigilance.* Dublin: Gill and MacMillan, Ltd.

Cooper, B. (1989) "Prostitution: A Feminist Analysis," *Women's Rights Law Reporter.* Vol. 11, p. 99.

Decker, J.F. (1979) *Prostitution: Regulation and Control.* Littleon, N.J: Rothman & Co.

Freeman, J. (1989) The Feminist Debate over Prostitution Reform: Prostitutes' Rights Groups, Radical Feminists and the [I]mpossibility of Consent," 5 *Berkeley Women's Law Journal*, p. 75.

Gomme, I.M. (1993) *The Shadow Line: Deviance and Crime in Canada.* Toronto: Harcourt Brace.

Greenwald, Harold (1970) *The Elegant Prostitute.* New York: Walker Publishing Co.

Hollis, P. (1979) *Women in Public: The Women's Movement 1850–1900.* London: George Allen & Unwin.

Hutt vs. the Queen. (1978) 32 CCC (2d) 418.

Jenness, Valerie (1993) *Making It Work: The Prostitutes' Rights Movement in Perspective.* Hawthorne, NY: Aldine De Gruyter.

Larsen, N. (1991) *The Politics of Prostitution Control: A Qualitative Analysis of the Development and Implementation of Bill C-49.* Unpublished Ph.D. Dissertation: University of Manitoba, Winnipeg, Manitoba.

Larsen, N. (1992) "Time to Legalize Prostitution," *Policy Options*, (September, 1992) p. 22.

Larsen, N. (1993) "Canadian Prostitution Control Between 1914 and 1970: An Exercise in Chauvinist Reasoning," *Canadian Journal of Law and Society,* Vol. 7(2), p. 137.

Larsen, N. (1996) "The Limits of the Law: A Critical Examination of Prostitution Control in Three Canadian Cities," *Hybrid: The University of Pennsylvania Journal of Law and Social Change,* Vol. 3(1) pp. 19–42.

Little, C. (1995) *Deviance and Control: Theory, Research and Social Policy*. Itasca, IL: Peacock Publishers, Ltd.

Lowman, J. (1989) *Street Prostitution: Assessing the Impact of the Law — Vancouver*. Ottawa: Department of Justice.

Lowman, J. (1994) *Anywhere but here* (Video) Vancouver: BC Learning Resources Institute.

Lowman, J. and L. Fraser (1995) *Violence Against Persons Who Prostitute in British Columbia*. Ottawa: Solicitor General of Canada.

Moyer, S. and P. Carrington, (1989) *Street Prostitution: Assessing the Impact of the Law — Toronto*. Ottawa: Supply and Services, Canada.

Perkins, R. (1991) *Working Girls: Prostitutes, Their Life and Social Control*. Australia: Australian Institute of Criminology.

Richards, D.A. (1982) *Sex Drugs, Death and the Law*. New Jersey: Rowman and Littlefield.

Shaver, F. (1993) "Prostitution: A Female Crime" in E. Adelberg & C. Currie (eds) *In Conflict with the Law: Women and the Canadian Criminal Justice System*. Vancouver: Press Gang Publishers, pp. 153–173.

Shaver, F. (1994) "The Regulation of Prostitution: Avoiding the Morality Traps," *Canadian Journal of Law and Society,* Vol. 9(1), p. 123.

Thio, A. (1995) *Deviant Behavior*, (4th ed.). New York: Harper Collins.

Walkowitz, J. (1983) *Prostitution in Victorian Society: Women, Class and State*. New York: Cambridge University Press.

ADDICTIONS AS DEVIANT BEHAVIOUR Normalizing the Pleasures of Intoxication

Chapter 4

Jennifer Butters
Patricia Erickson

INTRODUCTION

The social construction of drug use as deviance has served to stigmatize and criminalize many individuals, often causing more harm than drug use itself. Yet the consumption of psychoactive, mood modifying, intoxicating substances has been part of human society for over 10 000 years (Goode, 1997). The acceptability of different forms of drug-use behaviour has varied widely across, culture, substance, and time (Erickson, 1993). This century in particular has seen some forms of drug use transformed from a private indulgence to a public evil (Boyd, 1988).

The creation of drug use as a deviant behaviour has been a dynamic process involving three key social movements each emphasizing a specific form of "control" over substance use: moral, medical, and criminalization. Although originating from different concepts of addiction, all three movements describe the morals and values reflecting the "canons of decency" and respectability. These are essential to the perception of deserved rewards that distinguish one class from another, as well as serving as guidelines for proper behaviour (Gusfield, 1998).

This chapter outlines and contrasts the moral, medical, and the criminalization models of deviance as they pertain to drug use. Then the emerging concept of harm reduction is discussed as a counter balance to the deviant construction of the drug user and as a progressive step in the re-normalization of this universal human activity.

The views expressed by the authors do not necessarily reflect those of the University of Toronto or the Centre for Addiction and Mental Health.

67

THE MAKING OF "ADDICTION" — CREATING DEVIANCE

Cultures generally label particular lifestyles as "deviant" in order to define and dramatize standards of conduct that maintain the status quo (Alexander, 1990). The social construction of drugs as deviant created a new class of marginalized lifestyles contributing to the expectations of how people should live, and not live, their lives. Indeed substances that society now perceives to be threatening have at various times all been freely available, medically prescribed, aggressively marketed, severely restricted, and candidates for both prohibition and legalization (Heath, 1992). Considering this reality, the question becomes how and why we attribute a deviant status to the users of different substances.

While there are many ways to understand the concept of "deviance," two orientations encompass specific definitions: the positivist and the interactionist approach (Conrad and Schneider, 1980). The positivist approach assumes that deviance is real and exists not only in the objective actions of individuals but also is shared by those who observe these measurable experiences. Deviance is thus a behaviour that falls beyond conformity to dominant social norms. Furthermore, given that this perspective is premised on the belief that the social norms of society are known and shared, there is a corresponding perception that a consensus exists regarding the behaviours that constitute deviance.

In contrast, the interactionist perspective takes the stance that morality is not a constant, but rather a product of the process of social construction that is influenced by context, actors, and time. What constitutes deviance is a product of certain groups, generally those with more power, making claims regarding the acceptability of certain behaviours (Becker, 1963). These claims are typically based on personal interests and particular values. Thus from an interactionist perspective deviance is an action or a condition defined as inappropriate or in violation of certain powerful groups' conventions or rules.

Symbols and Language

Among the many forces that affect the social constructions of deviance, two important aspects to consider are symbols and language. Manderson (1995) argues that understanding the symbolic nature of objects associated with drug use provides a greater understanding of the social construction of drug use. Perhaps the most pervasive symbol is that of the needle. This image and emblem plays a key role in the generation and perpetuation of hostility and fear associated with drug use. Societal reaction to drug use is thus stimulated by the response to particular images that centre on objects of use and objects of ritual.

Regardless of whether the needle is self-administered or given by a medical professional, the discomfort of the piercing and visual image of it disappearing under your skin cannot be ignored; yet, depending on circumstance we perceive different levels of revulsion associated with this act. We must ask ourselves why. The answer to this question is directly related to one of the predominant ideologies of our society: trust and faith in the medical system. Therefore in medicalized contexts, because we assume there is a "valid" medical reason for the injection, we can ignore the discomfort and suspend our revulsion associated with injection. A similar tolerance however is not afforded the drug user. Another illustration of differential tolerance pertains to solvent use. For example, substances such as solvents, e.g. Pam cooking spray and glue, have been assigned a safe role in the home; however, when used for different purposes such as getting high, the boundary between what we know to be normal and that which is deviant is violated, creating feelings of discomfort. The underlying commonality to these examples is that these objects carry with them the important image of "violation" (e.g., the visual and tactile violation of injection drug use; the olfactory violation of smoking; the violation of normal usage of glue sniffing).

The issue of the symbolic violation of boundary is further perpetuated with respect to the perceived threat drug use poses to the mind/body and reason/emotion distinctions. Drugs threaten the integrity of the self, they carry with them the possibility of loss of control and disorder. Drug use thus blurs the line between rational and irrational, and it is this troublesome blurring of these boundaries upon which their deviant status is built (Manderson, 1995).

WHAT IS ADDICTION?

In addition to symbols, language is a powerful tool in the social construction of what becomes defined as deviance. The terminology, history, and connotations that are used when discussing drug use and addiction shape our perceptions of the "problem." How often do you hear or find yourself saying that you or others are *addicted* to something — coffee, chocolate, exercise? The word addiction is used rather liberally but has developed more precise meanings in its relationship specifically to drugs.

The root of the word addiction stems from the Latin verb *addicere,* meaning "to give over," where it connoted both negative and positive situations. For instance, in Roman times a person who was legally given over as a bond slave to his creditor was called an *addictus*; however, *addicere* also had positive connotations when used to denote strong devotion to a cause or activity.

Similarly in English, the term addiction is defined in the Oxford English Dictionary (1933: 104) as a "formal giving over or delivery by sentence of court. Hence, a surrender or dedication of any one to a master.... The state of being (self)-addicted or given to a habit or pursuit; devotion." Clearly this traditional definition had absolutely no direct connection with drugs. Indeed the association of the word "addict" with substance use did not occur until the nineteenth century when the temperance and anti-opium movements began. Applied to the habitual use of opium and perpetual drunkenness, the meaning of addiction was modified in four ways so that the new definition of addiction was (1) linked to specific drugs (opium and alcohol); (2) attributed the cause of addiction to exposure to the drug itself; (3) identified tolerance and withdrawal symptoms as criteria for addiction; and (4) ultimately ascribed an unfavourable meaning to the term as an illness or vice (Alexander, 1990). In essence, it was perceived that the addict had lost self-control and was instead controlled by the drug.

More recently the word addiction is defined, according to Jaffe (1985: 533), as a "behavioural pattern of drug use, characterized by overwhelming involvement with the use of a drug ... the securing of its supply, and a high tendency to relapse after withdrawal." This definition of addiction is also not without its ambiguity (Alexander, 1990). For example is overwhelming involvement a good or a bad thing? When considering the image of the street addict there is little doubt that overwhelming involvement may be associated with harm, though this may be attributed more to the lifestyle than the drug's effects. However, users also describe their involvement in positive terms and acknowledge many benefits from their drug use experience. This area of ambiguity has resulted in Alexander's (1990) suggestion of refining the term by identifying "negative" and "positive" addiction, reflecting the contrasting outcomes.

Another confounding feature associated with this definition is that "addiction" is frequently thought of as the *effect* of using drugs rather than the way of using drugs and ignores *how* this pattern was caused (Alexander, 1990). These examples serve to highlight the complexities and ambiguities surrounding a term that has become a common element in our everyday language.

WHAT IS A DRUG?

Although a taken-for-granted distinction, the categorization of substances into licit and illicit drugs originated in this century. There are many ways to define a drug including religious (sacramental substances), medical (medicines versus non-medicines), scientific (active chemical substances), and social (recreational substances) (Erickson, 1993). Central to these definitions however is the fact that the concept of "a drug" has been largely shaped by popular culture, and the categorization of substances as drug/non-drug generally represents an ideological rather than pharmacological position (Boyd, 1988).

When considering the question, "What is a drug?" it is important to examine the distinction between definitions based on psychoactive criteria and those based on legal status.

Legal Status

A legalistic definition implies that a drug is that which is prohibited by the law. As in Canada's Controlled Drugs and Substance Act, this definition suggests that drugs consist solely of illegal substances. Therefore, according to the legalistic definition, alcohol and tobacco, although potentially harmful and destructive, are not considered to be drugs. By extension, alcohol, tobacco, and their associated problems are not contributing to the "drug problem" in our country today; in effect, they are irrelevant substances for legal policy.

Thus a legalistic definition of drugs focuses on the violation of the law rather than potential or actual harm to the individual or society. The central concern underlying the legalistic definition revolves around the threat that illegal drugs are believed to pose to the state and the established order, undermining the basic social fabric of society (Zimring and Hawkins, 1992). This definition is therefore based on ideology and morality rather than the effects of drugs themselves.

Psychoactivity

While it is not the purpose of this chapter to discuss in detail the pharmacological properties and effects of different substances, a brief overview is provided. From this perspective a drug is any substance (other than food) that by its chemical or physical nature alters the structure or function in a living organism. The definition of drugs based on *psychoactivity* implies that a drug is a substance that influences or alters the workings of the human mind (Goode, 1997). This definition classifies a psychoactive drug as one that stimulates the central nervous system, acting on the brain to enhance or influence the user's emotions, mood, perceptions, and thinking.

Although capturing very different aspects of constructs underlying definitions, pharmacological and legal definitions of what constitutes a drug should not necessarily be seen as mutually exclusive categories. Indeed, although the logic of this process is questionable, perceptions of psychoactivity are influential in the process of assigning legal and illegal status to different substances.

For example, there are several different classes of drugs including stimulants, depressants, analgesics, or hallucinogens, which have a specific impact on the brain and subsequent behaviour through the central nervous system. Drugs that have been classified as *prohibited/illicit* substances, including cocaine, LSD, cannabis, and heroin, each fall into a different class of drugs. However, *legally available* substances, including alcohol (a depressant), nicotine (a stimulant), and codeine (an analgesic), are also distributed in the general drug categories. Therefore it would appear that the mere pharmacological classification (e.g., stimulant, depressant) system reveals very little about the appropriate legal or illegal status of a substance.

Conversely, when considering how we come to view certain drugs as deviant while tolerating others, it is necessary to understand how the perceptions of psychoactivity affect social definitions. Perhaps those drugs to which we assign greater potential harmful consequences are those that merit the illegal status. To this end our understanding of drug use as deviance and the related social policy is in part a reflection of differing psychoactive effects.

However, to assume that because tobacco and alcohol are legal substances (not classified as drugs) they are consequently harmless, while illegal drugs are dangerous, is a tremendous fallacy (Goldstein, 1994). Indeed, drugs with known acute and long-term harmful consequences are just as likely to be classified as legal and/or medically prescribed as they are illegal (Erickson, 1993; Addiction Research Foundation, 1987–1988). Alcohol and medically prescribed barbiturates are just two examples of substances that have potentially lethal short-term effects, and fatal long-term effects are strongly associated with tobacco use.

Furthermore, based on the 1997 Canadian Profile: Alcohol, Tobacco and Other Drugs (Canadian Centre on Substance Abuse), the highest drug-related mortality rates among the Canadian population were attributed to tobacco, followed by alcohol, and then illicit drugs. Specifically in 1992, 33 498 deaths were attributable to tobacco (lung cancer, heart disease, and pulmonary disease) while 6701 deaths were attributable to alcohol (impaired driving, liver cirrhosis, and alcohol-related suicides). Finally, illicit drugs accounted for 732 deaths resulting from suicide, opiate poisoning, cocaine poisoning, and AIDS-related deaths due to intravenous drug use.

Moreover, in that use patterns may become destructive and compulsive in nature for cocaine, heroin, alcohol, and nicotine, all "addictive" drugs (Akers, 1991), the dependency-producing properties of these drugs are quite varied (Erickson, 1993). Therefore just as the legal/illegal distinction reveals little about the nature of a substance's pharmacology, the effects of a drug on one's health and mental state reveal little about the legal status of a drug.

So how should we think of something we refer to as a "drug"? Social constructionists argue that an illegal drug should be conceptualized as something arbitrarily defined as "bad" and subjected to extreme disapproval by certain segments of society (Goode, 1984). Thus not only is the concept "drug" socially created but the connotations associated with the word "drug" are also socially determined and are generally negative.

THE TEMPERANCE MOVEMENT: MORALITY RULES

The temperance movement, most commonly associated with alcohol, was driven by the perception that drinking was a weakness ultimately resulting in the decline of moral behaviour (Single, 1997). This movement emerged in the nineteenth century and over time escalated from attempts to reduce drinking through persuasion to enforced abstinence of the total population (Alexander, 1990).

The temperance movement in Canada became increasingly popular as it provided one of the few commonalities between the French and English (Woods, 1983). By strategically aligning themselves with other popular movements of the times, such as women's suffrage, temperance societies managed to integrate themselves as a central part of social life (Smart and Ogborne, 1986). Support for the temperance philosophy was also reinforced through the use of language. Specifically warlike terminology became a tool for the movement with slogans such as "war to the death with the Demon of intemperance" (Chiniquy, 1847: 26) and the development of a Canadian temperance song book including such pieces as "The Temperance Army" and "Sound the Battle Cry" further empowered this movement (Alexander, 1990).

The crux of the temperance movement was the proclamation that drunkenness was the source of society's evils and that one single alcoholic had the power to convert others over to dark, immoral ways (Smart and Ogborne, 1986). As such the only way to prevent the moral decay of Canadian society was through the widespread prohibition of alcohol. Initially this prohibition was enforced by the North-West Mounted Rifles, a group that eventually came to be known as the North-West Mounted Police (NWMP) (Alexander, 1990). Although camouflaged under relatively benign terminology such as constables and commissioners, the NWMP served as a militaristic force, upholding the law with powers to search and make arrests without warrants, all in the name of prohibition (Gray, 1972).

Although the movement enjoyed a period of popularity, this was soon overshadowed by the excessive violence it spawned. The violent outcomes of American prohibition in the Al Capone era are well known as they have been dramatized in many movies and TV series (e.g., *The Untouchables*). Canadian prohibition gave rise to its own assortment of legendary individuals including the "Spracklin Gang" in Ontario. The leader of the Spracklin Gang was Reverend J.O.L Spracklin, a Minster of a Methodist church. As an avid supporter of prohibition enforcement, Spracklin was appointed head of a special force of liquor licence inspectors and soon implemented a martial-law style of enforcement. The enforcement efforts of the Spracklin gang included using their guns, delivering severe beatings (at least one person died), and carrying blank search warrants the Reverend could fill out on an "as needed" basis. Whether based on his popularity or perhaps the blinding belief in "all in the name of prohibition," Spracklin even managed to be acquitted of murdering a roadhouse owner in spite of eyewitness testimony to the contrary. In fact he was only stripped of his title and position when he was charged by members of his own congregation for "sexual propositions" to female parishioners (Gervais, 1980).

Although Spracklin represents an extreme example of the degradation of ideals associated with prohibition, general corruption became synonymous with prohibition efforts. A good example of this is the story of W.C. Findlay. Findlay was an eminent member of the political movement advocating prohibition in British Columbia and was ultimately appointed the prohibition commissioner of that province. Ironically, however, in just a short time following this designation Mr. Findlay was brought up on charges and found guilty of involvement in bootlegging (Hiebert, 1969).

Although not nearly as excessively violent as prohibition in the United States, it soon became apparent that the costs of prohibition in Canada far outweighed the rewards. Therefore, through a series of provincial plebiscites alcohol prohibition was soon abandoned as a social movement. The final provinces to relinquish prohibition endeavours were Nova Scotia (1929) and Prince Edward Island (1948) (Smart and Ogborne, 1986).

Tobacco has belatedly been subjected to a neo-temperance critique in the latter part of the 20th century. As the toll taken not only on users themselves but on their families and co-workers, through second hand smoke, has become publicized, a new basis for serious social disapproval of what had been a well-tolerated habit has been formed. Signs for smoke-free homes and sweeping workplace restrictions forced Canadian smokers into the great outdoors for their puffs. Although the prohibition of selling tobacco to minors (persons under the age of 16) has been on the books since the 1908 Tobacco Restraint Act, this law began to be enforced in Canada for the first time as the 1990s progressed and talk of a more sweeping tobacco prohibition was discussed publicly.

Practically speaking, since even a ban on tobacco advertising could not pass Supreme Court rulings on freedom of speech, and the federal government withdrew from its earlier tougher taxation stand, the weight of moral, if not legal, censure seems likely to remain the dominant form of social control. Nevertheless, the fairly widespread use of tobacco and its continued recruitment of young smokers keeps its deviant status on a milder level than that associated with the complete rejection embodied in the criminalization approach.

CRIMINALIZATION: FROM BAD TO WORSE

It may be difficult to conceive of a time when opium-smoking merchants operated their establishments in British Columbia with little public or legal outcry. This however was the case for roughly 40 years until 1908 when the criminalization of substance use first occurred prohibiting opium manufacturing, import, and sale. This criminalization however was prompted less by concerns regarding substance use and more so by the overarching anti-Asiatic sentiment. This new anti-drug ideology (specifically directed toward marijuana, cocaine, and opium) was further reinforced by the creation of a new enforcement sector of the RCMP in the 1920s. Indeed it has been suggested that nearing disbandment, the RCMP was effectively "saved" by the discovery of the drug menace in Canadian society (Alexander, 1990).

To use the criminal law in an effort to completely suppress certain behaviour requires the assumption that a moral consensus exists that this behaviour cannot be tolerated, that, as portrayed by Durkheim, it offends the collective conscience of society. The drug user is a depraved "dope fiend" without conscience or morals, living only to corrupt others and get that next fix. For such an evil menace to society, the appropriate response becomes the detection and harsh punishment of such wrongdoers. A strong law enforcement apparatus and efficient prosecution, sentencing, and incarceration are required. The very fact of an episode of illicit drug use or sale are all that is required to lay a charge — the experience of the individual, the amount, or the social circumstances are irrelevant in the criminal model. The offender is responsible for his or her own behaviour and must bear the consequences.

The vigorous application of criminalization has been the dominant approach since the upsurge in cannabis and other psychedelic drugs in the 1960s. The result has been large increases in the number of criminalized individuals, estimated at over half a million in Canada alone, for the simple possession of cannabis. The proportion of prison inmates jailed for drug law violations has soared, and the customs and criminal justice resources devoted to the suppression of drug use and sale has also grown. The consequences of conviction are numerous as well, as a criminal record bars the individual from many jobs, travel, and potential claims on a legitimate place in society (Erickson, 1980). At the end of 90 years of criminalization and about 30 years of evaluation, some detailed assessments have been made of its "success."

Indeed, these criticisms of an aggressive prohibition and the criminalization of drug users are numerous. They include its moral arbitrariness in selecting some drugs for punishment and not others, its insensitivity to differential consequences of drug use, the pharmacological naivety, the stigmatization and systematic marginalization of drug users, the manufacturing of a "moral panic" against drugs and drug users, the resultant infringement on the civil rights of citizens, the overburdening of the criminal justice system, the sustenance of a violent black market, and most telling of all — the failure to deliver what it promises: the control and reduction of illicit drug use and availability (Erickson et al., 1997). The lessons of drug prohibition appear to have been constantly re-learned and new ways sought to contain the most dangerous expressions of drug use behaviour and its harmful impacts on society.

COSTS OF SUBSTANCE ABUSE IN CANADA

Although studies have looked at individual costs associated with tobacco, alcohol, and illicit drugs, with the exception of the study reported on here, there have been few attempts to gauge the total costs associated with the use and abuse of drugs in Canada. *The Costs of Substance Abuse in Canada* (Single et al., 1996) presents an estimation of the costs associated with drug use that extend beyond those related to government accounts reporting on costs pertaining to the whole society. The authors acknowledge that this report presents a conservative approach to the estimation of these figures, thus any bias will reflect an underestimation of actual costs.

This study examined a variety of costs including, tangible costs (those borne to those other than the users, including the user's family), intangible costs (costs associated with pain, suffering, bereavement, and numbers of life-years lost), welfare costs, non-workforce death and illness costs, research, education and law enforcement costs, and an estimation of avoidable costs. Not included are those costs pertaining to the purchasing of psychoactive substances incurred by the user and the transfer payments including welfare benefits to those disabled by substance abuse.

In 1992 the estimated cost of substance abuse in Canada was more than $18.45 billion, representing $649 per capita and approximately 2.7% of the gross domestic product (Single et al., 1996). Recall these figures represent the most optimistic estimates and it is likely the actual costs are higher. A breakdown of the estimated costs associated with the three main categories of drugs (alcohol, tobacco, and illicit drugs) reveals interesting results.

The most significant costs to Canadian society are those associated with tobacco, followed by alcohol, and then illicit drugs. Interestingly, policy costs (those incorporating prevention, research, and enforcement costs) are highest for alcohol ($1.5 billion), followed by illicit drugs ($442 million), and essentially negligible for tobacco. The policy costs in 1992 for tobacco represented less than 1% of the total economic costs associated with tobacco. Ironically, it appears that the least amount of financial resources are directed toward the substance that causes the greatest harm to our society.

THE MEDICAL MODEL: THE "SICK" AND "DISEASED" DRUG USER

What Is the Medical Model?

Modern medicine based on the germ theory of disease (each illness is believed to be governed by a unique or specific etiology) is the dominant and mainstream school of medicine in Western societies. The confidence placed in the abilities of modern medicine coupled with the tremendous technological advances that have been made have created an environment in which the medical profession has secured a hold over health matters. This domination facilitated the transfusion of this profession into the realm of other "deviant behaviours" that previously fell outside its boundaries. This process of the medicalization of deviance (Conrad and Schneider, 1992) has resulted in the proliferation of deviant behaviours being defined and treated as medical problems; this process has included alcoholism and drug abuse. As initially described by Conrad and Schneider (1980), to medicalize deviance is to redefine it from "badness" to "sickness," thereby eliminating the criminal or moral stigma from the individual. The medical model thus sees the deviant as a patient. Occupying the sick role, the individual is not held responsible for illness, is exempt from normal social roles, but is also obligated to seek treatment and co-operate (Parsons, 1951).

The medical model of illness is generally considered to be the dominant concept of "illness" in the medical world (Weitz, 1996). This model comprises five components, each specifying a different facet pertaining to how illness is defined. According to the medical model, illness is:

a. A deviation from normal

b. Specific and universal

c. Caused by unique biological forces

d. Parallelled to the breakdown of a machine

e. Defined and treated through neutral, scientific processes (Weitz, 1996)

The medical model is based on the notion that a disease is caused by physiological difficulties found within the body. The emphasis of the medical model highlighted the importance of the bio-physiological and internal environment rather than social psychological and other external factors. Extending this definition to deviance, the medical model thus locates the source of deviant behaviour within the individual, its cause assumed to be an organic, constitutional, or psychogenic agent. Given this biological basis, the medical model of deviance stipulates that medical personnel and medicine are generally thought to be the necessary means of treatment for these "illnesses." Thus deviance is a symptom of an underlying psychological sickness that can only be detected and treated by medical professionals.

The Medical Model and Drug Use

Following the repeal of Prohibition, the temperance movement was succeeded by the disease concept of drug use. While the temperance movement focused on the moral weakness of individuals who used alcohol and argued for abstinence as the goal of prevention to be achieved through legal prohibition, the disease concept offered a new ideology.

The medical model perspective targets the *disease* of alcoholism as the primary problem. To this end there is only a specific segment of the population who is "at risk." These individuals are the "alcoholics" and are regarded as fundamentally different from the normal, social drinking proportion of the population (Single, 1997). In contrast to the temperance model, where blame was focused on the bottle in general, the medical model shifts the blame to the unfortunate, susceptible individual. Thus while abstinence is still the outcome treatment goal for those afflicted with the alcoholism disease, access to alcohol is not denied to those who do not suffer from alcoholism.

The modern application of the medical model to alcoholism essentially began in the 1930s with the development of the Yale Research Centre of Alcohol Studies (Conrad and Schneider, 1992). At this time the interest in alcoholism as a disease was not confined to medical personnel but the general community was also becoming concerned with the "disease" of alcohol. Indeed Alcoholics Anonymous (AA), founded in 1935, was established by two men who were personally experiencing alcohol-related problems.

Alcoholism, according to the AA philosophy, is equated to an "allergy" that essentially triggers uncontrolled drinking in susceptible people (much like pollen triggers uncontrollable sneezing in allergy sufferers) (Lisowski, 1996). Thus in the process of equating alcoholism to an allergy, the individual is not to blame for his or her illness. Research at the Yale Centre established a stage model of alcohol addiction. In doing so medical professionals were provided a diagnostic system facilitating the identification of those individuals with the "disease" of alcoholism (Conrad and Schneider, 1992).

The extent to which drug use is regarded as deviant is not really a function of the properties or characteristics of a particular drug inasmuch as it is the *purpose* of the drug use that defines the deviant quality. For example, the same drug used for medical purposes (e.g., opiates as pain killers) may not be regarded as deviant; however, if used to avoid withdrawal symptoms deviant connotations are immediately applied. Thus the deviant nature of drug use is not related to the physical properties of the drug but rather the norms associated with appropriate use. Under the umbrella of the medical model, the socially constructed norms related to drug use define the use of a drug for medical purposes as appropriate use.

There is nothing particular to the chemical nature of opiates that ultimately makes them either good or bad. Rather it is the social definition that separates the reputable from the disreputable. For example, heroin and morphine are two opiate drugs that are nearly identical with respect to their pharmacological properties and physiological effects. However one is regarded as a boon to medicine, while the other is a "junkie drug." In effect, one drug is licit and the other illicit, a distinction based not on the drug's chemical nature or bio-physiological effects but rather who prescribes and who denies use (Conrad and Schneider, 1980).

Critique of the Medical Model

The physiological and medical realities of prolonged drinking and other drug use cannot be ignored and it is indeed appropriate to discuss these aspects within the context of the medical model. However the medical model can be criticized on many grounds (for greater detail see Conrad and Schneider, 1980; Weitz, 1996).

First, in defining illness as a deviation from what is considered biologically normal (Weitz, 1996) the medical model assumes that "normal" is both known and recognizable. However perceptions of what constitutes normal are not fixed and invariant; rather, normality varies from person to person and group to group. Furthermore, this model is narrowly restricted to biological functioning and thereby negates the importance of the interaction between the person and the social context in which he or she lives.

A second critique is that the medical model sees the body as a machine, adopting a mechanistic approach to treatment and intervention. The outcome of this ideology is that doctors and researchers utilize a reductionist treatment approach that focuses on each part of the body individually, separate from the whole. Thus, this mechanistic approach fails to see the interconnectedness of an individual's life and body; emphasis remains concentrated on the body, negating the social environment.

Third, the medical model is premised on an assumption of unique etiology. In presuming that each illness is caused by a unique micro-organism, the medical model discourages scientists and researchers from exploring the reality that individuals respond in different ways to the same illness-causing factors. Instead the search remains for the "magic bullet" (a term first used by Paul Ehrlich in the discovery of a syphilis vaccine) treatment that will cure the illness by destroying a specific causal factor.

The medical model and the subsequent use of medicine in treatment are perceived to be morally neutral (Waitzkin, 1983). As such, these "illnesses" are considered to be scientifically verifiable and rational conditions not based on moral judgments. The accuracy of this element of the medical model however is questionable. Medical designations are indeed social judgments and are far from politically neutral. Several historical examples illustrate how the association of medical designations to deviant behaviour are intimately tied to the moral climate of society at the time. For example, Samuel Cartwright, a physician in the southern United States, published an article in 1851 detailing the characteristics of a disease known as "drapetomania." This "disease" affected only slaves and the major symptom was identified as the tendency to run away from the plantation of their master. Homosexuality and masturbation have also been defined and treated as illnesses in need of treatment. In the former Soviet Union political nonconformists have been diagnosed with "mental illness" such as manic reformism and counter revolutionary delusions, and hospitalized for their opposition to the political order (see Conrad and Schneider, 1980). These examples call into question the notion of the moral neutrality of the medical model and indeed illustrate how the medical designation of deviance is significantly influenced by moral undertones of society. In addition to these inadequacies and limitations of the medical model, scientific evidence has also been generated that calls into question several aspects of the medical model as it applies to alcoholism.

One proposition of the medical model of deviance is that alcoholics have a predisposing characteristic toward alcoholism that differentiates them from non-alcoholics. This notion of an "alcoholic personality" has however failed to be adequately supported by scientific research (Fingarette, 1988; Pattison et al., 1977; Mansell, Sobel and Sobel, 1977). Indeed, although studies of identical twins raised in different environments reveal differences in the rate of alcoholism between those with biological alcoholic parents and non-alcoholic parents, these studies do not offer a satisfactory explanation as to why some children of alcoholics do not become alcoholics and why some children of non-alcoholics do (Fingarette, 1988). Thus research does not seem to support the notion of a single predisposing characteristic that provides a distinction between alcoholics and non-alcoholics.

Further, the medical model suggests that alcoholism is a progressive disease ending with chronic alcoholism. However, research indicates that individuals move in and out of what can be thought of as deviant drinking. Indeed many alcoholics have been noted to experience periods of binge drinking and periods of recovery (Conrad and Schneider, 1992), while others stop drinking completely without medical intervention (Fingarette, 1988).

The notion that a sober alcoholic who begins drinking again will not be able to stop drinking has also been questioned. Providing contradictory evidence regarding the notion that alcoholism is an "allergy," some research suggests that it is possible for certain former alcoholics to resume controlled drinking without returning to their problem drinking behaviour patterns (Conrad and Schneider, 1992). Finally, another criticism of the medical model and its applicability to drug use is that medicine has failed to develop a "cure" for this disease (Conrad, 1992; Fox, 1977).

HARM REDUCTION: DEVIANT NO MORE?

Since the 1960s public health has developed into a perspective that encompasses environmental, psychological, and societal factors (Ashton and Seymour, 1988). Drawing from this evolved public health approach, a new drug perspective has emerged called "harm reduction." While harm reduction attempts to avoid the moral, medical, and legal reductionist biases that have characterized the previous approaches to drug use, whether this approach is yet another social construction of deviant behaviour remains to be assessed.

Major Features of Harm Reduction

Details regarding the underlying concepts of the harm reduction paradigm can be found in other sources (Erickson and Butters, 1998; Riley et al., 1999); however, a brief overview of the central features of harm reduction is provided in this chapter.

Perhaps one of the most important and central aspects of harm reduction is that this paradigm makes no assumptions regarding the moral and legal nature of drug use. At the conceptual level, harm reduction adopts a value-neutral approach to both the user and drug use in general. To this end, while moral judgments are not passed on the drug user, this framework does acknowledge the user's role. Specifically, the user is perceived as an active participant, capable of making choices, who also must take responsibility for these choices (Erickson et al., 1997).

Unlike the medical and criminal models that regard drug *use* as inherently problematic, a harm reduction approach focuses on the harmful *consequences* of use. Indeed the overarching goal of this approach is to reduce the adverse consequences of drug use without requiring necessarily decreased drug use (Riley, 1993). Under the framework of harm reduction, "adverse consequence" is a multidimensional construct. The harm reduction framework acknowledges the interaction between physical, social, psychological, and cultural factors in the development of intervention and treatment strategies. As such, unlike the medical and criminal models that hold abstinence as the ultimate outcome goal, this is not a requirement under harm reduction. Instead harm reduction seeks to decrease adverse health consequences, social consequences, and economic consequences of drug use without requiring reduced drug use (Erickson and Butters, 1998).

Furthermore, also in contrast to previous approaches of drug use, harm reduction recognizes the positive aspects of drug use, understanding that there are inherent "attractions" to using that cannot be negated if we are to develop effective prevention and intervention efforts. Indeed there are many pleasurable aspects of drug use that pertain to both licit and illicit drugs. For example, users report enjoyable aspects of cocaine to include physical energy, sociability, controlled high, and euphoria (Erickson et al., 1987). Moreover, in a recent study of female crack addicts, the "rush," the "ritual" associated with obtaining crack, the escape, and the calming effects of crack were cited as positive elements of using (Butters, Hallgren and McGillicuddy, 1997). These are all positive, desirable states and it is reasonable to understand why some individuals do not want to stop using. As such, harm reduction recognizes that abstinence may not be a reasonable goal for all drug users nor should it be the only *acceptable* outcome for intervention efforts.

Furthermore, where the medical and criminal models emphasize the individual, harm reduction draws on its association with public health and extends its scope to encompass the family, community, and society in general. In short, harm reduction — while emphasizing the individual — also acknowledges the impact of the broader social context. Unlike either the medical or criminal model of deviance that focus on the individual only as an entity requiring treatment or punishment, harm reduction acknowledges the role of the interrelationship between these factors and the individual (Zinberg, 1984).

For harm reduction to be adopted as the predominant approach to drug use, there are certain prerequisites that must occur. Foremost, there must be a shift away from criminal prohibition toward a more medically defined regulatory emphasis (Glaser, 1974). The aim is not a return to the extreme medical model approach whereby personal responsibility for one's actions is negated and blamed on the "disease" and treatment becomes controlled by the medical profession. Rather, a shift to a health-oriented approach respects the decisions made by the individual drug user and works with him or her to find less harmful ways to help the user adapt to his or her chronic drug use condition, until and if he or she wishes to cease use.

In addition to a shift towards health definitions of drug-related problems, Glaser (1974) also stipulated that the view of users as marginal deviants must be replaced with the recognition that users are mainstream, potentially functioning members of society. In addition, it is imperative to recognize that many of the health consequences perceived to be associated with drug use have been overstated and are not as devastating as once perceived to be. Finally, for harm reduction to be truly successful there needs to be much less criminalization, either by selective non-enforcement of drug laws or major drug law reform (Erickson and Butters, 1998). In short, if harm reduction is to become accepted as a viable and practical framework in which to structure the development and implementation of programs and policies, society must change the way the drug problem is constructed.

THE NORMALCY OF DRUG USE

Drug use is not a static phenomenon; rather there is a continuum or spectrum of drug users that extends beyond a simple dichotomy of users and non-users. Indeed, much illicit drug use is occurring in the non-deviant population where most social recreational use is *not* visible, *not* dependence-producing, and *not* harmful (Erickson and Butters, 1998). An illustration of this is the widespread use of cannabis in the 1970s and 1980s to the point where whole generations have, in effect, aged with the regular cannabis use (Erickson, 1980).

Based on information taken from the *1997 Canadian Profile: Alcohol, Tobacco and Other Drugs Report* (Canadian Centre on Substance Abuse), 72% of the Canadian population in 1994 indicated alcohol consumption and 27% or 6.1 million Canadians over 15 years of age were using tobacco. Regarding illicit drugs, almost one in four Canadians (5 500 000 people) report having used an illicit substance. The most widely used illicit drug is cannabis, whereby 23.1% (or 5 320 000) of the Canadian adult population indicate using it at some point in their life. In comparison, about 3.8% (875 000) indicate ever using cocaine or crack, 1 200 000 (5.2%) LSD, and 115 000 (0.5%) using heroin in their lifetime. Thus there is evidence that drug use is not a rarity among Canadians.

To this end, a harm reduction framework would suggest the recognition that a certain amount of drug use is inevitable and "normal" for any society, while only particularly excessive, destructive forms remain in the realm of deviant behaviours. Social drinking and the social smoker are expressions we are familiar with, and they embody the understanding that the use of alcohol and tobacco can be maintained in a controlled manner. A less portrayed image however is that of the controlled illicit drug user. Nonetheless, research illustrates that even the most feared, addictive drugs can be used safely and in a controlled way by the majority of users.

In a study of 111 cocaine users, one of the striking findings revealed was that for many users, controlled cocaine use in leisure hours (evenings, weekends, and special occasions) was possible (Erickson et al., 1987). These individuals were productive, contributing adult (each respondent was 21 years of age or older) members of society. They were not instantaneously turned into "coke heads" living life for their next hit. Thus the social distance between users and mainstream society members is much narrower than might be assumed. Indeed, heroin has also been demonstrated to be used in a controlled and pleasurable way by those who lead otherwise "normal" lives (Blackwell and Erickson, 1988), and it is no longer possible to argue persuasively that moderate cannabis use, in either one's youth or adult life, interferes with the achievement of conventional success (Erickson, 1989). This is not to say that drug use cannot become problematic; however, these findings are illustrative of the possibility of managed and controlled drug use.

In answer to the question put forward at the beginning of this section: Does harm reduction move beyond the social construction of drug use as deviant? The simple answer is yes. Harm reduction encourages the recognition of this behaviour as a normal part of life for many members of society. Harm reduction neither condemns or condones drug use or the user, *nor* does it imply widespread legalization of all substances. Instead it is the consequences of the behaviour that are the focus of intervention efforts, with the understanding that steps can be taken to reduce the harms associated with drug use that do not necessarily involve abstinence and/or criminalization. Harm reduction also implies that much drug use is nonproblematic and should simply be left alone.

Another question that needs to be asked is whether harm reduction has been successful in achieving its goals. To this, a qualified yes is given. Although more evaluation and empirical research must be done, preliminary studies and programs adopting a harm reduction framework show signs of success. For example, needle exchange programs have been successful in reducing risky behaviours associated with injection drug use, and long-term studies will document the impact these programs have on reducing the spread of HIV. Perhaps more telling however are the HIV statistics for those cities in which needle exchange is illegal or have experienced short supplies of clean syringes: 60% HIV rate in New York, 52% in Geneva, 51% in Edinburgh, and 40% in Bangkok (Binder, 1994).

Merseyside, England, represents an illustration of harm reduction in action. The implementation of the response, called Demand Enforcement, occurred in 1986. This strategy, involving the widespread co-operation among the police, the social/health care workers, and the users, resulted in a noticeable reduction in drug-related crime, the demand for street-level heroin has been decreased, and Merseyside also boasts the lowest rate of HIV cases in all of the United Kingdom (Cappell et al., 1993). These findings are particularly important when considering the failure of both the medical model approach and, even more prominently, prohibition/criminalization.

Another early sign of harm reduction's application is the increasing willingness of Canadian society to "try" new approaches regarding the treatment of drug users. This climate of acceptance or openness has even extended to one of the "scarier" substances — heroin. Based on the preliminary successes of the Swiss heroin prescription trials, some consideration is underway for the implementation of such a program in parts of Canada.

CONCLUSION

Drug use has been regarded as an immoral behaviour, a disease, and an act worthy of harsh punishment. These beliefs and perceptions have been guided less by empirical evidence than by political and social forces of the times. Unique in many ways, moral, medical, and criminal models have shared the goal of defining drug use and its users as deviant. Although perhaps guided by the intent to ameliorate some perceived harm, the actual outcomes of these initiatives have resulted in numerous negative consequences and failed to bring about their overarching intent to eliminate drug use. Moreover if these differential forms of social control were to be evaluated with respect to improving the health of Canadians, they have undeniably failed. The creation of a black market for illicit drugs coupled with drug trafficking networks, the disregard of potential therapeutic uses, and the failure to provide adequate servicess for those in need are just a few of the outcomes associated with the construction of drug use as deviant.

In the face of these realities, we need to question why our society clings so strongly to the belief of drug use as deviant? How is it that, in the face of empirical evidence regarding the failure of the current criminalization approach, new drug laws are passed that maintain the status quo? Perhaps the answer to this question stems in part from the understanding of what it is that deviance offers society. Defining behaviours as deviant has served as a means of separating the "good" from the "bad" and therefore if not drugs, what will take its place as a source of exclusion? Who will become society's scapegoats facilitating social cohesion and unity? If we adopt the Durkheimian belief that society "needs" deviance, with so many other taboos being broken (e.g., gambling, homosexuality) is drug use merely the last bastion of deviance? For several decades drugs have been portrayed as the root of social evils, thereby creating a "reality" which citizens can blame and target as the cause of other social problems (e.g., poverty, violence). It is much easier for governments to blame drugs and thereby offer a "solution" of social control through prohibitionist activities than to address other social realities.

Acknowledging the negative consequences associated with previous and current social control responses to drug use, the question remains "where do we go from here?" As presented in this chapter, harm reduction offers a new framework and perspective from which to consider drug use. In recognizing that for some, drug use is a "way of life," a behaviour that is valued and subsequently repeated, a harm reduction paradigm strives toward demystifying this behaviour. Demystification however implies neither widespread legalization nor the overall negation of some forms of drug use. Rather, harm reduction encourages the deconstruction or the re-normalization of drug use in an attempt to move beyond moralistic and punitive approaches toward effective interventions.

Canada's orientation toward health promotion policy (encouraging autonomy over one's health) contributes to a readiness to adopt harm reduction initiatives and steps away from the more repressive policy approach in the United States. However there is a delicate balance between a necessary orientation toward health and a return to an overly medicalized approach to drug use and users. The medical model alone is not sufficient to address the multiplicity of factors underlying the issues surrounding drug use. Use, treatment, and rehabilitation are not solely based on physiological factors but rather social, cultural, and psychological forces must all be considered in an attempt to understand substance use.

Drugs in and of themselves are not a great menace to our communities; rather it is this illusion that poses the greater threat. Making an enemy of drugs blinds us to and prevents us from addressing the real (albeit more politically challenging) issues underlying current social problems that directly pertain to the social economy of our society. While the potential personal and social harms associated with drugs are real, aggressive criminalization against use and users only serves to magnify the harms — other solutions are needed.

REFERENCES

Addiction Research Foundation (1987–1988). *Annual Report*. Toronto: Addiction Research Foundation.

Akers, R. 1991. Addiction: The troublesome concept. *Journal of Drug Issues* 21:777–792.

Ashton, J. & H. Seymour. 1988. *The New Public Health*. Bristol, PA: Open University Press.

Alexander, B. 1990. *Peaceful Measures: Canada's Way Out of the 'War on Drugs'*. Toronto: University of Toronto Press.

Becker, H. 1963. *Outsiders: Studies in the Sociology of Deviance*. Glencoe, Il.: Free Press.

Binder, H. 1994. "Syringe exchange in Australia." *ICAA News*, 3(4).

Blackwell, J., and P. Erickson. 1988. "Concluding Remarks: a Risky Business." In J. Blackwell and P. Erickson (eds.), *Illicit Drugs in Canada: a Risky Business*. Scarborough, Ontario, Nelson Canada.

Boyd, N. 1988. Legal and Illegal Drug Use. In V. Sacco (ed.) *Deviance: Conformity and Control in Canadian Society*. Scarborough, Ontario: Prentice-Hall Canada Inc.

Butters, J., A. Hallgren and P. McGillicuddy. 1997. *Poor women and crack use in Downtown Toronto: Research report*.

Canadian Centre on Substance Abuse and Addiction Research Foundation. *Canadian Profile: Alcohol, Tobacco and Other Drugs 1997*.

Cappell, D., T. Reitsma, D. O'Connell and H. Strang. 1993. Law enforcement as a harm reduction strategy in Rotterdam and Merseyside. In N. Heather, A. Wodak, E. Nadelmann & P. O'Hare (eds.), *Psychoactive Drugs and Harm Reduction: From Faith to Science*. London, England: Whurr.

Chiniquy, C. 1847. *Manual of the Temperance Society*. Montreal: Lovell and Gibson.

Conrad, P. and J. Schneider. 1980; 1992. *Deviance and Medicalization: From Badness to Sickness*. Philadelphia; Temple University Press.

Cooperstock, R., and J. Hill. 1982. *The Effects of Tranquillization: Benzodiazepine use in Canada*. Ottawa: Ministry of Health and National Welfare.

Cooperstock, R., and P. Parnell. 1982. Research on psychotropic drug use: a review of findings and methods. *Social Science Medicine* 16:1179–1196.

Erickson, P. 1980. *Cannabis Criminals: The social effects of punishment on drug users*. Toronto, Ontario: Addiction Research Foundation.

Erickson, P. 1989. Living with prohibition; Regular cannabis users, legal sanctions and informal controls. *International Journal of the Addictions*, 3:175–188.

Erickson, P. 1993. The law, social control and drug policy: Models, factors and processes. *International Journal of the Addictions* 28:1155–1176.

Erickson, P. and J. Butters. 1998. The emerging harm reduction movement: the de-escalation of the War on drugs? In E. Jensen and J. Gerber (eds.), *The New War on Drugs: Symbolic Politics and Criminal Justice Policy*. Cincinnati: Anderson Publishing.

Erickson, P., D. Riley, Y. Cheung and P. O'Hare. 1997. *Harm Reduction: A New Direction for Drug Policies and Programs*. Toronto: University of Toronto Press.

Erickson, P., E. Adlaf, G. Murray and R. Smart. 1987. *The Steel Drug: Cocaine in Perspective*. Toronto: Lexington Books.

Fingarette, H. 1988. *Heavy Drinking: The Myth of Alcoholism as a Disease*. Berkeley: University of California Press.

Fox, R. 1977. The medicalization and demedicalization of American Society. *Daedalus* 106:9–22.

Gervais, C. 1980. *The Rumrunners: A Prohibition Scrapbook*. Thornhill, Ontario: Firefly Books.

Glaser, D. 1974 "Interlocking dualities in drug use, drug control and crime," In J. Inciardi and C. Chambers (eds.) *Drugs and the Criminal Justice System*. Beverly Hills, CA: Sage Publications.

Gray, J. 1972. *Booze: The Impact of Whisky on the Prairie West*. Toronto: Macmillan of Canada.

Goldstein, A. 1994. *Addiction: From Biology to Drug Policy*. New York: W.H. Freeman.

Goode, E. 1989. *Drugs in American Society*. 3rd Edition. New York: Knopf.

Goode, E. 1997. *Between Politics and Reason: The Drug Legislation Debate*. New York: St. Martin's Press.

Gusfield, J. 1998. *The three American prohibitions; Culture and social structure in anti-alcohol, tobacco and "drug" movements*. Presented at the Kettel Bruun Society Annual Meeting, Florence, Italy, June.

Heath, D. 1992. US Drug control policy: A cultural perspective. *Daedalus* 121:269–291.

Hiebert, A. 1969. 'Prohibition in British Columbia.' Unpublished MA Thesis, Department of History, Simon Fraser University, Burnaby, BC.

Jaffe, J. 1985. Drug addiction and drug abuse. In A. Gilman, L. Goodman and A. Gilman (Eds.), *Goodman and Gilman's The Pharmacological Basis of Therapeutics*. 6th edition. New York: Macmillan.

Kalant, O. 1987. *Maier's Cocaine Addiction* [Der Kokainismus 1926], Addiction Research Foundation, Toronto.

Lisowski, C. 1996. The Medicalization of Alcoholism. In R. Weitz (ed.), *The Sociology of Health, Illness and Health Care: A Critical Approach*. Wadsworth Publishing, An International Thomson Publishing Company.

Manderson, D. 1995. Metamorphoses: Clashing symbols in the social construction of drugs. *The journal of drug issues* 25: 799–816.

Murphy, E. 1922. *The Black Candle*. Toronto: Coles.

Parsons, T. 1951. *The Social System*. New York: Free Press.

Pattison, E., M. Sobel and L. Sobel. 1977. *Emerging Concepts of Alcohol Dependence*. New York: Springer.

Riley, D. 1993. *The policy and practice of harm reduction: the application of harm reduction measures in a prohibitionist society*. Ottawa: CCSA.

Riley, D., E. Sawka, P. Conley, D. Hewitt, W. Mitic, C. Poulin, R. Room, E. Single and J. Topp. 1999. *Substance use and misuse* 34 (1): 9–24.

Single, E. 1997. Toward a harm reduction approach to alcohol-problem prevention. In P. Erickson, D. Riley, Y. Cheung and P. O'Hare (Eds.), *Harm Reduction: A New Direction for Drug Policies and Programs*. Toronto: University of Toronto Press.

Single, E., L. Robson, X. Xie, and J. Rehm. 1996. *The costs of substance abuse in Canada: highlights of a major study of the health, social and economic costs associated with the use of alcohol, tobacco and illicit drugs*. Ottawa: Canadian Centre of Substance Abuse.

Smart, R., and A. Ogborne. 1986. *Northern Spirits: Drinking in Canada Then and Now*. Toronto: Addiction Research Foundation.

Waitzkin, H. 1983. *The Second Sickness: Contradictions of Capitalist Health Care*. New York: Free Press.

Weitz, R. 1996. *The Sociology of Health, Illness and Health Care: A Critical Approach*. Wadsworth Publishing, An International Thomson Publishing Company.

Woods, S. 1983. *The Molson Saga: 1763–1983*. Toronto: Doubleday Canada.

Zimring, F. and G. Hawkins. 1992. *The Search for Rational Drug Control*. Cambridge, England: Cambridge University Press.

Zinberg, N. 1984. *Drug, Set and Setting: The Basis for Controlled Intoxicant Use*. New Haven, CT: Yale University Press.

THE CRIMINALIZATION OF MENTAL ILLNESS A Complex Process of Interpretation

Danielle Laberge

Pierre Landreville

Daphné Morin

INTRODUCTION

This study examines two deviance designations — mentally ill and criminal — and a number of related concerns. Rather than these situations in themselves, the focus of this discussion is their quality as a transgression of the normative model. Normative models overlap (law-abiding, responsible, healthy, normal) and to find the appropriate designation for a transgression may be difficult in concrete situations.

NORMS, INCIDENTS, AND NORMATIVE INTERPRETATIONS

Every society uses a range of norms to regulate the form, nature, frequency, intensity, and other characteristics of social interactions. Resultant codes of conduct and their underlying norms, contrary to popular belief or widespread adherence, are neither natural nor universal. A norm is a generalization, an abstract, but its respect or transgression is concrete, occurring in a real situation and as real behaviour. Designations such as "deviance," "conformity," "madness" arise only with reference to abstract norms, just as the designations conforming or mentally healthy are made with reference to a projected normative model (Conrad and Schneider, 1980; Fichelet and Fichelet, 1979). Deviance always represents a departure from projections of what is normal and predictable. The projection will of course vary from group to group; deviance, conformity, and mental health are not constants, as is apparent from many anthropological as well as sociological studies.

This paper has been translated by Marian Crowe.

Normative systems may be analyzed from a variety of perspectives and within a variety of theoretical frameworks. A normative system may be defined briefly with reference to its component norms, their interrelation, their mechanisms of maintenance, and reactions to their transgression. A full understanding of normative systems in all their complexity would require a multi-level analysis, with variations apparent in every dimension of studies from a generalized historical or comparative perspective. Various normative systems, more or less structured or formalized, may develop within a single society. The capacity of these systems to control behaviour varies further according to their form, and in relation to prevailing social conditions. Finally, norms are interpersonal. The reaction deemed appropriate with regard to prevailing social conditions, or effective within the framework of familiar models, is not abstract. It occurs in a situation of concrete interactions and implies a series of interpretations and decisions on the part of an observer (Holstein, 1993; Zauberman, 1982; Faugeron, Fichelet and Robert, 1977).

Norms constitute a framework that is both interpretive and prescriptive. As an interpretive framework, norms provide the standard by which to judge behaviour and situations, one's own and those of others, and the abstract rules that apply to concrete situations. As prescriptive rules, norms constrain actions or even thought about how a person should act in a variety of situations. Differing normative systems permit members of a society or a group to recognize what is "normal," "desirable," "correct," "appropriate" or, on the contrary, "shocking," "inappropriate," "unacceptable," "abnormal," and "intolerable."

"Norm" is clearly a very broad concept that includes a broad range of behaviours and situations. Each of the latter is regulated by a normative system, but the nature of regulation may vary greatly. Their diversity can be illustrated by comparing norms of polite behaviour, child education, medical ethics, or even norms of diagnosis of mental illness.

A number of propositions will be advanced to outline the analytical premises underlying this essay. These propositions provide an overall response to some general questions concerning the phenomenon of marginality or deviance, outlining the shift in designation from "mentally ill" to "criminal." These questions are: What makes a concrete situation deviant? What is a social reaction to deviance? What is the context or broader social framework in which both the deviant situation and the appropriate social reaction are defined?

THE ATTRIBUTION OF DEVIANCE

Marginality or deviance is not a quality inherent in a behaviour or social interaction. This quality can exist only with respect to a norm, the rule that defines the appropriate behaviour in that situation. When actual behaviour, in a situation that is always more complex than the regulation allows, is examined in the light of ideal behaviour according to some regulation, the comparison permits an interpretation to be made and meaning to be attributed. In every incident of interest to this study, an interpretation has been made by an agent of intervention authorized to make judgments, define situations, and more specifically, to assess the undesirable or problematic nature of the incident (Hulsman, 1981). Responsibility for the incident may be attributed to persons, to bad luck, to accident, and to other natural, supernatural or structural "causes" (Hulsman, 1981). Incidents attributed to persons become unacceptable behaviours, conflicts, interpersonal problems with mutual responsibilities or due to a deviant act by one or the other (Horwitz, 1990; Black, 1976; Aubert, 1965). The interpretation requires particular designations not dependent on any real or natural quality. These designations provide an additional meaning that becomes attributed to the incident.

As has frequently been demonstrated with mentally ill or criminal designations, behaviours defined as symptoms or offences are not inherently one or the other. Various stages in the construction of an incident permit the translation of a social act into a medical or criminal matter (Holstein, 1993; Cousineau, 1992; Acosta, 1987; Lévy, 1987; Warren, 1982; Zauberman, 1982; Faugeron, 1978; Scheff, 1966). Talking to oneself, speaking loudly in public, accosting strangers, for example, are by themselves insufficient for an interpretation of mental illness. These behaviours must also occur in a specific context. For an auctioneer, such behaviours are appropriate. Similar behaviour for no apparent reason in a crowded subway suggests a mental health problem. When comments to fellow passengers are, furthermore, incoherent, insulting, or threatening, the likelihood of mental illness interpretations is increased. The behaviours are not appropriate in that situation.

The notion of normal or appropriate behaviour is neither simple nor self-evident. Behaviour that is correct in one situation may be unacceptable in another. Whether an additional meaning such as illness or offence will be attributed will vary with the qualities of the situation: type of activity, social identity of its author (gender, age, civil status, etc.), social representations of the activity, the legal framework regulating such situations, human and financial resources allocated for interventions. These qualities also determine interpretations made and reactions by intervening agents. The deviant label is not predetermined for particular situations (Holstein, 1993; Zauberman, 1982).

The process of attributing meaning, in cases of mental illness, has been examined by labelling and social reaction theorists (Scheff, 1975, 1966; Goffman, 1968), from a social representation perspective (Jodelet, 1989), and by certain feminist authors from the perspective of women's experience (Carlen, 1985). The current study examines the application of deviance designations from a social interactionism perspective. Social interactions are the material from which a concrete deviant identity or situation is constructed.

It is through social interaction that concrete deviant identities are constructed. No person labelled mentally ill acquired that designation in isolation. One or more observers, whatever their qualifications, must have judged the person's behaviour as aberrant, dangerous, or inappropriate. In addition, deviance designations and social reactions occur at various levels: within the social unit, by private agencies, or by state authorities. The type of designation will vary, according to relationships between actors, their status, and their resources (Horwitz, 1990; Black, 1976). The concrete conditions that result in certain persons or behaviours being designated as deviant are not those found in abstract provisions, however formally codified.

It should be noted, however, that these phenomena do have an objective basis. That a label of mental illness is a social construction does not make it imaginary, unfounded, unwarranted, or irrelevant, nor its effect without consequences for persons so designated. Construction is not invention, speculation, creation *ex nihilo*; it is building and producing a completed structure from the materials at hand. The illness, deviance, or offence designation is constructed from qualities that define an incident as not normal, according to at least one observer. One extension of this fact is frequently ignored: while mental illness is a social construction, the person so designated may in fact be truly suffering. The same is true of crime: an offence is also a construction, not a fact of nature, but nevertheless may reflect a behaviour that causes damage, loss, and pain.

SOCIAL REACTIONS TO DEVIANCE

Where there is a social reaction, there is an observer who has recognized the problematic or deviant quality of a situation. While this may seem self-evident, it is an important reminder. This essay concerns only cases where mental illness was attributed, since it would be difficult to examine the effect of criminalization on mentally ill offenders who are not so designated.

When behaviour is judged deviant or problematic, an observer may choose one of three reactions: ignore the situation, find an informal solution, or request intervention by a specialized authority. The first is the most common reaction (Horwitz, 1990: 99). "Don't get involved," "mind your own business," "live and let live"; many other popular expressions counsel non-intervention. An observer may choose this non-reaction because of tolerance, fear for personal safety, unwillingness to be associated with such a situation, or not knowing what to do. The second option involves setting in motion a number of informal processes: parental discipline, consulting other family members or friends, consultations with less official agencies (counsellor, therapist, family doctor). In general, family members and friends who are aware of "episodes" or concerned by symptoms manifested by a loved one, choose informal resolution. In the exercise of police discretion, the officer chooses informal resolution by giving the person a "talking-to" or "warning-off" (Bittner, 1967). The third option is referral to the "proper authorities." This process consists of either reporting a situation or person, or requesting that agents intervene to take control. Cases of interest to this study were referred to police, the courts, a hospital or psychiatric emergency ward, or another social agency as complaints or requests for intervention. Lateral referrals may also be made, between agencies, according to jurisdiction and interpretation of the situation (Emerson, 1991). Social reactions may escalate over time; they may be repeated or modified as situations stabilize or change (Rogers, 1990). To examine a social reaction as a discrete or unique event provides only an artificial explanation. Except for single or accidental incidents that are never repeated, the social reaction to transgressions of the normative model may be hypothesized to be complex, and to vary over time.

The way a situation or the nature of a problem is interpreted becomes central to the choice of reaction, and particularly to the type of referral (Loseke, 1995; Horwitz, 1990; Zauberman, 1982). The perceptions of the actors present, their negotiations concerning the type of incident, how the behaviour is justified and who is at fault, each contribute to assigning the appropriate label (delinquent, ill person, dangerous offender) and to determining the "style of social control" (Black, 1976) to be applied (Horwitz, 1990; Scott and Lyman, 1970).

The reaction an incident or problem inspires will depend greatly on the interpretation the observer is likely to make. This interpretation has two separate effects: first on the type of social reaction that will occur, as demonstrated in the foregoing discussion, and secondly in orienting the direction of the referral. Interpreting a behaviour as harmless or banal increases its likelihood of being ignored or informally resolved. An example of such a case would be a parent deciding to take a firmer hand with a child. The observer who interprets the problem as serious is more likely to choose a more structured reaction. Beyond its relative seriousness, an interpretation will focus on the content and implied meaning of a situation. Many apparently unacceptable social situations cannot readily be labelled deviant, and interpretation takes a wide range of concerns into account: the objective qualities of the situation, the social identities of actors and observers, the context in which it occurs, the types of resources available, etc. Identical situations may result in widely varying interpretations, such as drunkenness, delinquency, mental illness, poor social skills, homelessness, or mere eccentricity.

Even the interpretive variables are not consistent. The more ambiguous a situation or a behaviour, the greater is the range of interpretations. A more apparent correspondence with popular conceptions, associated images, and established regulatory procedures will reduce the ambiguity in interpreting a situation, as well as the range of appropriate reactions. To a great degree, ambiguity and imprecision are qualities common to the situations examined by this study, and for this reason such situations are likely to result in contradictory and inappropriate apprehensions and interventions.

Other considerations significantly affect the definition of "troubles" (Emerson and Messinger, 1977) or "disputes" (Emerson, 1992) and the social reaction of "mobilizing the law" (Black, 1976) or psychiatric or social service agencies in the referral process (Zauberman,1982; Faugeron et al., 1977). A third-party intervention may determine the defining of a problem and the appropriate reaction (Emerson, 1992; Horwitz, 1990; Emerson and Messinger, 1977). A "symmetrical" intervention in a "dispute" or conflict, taking grievances of both parties into account, contributes to a definition of interpersonal conflict of shared responsibility to be resolved by negotiation (Emerson, 1992; Horwitz, 1990). In the opposite case, an "asymmetrical" intervention that considers the grievance of only one party readily redefines a "dispute" or conflict into deviance, either by qualifying the claims of one party as symptomatic of mental illness, or that person's behaviour as morally offensive and delinquent (Emerson, 1992). Access to resources to correct a problem is also an essential consideration in the defining and resolving process (Horwitz, 1990; Emerson, 1983; Zauberman, 1982); Aubert (1965) emphasizes that "the form of conflict may ... be determined by the available means of solution" (p. 83). In the same way, difficulties of access to social or mental health services may lead to definition as criminal, and referral for formal criminal justice rather than mental health interventions.

Intervening agents may adopt varying strategies, conforming to a variety of motives, when referring a person to a specialized authority (Landreville et al., 1998; Laberge and Landreville, 1994; Emerson, 1991; Zauberman, 1982). The cited studies examine the specific logic or motives to which activation of the criminal process is an appropriate response. It varies according to the category of social actor making the referral and with stages of processing of an incident. These studies identified motives for criminal justice interventions that included humanitarian concerns, desire to exclude the person from other services, social control as a last resort, the maintenance of law and order, etc.

The extremely public nature of an official reaction to an incident adds weight to the assigned deviant quality of the incident in subsequent social representations, in spite of the ambiguous or temporary nature of the original incident and in spite of the inappropriateness of the original reaction. The intervention of a specialized agency to some extent validates the decision to refer in the first place. In the context examined here, these dynamics are particularly apparent. Where a criminal justice intervention has been made, whatever the reason or nature of the original incident, the person acquires a label such as "criminal" or "offender." The official and stigmatizing qualities of such interventions obscure the harmlessness of originating incidents, as well as administrative limitations that produce a reaction considered at best "the lesser of two evils" by most intervening agents. Thus, the intervention becomes the source of the interpretation (Faugeron, 1979).

MENTAL ILLNESS AS A DEVIANCE DESIGNATION

To designate deviance in terms of mental illness requires a classification process that categorizes situations or persons with regard to representations of normal or acceptable, and thereby justifies intervention (Loseke, 1995; Holstein, 1993). The process requires a hierarchy of behaviour and persons that cannot be constructed, according to Brown (1993), without a social and moral interpretive framework:

> In short, once cast into a category, the incumbents are conventionally regarded as being governed not by experiential contingencies, but by maxims of conduct inherent in the categories themselves. Thus, classifications — such as true or false, good or bad, legal or criminal, sane or mad — also are definitions of personhood, hierarchies of value, and forms for power.
>
> Because categories are used not as mere labels but as methods for organizing perceptions, knowledge, and moral relationships, modification of the category in which a person is placed alters the meaning of his or her behaviour. (p. 504)

On a mundane level, "socio-interactional" criteria serve equally well for casual observers or intervening agents who are not mental health professionals to "recognize" certain behaviours as symptomatic of mental illness.[1] These socio-interactional criteria have inspired labelling theorists, and were broadly those adopting a constructivist perspective, to emphasize the importance of popular beliefs and "common knowledge" concerning mental illness when studying its recognition, classification, and labelling. Ultimately, the common quality among this group of criteria concerns inappropriate behaviour. There is no ambiguity about incoherent speech, not knowing where one is, ideas and actions that are totally out of context, conversations with invisible respondents, self-destructive actions, and a host of other behaviours and states that transgress norms. Thus particular norms may be differently perceived according to the group, or associated with originality or the desire to be different. This does not concern the type of norm as much as those to whom alternative definitions may be applied. Some of these norms affect only the person in question; others occur in social interactions and have consequences for other persons. Both types of situations are designated as "incidents." The expression indicates an activity that is first of all outside the norm, and secondly gives rise to measures to change or stop the activity.

An incident must meet a number of conditions to be designated in terms of mental illness. Mental illness must be attributed as the cause of the situation; behaviours or interactions must be interpreted as symptomatic of mental illness; a psychiatric intervention must occur. In the process of labelling and controlling, whether mental illness is designated and the person apprehended depends more on the social reaction to the incident than on the incident itself. Without a reaction, whether or not such situations incur suffering or other consequences, they receive no formal attention from authorities and no specific attribution of meaning will be made (Scheff, 1975; 1966).[2] Horwitz (1982) states that "the concept of mental illness is located in observers' categories rather than in actors' symptoms" (p. 4). In the same way that social reaction to a single behaviour varies, behaviour that will be designated in terms of mental illness varies. The designation is not a concrete quality of the incident; it is socially constructed.

The recognition of mental illness is the first step toward designating, and determining the social reaction to, mental illness. It is more readily attributed if the social distance between observer and observed is great. Social distance is a key variable according to Horwitz (1982), who examines two of its dimensions — relationship and culture — to hypothesize that "when people share many common life experiences, world views, norms and values, this distance is small; when they share few or none of these traits, the social distance is large" (p. 34). This viewpoint explains why family members and close friends are the least ready to acknowledge and label mental illness, and the most likely to "normalize" bizarre behaviour. Reluctance to label has been linked to the "contagious" nature of stigma for other family members, "the tendency of stigma to spread" (Goffman, 1975), which favours rejection of the label.

If observer and observed know each other (i.e., where social distance is small), other variables determine whether the mental illness label will be applied: socio-economic status, deviant role within the family, and access to psychiatric information. Middle-class families seem less reluctant to attribute and label mental illness than lower-class families. The capacity to neutralize the social cost of stigma does not appear to be equally distributed, and members of the least privileged classes are the most vulnerable to control mechanisms. Persons who assume a deviant role within the family are also readily labelled. Finally, exposure to psychiatric information favours labelling; the common tendency among intimate acquaintances to deny mental illness disappears when an official psychiatric designation has been made (Horwitz, 1982).

Where observer and observed are strangers, other factors enter into the process of attribution and labelling. The essential factors tend to be the public nature of the behaviour, judgment that behaviour is socially unacceptable, fear that a person may be dangerous, and the desire "to guard the community standards of decency and order" (Horwitz, 1982: 45).

The greater the cultural distance between observer and observed, the greater the likelihood that misunderstandings will occur, and consequently that a mental illness label will be applied. Horwitz (1982) states: "Since the norms used by psychiatric professionals to define mental illness reflect those of the dominant culture, the application of these norms results in a greater probability that unconventional behaviour will be labelled mentally ill" (p. 48). In addition: "Labellers of mental illness employ the familiar norms of their own culture and assume that they are universal" (p. 51). Thus, according to Horwitz (1982), the apparent difference in willingness to label mental illness between persons of higher and lower socio-economic status does not reflect a difference in access to material resources, but rather their cultural orientation as a result of "a liberal and humanistic type of education." The author hypothesizes that certain cultural attitudes are more the norm among the more favoured classes: introspection, familiarity with psychiatric knowledge, and a favourable attitude toward professional persons in general.

Gender is an essential dimension in understanding the process of labelling mental illness and orienting persons toward psychiatric treatment. Social representations of deviance (and mental illness) are gender-specific. They are linked to social constructions of masculinity and femininity, to male and female social roles. This linkage results in appropriate social reactions that differ according to the deviant person's gender. Social distinctions between men and women further affect reactions to mental illness which in turn reinforce the initial social distinctions (Horwitz, 1990). These are extremely important considerations in explaining the traditional gender dichotomy in deviance designations: mentally ill for women and criminal for men (Horwitz, 1990; Allen, 1986). A women's deviant behaviour is more easily defined as a psycho-affective abnormality than a man's identical behaviour. When orienting the direction of social controls, therefore, intervening agents tend to favour mental illness designations for women's deviance and to direct women toward psychiatric institutions. This selectivity at least partly explains the comparatively lower representation of women than men among incarcerated populations. This tendency also operates on another level, that of psychiatric orientation within the custodial context (Menzies, Chunn and Webster, 1992; Ryan, 1992; Allen, 1987a, 1987b; Gavigan, 1982). In criminal law and within criminal justice processing there are in fact several mechanisms by which an accused is redefined as "mentally ill," rather than, or as well as "criminal." The psychiatrization of women's deviance is thus driven by two factors: first, women are diverted from justice-processing by favouring apprehension by medical authorities; secondly, by favouring an interpretation of illness or mental disorder for the deviant activities with which women are charged.

Distinctions in the attribution and labelling of men's and women's deviant behaviour are closely related to the transgression of gender roles. Since roles differ according to gender, the interpretation and labelling of a transgression will also differ according to gender.

Women furthermore tend to direct themselves and their entourage toward psychiatric intervention. This orientation is explained in a number of ways. Women are supposedly "more introspective," more "in touch with their emotions," more inclined "to avoid confrontations," more likely to consider psychiatric intervention as a resource rather than a source of stigma. Horwitz (1990) states that the "preponderance of women in therapeutic settings across wide cultural and historical settings indicates a structural basis for therapeutic control that is rooted in interpersonal dependency" (p. 92). This argument is based on the inability of powerless groups to access other forms of control in regulating their conflicts. Horwitz (1990) includes women with children and men without positions of power as socially dominated groups:

> Defining themselves as victims who suffer from an illness elicits sympathy and pity for afflicted parties. In addition, the lack of autonomy and capacity that are associated with entry into therapy are more congruent with the roles of dependents than of dominants. The result is that dependency and therapeutic control are closely associated when problems arise among intimates. (p. 93)

The images used to designate deviance as mental illness significantly affect the elaboration and utilization of social policies, and thereby the social reaction to this type of behaviour (Loseke, 1995). These images are part of a representational world that associates certain ideas and suggests appropriate responses. The mental illness label is associated with the notion that the problem is caused by an illness, that its cause is biological, that its management is the jurisdiction of medicine and thus, that doctors of psychiatry are the appropriate authority to resolve the problem (Loseke, 1995; Holstein, 1993; Gallagher, 1980).

PSYCHIATRY, ANTI-PSYCHIATRY, AND MENTAL HEALTH EVOLUTION

In the last thirty years, psychiatry has been subjected to numerous criticisms of its make up and nature. According to Miller (1986) these challenges are an essential part of the psychiatric discipline. This debate is not the topic of this examination, nor will psychiatry be tried. Rather, we wish to explain how these challenges affect the evaluation of a variety of social situations and the social reactions considered appropriate to their management. It is noteworthy, however, that the deinstitutionalization movement that has affected North America generally, as well as a significant portion of Europe, became inscribed in a broader criticism of psychiatry, its scientific bases, and its treatment methods.[3] Consideration of this factor is relevant. The anti-psychiatry movement has created doubt concerning the very existence of mental illness as a biological and pathological designation (Castel, 1981; Conrad and Schneider, 1980; Goffman, 1968; Scheff, 1966; Foucault, 1961). In addition to the anti-psychiatry debate, debate within the discipline has demonstrated the highly normative qualities of some "illnesses." This does not suggest that psychiatrists, or the general population, acknowledge the cultural nature of many "illnesses." Former illnesses such as female hysteria and homosexuality have changed status and, more recently, various behaviours have acquired the status of illness or disorder ("abusing" food, solvents, or medications; compulsive gambling). While this evolution may not automatically invalidate the knowledge developed in the field, it highlights both its cultural qualities and the central role played by interpretations (Peyrot, 1995; Holstein, 1993; Hak, 1992; Barrett, 1988).

There have been considerable changes over the years in both the policies and practices of psychiatry. From a standpoint of policy, many persons who formerly would have received a psychiatric diagnosis are no longer referred to or supervised by psychiatrists. Many therefore never receive an in-depth assessment and a precise diagnosis. Others were assessed or supervised in the past, but lack of follow-up makes their current state impossible to determine. Meanwhile, conceptions of illness and symptomatic criteria have evolved as a result of both research and changing social definitions with regard to certain practices and behaviours. Finally, while some behaviours or behavioural profiles cause significant problems in terms of social functioning, many psychiatrists consider them not relevant to their field of expertise. "Personality disorders" are a case in point (Carlen, 1985).

Two major social transformations have greatly affected the living conditions of a large number of persons who, until recently, would have lived completely or partially under the supervision of psychiatric authorities. The first transformation, generally known as "deinstitutionalization," refers to a broad movement that gained tremendous momentum in the 1960s and '70s, with its goal being the removal of many persons from psychiatric and other institutional jurisdictions. The movement heralded changes in mental health policies, similar to recent policies of "independent living" or "community integration," which constitute a new wave of de-hospitalization. This second phase of deinstitutionalization arouses the same concern whether resources, the missing components targeted as the cause of past failures of deinstitutionalization, will ever be transferred to and used in the community (Cardinal, 1997).

The second and concurrent social transformation involves changed legislation with regard to involuntary commitment. These changes are variable, both among American states and Canadian provinces, but have fairly consistently been directed toward making the conditions of involuntary commitment more stringent in defining specific criteria for determining danger to oneself or others. These have resulted in prolonged procedural delays, judicial or quasi-judicial procedures, the right to legal representation and subsequently adversarial review procedures (Gordon, 1993; Bagby and Atkinson, 1988; Hiday, 1988; Bagby et al., 1987; Robertson, 1987; Gordon and Verdun-Jones, 1986). This second aspect of transformation increases the difficulty of determining an appropriate reaction to a person whose behaviour seems disorganized, erratic, or dangerous to himself or herself, or another.

Out of the upheaval caused by these transformations, many persons actually suffering from mental heath problems found themselves isolated, without community or family supports. The communities to which such persons were assigned did not know how, or were not as a community willing, to integrate these persons (Cardinal, 1997; Dorvil, 1988; Dear and Wolch, 1987). Consequently, extremely vulnerable persons, incapable of functioning socially and adequately without support, suddenly and literally found themselves on the street.

This context defines both the general parameters of the provision of health services and the immediate social reaction to an apparent emergency, which have increased the attractiveness of criminal justice solutions (Gingell, 1991; Freeman and Roesch, 1989; Roesch and Golding, 1985; Teplin, 1984a, 1984b; Teplin, 1983; Whitmer, 1980). This context has been somewhat modified since the era of deinstitutionalization, but generally in the direction of increased recourse to criminal justice processing. A socio-demographic profile of recipients of such interventions would be characterized by poverty, frequently with a marked inability to find or maintain stable employment, and by significant social isolation (Laberge et al., 1995). They were and continue to be persons who should, at least periodically, have recourse to psycho-social services. The "cuts" experienced by all psycho-social services throughout North America have increasingly deprived such persons of services, and particularly of appropriate services.

THE CRIMINALIZATION OF MENTAL ILLNESS

The concept of criminalization has been used for two decades to explain a variety of phenomena, including criminal justice intervention to resolve social problems. According to Abramson (1972), the concept particularly targets the actual or apparent shift from therapeutic or medical to criminal justice control of persons perceived as mentally ill.

A significant number of studies concerning the criminalization of mental illness have led, and continue to lead, the debate concerning the size and nature of a mentally ill population subject to criminal justice controls. These studies not only inspire discussion; their number also bears witness to the extent of this phenomenon. This study of the criminalization process further examines the elements or mechanisms of this shift in deviance designation from mentally ill to criminal. To understand these mechanisms requires an interpretation from the perspective of concrete situations.

For an incident to be defined as an infraction, criminal justice authorities (particularly police officers) must be involved. Police officers are frequently required to intervene with persons whose behaviour is erratic and who appear to be a danger to themselves. Studies concerning police activities demonstrate their discretionary power to manage some incidents officiously and others officially; decisions in some cases involve criminal justice processing and others are diverted elsewhere. Police discretion has often been interpreted as an abuse of power. While this discretion must clearly be structured to prevent abuses, it is essential to an officer's role as an agent of social control. Accepting the premise that all problematic behaviours are subject to interpretation, that behaviour is not inherently deviant, police discretion takes on great significance.

In incidents such as those examined in these studies, officers must in each case choose from a variety of solutions: tolerating the behaviour, friendly resolution of a conflict by encouraging the person to change his or her behaviour, referral to community or state psycho-social resources, immediate transportation to a psychiatric facility for an assessment, or apprehension following a decision that criminal justice processing is appropriate. For the latter decision, the seriousness of the incident is not the deciding factor. Instead, decisions are based on the lack of options to choose from, or a rejection of those options. The decision may be based on repeated failures of other options to manage the problem, the particular interests of certain actors, or even the fact that police were called first. Police decisions to direct a matter toward criminal justice resources are determined by a variety of considerations and various types of constraints, and cannot be analyzed in isolation.

The most important considerations of the referral process, as identified by this study, were the social role and identity of the person whose behaviour is judged deviant, his or her social network, the social identity and interests of the referring person, situation characteristics (place, nature of incident, the person's attitude), resources (availability of, access to, suggested alternatives), expertise, a variety of institutional constraints (administrative and legal) limiting each of the agencies that may intervene, and the quality of networking between agencies and resources.

Social Role and Identity

The social reaction to deviant behaviour apparently associated with mental illness varies according to the social identity of the observed person. This identity is neither self-evident nor inherent. It is a social construction that integrates, rejects, favours a variety of experiences throughout life and within social interactions. Identity always has two sides: the subjective — the way a person perceives himself or herself, self-image, projected image in interactions with others; and the objective side — the way he or she is really perceived. These two dimensions may be in harmony and reinforce each other, or clash when self- and other-perceptions are at odds.

Social status, gender and age, because visible, are extremely important components of identity in terms of social interactions. Less visible components may become equally important when known and interpreted by intervening agents. Interventions by social control agencies, especially when these are numerous, frequent, or intense, particularly mark and transform a person's identity. A record of psychiatric and criminal justice custody in a person's file becomes a structural component of his or her identity, and of the social reaction to his or her behaviour. These experiences transform not only a person's self-image, but also the image held by others. The person becomes a "nut-case," someone with a "chronic mental illness," a "dangerous offender," a "youth at risk." Identity is adjusted throughout a person's life. It visibly orients the direction of social reaction to deviant behaviour, which in turn contributes to affirming the deviant identity (Emerson and Messinger, 1977). As a result of this stigmatization process, the person becomes locked in a rigid category, repeatedly reaffirmed as institutional agents repeatedly define and respond to behaviour in the same way, from incident to incident.

Different people respond differently to images others hold of them; their access to resources with which to respond also varies. Some resist the deviant identity, some are ambivalent, some conform entirely (Warren, 1982). Furthermore, the social reaction may change during the course of an experience of contact with social control agencies. A person has a role in "negotiating" his or her identity (Margolin, 1992). Accepting the "mentally ill" identity and treatment increases the likelihood of therapeutic controls. Where there is resistance, a criminal identity is more readily assigned.

When referred to the criminal justice system, definition of a situation and social reaction are not so much a function of the person's identity as of the process by which it is constructed. In some circumstances, some facets of a person's identity are known at the time of the intervention; in others they become attached throughout the process. Some facets of identity will be known to some social actors and not to others. Generally, known dimensions, those that are the focus of the intervening agent, those in accord with the defining criteria of an intervening agency, and the self-image that the person holds and upholds, are also variables that influence how a situation will be defined, and the social reaction to it.

Persons referred to the criminal justice system have a number of qualities in common: most are poor, alone, without possessions, work or resources, and known in social control agencies for previous interventions of relative or immediate urgency. Many resist treatment. They frequently make a very poor impression. Most are perceived not only as suffering from a chronic mental illness, but a chronic mental illness accompanied by lack of compliance, resistance to treatment, vindictiveness, and dangerousness.

The Social Network

In the context of a criminal justice referral, the social network has a dual role. It participates in defining the deviant identity. Almost all persons define themselves, and are defined by, the social milieu with which they are familiar and with which they identify since it is their immediate universe. It may be a source of opposition or an ally in committing a person to restrictive categories such as mentally ill person or offender. It may also represent a person's most important resource, and as such may be represented by agencies of social control as an appropriate and acceptable recourse in resolving the incident.

The ability to mobilize a protective social network varies from person to person. Generally, the higher the socio-economic status, the broader and more diversified is the social network. Some persons, for example, will find a competent psychiatrist more readily than others. Persons apprehended by criminal justice authorities whose behaviour is defined as symptomatic of mental illness, however, are generally isolated and powerless, lacking or no longer having even the most basic social skills. For many, the social network — family, friends, entourage — is the principal resource permitting criminal justice processing to be avoided or diverted, or even neutralized to the point of eliminating its negative effects. Those without such resources have no such alternatives to offer. Their social isolation increases their vulnerability to criminal justice controls.

Referent Identity

The social identity, position, resources and aims of the referent who calls police attention to an incident also have a role in defining the officer's response. A nurse's complaint of assault when shoved, while on duty, by a patient is very differently received than a citizen's complaint of assault when shoved, on the street, by a stranger. Similar differences hold in the case of indecent exposure, depending on whether the offender exposes himself (or herself) to an adult or to children. In such cases, the seriousness of an incident will be determined by the identity of the "victim."

Officers may also interpret the aims of referents and decide whether or not to respond based on their attribution of motive for the referral. Such motives may vary widely. Some persons call police because they have been disturbed, but with no intention of registering a complaint; some call police to effect a psychiatric commitment when their own efforts on behalf of a family member have failed. A psychiatric facility may report an incident in order to label a patient undesirable, or to reinforce the patient's responsibility with respect to *the law* for his or her illness.

Personnel of many psychiatric institutions have reported that police do not take seriously their complaints concerning patients (Laberge and Morin, 1992). For police, these complaints are the business of the facility itself. On the other hand, police may be sensitive to pressure groups who adopt strategies such as systematic reporting of situations they define as problematic in their neighbourhoods. The case of business persons and citizens opposed to operating or living in the same downtown areas as homeless persons automatically comes to mind, as well as the case of residents who are unprepared to welcome or to integrate ex-psychiatric patients and who oppose the establishment of residential facilities in their neighbourhoods.

Situation Characteristics

The place, type of incident, types of observers, the social status of observer and observed, the known "facts" of the case, and the attitude of the referred person are all qualities that contribute to the definition of a situation and the decision to request police assistance. The visibility of incidents reported to police certainly contributes to their being flagged as psychiatric cases (Teplin and Pruett, 1992; Rogers, 1990). Behaviour that is inappropriate and disturbing, in a public place, is more likely to be observed, to attract attention, to cause fear and thereby to necessitate an intervention. The presence at the scene of vulnerable persons (children, elderly persons) equally predisposes a response toward one type of intervention or another. Informants may also influence the direction taken. For example, Rogers (1990) relates an incident in which a neighbour who is present informs police officers of numerous failures by social service workers who had previously intervened with the person whose behaviour is at issue. Officers therefore rejected this option and transported the person to the police station, illustrating the importance of access to alternative options.

Erratic speech, threatening actions, screaming, resisting police authority (lack of respect, non-compliance, resisting arrest), property damage, physical assaults, bizarre behaviour (talking to oneself, wandering aimlessly), etc., evidently influence how a situation will be interpreted. These behaviours are often specifically noted by police officers when requesting further criminal justice processing. They represent the basic elements justifying apprehension and "flagging," recommendation for psychiatric assessment of mental fitness. These notations may even influence the outcome of subsequent court-ordered psychiatric assessments (Menzies, 1987).

Available Resources

Knowledge of resources, types of services offered, and access to services are also aspects that influence police response to an incident (Teplin, 1984b). Knowledge of a range of resources opens doors to alternative options in any given situation. When an incident is flagged as psychiatric, hospital emergency facilities are often the only non-penal resource to which an apprehended person may be referred. Those who respond to assess an emergency situation (police officers, ambulance attendants) may also perceive that the hospital emergency response is inappropriate, oppressive, and constraining (Teplin and Pruett, 1992; Murphy, 1986). The options are thus perceived as limited, and cases may be criminalized if intervening agents are unfamiliar with available resources or consider them inappropriate to the needs of the situation. Furthermore, psychiatric emergency services are relatively autonomous and may dissuade or refuse the person admission (Rogers, 1990; Fox and Erickson, 1972). The absence of alternative social control options often favours criminal justice processing (Horwitz, 1990; Teplin, 1984b).

Expert Assessment

Few would disagree that in criminal justice processing, expert assessments perform a definitive role in constructing a person's deviant identity. Their impact varies with the amount of information concerning their expertise and their assessment that is available to intervening agents. Access to psychiatric information requires that intervening agents at the point of entry for criminal justice processing follow particular protocols. Readily available information is that which can be drawn from reports filed by experts during previous apprehensions

(Laberge et al., 1995). These were frequently biased to meet the expectations of the requester (Laberge, Morin & Armonry, 1997; de Bonis, 1985; Debuyst, 1984). They present an image of the assessed person that is constructed from various types of information provided (offending behaviour, attitude toward psychiatric treatment, previous involuntary commitments, etc.). The image thus created is polarized: mentally ill person, dangerous mentally ill person; offender, dangerous offender.

These identity constructions are continued by criminal justice agents. Following the first apprehension, police officers have access to such records and may orient their reaction (recommend withdrawing the complaint, refer to court doctors, charge the person with an offence without noting psychiatric antecedents) according to the expert reports on file (Laberge et al., 1995).

Agency Constraints

Each of the agencies involved in medical/criminal justice apprehensions operates under a number of self-limiting constraints. These may be administrative or structural (organization of police activity, structure of access to psychiatric services, availability of resources); other constraints are of a legal nature.

Legal Constraints

While legislation differs among the United States, Canada, and Great Britain, and even among different states and provinces of these nations (Gratzer and Matas, 1994), similar acts directly or indirectly regulate police activity in emergency situations of a psychiatric nature. At their most basic, a similar set of "umbrella" laws can be identified based on charters of rights and freedoms or constitutions that articulate principles regulating interactions between the state and civil society, its citizens, and the state's capacity to exercise coercive control. Charters and constitutions are so designated because in theory they are the basis of all other state laws. On another level, other laws express the rules, responsibilities, modalities of access, organization, and distribution of services, particularly health and mental health services. These laws also vary greatly based on whether or not services are completely or partially controlled by the state. Still another level of law provides the principles and dispositions that define circumstances in which coercive state powers may specifically be exercised to determine a person's mental state.

In a just society, the laws protect each citizen from arbitrary police intervention. Generally speaking, police officers may not constrain a citizen without a valid reason and may not keep a person in custody without a charge. An officer who judges a person's mental state to be such that he or she will not be safe if left alone, when no alternative services are available (either the hospital or the person refuses treatment), cannot simply keep the person at the police station until a solution is found; the person must be charged with an offence.

The officer who attributes an incident to a person's mental state, and thus appropriately a case for psychiatric authorities (through a hospital's emergency service), faces several difficulties. Most importantly, a person cannot be forced to receive treatment, nor a psychiatric professional to provide it. Laws in this context favour the promotion and protection of civil rights and freedoms, affirming principles of voluntary consent both to treat and to be treated (Madigan, Checkland and Silberfeld, 1994): the right to be treated by the professional and at the institution of choice[4] or to refuse all treatment,[5] and a professional person's right to accept or refuse the person to be treated (Molinari, 1991). In this context, an officer clearly may not in any way force a person to receive treatment, however problematic the behaviour and whatever the perceived need for treatment. Nor can an officer force a doctor to treat the person, or an institution to assume responsibility. This becomes a major obstacle when managing difficult cases of persons who are not gratifying to work with, and whose prognoses are poor. Depending on their classification, even those willing to be treated may be "rejected" or "bounced" from one agency to another.

Police may, as a final recourse, attribute dangerousness (to oneself or another) and thus rescind a person's right to refuse hospitalization.[6] This same attribution of dangerousness may be used by the hospital to justify refusing treatment to persons referred by police. Presumption of dangerousness, in most North American states and provinces the critical element of mental health legislation that authorizes involuntary commitment, is regularly invoked by psychiatric emergency facilities to refuse admissions accompanied by police officers (Teplin, 1984b).[7] Complex legislative provisions govern the means of obtaining consent to treat a person who has been involuntarily committed, since involuntary status in no way obviates the need to obtain informed consent prior to administering medical or psychiatric treatment (Gratzer and Matas, 1994; Gordon, 1993; Rozovsky and Rozovsky, 1990; Biron, 1988; Ménard, 1988; Québec, 1997).[8]

If the patient is legally or practically incompetent to provide consent to treatment, the treating facility must take legal steps to obtain consent from a substitute. These steps further complicate legal proceedings (Cournoyer and Monette, 1991; Ménard, 1988). Refusal to be treated, typical of police referrals of persons involuntarily committed for psychiatric assessment, is a potential source of problems in the hospital environment (Gratzer and Matas, 1994; Cournoyer and Monette, 1991), even when the law has been followed to the letter. This certainly affects the perceptions of police and other emergency personnel concerning the most appropriate response, and concerning access to mental health treatment.

Finally, the right to receive treatment and to choose the place of treatment is far from absolute. These rights are limited by organizational constraints and by institutional allocation of resources (human, material, and financial) (Molinari, 1991).

Decisions, Police Activities, and Interorganizational Networking

Studies that have examined the criminalization of mental illness have supposed that police officers either did not consider other solutions, or that alternative solutions were not available or not appropriate.

The decision to proceed with criminal justice processing is made in a highly specific and immediate context (Rogers, 1990). These decisions are made in the "heat of the moment": officers are called to manage crises rapidly, generally in very public situations, with limited and often contradictory information, in situations where a person's behaviour is unpredictable, with very little organizational support, and most importantly, with very little time to reflect on or discuss the most appropriate solution in the circumstances. In addition, the organization of police activity has no correspondence with concrete intervention requirements when a person's problem appears to be of a psychiatric nature. Each situation, however, must be managed in conformity with the legal constraints implicit in police work. It becomes difficult for officers to stay involved with the same case for any length of time as other requests for assistance or intervention are continually being logged. Police naturally prefer to respond to the most straightforward requests in the least amount of time (Murphy, 1986; Bonovitz and Bonovitz, 1981; Sims and Symonds, 1975; Matthews, 1970; Bittner, 1967). The great distance between this logic and that which directs medical interventions is a source of frustration for police officers. Numerous studies have demonstrated how frequently the "psychiatric route" is abandoned, even when officers believe that the person's most pressing need is for psychiatric treatment. Criminal justice processing, according to many officers, guarantees that the person will eventually be treated in compliance with a court order. Generally, this is an order for an assessment of fitness to stand trial. In the United States, this practice has been widely studied in the context of the criminalization of mental illness (Miller, 1992; Geller and Fisher, 1991; Arvanites, 1988; Dickey, 1980; Bonovitz and Guy, 1979; Geller and Lister, 1978).

Police decisions of necessity take into account the response they may expect from the agencies to whom they refer persons. Depending on how well they know the way the criminal justice system treats such cases, on their expectations concerning reception in psychiatric treatment environments, and on their perceptions of the quality of medical management of such referrals, officers will draw on their interorganizational knowledge before orienting a case in one direction or another (Teplin and Pruett, 1992; Emerson, 1991; Rogers, 1990).

The Functioning of Psychiatric Services

Regionalization

An outcome of mental health reform in various North American states and provinces has been to regionalize psychiatric services, to organize them according to principles of geographic responsibility. While such models of care distribution have certain advantages from a perspective of workload efficiency and quality of care for some types of clients, they are problematic in many other cases. The clientele with which this study is concerned may be distinguished by lack of a fixed address, often because of periods of commitment in institutions and other facilities. Lack of a stable address is frequently used by hospitals to justify a refusal to administer the full range of treatment. The attitude toward treatment and the psychiatric hospital, of a person who fails to conform to the model (stable, compliant, voluntary patient), serves just as well to exclude the person on the basis of temporal criteria. If the person is treated once and not again during a specified period, the file is closed and the institution relinquishes responsibility for the person. These two conditions, stability and recent treatment, reinforce each other to exclude marginal clients from treatment by medical authorities.

Specialization

Much of the medico-social network was developed with specified target clienteles, and specialized problem management strategies. Resources were thus allocated according to specific problems: addiction, severe psychosis, developmental delays, sexual deviance, etc. The nature of this specialization corresponds with various imperatives: financial constraints, available expertise, competence, resources, and response to current research. Clients defined by a dual specification (mentally ill offender, "psychopathic" criminal) are frequently excluded from such resources since they do not meet highly specialized eligibility criteria (Teplin,

1984b). They rarely correspond to "ideal" client profiles defined by such resources; on the contrary they generally present several problems simultaneously.

Networking

Each agency has its own organizational logic. Each may be required to intervene with persons who move between criminal justice and mental health systems, and who may even be successively or simultaneously in the custody of various agencies of both systems, without either system taking the conditions imposed by the other into account in its organization, or in its means of intervention. While even among agents of the same system there is resistance to sharing information, the law itself may mandate the lack of interagency communication. Failure to share information may be due to organizational constraints (lack of resources); more often it occurs because agents are simply unaccustomed to collaborating, and due to systemic resistance (no known communication channels, "turf" barriers) (Steadman, 1992).

In concluding this discussion, we would like to emphasize that criminal justice involvement is based on a complex decision-making process with a variety of criteria that orient the trajectory of a case from its outset. In this context, the role of the apparently deviant behaviour in the construction of a social reaction is only relative. Other elements influence criteria for defining both the situation and the appropriate intervention. Furthermore, the intervention of one system cannot be understood or analyzed without consideration of the organization and range of practices of the other (Laberge and Morin, 1995; Teplin and Pruett, 1992; Roesch and Golding, 1985).

CONCLUSION: THE DOWN SIDE OF CRIMINALIZATION

Intervention and apprehension by criminal justice authorities has serious consequences. Most agree that this is a form of punishment, but at the moment of apprehension few stop to consider the negative medium- and long-range effects of criminal justice processing. In the short term, of course, the person whose behaviour cannot be tolerated is immediately incarcerated. This is the justification for criminal justice intervention with mentally ill persons: to keep an eye on the person and to direct him or her toward health improvement and treatment. When such persons are taken into custody, however, their incarceration frequently leads to much greater hardships than would the incarceration of an ordinary citizen. If incarcerated for more than a few days, they may lose their stable residence or their few possessions, and find their difficulty of access to social resources increased due to missed appointments. These considerations are rarely mentioned in studies examining the effect of imprisonment, although they are a matter of systematic comment by intervening agents. Persons who miss appointments are penalized by labels such as "bad patient," "unmotivated," "a waste of everyone's time" and by being placed back on waiting lists. In some cases this may even be a matter of fines.

In general, a criminal record produces obstacles in many situations including difficulties in finding work or lodging immediately come to mind. In particular, a criminal conviction becomes an obstacle to obtaining access to a range of psycho-social resources. A conviction carries a generalized stigma. Labels such as "delinquent," "criminal," "offender" are indiscriminately associated with dangerousness, aggressiveness, threat. This association does not depend on the type of conviction. The terms are generalized without consideration of the broad range of behaviours, from shoplifting to first-degree murder, that may lead to apprehension and conviction and have in common only the fact that they are against the law. Immense differences are obscured by the criminal classification.

Medium- and long-term negative effects of criminal justice processing are apparent even within criminal jurisdictions. The person may be held in custody without bail due to the belief that a person who is incompetent or "of no fixed address" will disappear before the trial. If released, he or she may in fact fail to make the mandatory court appearances, held weeks or months later, and a bench warrant may be issued. If found guilty, which is quite likely, the sentence often consists of probation with several conditions, including treatment. Non-compliance with such orders constitutes another infraction and increases the momentum of the criminal trajectory. If police receive reports of bizarre, erratic behaviour for a person for whom a bench warrant has been issued, or who has violated court conditions (for bail or probation), he or she will be labelled "recalcitrant" rather than "person in need of help." In the very long term, a criminal conviction results in the label "recidivist" and increases the range of restriction of freedom and the severity of punishments. In some cases, multiple apprehensions inspire in intervening agents the desire to see the person "put away," resulting in extremely severe sentencing recommendations with respect to the seriousness of the offence.

In the best of circumstances, where criminal justice processing is successfully used to refer an apprehended person for psycho-social intervention, the strategy nevertheless carries medium-term negative effects of which the costs may well outweigh any benefits.

In recent years, Canadian policy has moved toward a more parsimonious use of criminal charges in the types of cases of interest. The human and financial cost of using the courts, particularly the criminal courts, is high and does not obtain the desired results. While some fear that a strategy of parsimony equates with accepting the unacceptable, and absolving persons of self-responsibility, it is rather a search for alternatives to minimize recourse to criminal justice processing.

In cases where the intervening criminal justice agency takes a person's psychiatric disposition into account, intervention can be minimized in a number of ways. The aim of decriminalization is to adopt measures outside of criminal justice processing, to reduce or eliminate the use of prisons in these cases. The practice of decriminalization in every case acknowledges that there is a problem and that it affects the person who experiences the problem as well as others in his or her environment. The need to find solutions that reduce these effects is urgent.

ENDNOTES

1. Mental illness attributions were not created in a vacuum, without reference to legal or psychiatric criteria Warren (1982, p. 139) citing Santos (1977), refers to the "concept of Topos".

2. Holstein (1993) cites a lively debate between Scheff and Gove concerning the relative importance of social reaction *versus* the behaviour in itself.

3. Financial considerations also play a role in this development; challenges to the foundation of psychiatry were not the only impulse toward reducing hospital populations (Dear & Wolch, 1987; Warren, 1981; Rose, 1979) The distinct rationales that justified deinstitution were not jointly shared.

4. This right may be restricted by the application of various residential policies.

5. Laws requiring informed consent by self or other with regard to psychiatric matters are a "prickly subject" (Winick, 1994; Gordon, 1993; Rozovsky & Rozovsky, 1990; Robertson, 1987; Gordon & Verdun-Jones, 1986), and the constraint implicit in criminal justice referrals complicates the issue of obtaining consent (Migneault & O'Neil, 1988). Within the context of these laws, a police officer has no means whatever to force a person whose behaviour is judged problematic and who is deemed to require some intervention, to receive treatment.

6. In Quebec, this option is regulated by a new statute (in force since June 1, 1998) regarding persons whose mental state presents a danger for themselves or others. Article 7 is more specific than previous legislation, requiring that this danger be both serious and imminent. Articles 8.1 and 8.2 of this law require that police referrals for involuntary commitment due to dangerousness be made only at the request of a third party (Québec, 1997).

7. While no systematic examination of this response has been made in Quebec, interview respondents who are involved in such interventions have emphasized dangerousness and unpredictability as reasons to refuse treatment; their views are supported by administrative documents concerning psychiatric-criminal justice clientele (Decoste et al., 1985; Groupe de travail interministériel (MSSS, MJQ, MSGQ), 1986; Table de concertation psychiatrie-justice de Montréal, 1989).

8. Canadian mental health legislation varies from province to province (Segal, Tefft & Trute, 1991; Rozovsky & Rozovsky, 1990), but in each province treatment without consent of involuntary patients may be contested as inconsistent with the *Canadian Charter of Rights and Freedoms* (See Robertson, 1987, p. 403–7).

REFERENCES

Abramson, M. (1972). The Criminalization of Mentally Disordered Behavior: Possible Side Effect of a New Mental Health Law. *Hospital and Community Psychiatry, 23*(4), 101–105.

Acosta, F. (1987). De l'événement à l'infraction: le processus de mise en forme pénale. *Déviance et Société, 11*(1), 1–40.

Allen, H. (1987a). *Justice Unbalanced: Gender, Psychiatry and Judicial Decision*. Milton Keynes, UK: Open University Press.

Allen, H. (1987b). *Rendering them Harmless: The Professional Portrayal of Women Charged with Serious Violent Crimes*. In P. Carlen, & A. Worrall (Eds), *Gender, Crime and Justice*, (pp. 81–94). Milton Keynes, UK: Open University Press.

Allen, H. (1986). *Psychiatry and the Construction of the Feminine*. In P. Miller, & N. Rose (Eds), *The Power of Psychiatry*, (pp. 85–110). Cambridge: Polity Press.

Arvanites, T. M. (1988). The Impact of State Mental Hospital Deinstitutionalization on Commitments for Incompetency to Stand Trial. *Criminology, 26*(2), 307–320.

Aubert, V. (1965). *The Hidden Society*. Totowa, N.J.: The Bedminster Press.

Bagby, M. R., & Atkinson, L. (1988). The Effects of Legislative Reform on Civil Commitment Admission Rates: A Critical Analysis. *Behavioral Sciences and the Law, 6*(1), 45–61.

Bagby, M.R., Silverman, I., Ryan, D.P., & Dicksens, S.E. (1987). Effects of Mental Health Legislative Reform in Ontario. *Psychology/Psychologie canadienne, 28*(1), 21–29

Barrett, R. J. (1988). Clinical Writing and Documentary Construction of Schizophrenia. *Culture, Medicine, and Psychiatry, 12*, 265–299.

Biron, A. (1988). *La doctrine du consentement éclairé.* In P. Migneault, & J. O'Neil (Eds), *Consentement éclairé et capacité en psychiatrie. Aspects cliniques et juridiques. Actes du colloque tenu à Verdun le 17 octobre 1986,* (pp. 101–121). Verdun: Éditions Douglas.

Bittner, E. (1967). Police Discretion in Emergency Apprehension of Mentally Ill Persons. *Social Problems, 14*, 278–292.

Black, D. J. (1976). *The Behavior of Law.* London: Academic Press.

Bonovitz, J. C., & Bonovitz, J. S. (1981). Diversion of the Mentally Ill into the Criminal Justice System: The Police Intervention Perspective. *American Journal of Psychiatry, 138*(7), 973–976.

Bonovitz, J. C., & Guy, E. B. (1979). Impact of Restrictive Civil Commitment Procedures on a Prison Psychiatric Service. *American Journal of Psychiatry, 136*, 1045–1048.

Brown, R. H. (1993). *Moral Mimesis and Political Power: Toward a Rhetorical Understanding of Deviance, Social Control, and Civic Dicourse.* In J. A. Holstein, & G. Miller (Eds), *Reconsidering Social Constructionism,* (pp. 501–522). New York: Aldine De Gruyter.

Cardinal, C. (1997). 35 ans de désinstitutionnalisation au Québec 1961–1996. In Le Comité de la santé mentale du Québec (Sous la dir. de), *Défis. De la reconfiguration des services de santé mentale.* Québec: Ministère de la Santé et des Services sociaux.

Carlen, P. (1985). Law, Psychiatry and Women's Imprisonment. A Sociological View. *British Journal of Psychiatry, 146*, 618–621.

Castel, R. (1981). *La gestion des risques: de l'antipsychiatrie à l'après psychanalyse.* Paris: Editions de Minuit.

Comité des coordonnateurs des urgences psychiatriques de la région 6-A. (1992). *Protocole pour l'application de la sectorisation dans les urgences psychiatriques de la région 6A,* Montréal: Comité des chefs de départements de psychiatrie.

Conrad, P., & Schneider, J. W. (1980). *Deviance and Medicalization. From Badness to Sickness.* St-Louis: The C.V. Moosby Company.

Cournoyer, J., & Monette, Y. (1991). La judiciarisation du traitement du malade psychiatrique inapte qui refuse catégoriquement de consentir. *Revue canadienne de psychiatrie, 36*(5), 339–343.

Cousineau, M. (1992). *Processus décisionnel et détermination des trajectoires judiciaires: analyse du cheminement d'une cohorte de justiciables.* Thèse de doctorat, Université du Québec à Montréal, Montréal.

De Bonis, M. (1985). Psychologie et évaluation de la responsabilité dans l'expertise psychiatrique. *Déviance et Société, 9*(3), 201–214.

Dear, M. J., & Wolch, J. R. (1987). *Landscapes of Despair.* Princeton, N.J.: Princeton University Press.

Debuyst, C. (1984). La notion de dangerosité, maladie infantile de la criminologie. *Criminologie, 17*(2), 7–24.

Decoste, G., Gaudet, D., Bédard, G. P., & Blais, J. (1985). *Les services psychiatriques en milieu correctionnel: une nécessité d'agir.* Services correctionnels québécois.

Dickey, W. (1980). Incompetency and the Nondangerous Mentally Ill Client. *Criminal Law Bulletin, 16*(1), 22–40.

Dorvil, H. (1988). *De l'Annonciation à Montréal. Histoire de la folie dans la communauté. 1962–1987.* Montréal: Editions Emile-Nelligan.

Emerson, R. M. (1992). Disputes in Public Bureaucracies. *Studies in Law, Policics, and Society, 12,* 3–29.

Emerson, R. M. (1991). Case Processing and Interorganizational Knowledge: Detecting the "Real Reasons" for Referrals. *Social Problems, 38*(2), 198–212.

Emerson, R. M. (1983). Holistic Effects in Social Control Decision-Making. *Law and Society Review, 17,* 425–455.

Emerson, R. M., & Messinger, S. L. (1977). The Micro-Politics of Troubles. *Social Problems, 25*(2), 121–134.

Faugeron. C. (1978). *Du simple au complexe: les représentations sociales de la justice pénale.* Déviance et Société, 2 (4), 411–432.

Faugeron, C. (1979). Le renvoi: idéologisation des pratiques ou pratiques idéologiques. Le contrôle social de la déviance. *Actes du colloque tenu à de Vaucresson le 24 octobre 1978,* (pp. 79–98). Vaucresson: Délégation générale à la recherche scientifique et technique.

Faugeron, C., Fichelet, M., & Robert, P. (1977). *Le renvoi du déviant. Des modes informels aux systèmes institutionnels de contrôle de la déviance.* Paris: C.O.R.D.E.S.

Fichelet, M. & R. Fichelet (1979). Réflexion sur la déviance dans ses rapports au pouvoir et à la société. Le contrôle social de la déviance, Actes du colloque de Vaucresson tenu le 24 octobre 1978, (pp. 99–109). Vaucresson: Délégation générale à la recherche scientifique et technique.

Foucault, M. (1961). *Histoire de la folie.* Paris: Plon.

Fox, R. E., & Erickson, P. G. (1972). *Apparently Suffering from Mental Disorder.* Toronto: University of Toronto Centre of Criminology.

Freeman, R. J., & Roesch, R. (1989). Mental Disorder and the Criminal Justice System: A Review. *International Journal of Law and Psychiatry, 12*(2–3), 105–115.

Gallagher, B. J. (1980). *The Sociology of Mental Illness.* Englewood Cliffs, N.J.: Prentice-Hall.

Gavigan, S. (1982). Women's Crime and Feminist Critiques: A Review of the Literature. *Canadian Criminology Forum — Le forum canadien de criminologie, 5,* 40–53.

Geller, J. L., & Fisher, W. H. (1991). Effect of Evaluations of Competency to Stand Trial on the State Hospital in an Era of Increased Community Services. *Hospital and Community Psychiatry, 42*(8), 818–823.

Geller, J. L., & Lister, E. D. (1978). The Process of Criminal Commitment for Pretrial Psychiatric Examination: An Evaluation. *American Journal of Psychiatry, 135*(1), 53–60.

Gingell, C. R. (1991). *The Criminalization of the Mentally Ill: An Examination of the Hypothesis.* Unpublished doctoral dissertation, Simon Fraser University, Vancouver.

Goffman, E. (1968). *Asiles. Etudes sur la condition sociale des malades mentaux*. Paris: Les Editions de Minuit.

Goffman, E. (1975). *Stigmate*. Paris: Editions de Minuit.

Gordon, R. M. (1993). Out to Pasture: A Case for the Retirement of Canadian Mental Health Legislation. *Canadian Journal of Community Mental Health*, *12*(1), 37–55.

Gordon, R. M., & Verdun-Jones, S. N. (1986). *Mental Health Law and Law Reform in the Commonwealth: The Rise of the "New Legalism"?* In D. A. Weisstub (Ed.), *Law and Mental Health. International Perspectives. vol. 2*, (pp. 1–82). Toronto: Pergamon Press.

Gratzer, T. G., & Matas, M. (1994). The Right to Refuse Treatment: Recent Canadian Developments. *Bulletin of the American Academy of Psychiatry and the Law*, *22*(2), 249–256.

Groupe de travail interministériel (M.S.S.S - M.J.Q. - M.S.G.Q.). (1986). *Plan d'action relatif aux services requis par la clientèle présentant le double problème de la maladie mentale et de la délinquance*. Québec: Ministère de la Santé et des Services Sociaux, Ministère de la Justice, Ministère du Solliciteur général.

Hak, T. (1992). *Psychiatric Records as Transformations of Other Texts*. In G. Watson, & R. M. Seiler (Eds), *Text in Context. Contributions to Ethnomethodology*, (pp. 138–155). Newbury Park: Sage Publications.

Hiday, V. A. (1988). Civil Commitment: A Review of Empirical Research. *Behavioral Sciences and the Law*, *6*(1), 15–43.

Holstein, J. A. (1993). *Court-Ordered Insanity. Interpretive Practice and Involuntary Commitment*. New York: Aldine de Gruyter.

Horwitz, A. V. (1990). *The Logic of Social Control*. New York and London: Plenum Press.

Horwitz, A. (1982). *The Social Control of Mental Illness*. New York: Academic Press.

Hulsman, L. H. C. (1981). *Une perspective abolitionniste du système de justice pénale et un schéma d'approche des situations problématiques*. In C. Debuyst (Sous la dir. de), *Dangerosité et justice pénale. Ambiguïté d'une pratique*, (pp. 7–16). Genève, Paris: Médecine & Hygiène, Masson.

Jodelet, D. (1989). *Folies et représentations sociales*. Paris: Presses Universitaires de France.

Laberge, D., & Landreville, P. (1994). Beyond Law and Order: Motives in the Mobilization of the Penal System. *Journal of Human Justice*, *5*(2), 84–97.

Laberge, D., Landreville, P., Morin, D., Robert, M., & Soullière, N. (1995). *Maladie mentale et délinquance: deux figures de la déviance devant la justice pénale*, Collection Perspectives criminologiques. Bruxelles, Ottawa et Montréal: De Boeck Université, Les presses de l'Université d'Ottawa et Les presses de l'Université de Montréal.

Laberge, D., & Morin, D. (1995). The Overuse of Criminal Justice Dispositions. Failure of Diversionary Policies in the Management of Mental Health Disposition. *International Journal of Law and Psychiatry*, *18*(4), 389–414.

Laberge, D., & Morin, D. (1992). *Les clientèles "psychiatrie-justice": problèmes de prise en charge et d'intervention*. Montréal: Les cahiers du groupe de recherche et d'analyse sur les politiques et les pratiques pénales (G.R.A.P.P.P).

Laberge, D., Morin, D., & Armony, V. (1997). Les représentations sexuées dans les discours d'experts psychiatres. *Déviance et Société*, *21*(3), 251–272.

Landreville, P., Laberge, D., Morin, D., & Casavant, L. (1998). *Logique d'action et fonctions de la prison: l'exclusion des itinérants par le droit pénal.* In P. Robert (sous la dir. de), *La gestion sociale par le droit pénal. La discipline du travail et la punition des pauvres. Actes de la 8e journée de droit social et du travail,* (pp. 153–171). Cowansville: Les Éditions Yvon Blais inc.

Lévy, R. (1987). *Du suspect au coupable: le travail de la police.* Genève: Médecine et Hygiène.

Loseke, D. R. (1995). *Writing Rights: The "Homeless Mentally Ill" and Involuntary Hospitalization.* In J. Best (Ed.), *Images of Issues. Typifying Contemporary Social Problems,* (pp. 261–285). New York: Aldine de Gruyter.

Madigan, K. V., Checkland, D., & Silberfeld, M. (1994). Presumptions Respecting Mental Competence. *Canadian Journal of Psychiatry, 39*(3), 147–152.

Matthews, A. R. (1970). Observations on Police Policy and Procedures for Emergency Detention of the Mentally Ill. *Journal of Criminal Law, Criminology, and Police Science, 61,* 283–295.

Ménard, J. (1988). *Capacité et consentement éclairé: les droits du patient psychiatrique.* In P. Migneault, & J. O'Neil (Eds), *Consentement éclairé et capacité en psychiatrie. Aspects cliniques et juridiques. Actes du colloque tenu à Verdun le 17 octobre 1986,* (pp. 123–143). Verdun: Éditions Douglas.

Menzies, R. J. (1987). Psychiatrists in Blue: Police Apprehension of Mental Disorder and Dangerousness. *Criminology: An Interdisciplinary Journal, 25,* 429–453.

Menzies, R. J., Chunn, D. E., & Webster, C. D. (1992). Female Follies: The Forensic Psychiatric Assessment of Women Defendants. *International Journal of Law and Psychiatry, 15*(2), 179–194.

Migneault, P., & O'Neil, J. (Eds). (1988). *Consentement éclairé et capacité en psychiatrie. Aspects cliniques et juridiques. Actes du colloque tenu à Verdun le 17 octobre 1986.* Verdun: Editions Douglas.

Miller, P. (1986). *Critiques of Psychiatry and Critical Sociologies of Madness.* In P. Miller, & N. Rose (Eds), *The Power of Psychiatry,* (pp. 12–42). Cambridge: Polity Press.

Miller, R. D. (1992). Economic Factors Leading to Diversion of the Mentally Disordered from the Civil to the Criminal Commitment Systems. *International Journal of Law and Psychiatry, 15*(1), 1–12.

Molinari, P.A. (1991). Le droit aux services de santé: de la réthorique à la mise en oeuvre judiciare. In Barreau de Québec. Service de la fromation permanente (Sous la dir. de) Développements récents en droit de la santé, (pp. 73–99). Cowansville, Québec: Les éditions Yvon Blais inc.

Murphy, G. R. (1986). *Special Care: Improving the Police Response to the Mentally Disabled.* Washington, D.C.: Police Executive Research Forum.

Peyrot, M. (1995). Psychological Testing and Forensic Decision Making: The Properties-in Use of the MMPI. *Social Problems, 42*(4), 574–586.

Québec. *Loi sur la protection des personnes dont l'état mental présente un danger pour elles-mêmes ou pour autrui,* Lois du Québec, 1997, c.75. (An act regarding the protection of persons whose mental state presents a danger to themselves or to others, Law of Quebec, 1997 chapter 75.)

Robertson, G. B. (1987). *Mental Disabililty and the Law in Canada.* Toronto, Calgary, Vancouver: Carswell.

Roesch, R., & Golding, S. L. (1985). *The Impact of Deinstitutionalization.* In D. P. Farrington, & J. Gunn (Eds), *Aggression and Dangerousness,* (pp. 209–239). Toronto: Wiley.

Rogers, A. (1990). Policing Mental Disorder: Controversies, Myths and Realities. *Social Policy and Administration, 24*(3), 226–236.

Rose, S. M. (1979). Deciphering Deinstitutionalization: Complexities in Policy and Programme Analysis. *Milbank Memorial Fund Quarterly/Health and Society*, *57*(4), 429–460.

Rozovsky, L. E., & Rozovsky, F. A. (1990). *The Canadian Law of Consent to Treatment*. Toronto and Vancouver: Butterworths.

Ryan, K. A. (1992). *Mad or Bad? Women and the Forensic Psychiatric Process*. Master of Arts, Simon Fraser University, Vancouver.

Scheff, T. J. (1966). *Being Mentally Ill. A Sociological Theory*. Chicago: Aldine Publishing.

Scheff, T. (Ed.). (1975). *Labeling Madness*. Englewood Cliffs, N.J.: Prentice-Hall.

Scott, M. B., & Lyman, S. M. (1970). *Accounts, Deviance and Social Order*. In J. D. Douglas (Ed.), *Deviance and Respectability. The Social Construction of Moral Meanings*, (pp. 89–159). New York: Basic Books.

Segall, A., Tefft, B., & Trute, B. (1991). Community Attitudes and Mental Health Law. *Canadian Journal of Community Mental Health*, *Special Supplement*(2), 17–72.

Sims, A. C. P., & Symonds, R. L. (1975). Psychiatric Referrals from the Police. *British Journal of Psychiatry*, *127*, 171–178.

Steadman, H. J. (1992). Boundary Spanners: A Key Component for the Effective Interactions of the Justice and Mental Health Systems. *Law and Human Behavior*, *16*(1), 75–87.

Table de concertation psychiatrie-justice de Montréal. (1989). *Plan d'organisation des services de santé mentale dans le secteur psychiatrie-justice pour la région 06-A. Bilan et recommandations soumis aux CRSSSMM. Document de travail*. Montréal.

Teplin, L. A. (1983). The Criminalization of the Mentally Ill: Speculation in Search of Data. *Psychological Bulletin*, *94*(1), 54–67.

Teplin, L. A. (1984a). Criminalizing Mental Disorder: The Comparative Arrest Rate of the Mentally Ill. *American Psychologist*, *39*(7), 794–803.

Teplin, L. A. (1984b). *Managing Disorder. Police Handling of the Mentally Ill*. In L. A. Teplin (Ed.), *Mental Health and Criminal Justice*, (pp. 157–175). Beverly Hills: Sage.

Teplin, L. A., & Pruett, N. S. (1992). Police as Streetcorner Psychiatrist: Managing the Mentally Ill. *International Journal of Law and Psychiatry*, *15*(2), 139–156.

Warren, C. A. B. (1981). New Forms of Social Control: The Myth of Deinstitutionalization. *American Behavioral Scientist*, *24*(6), 724–740.

Warren, C. A. B. (1982). *The Court of Last Resort. Mental Illness and the Law*. Chicago: University of Chicago Press.

Whitmer, G. E. (1980). From Hospitals to Jails: The Fate of California's Deinstitutionalized Mentally Ill. *American Journal of Orthopsychiatry*, *50*, 65–75.

Winick, B. J. (1994). The Right to Refuse Mental Health Treatment: A Therapeutic Jurisprudence Analysis. *International Journal of Law and Psychiatry*, *17*(1), 99–117.

Zauberman, R. (1982). Renvoyants et renvoyés. *Déviance et Société*, *6*(1), 23–52.

SEXUAL ORIENTATION AND IMAGES OF DEVIANCE Report on a Needs Assessment Survey of Senior Gays And Lesbians*

Sandra Kirby and the Sum Quod Sum Foundation Inc.

INTRODUCTION

We conducted a needs assessment of lesbian and gay seniors in Winnipeg to make visible the "taken for granted" assumptions about older people, and in particular, older homosexuals. This group of people have lived through a time when being a homosexual was a criminal offence, a psychiatric illness and/or a sin. Now, with human rights protections in place, our objectives were to identify the apparent needs of the elderly gay and lesbian community in Winnipeg and the surrounding area and to determine possible solutions which are most likely to meet these needs. There were two distinct parts to the research: a survey of gay and lesbian seniors and those not yet seniors, and a survey of selected mainstream organizations providing services to older persons. Funding was provided from *New Horizons, Health Canada,* and various community groups and individuals in Winnipeg. The needs, in order of priority and identified by the survey participants were: health, economics, housing, social and recreational opportunities, crime and safety, transportation, and spirituality; although in this chapter we present only the health issues in detail. The survey of organizations was conducted to bring to the attention of these organizations the existence of this community in need and to determine if and/or how the needs of gay men and lesbians were currently being met. Twenty-seven seniors' organizations were contacted and eight in-person interviews were conducted. We conclude that the needs of senior gay men and lesbians for housing and social and recreational opportunities are not being met by the existing seniors' organizations. For health care in particular, we conclude that the gay and lesbian community perceives that health care providers are not informed on matters relating to aging and even less informed on matters relating to being gay and lesbian.

*The SQS Report, some of which is contained verbatim in this chapter, was prepared for the funder in September of 1997 and released to the public in September of 1998 after a thorough consultation with participants, the SQS Board of Directors and the Advisory Committee.

THE CONTEXT

In Canadian law, lesbians and gay males have always been invisible. For example, the words lesbian and gay do not appear in any statute or regulation anywhere (Riley, 1997). This invisibility is not limited to the law. As communities, gay males and lesbians are invisible across Canada and many still live with the enduring stigma and socio-economic sanctions of the communities in which they live (Stebbins, 1988). "Although the Court (the Supreme Court of Canada) confirmed that sexual orientation was an analogous ground under s.15 (of the *Charter of Rights and Freedoms)*, leaving no doubt about gay and lesbian access to legitimate Charter equality challenges, the Court still managed, by the slimmest of majorities (5 to 4) to justify such discrimination in the impugned legislation in that case ... by arguing that parliament had the right to change legislation slowly when responding to social policy changes." (Fisher, J. in Riley, 1997: 28). This official acknowledgment that social attitudes are changing and having an effect on social policy is encouraging for lesbian and gay activists.

However, the pressure for lesbians and gay males to conform to heterosexual lifestyles and to hide their sexual orientation, to be closeted, remains intense despite the reading of protection for lesbians and gay males into the *Charter of Rights and Freedoms*. Some heterosexuals are willing to accept homosexuals as long as gay sexual and romantic expression is kept to bedrooms. This is a form of "tolerance" rather than the more true acceptance. Public sexual and romantic display is, and mostly remains, the domain of heterosexuals. In general, heterosexual society still feels itself superior to homosexual society because heterosexuals can form "natural" relationships and can produce children. These arguments fall flat when the word "natural" is changed to "majority," with homosexuals being the minority. Many gay men and lesbians form partnerships, some of them lifetime partnerships. Further, producing children is not the sole domain of heterosexuals. Many homosexuals have children, some of them from within their homosexual partnerships. As Reid (1975) writes, if homosexuality was not so important, why are lesbians and gay males being oppressed so much for it?

Sum Quod Sum Incorporated (SQS) was formed as a charitable foundation in Manitoba in 1992 to provide, among other things, facilities, services and/or educational programming for older gay men and lesbians. Blye Frank (1991: 1) was concerned about the "set of social and sexual relations that produce and hold in place, 'the everydayness of heterosexism'." SQS's concern has been to make visible this set of social relations for older lesbians and gay males, social relations which are, in Frank's terms, saturated with heterosexism and work to oppress and marginalize gay males and lesbians. In addition, in discussing the needs of older lesbians and gay males, SQS repeatedly came back to our own uncertainties about what older lesbians and gay men needed and how and by whom they might best be met.

It is from this uncertainty that SQS decided to conduct a needs assessment of lesbian and gay seniors in Winnipeg. What are the "taken for granted" assumptions about older people, and in particular, older homosexuals? This group of people spent their formative years in a society that criminalized their conduct, branded their orientation a psychiatric illness, and pronounced them sinners. We recognized that, notwithstanding recent changes in the law and recent progress in societal attitudes, homophobia remains a fact of life. We further questioned whether senior lesbians and gay men were likely to demand from persons in positions of power — those who control housing, medical, recreational, spiritual, and social services for the elderly — recognition, respect, or even satisfaction of their basic needs. That is, if SQS could create better access to existing programs, would senior gay men and lesbians then make use of them? We didn't know.

In 1996–97, Sum Quod Sum Inc. conducted a needs assessment of lesbian and gay seniors. There were two distinct parts: a survey of gay, lesbian, and bisexual seniors and those not yet seniors; and a survey of selected mainstream organizations providing services to older persons.[1] The second was a survey guide for mainstream organizations to bring to their attention the existence of a community in need. Information from these two sources was then compared to determine priority areas of needs and ways in which those needs are or can be met.

METHODOLOGY

With the assistance of an Advisory Committee formed specifically for the project, a questionnaire was developed and used for both in-person and mail-in surveys. This committee included invited persons from the gay male, lesbian, and bisexual community, the seniors' community, the SQS board of directors, academics, and activists and administrators concerned with aging. The Advisory Committee was essential because it created a sense of project-ownership in the gay and lesbian community and helped seniors who were "deep in the closet" to feel confident that they could participate safely. This committee had critical input to the various survey drafts, made connections with individuals and groups for possible participation, and approved the final needs assessment survey for use.[2] Questions for the surveys were developed through a review of literature and extensive consultation with the SQS board of directors. They were then piloted with the board and several individuals.

The criterion for participation in the survey was self-identification as gay men, lesbians, or bisexuals in the designated age groups, over 55 years of age and those younger than 55 years of age. These younger individuals were included to provide some sense of future needs. Locating participants required ingenuity, sensitivity, and prudence on the part of SQS. To invite participation, several steps were taken. A mailing list was constructed. This was a compilation of names and addresses from sheets gathered from gay, lesbian, and bisexual groups in Winnipeg. Names were included only with the express consent of individuals, many of them "deeply closeted," who were willing to receive a survey to complete. Very careful attention was paid to the security of the mailing list and only the research team had access to this list. SQS also held social events and attended lesbian and gay pride education events and socials with information about the project for distribution.

The participant's survey package contained an introductory letter, invitation to participate, guarantees of confidentiality and anonymity, and the right to withdraw at any time, a contact name in case of further questions, and a stamped return envelope to the SQS Foundation Inc. office. Everyone on the participant list received a survey. Some surveys were also distributed at meetings of selected groups and some key individuals took multiple copies for distribution to others who did not want, for whatever reasons, to be identified on a list. Slightly over 400 surveys were distributed and 123 returned, a return rate of 28.9%. For quantitative analysis, we relied upon the SPSS (Statistical Package for the Social Sciences), preparing descriptions and comparisons on the data available. For the qualitative analyses, written information from the questionnaires was transcribed verbatim, then subjected to the constant comparative method (Kirby and McKenna, 1989). All quotations which appear in this chapter are drawn directly from the qualitative analyses.[3]

A separate survey was developed for mainstream seniors' organizations. The purpose of this survey was primarily to find out what programs and services were available, if any, to senior gay men and lesbians and to raise awareness about lesbian and gay issues. Twenty-seven seniors' organizations and groups were contacted first through an introductory letter, then by follow-up phone calls. None of the telephone calls was a "cold call" and all attempts to organize interviews were documented. In-person interviews were conducted with eight individuals who represented their organization or group. The results are summarized here in the section entitled "Interviews with Seniors' Organizations."

RESULTS OF THE SURVEY OF GAY MEN AND LESBIANS

Demographics

Of the 123 participants, 46% were under 55 years of age, 29% were aged between 55 and 64 years, and 24% were over 65 years of age. The average age of all participants was 57.2 years, with an age range of 38 to 80 years. Slightly over half of the participants were male, 54%. Females were more represented in the younger groups and males more represented in the older groups (Sig. <0.03). Over one-half (56%) of the participants were in a current relationship with a person of the same sex. Of these, 30% had been in this relationship for 15 or more years. The average length of that relationship was calculated to be 10.2 years. The partner, on average, is 8 years younger than the survey participant. 44% of all participants live with a same-sex partner/lover. 42% live alone.

Statistics Canada defines ethnic origin as the ethnic or cultural group(s) to which our ancestors belonged (1993: 184–191). Over half (51%) the participants identified their ethnic or cultural origin as English. The second most frequently reported group was Scottish (23%), followed by Irish (15%); Ukrainian (12%); French (11%); German (10%); Polish (7%); Métis, Dutch and Jewish (each 2%); Aboriginal/Native and Italian (each at 1%); unspecified (17%). English was the language spoken most often in the homes of 97% of the participants.

In terms of education, 4% of the participants have less that grade 9 education; 51% have completed grades 9–12; 14% have some non-university formal education; and 44% have some university education. Of those with some university education, 79% have at least one university degree.

For the purposes of the survey, total yearly income of the respondents was defined to include wages and salaries, self-employment income, investment income, government transfer payments, pensions, and miscellaneous income. The average yearly income was calculated to be $27 934 but ranged from under $5000 to over $60 000 annually. With the official poverty line, the low income cut off for the year 1996 for one person in a city the size of Winnipeg, at $17 132 (LICOs, 1992 base), our results show that 24% of the participants have incomes which fall below this poverty line. Even more important, 42% of the female respondents, compared to only 14% of male participants, report incomes which fall below this line.

How the Participants See Themselves

When asked to use their own words to describe their emotional and/or sexual orientation, the majority of participants chose the word "gay." Next often used is the word "homosexual," sometimes linked with "homosexual man" or "gay homosexual." The participants did, however, display a variety of responses, including:

- In my will, it is obvious that I am a homosexual. I want to be buried close to my male lover who died ten years ago. (51-year-old male)
- Just because I have children does not make me a bisexual. (47-year-old male)

They do not like words such as "fag or faggot," "puff," "fruit," "Nancy boy," "queer," "dyke," "pansy," "auntie," "pervert," "homo," "lezzie," "patsy," and "fairy." These words were felt to have negative connotations.

When asked how long they considered themselves to be gay or lesbian, they responded with a specific number of years or with a specific event in their lives:

> (I have been gay)
>
> ... all my life, except for a period that a shrink convinced me I wasn't gay. (47-year-old male)
> ... since 1945. 51 years. But I was not active til age 54. (71-year-old male)
> ... since puberty. (69-year-old female)
> ... since I remember having feelings for another person. (57-year-old female)

When asked how they feel about being lesbian or gay, the majority used very positive language to describe their feelings: words such as "great," "terrific," "fabulous," and "satisfied." Some qualified that they felt good about their sexual orientation, but had to hide it in their workplace or from their biological family. A few were not overly positive about how they felt:

> Still mixed up and fearful of family, especially children and grandchildren finding out. (63-year-old male)

When asked why they feel the way they do, most said it was because they were able to be themselves, to be comfortable with themselves and because they live happily, recognizing that there would be some difficulties. Others said they were having difficulty accepting themselves but were working towards it.

- I have become more comfortable as I have decided to live without secrecy. (47-year-old female)
- I denied my orientation for forty years, now I can celebrate who I am. (55-year-old male)
- I used to be very paranoid. I guess being a member of such a small group and experiencing discrimination, I guess I brought on the paranoia, which I've tried to combat. (65-year-old female)

Coming out is a continual process. Many participants indicated that they had never come out to anyone and, in fact, responding to the survey made them feel at some risk of coming out unintentionally. Others stated that they had been out for a long time to family, friends, co-workers, and the public at large.

A component of the questionnaire asked the participants questions about the people with whom they socialized. They socialize with people of various ages (63%), same age (15%), younger people (9%), and with older people (4%). They socialize with both men and women (73%), mostly women (17%), and mostly men (10%). They socialize with gay and straight people (66%), gay/lesbian/bisexuals (25%) and heterosexual/straight people (9%).

Our analysis shows that this is a group who think of themselves as different. They see themselves as "not heterosexual" and as having different needs as they grow older. Some have lived the equivalent of two lives, one in the closet for many years. They value their difference. Some speak of fears, both of aging and of coming out. Others say they look forward to aging with great enthusiasm and optimism. They share many things in common with lesbians and gays who are not seniors but because they are gay or lesbian, they are also different from them.

Needs of Older Lesbians and Gay Males

The participants ranked health care as being the most serious issue facing them, followed by economics (employment and/or income), housing, and social/recreational needs. The last three issues were identified as crime and safety, transportation, and outlets for spirituality, but all were seen as less serious and of much lower priority. For the purposes of this chapter, only the first priority is discussed in detail.

Health is an issue which includes the health care and prospects of the participants, their access to appropriate health care, and support for health care of their partners/lovers. First, 18% of all participants said they had encountered health care practices and/or policies which excluded them as a lesbian or gay male:

- The medical/dental insurance forms are limited to spouse of the opposite sex. (69-year-old male)
- On a form giving new information where you have to check off marital status. (46-year-old female)
- When my first lover was dying, home care services told me I was not eligible for help. It was a nightmare. Yet the straight world enjoys endless programs of support which we, as gays, pay for. (61-year-old male)

Second, when asked who would take care of them if they were very sick or had a disability and needed help or support, a partner/lover is the overwhelming choice. Next is a family member, then a friend. Fully 22% did not know to whom they would turn. Three percent said they would turn to no one.

Third, we asked whether participants needed help with daily living. Age is a significant predictor of whether survey participants are able to perform certain daily activities. For example, those who need help or are unable to do activities such as yard work, heavy housekeeping, transportation, going up and down stairs, and laundry, tend to be older. Those with lower incomes tend to need more help with transportation, with moving around the house, and with walking up and down stairs.

One of the health concerns is that some participants (20%) find that their sexual orientation acts as a barrier in their decision to voice concerns or ask questions about health issues which affect them. Only 78 of the 123 participants have disclosed their sexual orientation to their family practitioner:

- Until I had come out to my present G.P., I didn't feel that I was getting thorough or proper care ... (65-year-old female)
- My former doctor was very supportive. My current one — questionable???. (54-year-old male)

We believe that this increases the risk for individuals to be treated for problems which do not affect them or, conversely, not to be treated for problems for which they may be particularly at risk.

While 59% of the participants said their sexual orientation made these issues no different than those of other seniors, fully 40% offered specific comments about the relationship between being gay and growing older. Five overlapping themes emerge from the comments made by participants. The first is a sense of difference related to who are one's peers and loved ones:

> To live together in 'seniors' housing, we would probably have to announce that we are gay. This would lead to bigotry afterwards and make the situation unpleasant to say the least. (56-year-old female)

The second theme is a sense of difference related to one's role in a family:

> Pleasant and quiet surroundings compensate for lack of immediate relationship with family. Things would be less important if I had a lover or companion. (51-year-old male)

The third theme involves a sense of difference related to financial planning — how lesbians and gay men access pensions, benefits, and allowances which would be their due if they were heterosexual:

> Shared income for two women living together does not equal what might be expected in a heterosexual relationship. Without the monetary benefits of socially sanctioned relationships (health, pension, taxation), finances are further compromised. (47-year-old female)

The fourth theme involves a sense of difference directly connected with a sense of discrimination gays and lesbians feel in society. Whether such discrimination is due to homophobia or heterosexism or just plain invisibility, lesbians and gays have difficulty sensing that they are a valued and accepted part of society.

> I often feel that "straight" society doesn't include my being a lesbian as a valid reason for any concerns I may have, so I need to find, within the gay community, my own support and community. I may even have to help create it. (55-year-old female)

The fifth and final theme is a sense of difference which emerges from recreational and social needs:

> I think only in as much as I don't have a family to rely on. I also know I will never meet anyone special again because it's too hard to meet people when you get to my age. (72-year-old female)

Together, these themes illustrate how the sense of family and access to resources may be quite different for gay males and lesbians than for those who are heterosexual. The sense of community is also different and many senior lesbians and gay males feel part of a lesbian and gay community (42%). Some look forward to growing older, thinking about time with grandchildren, good health, friends, and as one participant stated, "to outlive some of my so-called problems" (66-year-old male). Others are afraid of decreasing health and/or libido, feelings of mortality, and/or specific issues related to death and dying (wills, life insurance, power of attorney, living will or funeral arrangements).

Finally, we asked participants if they had anyone they could go to or rely on for emotional/social support in time of need. Ninety-four percent said yes. In order of priority, the participants confide in or rely on the following for support:

- Friends (82%)
- Lover/partner (51%)
- Medical doctor (30%)
- Pets (26%)
- Siblings (23%)
- Past lovers/partners (21%)
- Gay/Lesbian group/community (19%)
- Children (18%)
- Extended family (18%)
- Counsellor (15%)
- Parents (9%)
- Psychiatrist (9%)

The picture painted here is that many participants face barriers in being able to find and use various resources which would help them and/or their partners be well cared for. Some are related to feelings of embarrassment or shame about being gay or lesbian, fear of getting a negative reaction because of being gay or lesbian, lack of money, and insufficient access or knowledge of available services. Other barriers are related to being "different" or "other" in a society which is prepared to treat all people as heterosexual.

Interviews with Seniors' Organizations

Of the 27 seniors' service organizations selected for the purpose interviewing, only eight were interviewed. The responses were, at best, seriously disheartening. Despite serious attempts to organize interviews with all 27 groups, all of which to a greater or lesser degree we believe to be publicly funded, some organizations responded with less than courtesy. Here are two unfortunately typical examples:

> We received a telephone call on September 6, from someone identifying herself as a staff member of _____ Senior's Housing. She asked that their organization be taken off our mailing list. She explained, "We are affiliated with a church that does not believe in this sort of thing — and frowns upon it. These people have enough rights already without spending any more government money — wasting government money. I am not alone. There are hundreds of thousands who believe the same thing!" She continued "I don't understand why anyone would parade themselves, or work for them, or why governments give money for rights they don't deserve. And we don't have anyone like that here!" She then hung up the phone. (Researcher's notes)
>
> The researcher left three messages at _____ organization before finally contacting the president. The president stated that she was temporarily acting as executive director. The president stated that she was very busy with moving. The researcher called back monthly for three months seeking an appointment. She was put off each time. (Researcher's notes)

In the context of that lack of welcome from many groups, it is not difficult to imagine how unwelcoming those same organizations would be of any senior gay man or lesbian who wishes to take advantage of their services, unless that individual is able successfully to hide the reality of who he or she is.

Those organizations which did grant an interview had never really considered the position of elderly gay men and lesbians in the seniors' community. All but one were unaware of any gay men or lesbians having used their services. Either none have used those services or are using the services but hiding their identity. The destructiveness of "passing" as heterosexual is multifaceted. It includes not speaking in public in the first person plural, not speaking about important things in one's life such as significant relationships and events. It means hiding who one loves, and ultimately in hiding oneself as if it is shameful to be gay.

We concluded that if senior lesbians and gay men who need services are not using them, then seniors' organizations which have a mandate and funding to deliver those services are failing — either intentionally or through oversight — an identifiable segment of the seniors' community. If senior gays and lesbians are using those services, but are having to hide who they are and what their needs are from the very people and organizations whose mandate it is to serve them, the use of those services by gay and lesbian seniors is being undertaken at a terrible cost to those seniors.

CONCLUSION

We conclude that there exist, among senior lesbians and gays, a substantial number of people who are seriously at risk. For example, only 56% of the respondents describe themselves as being in long-term relationships. Only 44% of the respondents live with their same-sex partners. Forty-one percent of the survey respondents live alone. Not only are they alone, but many are poor and 24% of the respondents and 42% of the female respondents have incomes which fall below the poverty line. The respondents do not generally rely on family members for support but are more likely to rely on friends. Further, while 82% are open about being lesbian or gay with all of the people they rely on for support, there is considerable evidence that the fear of discovery of one's sexual orientation and the fear of rejection and hostility upon discovery are very real to many of the respondents. Such fear isolates lesbian and gay seniors from the supports that could be offered by the larger gay and lesbian community and by the community service providers for seniors.

Further, the needs of senior gay men and lesbians for housing and social and recreational opportunities are not being met by the existing seniors organizations. For health care in particular, we conclude that the gay and lesbian community perceives that health care providers are not informed on matters relating to aging and even less informed on matters relating to being gay and lesbian. We believe that the existing seniors' community can, to some extent, meet the needs of aging gays and lesbians, particularly in the areas of educational and recreational services. However, we have also found that some of the gay and lesbian seniors do not use the services generally available and for those who do, many are being forced to compromise themselves and their relationships in order to do so. There is, encouragingly, a desire on the part of a fair number of gay and lesbian seniors to avail themselves of the services that exist for seniors generally, provided that they can be accepted with respect.

Under the provincial *Human Rights Act* in Manitoba, discrimination includes the failure to make reasonable accommodation for the special needs of any group if those needs are based on a number of listed characteristics, one of which is sexual orientation. Discrimination includes systemic discrimination, meaning that it includes any act or omission that results in differential treatment regardless of the form that the act or omission takes and regardless of whether the person responsible for the act or omission intended to discriminate (Section 19, *Human Rights Act*). There is, under the laws of this province, an affirmative duty on those who offer services and those who offer housing not themselves to discriminate on the basis of sexual orientation and not to permit others to harass on the grounds of sexual orientation. We believe that seniors' organizations can meet the needs of aging gay men and lesbians if there is a desire on their part and through education of the staff, volunteers and, ultimately, their other participants. And, if those services are offered in a respectful and safe fashion, we believe that a fair percentage of lesbian and gay seniors would use such services.

We wish to note, however, that there is a significant portion of the gay and lesbian seniors' community which does not wish to participate in integrated activities at all, either because of fear or because, as one of the participants put it, "too much water has passed under the bridge." Fighting this cause requires a degree of energy and resiliency that not everyone possesses.[4]

ENDNOTES

1. Funding was provided from *New Horizons, Health Canada,* and various community groups and individuals in Winnipeg.

2. These volunteers contributed many long hours to the project and the project owes much of its warmth, comprehensiveness, and acceptance in the lesbian and gay community to the Advisory Committee.

3. Please note that the survey was not randomly distributed. Survey results cannot be generalized to other lesbian and gay populations in other communities and should only be cautiously used when describing Winnipeg's older gay and lesbian communities.

4. Based on the findings of the Sum Quod Sum Inc. Needs Assessment Survey, we make a number of recommendations. Some are presented here in abbreviated form:

   * that a gay/lesbian only or gay friendly multi-service seniors' centre be established;

   * that research be undertaken to examine the existing support networks, formal and informal, among older gay men and lesbians in order to determine gaps in support/care structures;

   * that research be undertaken to look specifically into the relationship between the degree of "outness" of an individual and the access of the individual to current seniors' services and centres;

   * that ongoing education regarding the needs of gay and lesbian seniors be undertaken with those existing seniors' organizations which extend services to seniors comply in all respects with the requirements of the applicable human rights legislation.

REFERENCES

Frank, B.W. (1991) "Celebrating Our Surviving Heterosexism in the University". Paper presented at the Learneds Societies Meetings, Queens University, June 1, 1991.

Kirby, S.L. and A. Robinson (1997) *Lesbian Struggles for Human Rights in Canada.* Unpublished manuscript, Status of Women Canada, Ottawa.

Kirby, S.L. and K. McKenna (1989) *Experience Research Social Change: Methods from the Margins.* Toronto: Garamond.

LICOs, 1992 base, Statistics Canada, Regina.

Reid, C. (1975) "Coming out of the Women's Movement", *Lesbianism and the Women's Movement.* Eds. N. Myron and C. Bunch, Baltimore: Diana Press.

Riley, S.P. "Legal Analysis". In Kirby, S.L. and A. Robinson (1997) *Lesbian Struggles for Human Rights in Canada.* Unpublished manuscript, Status of Women Canada, Ottawa, Appendix 1.

Statistics Canada (1993) *Statistics Canada Report.* Ottawa: Queens Printer. Pp. 184–191.

Stebbins, R. (1988) *Deviance: Tolerable Differences,* McGraw-Hill Ryerson Limited, Toronto.

RE-EXAMINING
THE FOCUS

CRIME, PROPERTY, AND POVERTY IN THE 1990S Learning from the 1790S

Ted Schrecker

INTRODUCTION (AND DISCLAIMERS)

Many of us with an interest in sociolegal studies[1] either acquired that interest or saw it grow as the result of reading Douglas Hay's magnificent essay on "Property, Authority and the Criminal Law"[2] in England at the end of the eighteenth century. Hay's objective was to explain the content of criminal law during that period, and the way in which courts enforced it, with reference to class conflict. More specifically, he was interested not only in the proliferation of capital offences (hanging was a routine punishment in those days, sometimes for offences that we would today regard as petty thefts) but also in how changes in the law reflected the changing composition of the ruling class, as a power structure organized around agrarian production was eclipsed by an industrial elite whose interests required the effective defence of a different kind of property rights. Members of Parliament were at the time generally chosen by a small, propertied minority of the population, although the basis of the franchise varied widely across England; universal (male) suffrage was only achieved later, after widespread social disruption and threats of revolt in the nineteenth century. This brief summary cannot possibly do justice to the richness of Hay's writing, particularly in contrast to the threadbare nature of too many contemporary social scientific publications. Those who have not read Hay, or who have not explored the social history literature more generally, are therefore in for a treat.

In this chapter, I view myself as writing contemporary sociolegal history, and use that starting point to suggest that we can learn much about the way criminal law and the associated institutions (police, courts, prisons) define and reinforce existing inequalities of power and

Portions of the research for this chapter were originally conducted under a doctoral fellowship from the Social Sciences and Humanities Research Council of Canada. I have benefited from many conversations with Philip Corrigan, Laureen Snider, Sylvie Tourigny, and Richard Vernon about the issues discussed here, but they are all blameless with respect to the chapter's contents.

privilege in our own era from the way in which Hay approached his subject matter. Having said this, a number of warnings or disclaimers are in order. First, my aim is not to produce a comprehensive treatment of the politics of crime, but simply to make the reader think about the connections between crime and the economic structure of Canadian society in ways that go beyond headlines, cop shows, and entirely legitimate public outrage over atrocities like the murders committed by Paul Bernardo and his wife. Second, the 1990s in North America are not the 1790s in England ... and although I have used illustrations from both Canada and the United States to make the case for the contemporary relevance of Hay's approach, Canada is not (yet) the United States. The societies differ in a multitude of respects, not least of which is the relatively higher level of support provided by Canada's "safety net" programs, including employment insurance, welfare, and of course public health insurance.

However, just as England in the 1790s was beginning the transition from an agrarian society to an industrial one, so Canada and the United States are undergoing rapid change in the organization of economic activity, the sources of employment and the distribution of economic rewards. A subtext of this chapter, and the central theme of my current research, is that transnational economic integration ("globalization") is creating ever strengthening pressures for convergence. These pressures are already driving technological change, and promise (or threaten) to produce more far-reaching social effects as product and financial markets become further integrated across national borders and when the current period of sustained North American economic growth ends, as it almost inevitably must. I return to these points at the end of the chapter.

PROPERTY

Making the best use of Hay's historical analysis requires that we tease out two distinct but related themes and hypotheses in his essay. The first of these involves the argument that the "criminal law ... was nine-tenths concerned with upholding a radical division of property,"[3] along with ensuring the deference to authority necessary to securing that objective. It is not difficult to compare past and present with reference to the class biases of criminal law and its enforcement. Hay and fellow historian J.M. Beattie have both pointed out that, in historical terms, increases in prosecutions for theft correlate well with periods of high food prices, which meant hardship if not absolute starvation for significant numbers of people who simply could not afford to eat.[4] Now, having to steal to get food or fuel seems like a remote possibility for most of us, yet Nicole Hahn Rafter has argued that the increase in property crimes by women that was reported in the United States during the Reagan era "directly corresponds to a rapid feminization of poverty during the same time period."[5] In the United States, imprisoned women at the end of that decade were "overwhelmingly ... young, economically marginalized, women of colour (57 percent) and mothers of children (75 percent), although only a third were married at the time of the survey. ... Two-thirds had never earned more than $6.50 an hour for their labour."[6]

One of the few studies of its kind undertaken in Canada is compatible with a similar conclusion. It found that 42 percent of all the criminal charges laid against women in Halifax courts between 1984 and 1988 were for theft under $1000,[7] and that "a minimum of 33 percent and possibly as many as 49 percent of women charged in Halifax City Courts were at or below the poverty line," as determined by their eligibility for legal aid.[8] Howard

Hampton, Attorney-General in Ontario's then newly elected New Democratic Party (NDP) government, learned first-hand about the connections among gender, crime, and poverty when he visited a Toronto courtroom in September 1991. "The interesting thing that I saw," he was quoted as saying, "was the number of single mothers up on shoplifting charges ... They're stealing basic things, like supplies for their babies."[9] This observation is supported by other journalistic accounts,[10] which must often be relied upon given the limited academic research on the operation of the trial courts.

Despite its professed concerns about poverty and social justice (and a high-profile rhetorical commitment to gender equity), the government of which Hampton was a member did little to change the criminogenic situation he identified, although he was quoted as proposing an alternative measures program in which "an accused shoplifter might volunteer to attend a group session with retailers to learn about the impact of theft, instead of going through the courts."[11] In 1995, the stirrings of an economic recovery could not save the NDP government from being replaced by the Conservatives, whose leader appealed directly to the resentments of the rich by promising income tax cuts and reductions in income support for the province's growing number of poor individuals and families. (Hampton is now the leader of the Ontario NDP.)

On a national level, statistical data that would clearly provide the basis for an argument about the relations among class, crime, and property are not readily available. However, petty thefts (under $1000 until 1995, under $5000 thereafter) accounted for more than one-quarter of *all* reported *Criminal Code* offences in 1997. Not all such thefts are crimes of poverty, although a substantial number probably are. So, in all probability, are a subset of other offences including breaking and entering (which accounted for roughly another 15 percent of reported *Code* offences in 1997) and small-scale credit card frauds.[12] Even before any considerations of bias in either reporting or enforcement, then, the available data do not allow us to reject the hypothesis that a substantial proportion of crime and a larger proportion of property crime are either driven by or related to some degree of economic deprivation.

Another body of suggestive evidence comes from the United States, where both economic inequality and crime are more extreme than in Canada. Labour economist Richard Freeman recently argued that the expanding involvement of young men in criminal activity (including, of course, the drug trade) is directly related to changes in labour markets that have reduced, if not eliminated the demand for workers with limited skills.[13] Sociologists Bruce Western and Katherine Beckett have pointed out another dimension of the relation between crime and unemployment: official unemployment rates in the United States are artificially low as compared with those in other countries because they fail to take into account the uniquely high proportion of working age Americans who are in prison, and therefore excluded from the relevant baseline populations.[14]

If we think we need to know more about the division between the propertied and the propertyless as reflected in Canadian criminal justice, we might consider Michael Mandel's argument that the use of employment status as a criterion of sentence severity has the effect of reinforcing the equation of "good character" with "properly fulfilling a valued role in the productive apparatus,"[15] even if the role is a thoroughly subordinate one. (A 1996 study found that more than half of all adult inmates of Canadian jails and prisons were unemployed at the time of their admission.[16]) Conversely, consider the economically devastating effect of a criminal record for shoplifting on the employment prospects of, say, a Canadian single mother with limited skills, who is already one of society's most vulnerable workforce participants and is more likely than not already to be living in poverty.

The class-biased character of the institutions of criminal justice in the context of the overall functioning of the state can be inferred, as well, from allocations of state resources. In the US context, Chesney-Lind points out that while states spent hundreds of millions of dollars a year on new prisons for women during the 1980s, they were simultaneously cutting funding for the programs that would alleviate the poverty and associated risk of brutalization that drive women to theft and violence.[17] More recently, the budgetary politics of states like California have been organized around direct tradeoffs between building prisons to house an expanding population of inmates, which results from increasingly punitive sentencing policies, and supporting the public higher education that has historically provided both economic opportunity and social cohesion.[18] Prisons usually win, since at least in the United States what Norwegian criminologist Nils Christie has called the crime-control industry has become a major source of income, and therefore a significant political player in its own right.[19] Systematic assessments of similar changes over time among the various budgetary priorities of Canadian governments would be valuable.

SOME OBJECTIONS ANSWERED

It could be objected that the narrative I have just presented is based on anecdotal or at best unsystematic evidence. Of course it is. Despite the dramatic improvements in criminal justice information that have been achieved by the Canadian Centre for Justice Statistics over the last few years, one of the most valuable resources for research on crime and criminal justice in Canada remains a good clipping file. We just do not have the time-consuming qualitative studies of defendants' economic situations, details of the alleged offence, charging behaviour (by police and Crown attorneys) and dispositions in various trial courts across Canada that would be necessary to construct a more systematic and compelling class analysis of crime and criminal justice in Canada. Meanwhile, and as a more fundamental methodological point, when similar themes and patterns surface over and over again, anecdotal evidence can provide a sufficiently compelling picture of a set of social institutions consistently oriented around the defence of certain prerogatives and priorities that to ignore the evidence becomes simply irresponsible.

Based on these data limitations it could also be argued, along the lines of John Langbein's response to Hay's essay,[20] that I am basing conclusions on a small subset of offences unrepresentative of the broader universe of activity defined as criminal. However, the admittedly incomplete data I have provided do not support this criticism, given the prevalence of petty thefts. Only on the basis of an uncritical acceptance of certain "baselines" related to the status quo in terms of property rights[21] can we dismiss such crimes as lacking a political meaning that is worth deciphering. Indeed, I suggest in the conclusion to this chapter that it is also worth searching for political significance in violent crime that is superficially unrelated to deprivation or economic inequality.

A third potential objection to the linkage of crime and class politics is that crime victimizes the poor and vulnerable as well as the propertied. Indeed, it may do so disproportionately. Langbein makes much of this point in his critique of "Property, Authority and the Criminal Law,"[22] and Hay concedes that "[t]he poor suffer from theft as well as the rich, and in eighteenth-century England probably far more poor men lost goods to thieves, if only because the rich were few and their property more secure." Much the same is probably true today, if only because (to quote right-wing US criminologist John DiIulio, Jr.) "the law-abiding people of [inner city African-American] communities experience a relative lack of the financial and political resources needed to target-harden their homes, stores, parks and schools."[23] The political resources in question include, of course, the ability to demand more effective and less discriminatory policing. Thus, rather than establishing the consensual basis of the criminal law, a pattern of the kind identified by DiIulio might lead us to ask whether criminal laws are made and (especially) enforced with the consciously chosen objective of ensuring that poor or otherwise marginalized people victimize primarily each other. In other words, crime prevention may be less important for purposes of law and public policy than crime containment, defined with reference to class, geography, or both.

CRIME AND CONTAINMENT

Two examples from among many will suffice to support this conjecture. The first comes from the British newsweekly *The Economist*, which recounts how a Los Angeles policeman, "investigating a burglary in the prosperous Hancock Park area, recently told the white victim that the crime might not have happened before the [Rodney] King beating. The suspect — a young Hispanic — would have been spotted hanging around by a patrol car and shooed back south of Olympic Boulevard, in a poorer part 'where he belonged'."[24] Second, and closer to home, one of the major episodes in the history of recent legislative reform of the criminal law in Canada involved prolonged and ultimately successful efforts to amend the *Criminal Code* provisions governing street soliciting, to facilitate the arrest and conviction of prostitutes. My reading of the legislative record strongly suggests that these efforts were driven not by altruistic concerns for alleviating the desperation which might drive people to that way of making a living, but rather by the thoroughly self-interested motives of maintaining neighbourhood amenities and property values: soliciting was all right, as long as it happened somewhere else. The economic vulnerability that makes prostitution look better than the other available options[25] was (and still is) largely, although not entirely, peripheral to the politics involved. Subsequent enforcement of the anti-soliciting section of the *Code*, which has seen women convicted under its provisions much more likely to face prison or probation than their male clients, reflects this set of priorities as well.[26]

In somewhat different ways, both these examples lead us to the conclusion that the criminal law and the expanding apparatus of its enforcement are institutions explicitly and intentionally organized around defining and protecting a certain kind of community at least partly by excluding outsiders. These institutions certify certain actors or classes as deserving of protection from marginalized and sometimes demonized others, the "dangerous classes." In the body of historical evidence that supports this conclusion, particularly fascinating is Eric Monkkonen's correlation of increases in "public-order arrests" (for drunkenness and/or disorderly conduct) in the urban United States with periods of "internal war, unemployment and depression." All of the events that defined these periods " ... moved fifteen- to forty-five year old males out of their homes, communities, and jobs" and into a more-or-less rootless existence in which they posed at least a symbolic threat to "the basic social arrangement — the nuclear family — in an already stressful period."[27] Family values as a politically evocative trope, on this line of reasoning, are nothing new.

The importance of containment also emerges from a body of research on modern policing, exemplified by Richard Ericson's landmark ethnographic study of police patrol work in Peel Region (just outside Toronto) as an exercise in what he called the "reproduction of order."[28] Perhaps unwittingly, US political scientist James Q. Wilson and his collaborator James Kelling made the same point in 1982, when they defended the discretionary (and sometimes discriminatory) exercise of police powers at street level as necessary to protect against "the fear of being bothered by disorderly people. Not violent people, nor, necessarily criminals, but disreputable or obstreperous or unpredictable people: panhandlers, drunks, addicts, rowdy teenagers, prostitutes, loiterers, the mentally disturbed."[29] This contention was backed by the claim that police and the criminal law were acting on behalf of the values of "the community,"[30] but clearly the community as defined by Wilson and Kelling was one that included some and conspicuously, perhaps even coercively, excluded others.

Nothing in the Wilson/Kelling approach seriously calls into question the claim that much of the criminal law and its enforcement is organized around the protection of property. We might be talking about a propertied majority (a silent majority?) rather than the small propertied minority of early modern England, but property and its associated prerogatives are still very much the issue. When large numbers of people have *something* to lose, the appeal to support the local police gains salience by virtue of its direct relationship to their economic interests, as the lawyers for the Los Angeles police officers who were charged in the videotaped beating of Rodney King clearly understood. (After the cops' acquittal on state charges was announced, the prosecutor said the verdict "sends out a message that whatever you saw on that tape was reasonable conduct";[31] he was, of course, absolutely correct.) Over the past few years, the article by Wilson and Kelling has been cited as the inspiration for a high-profile crackdown on so-called lifestyle offences such as panhandling in New York City;[32] indeed, any number of cities have mounted programs aimed at incarcerating the homeless, or at least moving them out of the sight lines of local property owners and high-income tourists.[33] In 1998, Kelling's proposals for Toronto drew enough interest from Ontario's Conservative government to lead Chief David Boothby of the Metropolitan Toronto Police, a force not known as a colony of bleeding hearts, to wonder whether "in this day and age, we want to call a squeegee kid, a panhandler, a homeless person a criminal."[34]

THE WAR ON DRUGS: "ROGUES AND CRIMINALS"?

The war on drugs (a phrase that originated in the United States, but which has become commonplace in Canada) can be analyzed with reference to the politics both of economic vulnerability and of spatial and cultural exclusion. Economist Samuel Myers, comparing the labour market opportunities accessible to African-Americans and whites in three US states, concluded that the attractiveness of the drug trade is directly traceable to the drastically lower earnings African-Americans can expect in alternative pursuits. "If blacks earned the same legal and illegal wages as whites, the reduction in drug dealing would be nothing short of phenomenal — a 90 percent drop. In other words, much more can be said about the utility of examining drug dealing as a rational response to low wages in the labour market."[35] A similar point emerged from Philippe Bourgois's multi-year ethnography of crack selling in the *barrio* of New York City, in which the emergence of the crack trade was directly linked with the collapse of economic opportunity, leading to and reinforcing a degree of social exclusion Bourgois described as "inner-city apartheid."[36] To use an example from another, even more conspicuously de-industrialized city: in the former hub of the North American automobile industry, only one in four Detroit residents owns a car — making it difficult, if not impossible, for many to commute to jobs that have now shifted to the suburbs.[37]

It is worthwhile briefly to examine the ways in which the war on drugs simultaneously reflects and reconstitutes the exclusionary process identified by Bourgois and others. The spectre of the drug menace has effectively justified expansion of the realm of everyday life into which the state can intrude, with such literally Orwellian outcomes as turning 13-year-old children into informers against their parents,[38] as well as more mundane but similarly intrusive procedures like random workplace drug testing. Perhaps more significantly, the war on drugs erodes the possibilities for collective organization and opposition to state policies, as distinct from individual noncompliance. The use and sale of certain illegal drugs may be highly correlated with underclass membership; regardless of the actual situation, the state can plausibly establish the correlation for public consumption. Repressive, at least superficially drug-related policing and imprisonment policies provide both a context and pretext for isolating and brutalizing the people involved, while the political risks from those policies, which might otherwise alienate more politically effective ("taxpaying") citizens with egalitarian sympathies, are substantially reduced. Critics are in effect forced to defend a group defined in the prevailing discourse, and on national television, as parasites and predators.

Stating the issue this way oversimplifies a highly complex process, and requires more elaboration. However the oversimplification is not fanciful, as shown by Mike Davis's superb account of the relations among drug enforcement, class/race, and civil liberties in Los Angeles,[39] and more recently by William Chambliss and his students in ride-along studies in Washington, D.C. that closely resemble Ericson's work on policing in Ontario.[40] The dynamic in question may resemble the one identified in the eighteenth century context by Anthony Fletcher and John Stevenson, with the comment that: "So long as the general idea of the rule of law held firm, individual defiance and dissent could be regarded as the action of rogues and criminals. It was the reservoir of belief in the idea throughout society that made this ideology so effective."[41] Unfortunately, the inescapable role of race and racism in the social construction of "rogues and criminals," throughout the criminal justice system, must remain outside the scope of this chapter.

CRIME, AND LAW BEYOND CRIME: THE VARIETIES OF COERCIVE POWER

Hay's essay does not exhaust the ways in which the law served class interests, just as looking exclusively at the criminal law (Canada's *Criminal Code* and related federal statutes) would not give us a complete picture of this phenomenon today. Indeed, one could construct a far stronger case for the inseparability of state power and class power at the end of the eighteenth century by including in the scope of inquiry not only the criminal law, but also "another set of laws" that "affected the majority of the population in an equally fundamental way — the poor laws and their close relatives, the settlement, bastardy, master/servant and apprenticeship laws."[42] Also significant in terms of law as an instrument of class power was imprisonment for debt, which Paul Haagen has described as little more than "a form of legalized extortion," and one which was strikingly widespread.[43] Death in debtor's prison killed the offender just as dead, albeit with less ceremony, than the gallows about which Hay writes so eloquently.[44]

We no longer have debtors' prisons, although we do imprison people with some frequency for failure to pay fines levied not only under the *Criminal Code*, but also under a variety of provincial statutes. Indeed, Canadians were sent to jail for failing to pay a fine roughly 25 000 times in 1996–97; they accounted for one out of every four "admissions" to provincial and territorial jails and prisons.[45] A broader contemporary inquiry, which has not been undertaken in Canada, would look at the full range of situations in which the law organizes the deployment of state coercive power in ways that reinforce economic inequalities rooted in property rights. Such situations might include evictions of tenants after rents have been decontrolled or local authorities have approved the conversion of rental units into condominiums, as well as foreclosures resulting from homeowner defaults on poorly explained or misrepresented home equity loans, or from local increases in unemployment after a major employer has pulled out of a community and relocated production to Mexico or the US sunbelt. Expanding the inquiry further, we might want to look at situations in which charges are laid or threatened against women in domestic conflicts where women strike back against routinely abusive husbands or partners only because doing so seems the last or only resort given the precariousness of their economic status.

AUTHORITY

"Property, Authority and the Criminal Law" is also about a second theme, having to do with political authority as it relied on the myth[46] of equality before the law and the various ways in which the myth was propagated. Hay's classic formulation of the myth's importance is that "the criminal law, more than any other social institution, made it possible to govern eighteenth-century England without a police force and without a large army. The ideology of the law was crucial in sustaining the hegemony of the English ruling class."[47] However, neither the ruling class nor its expectations from the law were monolithic during this crucial period of economic change. Indeed for Hay, one of the phenomena that demands explanation is "the delay in reform long after a good case had been made that capital statutes allowed theft to increase by making prosecutions uncertain"[48] because juries, without which the myth of equality before the law would quickly have imploded, simply refused to convict knowing that the most probable outcome was a trip to the gallows for the offender. When "reform" efforts succeeded early in the next century, they did so at least partly because an expanding commercial class of "middling men" had considerably more to gain from the superior protection of property afforded by the reformers' proposals than they had to lose from the demise of a gentry-dominated social and legal order.[49]

For purposes of this chapter, the details of Hay's argument are less important that what we can learn (and what we should *not* infer) from Hay's description of "the private manipulation of the law by the wealthy and powerful" as a "ruling-class conspiracy" in which "the common assumptions of the conspirators lay so deep that they were never questioned, and rarely made explicit." Hay's choice of words perhaps promotes unnecessary confusion. He is by no means a conspiracy theorist in the colloquial modern sense; indeed he goes to some pains to point out that "the ideological structure surrounding the criminal law," rather like a pattern of market outcomes, "was the product of countless short-term decisions."[50] Neither does he mean to imply that legal and political choices are driven solely by class interest, or can be inferred from class positions. Rather, he has identified a key dynamic in the political discourse of law and order, which then as now is replete with code-words and shared understandings. Their importance can be illustrated with two examples from the recent past.

First, consider the case of William Bennett, a Republican former academic who entered United States politics as chairman of the National Endowment of the Humanities, where he generated diatribes about universities' failure to transmit the values of Western civilization. After serving as Ronald Reagan's Secretary of Education, he orchestrated George

Bush's anti-drug strategy as Director of the Office of National Drug Control Policy. Following Bush's defeat in 1992, he re-emerged as co-chair of something called the Council on Crime in America. The Council's first report, in 1996, combined a warning about increasing levels of violent crime in the future with an aggressive defence of the United States' uniquely high rates of incarceration.[51] Particularly in retrospect, Bennett's transition is emblematic of the political authoritarianism (which has been called "authoritarian populism" in the context of Thatcher's Britain[52]) and selective cultural nostalgia that made the New Right's agenda more than just an unapologetic economic revolt of the rich against the rest of us.

Second, and closer to home, consider the fact that Ontario's NDP government early in its mandate chose tax lawyer Susan Eng to chair the Metropolitan Toronto Police Services Board. This move signalled the fact that while accommodation with ethnic and women's elites might be on the agenda, a basic re-examination of the connections between law and class clearly was not. Tax lawyers, more or less by definition, help the rich keep more of their money. There is an interesting comparison to be made here between the political fate of Eng, who became a capable champion of expanded police budgets, and that of Mary Hogan, a provincial court judge and former director of a community legal services clinic. Appointed deputy minister in the Attorney-General's department, Hogan was apparently unwilling to abandon a commitment to reforms in criminal procedure that were seen by Crown attorneys as favouring defendants, and was dismissed by the government in short order.[53] There are lessons here, both about the limits of social democracy with respect to issues of crime and class and about the importance of further research on the internal distribution of power within the institutions of criminal justice.

CRIMINAL LAW AND FUNDAMENTAL VALUES

Once again, anecdotes are valuable: stories like these must be kept in mind when we consider such elements of contemporary criminal justice policy discourse as the claim that the criminal law "serves to underline those values necessary, or else important, to society."[54] The presumption is that there can be little disagreement about these values. However, confirmation from actual surveys of public opinion about the relative seriousness of various kinds of offences is at best partial.[55] Further, to the extent that a consensus can be observed about the values supposedly embodied in the criminal law, the consensus is carefully structured and nurtured by rulers and policy entrepreneurs who appeal not only to economic interests but also, and even more basically, to apprehensions about personal security.

Because "the desire of persons to escape internal violence and disorder may override virtually all countervailing considerations,"[56] the realistic fears of the vulnerable can be magnified and catalyzed in politically useful ways by exploitation of culturally resonant stereotypes like the spectre of the African-American rapist, used to great effect in George Bush's 1988 presidential campaign.[57] The content of such stereotypes is always revealing; Donna Haraway reminds us that "*monsters* have the same root as *to demonstrate*; monsters signify."[58] For present purposes, it suffices to point out the political efficacy of symbolic threats like DiIulio's warning about the coming demographic cohort of "super-predators,"[59] and to suggest that they are best viewed as elements both of state strategy and of class strategy, although the state is clearly forging and consolidating alliances with, among, and within some classes against others.

Maintaining either a consensus about shared values or a belief in the existence of such a consensus among the politically effective segments of the population (not necessarily co-extensive with the entire population, by any means!) is both a logical and a tactical requisite for the myth of equality before the law. That myth becomes incoherent if the values reflected in the substance of the law themselves constitute contested terrain. Apart from questions of coherence, particular strain is placed on the law's credibility when there are dissenters who cannot be effectively marginalized (hence, to return to a point made earlier in this chapter, the tactical importance of the war on drugs). The issue of credibility suggests why Hay attaches so much importance to such phenomena as "the extreme solicitude of judges for the rights of the accused";[60] the image of the law as "a power with its own claims" distinct from both those of class and those of state officials;[61] and the axiom that the law applied equally to rich and poor alike. This last element was, according to Hay, of special importance as a way of securing acquiescence to the rule of law and the interests it defended: "In a society radically divided between rich and poor ... the occasional victory of a cottager in the courts or the rare spectacle of a titled villain on the gallows made a sharp impression."[62]

In the contemporary context, we could go in at least two different directions, both provocative, with a version of this analysis. First, it could be argued that a similar set of myths characterizes popular attitudes toward the criminal law. Particularly salient are the axioms that the norms of due process must be observed, that innocence is presumed, and that guilt must be proved beyond a reasonable doubt. High-profile cases like those of David Milgaard, Donald Marshall, and Guy Paul Morin (each of whom was mistakenly convicted of murder and served many years in prison before eventually being freed), along with an indeterminable number of similar situations involving lesser offences,[63] demonstrate to the credulous that although justice may be delayed the system ultimately works. Conversely, not even a Colin Thatcher or a Peter Demeter can get away with murder. Second, there is a dramatic divergence between the content of the myth itself and the reality of criminal procedure. Both the limited Canadian research on the workings of the trial courts, where the overwhelming majority of cases are resolved, and similar studies in other jurisdictions consistently find those courts to be characterized (a) by a striking lack of attention to the formalities that are integral to the myth and (b) by an institutional division of power that effectively embodies the presumption of defendants' guilt, rather than their innocence.[64]

Richard Ericson has further suggested the importance of distinguishing between the "public culture," in which "law is a cultural performance for achieving legitimacy," and the "control culture" embodying the actual and often informal rules according to which the criminal justice system operates.[65] Ericson dramatizes the gap between the two cultures with an inventory of the multiple legal and institutional advantages enjoyed by police in their interactions with civilians, arguing that these advantages almost entirely negate whatever formal dimensions of equality are provided by case law, statute, and the *Charter of Rights and Freedoms* — all elements of the public culture of law and law reform.[66]

The gap between the illusion and the reality of criminal procedure likewise illustrates the exclusionary intent and effect of criminal law since, in most cases, "police can routinely control the process and accomplish the satisfactory disposition of cases, within an enabling framework provided by law and court organizational arrangements."[67] Put bluntly, people in a position to describe the immense discrepancy between the rhetoric and the reality either have a professional, institutional interest in concealing it or are already sufficiently marginalized that there is little they can do about it. The process of certifying them as rogues and criminals largely deprives them of voice — an outcome well understood by the editor of the *Canadian Police Chief* who worried in 1982 that the *Charter* was "exploding into a bonanza for the marginals of our society."[68] Subsequent case law has conspicuously failed to confirm his apprehensions. Instead, in the ensuing years the scope of state power associated with criminal law and its enforcement has if anything expanded, despite the *Charter* (the Supreme Court's 1998 decision to allow evidence found in warrantless staff searches of high school students to be used in criminal proceedings[69] is a particularly striking recent illustration) and despite a commitment from the political executive to the principle of restraint in application of the criminal law.[70]

CONCLUSION:
COMING SOON ... TO A COUNTRY AROUND YOU?

In early January 1999, the Mercedes driven by a Toronto corporate lawyer was rammed from behind, in a carjacking tactic common enough in parts of the United States that car rental companies routinely warn about it. He and his wife were then abducted, held for 12 hours, and robbed. Suspects, from one of Toronto's poorest areas, were quickly arrested and a brief but acrimonious debate ensued about whether the crime was a reflection of growing economic inequalities or simply, in the words of one letter to the editor, "an attack by three conscienceless criminals against two law-abiding citizens."[71]

Is this incident an early warning of things to come? Certainly, there are reasons to believe that US-style economic inequalities are coming to Canada. A recent report by Toronto's Centre for Social Justice, relying heavily on unpublished Statistics Canada figures, documented the increasing polarization of income in Canada and noted that the market income of the poorest Canadian families (that is, their income before the effect of direct government transfers) has declined dramatically over the past two decades.[72] The increase in inequality has been less dramatic than in the United States,[73] in part because of income transfers and other social programs that are less available south of the border, if indeed they exist at all. Even in today's economy, which is healthy according to most conventional indicators, those programs are under strain as Canada's governments are under pressure to cut spending and make their tax regimes more attractive for corporate investors and footloose, high-income taxpayers. The effect has been a social policy of "creating more desperate citizens," in the words of sociologist Laureen Snider.[74]

Some signs of that desperation are now readily visible, for instance in the increasing numbers of homeless people on the streets of our cities. A paradigm of official response is also emerging, in the form of anti-panhandling bylaws and stepped-up police harassment in cities like Winnipeg, Vancouver, and Toronto.[75] More explicit strategies of urban containment may well follow as the economic balance of power shifts to higher-income suburbs — a process that is already well under way in the Greater Toronto Area[76] — and as the residents of gentrified downtown enclaves seek to protect themselves and their property values. The *de facto* abandonment of Vancouver's downtown east side by both city and provincial governments, apart from periodic police sweeps of drug users and dealers, perhaps gives us a preview. (Like Ontario in the early 1990s, British Columbia now has an NDP government, again raising the issue of the limits to social democracy.)

Other, far more widespread dimensions of the increase in desperation include the rapidly rising incidence of child poverty: the number of poor Canadian children increased by 60 percent between 1989 and 1996, with increases in some provinces even higher (83 percent in British Columbia and 116 percent in Ontario). In Vancouver, the best available figures indicate that 36 percent of children are living in poverty; in Toronto, the figure is 37.9 percent for children under the age of 10.[77] The longer-term consequences of such effects of economic restructuring and social retrenchment cannot be anticipated just by looking at poverty and crime, although that linkage is important. Desperation may play out in the form of destructive (and self-destructive) behaviour of various kinds, which may or may not have anything to do with direct economic motivations[78]

Conversely, households at the top of the economic scale are likely to pursue the strategy Robert Reich has called the secession of the successful:[79] disengaging themselves from collective provision of a variety of services from which they do not directly benefit. In the United States and also in parts of England, both societies that have made a commitment to the unfettered market and the degree of economic inequality that is associated with it, gated and privately guarded communities are beginning to proliferate.[80] Such communities may indicate the contours of future patterns of settlement; more importantly, they serve as a powerful metaphor for the future of social policy more generally. In terms of crime policy, the image of secession is perhaps less apposite than that of a scramble for the best (and best defended) lifeboat, with the results reflecting the distribution of wealth and political aptitude. In any event, an analytical perspective that explicitly connects crime, class structure, and the character of state response will be more appropriate than ever.

ENDNOTES

1. A term that is not, I would emphasize, synonymous with the sociology of law.

2. D. Hay, "Property, Authority and the Criminal Law," in D. Hay et al., *Albion's Fatal Tree* (New York: Pantheon, 1975), 17–63.

3. Hay, "Property," 35.

4. J. M. Beattie, *Crime and the Courts in England, 1660–1800* (Princeton, NJ: Princeton University Press, 1986), 202–237; D. Hay, "War, Dearth and Theft in the Eighteenth Century: The Record of the English Courts," *Past and Present* no. 95 (1982), 117–160.

5. N. Rafter, "Crime and the Family," *Socialist Review* 19 (no. 1, January–February 1989), 124.

6. American Correction Association survey cited by M. Chesney-Lind, "Patriarchy, Prisons and Jails: A Critical Look at Trends in Women's Incarceration," presented at the International Feminist Conference on Women, Law and Social Control, Mont Gabriel, Québec, July, 1991, 19.

7. R. Skibbens, *Women in Halifax Courts: A Statistical Profile* (Halifax: Coverdale Court Work Services, November 1991), 17.

8. *Ibid.*, 27.

9. T. Tyler, "Judge calls his busy court a 'sausage factory'," *Toronto Star*, September 9, 1991, A8.

10. See e.g. T. Tyler, "Grim times fill court with more shoplifters," *Toronto Star*, January 13, 1992, A6.

11. *Ibid.*

12. Figures cited in this paragraph are drawn from R. Kong, "Canadian Crime Statistics, 1997," *Juristat* 18 (no. 11, July 1998). *Juristat*'s Statistics Canada catalogue number is 85-002-XPE.

13. R. Freeman, "Why Do So Many Young American Men Commit Crimes and What Might We Do About It?" *Journal of Economic Perspectives* 10 (1996), 25–42.

14. B. Western and K. Beckett, "The Penal System as a Labor Market Institution: The Dynamics of Jobs and Jails, 1980–1995," presented to the American Sociological Association, Toronto, Ontario, August 1997 (Princeton University, mimeo, 1997).

15. M. Mandel, "Democracy, Class, and Canadian Sentencing Law," *Crime and Social Justice* no. 21/22 (1984), 171.

16. D. Robinson et al., "A One-Day Snapshot of Inmates in Canada's Adult Correctional Facilities," *Juristat* 18 (no. 8, June 1998).

17. Chesney-Lind, "Patriarchy, Prisons and Jails," 21–27. For a chilling ethnographic account of some poor women's vulnerability in the inner city drug culture see L. Maher, E. Dunlap, B. Johnson and A. Hamid, "Gender, Power, and Alternative Living Arrangements in the Inner-city Crack Culture," *Journal of Research in Crime and Delinquency* 33 (1996): 181–205.

18. F. Butterfield, "Punitive Damages: Crime Keeps on Falling, but Prisons Keep on Filling," *The New York Times*, September 28, 1997 (s. 4), 1, 4; R. Walker, "California Rages Against the Dying of the Light," *New Left Review* no. 209 (1995), 42–74.

19. N. Christie, *Crime Control as Industry?* (London: Routledge, 1993); E. Schlosser, "The Prison-Industrial Complex," *Atlantic Monthly* 282 (December 1998), 51–77.

20. J. Langbein, "*Albion's* Fatal Flaws," *Past and Present* no. 98 (1983), 99–101.

21. On the importance of such baseline assumptions see C. Sunstein, "*Lochner's* Legacy," *Columbia Law Review* 87 (1987), 873–919.

22. Langbein, "*Albion's* Fatal Flaws," 97, 101–102.

23. J. DiIulio, Jr., "Help Wanted: Economists, Crime and Public Policy," *Journal of Economic Perspectives* 10 (1996): 3–24, at 11.

24. "A beating for the police," *The Economist*, July 6, 1991, 25.

25. The depths of that desperation can be gauged from the fact that between 1991 and 1995 alone, "63 known prostitutes were murdered" in Canada, most of them apparently by clients or pimps D. Duchesne, "Street Prostitution in Canada," *Juristat* 17 (no. 2, February 1997), 1.

26. *Ibid*, 10; J. Lowman, "Punishing Prostitutes and Their Customers," in L. Samuelson and B. Schissel (eds.), *Criminal Justice: Sentencing Issues and Reform* (Toronto: Garamond, 1991), 299–328. See also Larsen, this volume.

27. E. Monkkonen, "A Disorderly People? Urban Order in the Nineteenth and Twentieth Centuries," *Journal of American History* 68 (1981), 545–546.

28. R. Ericson, *Reproducing Order: A Study of Police Patrol Work* (Toronto: University of Toronto Press, 1982). For other studies in a similar vein see D. Black, *The Manners and Customs of the Police* (New York: Academic Press, 1980), 3–40; D. Smith and G.

Gray, *Police and People in London* (London: Gower, 1985), 82–140, 388–421; J. Skolnick, *Justice Without Trial* (New York: Wiley, 2nd ed., 1975), 80–88.

29. J. Wilson and G. Kelling, "Broken Windows," in D. Timmer and D. Eitzen (eds.), *Crime in the Streets and Crime in the Suites* (Boston: Allyn and Bacon, 1983), 358 (reprinted from *The Atlantic Monthly*, May 1982). For more recent elaborations of their views see G. Kelling, "Reduce Serious Crime by Restoring Order," *The American Enterprise*, May/June 1995, 35–36 and J. Wilson, "Just Take Away Criminals' Guns" [defending substantially expanded police stop-and-frisk powers], *The American Enterprise*, May/June 1995, 37–38.

30. Wilson and Kelling, "Broken Windows," 360.

31. Quoted by S. Mydans, "Los Angeles Policemen Acquitted in Taped Beating," *The New York Times*, April 30, 1992, A1.

32. For an extremely important critique of that campaign, which should be read by anyone interested in the future of Canadian cities, see H. Robins, "The Test of the City's Recovery — Is Life Better for the Average New Yorker?" *Social Policy* 27 (no. 4, Summer 1997), 2–29.

33. J. Zaslow, "A Tolerance Test for Affluent Americans," *The Globe and Mail*, December 8, 1986, B1, B12 [reprinted from *The Wall Street Journal*]; M. Hombs, "Reversals of Fortune: America's Homeless Poor and their Advocates in the 1990s," *New Formations* 17 (Summer 1992), 109–125; T. Egan, "In 3 Progressive Cities, It's Law vs. Street People," *The New York Times*, December 12, 1993, A16; C. Goldberg, "The Homeless Huddle at Land's Edge," *The New York Times*, November 12, 1995 (s. 1), 1, 22; J. Smith, "Arresting the Homeless for Sleeping in Public," *Columbia Journal of Law and Social Problems* 29 (1996), 293–335.

34. J. Duncanson, "Boothby Pleads for Compassion in Enforcing Law," *Toronto Star*, February 12, 1998, C1; J. Duncanson, "Petty Crime Crackdown Saves Cities: US Expert," *Toronto Star*, February 13, 1998: B3.

35. S. Myers, "Crime, Entrepreneurship, and Labor Force Withdrawal," *Contemporary Policy Issues* 10 (April 1992), 91.

36. P. Bourgois, "The Political Economy of Resistance and Self-Destruction in the Crack Economy: An Ethnographic Perspective," *Annals of the New York Academy of Sciences* 749 (1995): 97–118; Bourgois, "Confronting Anthropology, Education, and Inner-City Apartheid," *American Anthropologist* 98 (1996): 249–265; and Bourgois, "In Search of Horatio Alger: Culture and Ideology in the Crack Economy," in C. Reinarman and H. Levine, eds., *Crack in America* (Berkeley: University of California Press, 1997), 18–51.

37. R. Meredith, "Jobs Out of Reach for Detroiters Without Wheels," *The New York Times*, May 26, 1998, A12.

38. Associated Press, "Girl has parents arrested for drugs," *The Globe and Mail*, August 15, 1986, A1-A2 (on an incident in California); L. Jones, "Turned in by daughter, parents get probation," *Detroit News*, September 8, 1988, 3B (on an incident in Michigan).

39. M. Davis, *City of Quartz* (London: Verso, 1990), 223–322.

40. W. Chambliss, "Policing the Ghetto Underclass: The Politics of Law and Law Enforcement," *Social Problems* 41 (1994): 177–194.

41. A. J. Fletcher and J. Stevenson, "Introduction," in Fletcher and Stevenson (eds.), *Order and Disorder in Early Modern England* (Cambridge: Cambridge University Press, 1985), 16–26.

42. P. King, "Decision-Makers and Decision-Making in the English Criminal Law, 1750–1800," *The Historical Journal* 27 (1984), 54–55. See also J. Innes, "Prisons for the Poor: English Bridewells, 1555–1800," in F. Snyder and D. Hay (eds.), *Labour, Law, and Crime: Historical Perspectives* (London: Tavistock, 1987), 42–122.

43. P. Haagen, "Eighteenth-century English Society and the Debt Law," in S Cohen and A Scull (eds.), *Social Control and the State* (Oxford: Blackwell, 1985), 225, 223.

44. For the parallels between debt law and the criminal law, and an argument that they shared both an important ideological function (reinforcing "patterns of deference and dependence") and considerable practical importance as means of controlling the lower orders, see *ibid*, 229–237.

45. M. Reed and J. V. Roberts, "Adult Correctional Services in Canada, 1996–97," *Juristat* 18 (no. 3, February 1998), 1, 5.

46. Here I refer to myths against the background of Murray Edelman's observation that: "A 'myth' is not necessarily a fiction. The term signifies a widely accepted belief that gives meaning to events and that is socially cued, whether or not it is verifiable." Edelman, *Political Language* (New York: Academic Press, 1977), 3.

47. Hay, "Property," 56.

48. *Ibid*, 57.

49. *Ibid*, 57–62; M. Rustigan, "A Reinterpretation of Criminal Law Reform in Nineteenth-Century England," in D. Greenberg, ed., *Crime and Capitalism* (Palo Alto, CA: Mayfield, 1981), 255–278.

50. Hay, "Property," 53; on this point see also Hay, "The Criminal Prosecution in England and its Historians," *Modern Law Review* 47 (1984), 16.

51. M. Scully, "Endowment Chief Assails State of the Humanities on College Campuses," *Chronicle of Higher Education* 29 (November 28, 1984), 1, 16; M. Massing, "The Two William Bennetts," *New York Review of Books* 37 (March 1, 1990), 29–33; Council on Crime in America, *The State of Violent Crime in America* (Washington, D.C.: New Citizenship Project, January 1996).

52. J. Sim, P. Scraton and P. Gordon, "Introduction: Crime, the State and Critical Analysis" in P. Scraton, ed., *Law, Order and the Authoritarian State* (Milton Keynes: Open University Press, 1987), 60–62.

53. T. Wong, "Fire 'feuding' attorney-general and his deputy, Liberal urges Rae," *Toronto Star*, February 25, 1992, A1, A7; T. Tyler, "There's more trouble afoot in Hampton's ministry," *Toronto Star*, February 29, 1992, A1, A28.

54. Law Reform Commission of Canada, *Our Criminal Law* (Ottawa: Supply and Services Canada, 1977) 16, see also 5–6; Department of Justice, *The Criminal Law in Canadian Society* (Ottawa: Supply and Services Canada, August 1982).

55. F. Cullen *et al.*, "Public Support for Punishing White-Collar Crime: Blaming the Victim Revisited?" *Journal of Criminal Justice* 11 (1983), 481–494; L. McDonald, *The Sociology of Law and Order* (Toronto: Methuen, 1976), 226–235.

56. F. Allen, *The Crimes of Politics* (Cambridge, MA: Harvard University Press, 1974), 14.

57. K. H. Jamieson, *Dirty Politics: Deception, Distraction, and Democracy* (New York: Oxford University Press, 1992), 15–42, 129–135.

58. D. Haraway, "The Promises of Monsters: A Regenerative Politics for Inappropriate/d Others," in L. Grossberg *et al.* (eds.), *Cultural Studies* (New York: Routledge, 1992), 333, n. 16 (emphasis in original).

59. J. DiIulio, Jr., "The Coming of the Super-Predators," *The Weekly Standard*, November 27, 1995, 23–28.

60. Hay, "Property," 32.

61. *Ibid*, 33.

62. *Ibid*, 39; see generally 33–39.

63. See, *e.g.,* P. Watson and G. Oakes, "Judge denounces police for harassing immigrant," *Toronto Star*, April 25, 1989, A1 (repeated traffic charges based on tenuous or fabricated evidence as an instrument of harassment); "Police conduct 'reprehensible'," *The Globe and Mail*, October 25, 1990, A14 (damages awarded, after seven years, against police for assault and false arrest on dangerous driving charges following a car accident deliberately caused by police).

64. A. Blumberg, *Criminal Justice: Issues and Ironies* (New York: Franklin Watts, 2nd ed., 1979), 145–315; R. Ericson and P. Baranek, *The Ordering of Justice* (Toronto: University of Toronto Press, 1982), 76–215; Skolnick, *Justice Without Trial*, 164–229; on British trial courts see D. McBarnet, *Conviction: Law, the State, and the Construction of Justice* (London: Macmillan, 1981); M. McConville and J. Baldwin, *Courts, Prosecution and Conviction* (Oxford: Clarendon Press, 1981).

65. R. Ericson, "Legal Inequality," *Research in Law, Deviance and Social Control* 7 (Greenwich, CT: JAI Press, 1985), 36; see generally 33–39 and R. Ericson and P. Baranek, "Criminal Law Reform and Two Realities of the Criminal Process," in A. Doob and E. Greenspan (eds.), *Perspectives in Criminal Law* (Aurora, ON: Canada Law Book, 1985), 255–276.

66. Ericson, "Legal Inequality," 53–61.

67. *Ibid*, 60.

68. "The Charter of Rights and the Police," *Canadian Police Chief* 1 (no. 7, August 1982), 1.

69. *R.* v. *M.R.M.* (1998), S.C.J. no. 83.

70. Government of Canada, *The Criminal Law in Canadian Society* (Ottawa: Supply and Services Canada, 1982), 41–46, 59.

71. P. Cheney et al., "Lawyer Kidnapped in Rosedale Car Bump," *The Globe and Mail*, January 8, 1999, A1, A3; "The Rosedale Abduction," special section, Letters to the Editor, *The Globe and Mail*, January 13, 1999, A19.

72.   A. Yalnizyan, *The Growing Gap: A Report on Growing Inequality Between the Rich and Poor in Canada* (Toronto: Centre for Social Justice, October 1998).

73.   K. Larin and E. McNichol, *Pulling Apart: A State-by-State Analysis of Income Trends* (Washington, D.C.: Center for Budget and Policy Priorities, December 1997); <http://www.cbpp.org/pa-rel.htm>.

74.   L. Snider, "Towards Safer Societies," *British Journal of Criminology* 38 (1998), 19.

75.   M. Cernetig, "Crackdown on the Outstretched Palm," *The Globe and Mail*, May 18, 1998, A2; K. Honey and J. Mahoney, "Toronto Puts Squeeze on Squeegees," *The Globe and Mail*, July 29, 1998, A9; L. Monsebraaten, "Plight of the Homeless a 'National Disaster'," *Toronto Star*, October 8, 1998, A1, A7; A. Schafer, *Down and Out in Winnipeg and Toronto: The Ethics of Legislating Against Panhandling* (Ottawa: Caledon Institute of Social Policy, August 1998).

76.   J. Gadd, "Face of Metro Lined with Poverty," *The Globe and Mail*, November 19, 1996; D. Hill, *Metro Toronto: A Community At Risk — Demographic, Economic, Social, and Funding Trends in Metropolitan Toronto* (Toronto: United Way of Greater Toronto, July 1997).

77.   Campaign 2000, *1998 Federal Report Card* (Toronto: Family Service Association, December 1998) <http://www.campaign2000.ca>; "Beautiful B.C. Gets Poor Marks on Child Poverty Report Card," news release, B.C. Campaign 2000/B.C. Teachers' Federation, November 30, 1998 <http://www.bctf.bc.ca/pressreleases/archive/1998-11-30-html>; L. Monsebraaten, "Toronto Has More Poor Kids, Study Says," *Toronto Star*, December 8, 1998 (internet edition).

78.   J. Gilligan, *Violence: Reflections on a National Epidemic* (New York: Vintage, 1996); Gilligan is a psychiatrist and former director of mental health for the Massachusetts prison system.

79.   R. Reich, "Secession of the Successful," *The New York Times Magazine,* January 20, 1991, 16–17, 42–45.

80.   T. Egan, "Many Seek Security in Private Communities," *The New York Times*, September 3, 1995 (s. 1), 1, 10; J. Glancey, "A World Apart," *The Guardian Weekend*, August 29, 1998, 38–39; E. McKenzie, *Privatopia: Homeowner Associations and the Rise of Residential Private Government* (New Haven: Yale University Press, 1994); A. Travis, "Police Patrols Go Private," *The Guardian*, May 17, 1998, 1; E. Wilkins, "Demand Rises for Burly Bodyguards and Fortress Flats," *The Times* [London], April 18, 1997, 3.

SETTING THE STANDARD
Self-Sufficiency and Marriage Breakdown

Lori G. Beaman

INTRODUCTION

Women face many difficulties as they struggle to cope with marriage breakdown, not least of which is a re-assessment of their roles. The construction of the normal woman has many facets, and shifts depending on the social context. Women who work in the paid labour force are sometimes portrayed as bad mothers, who don't care enough about their children to stay at home with them. Women who stay at home with their children are painted as being lazy, or stupid, or both. Women who must turn to income assistance programs, or welfare, for financial assistance after marriage breakdown are viewed as unmotivated dependents on the state. These images are exacerbated by the media, which use language like "welfare queens" and "latchkey kids" to portray deviant images of women (Rivers, 1996). Marriage breakdown is an important site on which we can examine the multi-layered nature of the social construction of the deviant woman, and the ways in which those constructions are interpreted, and reinforced through the law. The social constructions of the good mother, the lazy welfare recipient, the greedy woman, all inform the ways in which women are constructed as deviant, setting up one "type" of woman as virtuous, the other as abnormal.

It is well known that marriage and relationship breakdown leaves men financially better off than women, and renders women financially dependent on either their former partners, the state, or both (estimated decline for women is 30%, Statistics Canada, 1997; see also Rogerson, 1991; Eichler, 1990). The majority of single-parent families headed by women live below the poverty line (Douglas, 1991). Despite these dramatic statistics, there has been little research that details the specificities of the diversity of impact amongst women. It is this

Acknowledgments: I am grateful for the research assistance of Nikki Skelly, particularly her meticulous attention to detail, and for the extremely helpful suggestions of Rebecca Johnson on an earlier draft of this paper.

latter aspect of women's lives which will be the focus of this paper. This paper will identify patterns of similarity and difference among different groups of women who seek financial support on marriage breakdown. For example, women who are now in their 50s find themselves in a different position before the courts than do other age cohorts. This group of women, typically born in the 1940s and now in their fifties, were socialized to reject their own career aspirations in favour of those of their husbands. Most of this group stayed at home, raised their children, and made it possible for their husbands to advance their careers. Yet, as they reach their fifties, many of them find themselves divorced and facing a bleak future as they enter their "golden years." These middle-class women are "only one man away from welfare" (Eichler, 1990: 62). While their disadvantaged position has been documented in relation to pensions (Grassby, 1991), there has been little research which builds an analysis from the vantage point of the women who have actually experienced marriage breakdown and its subsequent financial consequences.

This problem is located in a social context, which includes a climate of conservatism in Canada that promotes a strong base of support for family values rhetoric in popular culture, and in the promotion of that rhetoric through state policies which implicitly and sometimes explicitly recognize the importance of a stay-at-home mother and the desirability of keeping the family (narrowly defined) together. Yet the rhetoric of valuing the stay-at-home mother does not translate into any real support. This discussion is not intended to denigrate the role of women who are homemakers, but to investigate the ways in which the law constructs women in particular ways. It is therefore essential to document the intersection of law and the lives of a particular group of women, at a time when the law and the state are giving mixed messages about dependence and self-sufficiency.

Despite the Supreme Court of Canada's explicit statement in *Moge v. Moge* that self-sufficiency is only one criterion to be used in awarding support on marriage breakdown, lower courts continue to emphasize self-sufficiency when setting support amounts, as do lawyers in their negotiations. The legal system ignores the realities of the job market when it insists that women who have sacrificed their careers for family can retrain, find work, and become self-sufficient. The labour market is not receptive to women who have no experience in the paid labour force. Promotion of self-sufficiency also ignores the fact that on marriage breakdown many women continue to be assessed for eligibility for state programs on the basis of their partners' incomes (LEAF N.B., 1996).

This chapter examines the ways in which roles are socially constructed through legal decisions about financial support for women after marriage breakdown. Courts use notions of the normal woman to make decisions about who is worthy and who is not. These constructions of normal do not appear in the *Divorce Act*, nor are they always overtly expressed in case law. As sociologists, it is our task to deconstruct cases so as to reveal the underlying, often hidden, assumptions about who and what women are and should be. The focus on women is not to deny that there are role norms constructed around men, but because women are most often left in an extremely disadvantaged economic situation on marriage breakdown, we have chosen to analyze women's roles.

THE LAW

In Canada the rules of spousal support have shifted rather dramatically during the past three decades, even if the underlying assumptions about women and their roles have not been quite as quick to change. Until the *Divorce Act, 1985*, conduct and entitlement to support were bound together. In other words, adultery affected the ability to claim spousal support. The "innocent" wife could claim spousal support from the "guilty" (adulterous) husband, as long as she remained "innocent." Section 15 (7) of the *Divorce Act*, 1985 sets out the things a court must consider when making a support order:

> 15(7) An order made under this section that provides for the support of a spouse should:
>
> 1. recognize any economic advantages or disadvantages to the spouses arising from the marriage or its breakdown;
>
> 2. apportion between spouses any financial consequences arising from the care of any child of the marriage over and above the obligation apportioned between the spouses pursuant to sub-section (8);
>
> 3. relieve any economic hardship of the spouses arising from the breakdown of the marriage; and
>
> 4. insofar as predictable, promote the economic self-sufficiency of each spouse within a reasonable period of time.

While these provisions may seem straightforward, it is the ways in which lawyers and judges use them that is potentially problematic. Law is not just what is printed in statutes, but also includes case law, which is the law created when judges interpret statutes like the *Divorce Act*. We can use case law to look for patterns in how judges link the role of women to support on marital breakdown. One of the limitations of using case law as the basis for any sociological analysis is that court cases represent a small proportion of divorce cases. Case law, some of which is reported in different series, for example the Dominion Law Reports or the Supreme Court of Canada Reports, may not be very representative of divorce cases. The vast majority[1] of cases are settled before they even reach the courts, by way of negotiated settlement between lawyers on behalf of their clients. Carol Smart calls this the "mundane" aspect of law, or those day-to-day practices that are patterned, often in gendered ways, but which remain obscured from our view, and therefore our analysis as sociologists. Unfortunately, because of a paucity of research on these hidden aspects of law, we can only speculate as to the ways in which settlements are reached, and the assumptions used to reach them. The end result then, is that we must turn to case law to deconstruct the norms embraced by the law in relation to women.

The situation is further complicated by the fact that the ability to "make it" is determined by the particular circumstances of each women, as well as by her stage in life. As Miriam Grassby points out, women are often not fully apprised of the economic consequences of marriage breakdown. They assume that because they have been able to "make it" in their forties that they will be able to provide for themselves as they age. "They consider themselves self-sufficient and thus renounce support" (Grassby, 1991: 370). Yet interruptions in employment for care of the family and often lower education means that they severely underestimate the resources they will need to take care of themselves for the rest of their lives. As Helena Orton points out, "women who interrupt their employment experience losses in numerous employment related areas, including seniority, opportunity for advancement, development of job skills, opportunity to keep skills up-to-date or prevent them from deteriorating, fringe benefits and the ability to accumulate future benefits such as pensions and disability insurance" (1993: 73). Women often suffer these losses whether or not they are employed in the paid labour force, by virtue of the fact that they are most often in the role of primary caregiver (Payne, 1995: 269).

Not only are gendered patterns reified by lawyers at the mundane level of law, but some lawyers also struggle to help women to recognize the practical difficulties of living on their own. As a legal practitioner, I have found one of the most frustrating aspects of advising a woman client about support for herself was the often expressed desire to walk away with nothing. This frustration was not rooted in a desire to see my clients adopt an attitude of greed, but in the fact that many of my clients had never lived on their own, and thus did not have an appreciation of the costs associated with day-to-day living, even when they had been managing the household finances. One major concern was the child-blackmail often practised by their husbands. Women often told me that their husbands had threatened to "go" for custody if they attempted to secure support for themselves, or more than a minimal amount of the marital property. Despite the fact that more often than not their husbands had had no, or an extremely limited role, in the day-to-day care of the children, most women were unwilling to gamble on losing custody by taking the matter to court, or by holding out for more in negotiations between lawyers.

In addition to the complications added by individual circumstances, the *Divorce Act* itself, although setting out guidelines for support awards, is not always clear in their translation from law to practice. Carol Rogerson notes, "The absence of clear norms in the support provisions of the *Divorce Act, 1985* is also symptomatic of a more fundamental problem — the absence of a strong social consensus on the appropriate principles of support after marriage breakdown. Principles of support are ultimately rooted in social understandings of the meaning of marriage and parenthood" (1991: 383). Society is currently divided in its expectations and construction of the ideal woman. Women are alternatively supposed to be successful careerists, stay-at-home mothers, or combine both career and mothering and do it all. The rhetoric of the New Right has added another dimension to the social construction of women's roles by bringing political pressure to bear on such issues as state-funded childcare and other state assistance to single mothers. On the other end of the political spectrum is feminism, which has worked to promote women's equality, and more specifically to open job opportunities for women and to eliminate the glass ceiling. New Right advocates often point to the feminist movement as having made life more difficult, rather than better, for women, by making it shameful for women to choose to stay at home with their children. This of course implies that staying at home with children is somehow easy, and that women who do not want to stay at home with their children are deficient. Amongst all of this political rhetoric, conflicting images and norms of the "perfect" woman are constructed that impact on how the courts determine who is worthy to receive support.

Despite the fact that no one consideration is highlighted in the *Divorce Act,* a persistent problem in the interpretation of the support provisions has been the courts' tendency, until recently, to overemphasize self-sufficiency, found in the last clause of section 15. Even though the Supreme Court has now clearly stated that self-sufficiency is just one of four considerations in awarding support, separation agreements are negotiated to reflect an emphasis on "weaning women off" the income they receive from their ex-husbands, the assumption being that given a little time, and the right efforts, women can become self-sufficient. To compound the problem, the low levels of income that constitute self-sufficiency are scarcely above the poverty line. While their husbands live at the same or better standard of living than they are accustomed to while married, women are expected to live at a much reduced standard because they are living "off" their husbands. "While most women are economically disadvantaged on the termination of marriage, marriage has significantly benefited most men. The division of labour in most homes has enabled husbands to expand their knowledge and experience in work-related areas, develop a higher income potential than their wives and achieve more secure employment" (Orton, 1993: 75). Women who are at home full-time present one set of circumstances, and those who work full- or part-time in the paid labour force present another, for not only do women who work outside of the home contribute to the family income, but research has shown that they also take responsibility for the majority of home-related work as well. Thus the emergence of the term "double day" or the "second shift" (see Hochschild, 1989). How do we account for this double shift when the marriage breaks down? How can women recoup the losses they suffer either as full-time homemakers, or as participants in the paid labour force?

Another difficulty to emerge in this context is women's own feelings about asking for payment for something they may have seen themselves as doing out of a sense of responsibility and love for their husbands and children. Women themselves minimize the importance of their contributions to the family and feel guilty about seeking compensation. Joan Williams (1991) argues that the myth of the selfless mother is constructed in such a way that women are supposed to sacrifice everything for their families. Women are then blamed for their own suffering, and when they step outside of the role of sacrificial lamb by asking for support for themselves they are seen as being selfish. Moreover, Margrit Eichler argues that career decisions may not actually be made jointly. "Empirical data suggest that this may, in fact, be the norm. Legally, of course, spouses are not — and should not — be dependent on the consent of their spouses in order to accept a new job, leave an old job, go to school, leave school, etc. The joint decision-making, then, is a legal fiction created for a particular context, not a social and legal reality" (1990: 71). Thus a woman's own guilt and/or the possibility that she may have had very little say in the decisions around her participation in the paid labour force both work to limit her ability to seek out a level of support that will permit her to live beyond mere survival.

Underlying the emphasis on self-sufficiency is the assumption that women can catch up, that they don't suffer any lasting disadvantage from the sacrifices they make as wives and mothers. How does this link to images of women and what is constructed as the "normal" woman? The law creates an interesting paradox: while we want to think of women as being equal to men in today's society, and we want the law to promote and encourage women's equality, the reality is that women are still in a disadvantaged economic position in relation to men, often as a result of their assumption of childcare responsibilities and their sacrificing of their own career opportunities for the "good" of the family. Women who do not work toward their own financial independence are then painted as lazy, or as not trying hard enough. The paradox is illustrated by the majority judgment in the Court of Appeal[2] decision in *Moge:*

> Today, the dissolution of marriage also results in a fairer distribution of the assets the married partners have acquired together. No longer does a man have the advantage in a division of the family wealth. Provincial statues provide for equal sharing, enabling a woman, who might previously have been left with next to nothing, to start her new life as a formerly married person with a fair share of the joint assets.
>
> Women's gains have not been won without a price, a price most women gladly pay. A woman cannot be the equal of a man and expect maintenance from him if her marriage ends. Subject to transitional adjustments, particularly where children are involved, economic self-sufficiency has become the rule.

Orton points out that this statement "exemplifies how women's increasing legal rights and social opportunities become translated into an assumption of the de facto equality" (1993: 86). One senses a slight punitive attitude in the latter paragraph, in which the goal of equality becomes the basis to deny all women support. Women's desire to want that which they should not have then — equality — is deviance in that it abandons the narrowly pre-scribed roles traditionally reserved for women. The message of the second paragraph is that one cannot eat one's cake and have it too. The message in the first paragraph is also false — statistics show us that women are clearly disadvantaged economically by marriage, and by marriage breakdown. It has become obvious that provincial legislation, such as the marital property acts, which provide for an equal division of marital property, does not equalize women financially. Division of property does not account or compensate for inequities in earn-ing power. Treating women as though they are equal when they have suffered disadvan-tages because of their marital status and the decisions made within their marriages exacerbates their inequality.

The most famous cases to elevate self-sufficiency to the first priority in awards of spousal support are what is known as the "trilogy" of spousal support cases, *Pelech, Caron,* and *Richardson*, decided by the Supreme Court of Canada in 1985. These cases established what became known as the "clean break" theory of support, which promoted the principle of self-sufficiency. These were based on the notion that parties are freely contracting indi-viduals who may enter and leave marriages, and who do so as equals. Interestingly the Court ignored the disadvantaged position of women, and failed to recognize the long-term disability caused to women who had given up their careers in favour of their families. Self-sufficiency was set remarkably low, such that poverty-line income was an adequate marker for termination of support. This was often in "stark contrast to the standard of living she had before separation, and to the income of her former husband, whose material wealth in-creased significantly after separation in almost all cases" (Douglas, 1991: 8).

The trilogy cases set up employed, self-sufficient women as the norm — with the un-derlying assumption that any determined woman could find a job, and take care of herself. Her husband, therefore, had a limited obligation to provide for her financially once the mar-riage was terminated. The larger philosophical position here is rooted in one version of lib-eralism that sees women as having opportunities equal to those of men. Susan Engel summarizes the trilogy principles this way: "1. The requirement of a causal connection be-tween the need to be addressed by the maintenance award and the marriage; and 2. The pri-macy of the self-sufficiency objective" (1993: 400). This of course raised issues around what constituted a reasonable effort to become self-sufficient on the part of a woman — was she obliged to apply for work at fast-food restaurants, working for minimum wage? As Grassby has pointed out, women are expected to live in frugal comfort (1995: 195). She argues that women who are employed are caught in a double bind: those who were em-ployed but claim that their husbands supported them may be portrayed as greedy and self-ish, the penalty being no or low support. If a woman argues that she supported herself, she may be determined to be self-sufficient, and thus ineligible for support. "In fact, she was nei-ther totally supported by the husband, not totally self-sufficient" (1995: 211). There is often no recognition of the fact that men benefit from marriage economically — married men earn more over a lifetime than do those who are single (Grassby, 1995: 194)

Another interesting tension in the midst of determinations of support awards is the prob-lem that, building on the legal fiction identified by Eichler that women are often not equal participants in the decision making process around their own participation in the paid labour force, if men see the role of childcare as primary for women to the extent that they sup-port, and indeed sometimes insist, on women staying home to provide childcare, why does that commitment change on separation and divorce? In other words, marriage breakdown triggers a shift in attitude from "it is essential to have a caregiver (almost always the woman) in the home" to "get out and get to work."

Children become pivotal in the assessment of a woman's worthiness for support — where the payor's assets are limited, support for children is protected first. This may result in a woman being left with no support at all when the children leave home. Julien Payne argues that this is not right: "Although it is appropriate to terminate child support when the child is economically self-sufficient, it does not follow that spousal support should be terminated, or even reduced, because the custodial parent's responsibilities for the child have ceased to exist" (1995: 278). Although lip service may be paid to the separation of child and spousal support, in reality they are integrally linked, often to the disadvantage of women. One of the difficulties in talking about support as a distinct problem is that there is an artificial division of the issues involved in the legal resolution of marriage breakdown. Practically, these issues are generally negotiated at the same time, as part of a "package," in relation to how much the payor spouse can afford. By linking payments to children, women risk losing support once children move out, even if they have not been able to achieve a means to self-sufficiency, or if they have entered the workforce but are living at a much lower standard of living than they were at the time of their married life. Courts have explicitly stated that child support cannot be bargained away, that it is the right of the child, not the parent. The protection of children is an admirable goal, but it clearly gives paramount importance to child support that has the potential to disadvantage women.

In 1992, the Supreme Court of Canada examined the issue of spousal support again in *Moge* v. *Moge.*[3] The importance of the cases has been debated by legal scholars and practitioners, but Goodfellow summarizes it this way: "*Moge* offers a comprehensive philosophy for spousal support the basis of which is equitable sharing of the economic consequences of marriage." (1996: 1). Payne argues that although there is no data to support the following conclusion, "legal practitioners throughout Canada acknowledge that *Moge* v. *Moge* has strengthened the pre-existing trend towards higher amounts of spousal support and for longer periods of time" (1995: 277). The facts of the case are straightforward, although they slip between the cracks of the legal dichotomy of "traditional" and "modern" marriages (Sheppard, 1995). Zofia Moge was married in the '50s in Poland, came to Canada in 1960, had three children during the course of her marriage, separated from her husband in 1973, and was divorced in 1980. During the marriage she worked part-time cleaning offices and Mr. Moge worked as a mechanic. He paid $150.00 per month support from 1973–1987, $400.00 from 1987–1989, during which time Zofia Moge was laid off and found new temporary employment and continued to work when she could. In 1989 Mr. Moge applied to discontinue support payments, arguing that his former wife should be self-sufficient. At this time she was earning approximately $800.00 per month, and he was earning $2200.00. Her abilities in English and her job qualifications — she had completed grade seven — were limited.

The Court was clear on the need to consider *each* of the factors set out in the *Divorce Act*, rather than focusing only on self-sufficiency. In relation to Zofia Moge, it was found that she had suffered a substantial economic disadvantage from the marriage, that her care of the children had an impact on her ability to earn an income, that she continued to suffer economic hardship as a result of the marriage breakdown, and that although she had failed to become economically self-sufficient, she had made a conscientious effort to become so. The Court adopted a model of support which did not prioritize self-sufficiency, but rather looked at the consequences of the marriage as an ongoing process which does not simply end because the marriage does.

In a sense, *Moge* and the trilogy cases represent either end of the legal spectrum of possibilities, both in terms of the actual support award as well as in their underlying assumptions about women. While *Moge* has arguably re-set the standards used by courts in their determination of support, this is not always the case. Husbands' lawyers continue to raise various versions of the self-sufficiency criterion in their arguments against or to minimize support payments. There still exist multiple versions of what constitutes the "normal" woman, used by courts, but more importantly, by lawyers. As already mentioned, tracking the legal construction of normal at the mundane level is both necessary and difficult. Carol Rogerson suggests that "lawyers negotiating contracts on behalf of wives may assume a model of spousal support in which spousal self-sufficiency plays an even greater role than is actually accepted by the courts" (1991: 386). In the following section we will examine in greater detail legal constructions of the normal woman and their implications for spousal support.

THE NORMAL WOMAN

In her detailed examination of case law in Canada, Carol Rogerson identifies three types of approaches the courts use in determining support amounts — the income-security model, the clean-break model, and the compensatory model. Each of these approaches has underlying assumptions about women, their roles, and their worthiness for support. The first, the *income-security model*, is rooted in the notion that women are dependent, unable to care for themselves economically. In this model, worthiness for support is based on the very existence of the marriage, and the inherent dependence of women. Support is intended to provide economic security. What underlies this model? So-called traditional notions about women as homemakers, who give up any prospects of a career for the sake of the family. We will call this norm for women the "good mother" model. It is still held out as the ideal by some facets of society,[4] and is currently enjoying a revival thanks to new right political groups. The irony is that while this norm has been revived as rhetoric, there is little in the way of actual support for women who fit this "good mother" model.

One of the complications of this model is that it does in fact resemble the reality of some women's lives, particularly for, but not necessarily restricted to, women who are now in their late forties and older. Thus, while we need to recognize that some women are economically dependent on their husbands, we also need to be careful not to reify the notion that women should be economically dependent on men. This model constructs women who sacrifice as normal and good and guarantee their rewards of life-long security for their selflessness. Yet, even within this model women who meet the norm are likely to be constructed as deviant in some way upon divorce. They are likely to be caught in a bind of being financially dependent, and therefore needy. By asking for compensation for their sacrifice, they risk being constructed as selfish, and thus deviant and undeserving. In a sense, marriage breakdown for the good mother acts as a catalyst which transforms her from a selfless, self-sacrificing woman to a needy, selfish, demanding dependent.

This is complicated when women work part-time — they stray from the perfect homemaker model and are therefore less likely to be rewarded. The woman who goes out to work is less likely to be given an adequate support order, and she also calls into question her good mother status. In other words, homemaker status is not *carte blanche* to support. Stereotypical role constructions narrow the possibilities for women to fit into this category neatly. Women's lives are not neat packages which fit into preconstructed legal categories. Full-time homemakers take part-time employment, or they work out of the home. If a woman constructs her earnings as more than pin money[5], she risks being deemed self-sufficient, and sentenced to a life of low-wage labour to eke out a living. The model good mother cannot be seen to be earning a real income or she risks being constructed as deviant (and so too her bread-winning husband whose fulfillment of his role is threatened by any aberrations on the part of his wife).

In straying from the good mother model by working outside of the home, women have also faced problems in relation to custody. Women who choose to work undermine their status as the primary caregiver of their children, thus risking custody, and leaving themselves open to the threat of a custody application, even in the face of broader social science evidence which suggests that even women who work full-time in the paid labour force are still the primary caregivers, doing double duty as wage earners and caregivers. Such was the case for Judy Tyabji, who essentially lost custody of her children because of her active career as a member of the British Columbia legislature (Boyd, 1997). In her analysis of that case, Susan Boyd argues that men who enter politics "are not viewed as abandoning their families in the same way as women, precisely because the expectations of them in the family realm are lower" (1997: 255). Purported gender neutrality can be used in these cases to punish women for daring to have an interest in a career.

While full-time homemakers may be "rewarded" for their faithfulness to the ideal of the good mother and good wife, the reward often falls short of their previous lifestyle. As Grassby argues, "as each of the payor spouse's expenses are analyzed, the court is told that he needs a nice place to live, he has to have nice clothing, he has to have a nice car, pleasant leisure, a nice vacation, or why should he work. However, the wife just needs an apartment, basic clothing, has no need to eat in restaurants, does not need a car, requires little money for leisure because she doesn't work, and does not need a vacation because she is on holiday all the time" (1995: 196). Thus, the payment for adhering to the good mother model is enough support to live just above, or at, the poverty line. To see this model as a vehicle for a guaranteed life of leisure is therefore misleading.

The second model identified by Rogerson is the *clean-break model*, which is based on the premise that women should become self-sufficient as soon as possible after marriage breakdown. The premise which underlies this model is that we now live in a time when women have opportunities equal to those of men, and even after a lifetime of career interruptions or abandonment, with a little educational upgrading and an honest effort women don't need to "live off their husbands." The normative woman in this model will be referred to as the "liberated woman." This model is premised on a liberal notion of equality which is rooted in formal rather than substantive equality. Formal equality sees men and women as the same — equally capable of earning a living and providing for themselves. Systemic disadvantages, such as discrimination against women in the labour force, or the impact of child-bearing and child-rearing on women, are not taken into account. Women and men are seen as being essentially the same, with women simply needing a bit of time to catch up.

The single most significant impact of this model is the impoverishment of women. When the courts established self-sufficiency they set the levels so low that even earning wages at the poverty line was adequate to result in a determination that a woman was self-sufficient. The goal of self-sufficiency was established as the most important factor in setting spousal support. Women who had stayed at home to raise their children were presumed to be able to retrain and enter the workforce within a limited amount of time. Women who were successful at finding full-time employment at low-wage levels were effectively sentencing themselves to a lifetime of poverty, while their former husbands continued to live at a the same or a higher standard of living. Whether women's lives actually resembled that of the liberated woman or not, they were expected to fulfill or at least attempt to fulfill that role.

Like those women who do not fit neatly into the good mother category, women who wholeheartedly embrace the "liberated woman" model also suffer consequences in relation to custody. Again, women who go out to work call into question their role as the primary caregiver, thus opening the possibility of losing custody. This model fails to recognize the need for substantive equality, or equality which takes into account systemic disadvantages faced by women, or the unique contributions women make. Like the norm of the good mother, the "liberated woman" is set up for failure. She faces systemic disadvantages that limit her wages and her possibility for promotion. Courts may also limit her mobility by preventing her from moving farther away from the non-custodial parent, thus further limiting her employment options. While she is still called upon to be a good mother, she must also be self-sufficient. Like the good mother, the liberated woman is transformed on marriage breakdown into a self-sufficient woman, even if she is living at the poverty line. As we saw earlier in the Court of Appeal's comments in *Moge*, this model may be used punitively to set the standard for all women, regardless of their actual ability to support themselves. The trilogy cases were the beginning of a period of dominance of this model in Canadian courts, and the Supreme Court of Canada decision has finally begun to shift the balance to a more compensatory model.

The *compensatory model* sees support as a way to compensate for the economic consequences of marriage. At least on the surface, this model has the most promise in that it allows for all possible contingencies: stay-at-home mother, part-time in the paid labour force, full-time work outside of the home. The compensatory model recognizes the systemic disadvantages facing women, and attempts, as much as possible within the guidelines of the *Divorce Act,* to compensate women for economic disadvantages resulting from their marriages. The underlying assumption is that women should be, but are not always, equal. This approach attempts to redress systemic and individual disadvantages. The *Moge* case is an exemplar of the compensatory model.

While this model has some important advantages in terms of underlying notions about women and their equality in society, it does rest on some assumptions about who is responsible for human beings who are unable to support themselves. By looking to the family, the state divests itself of any responsibility for its citizens who are impoverished. Margrit Eichler points to a serious flaw which is inherent in the compensatory model — that individuals are responsible for their own care, with no role for the state in providing for those who cannot help themselves. She argues that this approach effectively privatizes support. In this model when marriage breaks down individuals are expected to take care of themselves, but if a woman cannot provide for herself, and her former spouse cannot assist, the state has no role in supporting her. Eichler argues that while this model is premised on equality between the sexes, it leaves open the possibility for a decrease in social support for families. She proposes a social responsibility model of the family in which the state is responsible for adults and children who cannot provide for themselves. Her proposal would not allow adults to abscond from responsibility for themselves, but it would see the state as a provider when an adult needs assistance (Eichler, 1990: 68).

CONCLUSION: REFORMING THE NORM

How can we think about reforming images of woman to incorporate the reality of women's lives? The law cannot take an essentialist view of women; women who separate and divorce are diverse, with different needs, cultural capital, and abilities. Women do not fit neatly into the "good mother" or "liberated woman" categories the law, and society, has constructed as normal women. The diverse ways in which gender and other experiences of race, ability, and age intersect to impact the ways in which women survive marriage breakdown need to be considered in the process of assessing spousal support. Although *Moge* has begun to alter the ways in which support is ordered, we need to be sure that those majority of cases which are dealt with at the mundane level are not prioritizing self-sufficiency to the extent that women are left to live in poverty. The social construction of the normal woman has a direct impact on the ways in which the law processes applications for support.

Social constructions of images of women must be based on the lived experiences of women, not a bifurcated vision of who women should be based on mythical images perpetuated from Victorian folklore, or through radical conceptualizations of the modern woman, and indeed modern men, who share equally in child-rearing responsibilities. Either ideal has an extremely limited basis in reality, and does not represent "normal" women who separate and divorce. If these ideals are accepted as normal, most women fall short, and are characterized as deviant.

At a broader level, the challenge is to value the multiple ways women live their lives, and to facilitate the full participation of women in decisions about child-bearing, and child-rearing, and employment. Legal rules need to be flexible enough to account for the multiple ways in which women live their lives, while offering some assurance that women do not risk impoverishment either by staying at home or by entering the workforce. By deconstructing socially constructed categories such as the good mother or the liberated woman, we can begin to reformulate how the law can effectively assist women on marriage breakdown, so as to foster independence while at the same time ensuring that they are not left living in poverty.

ENDNOTES

1. For example, Neilson reports that fewer than 4% of child custody or access decisions on divorce are finalized by a hearing (1997: 127).

2. Note that this is the Court of Appeal decision. The Supreme Court of Canada effectively overruled the Supreme Court. The point here though is that this sort of reasoning exists amongst judges in Canada.

3. It could be argued that *Moge* and the trilogy cases are very distinct on their facts. The trilogy cases involved separation agreements, *Moge* involved variation of a pre-existing court order. However, as Heeney points out, *B(G) v. G(L)* seems to have made the trilogy "old law" (1996).

4. Although not restricted to religious groups, this model is in some measure adopted by evangelical Christians, and by Mormons.

5. This term was originally used to refer to the extra money women made to purchase fancy hat pins. Even so, the "extra" money women earned was far more likely to go to household necessities than to frivolities.

REFERENCES

Boyd, Susan
1997 "Looking Beyond Tyabji: Employed Mothers, Lifestyles, and Child Custody Law," in *Challenging the Public/Private Divide: Feminism, Law and Public Policy*, ed. Susan Boyd, Toronto: University of Toronto Press.

Douglas, Kristen
1991 *Spousal Support Under the Divorce Act: A New Direction*. Background Paper: Library of Parliament.

Eichler, Margrit
1990 "The Limits of Family Law Reform or, The Privatization of Female and Child Poverty," *Canadian Family Law Quarterly*, 7:59–84.

Engel, Susan
1993 "Compensatory Support in Moge v. Moge and the Individual Model of Responsibility: Are we Headed in the Right Direction?" *Saskatchewan Law Review*, 57:397–413.

Goodfellow, W.R.E. J.
1996 "Spousal Support After *Moge* (S.C.C.) — Child Support After Thibaudeau (S.C.C.) and Levesque (Alta C.A.) – Do these Decisions Really Change Support Law?" *Canadian Family Law Quarterly*, 14: 81–104.

Grassby, Miriam
1995 "Spousal Support — Assumptions and Myths Versus Case Law," *Canadian Family Law Quarterly*, 12:187–239.

1991 "Women in their Forties: The Extent of Their Rights to Alimentary Support," *Reports of Family Law*, 30:369–403.

Heeney, Thomas A.
1996 "From Pelech to Moge and Beyond: The Test for Variation of a Consensual Spousal Support Order," *Canadian Family Law Quarterly*, 14:81–104.

Hochschild, Arlie
1989 *The Second Shift*. New York: Avon Books.

LEAF NB
1996 *Access to Justice: Domestic Legal Aid in New Brunswick*.

Neilson, Linda
1997 "Spousal Abuse, Children and the Courts: The Case for Social Rather than Legal Change," *Canadian Journal of Law and Society*, 12(1):101–145.

Orton, Helena
1993 "Using Constitutional Equality Principles to Shape Jurisprudence — *Moge v. Moge*, Spousal Support Under the *Divorce Act* and Women's Equality," Special Lectures of the Law Society of Upper Canada.

Payne, Julien D.
1995 "Spousal and Child Support After Moge, Willick and Levesque," *Canadian Family Law Quarterly*, 12:261–299.

Rivers, Caryl
1996 *Slick Spins and Fractured Facts: How Cultural Myths Distort the News*.

Rogerson, Carol J.

    1991 "Judicial Interpretation of the Spousal Support Provisions of the Divorce Act, 1985," *Advocates Quarterly*, 12(4):377.

Sheppard, C.

    1995 "Uncomfortable Victories and Unanswered Questions: Lessons from *Moge,*" *Canadian Family Law Quarterly*, 12:283–329.

Smart, Carol

    1990 "Law's Power, the Sexed Body, and Feminist Discourse," *Journal of Law and Society*, 17: 197–198.

Williams, Joan

    1991 "Gender Wars: Selfless Women in the Republic of Choice," 66 *NYU Law Review* 1559.

THE SOCIAL CONSTRUCTION OF WELFARE RECIPIENTS AS "LAZY"

Jason Doherty

INTRODUCTION

The purpose of this chapter is to examine the social construction of knowledge and determine how we come to know what a "fact" is. The social construction of knowledge is examined in relation to the construction of welfare recipients as "lazy." In addition, the process at work in the construction of knowledge and the role of social recipients is examined.

The creation of knowledge can enrich or degrade one's individual quality of life depending on one's social position. It is important that we examine, understand, and develop the construction of "fact" to increase the quality of all human life. It is imperative that the marginalized of society be included and empowered by knowledge. Considering this, it is important that we examine and evaluate the principles on which current understanding is based.

The body of this chapter is divided into four sections including the social construction of knowledge: structure and agency, "fact," process and exclusion, and the analysis. Section one explores the social construction of knowledge by placing emphasis on the role that actors do or do not play in constructing knowledge. The two perspectives outlined in reference to the role of the social actors in the construction of knowledge include structure and agency.

Section two is dedicated to a discussion of knowledge creation and the determination of "fact." What we consider a "fact" is related to the perspectives outlined in section one with the intent to bring attention to the various conceptions of "fact." Further, the perspectives are compared and contrasted with the intent of social analysis.

Section three places emphasis on the unequal power relations that exist in the social construction of knowledge. Critical theory is used to explain the empowering and disempowering characteristics inherent in the social construction of "fact." The role of formal organizations such as the legal, medical, and academic in the reproduction of "truth" is discussed, placing emphasis on the process of knowledge creation.

Section four contains an examination of the Canadian state agenda in relation to cuts to our social welfare system. The reduction of federal transfer payments and the subsequent social construction of welfare recipients as "lazy" is considered. The social construction of knowledge and the determination of fact is used to provide an understanding of the process through which the state legitimizes its actions.

THE SOCIAL CONSTRUCTION OF KNOWLEDGE: STRUCTURE AND AGENCY

The methodology of understanding is at the centre of debate in the social sciences. Social scientists share a common understanding of human interaction but disagree frequently on the construction of meaning within this interaction. Do social actors create their reality from moment to moment or are they constrained by a predetermined reality? Schutz notes the social nature of reality:

> All interpretation of this world is based on a stock of previous experiences of it, our own or those handed down to us by parents or teachers; these experiences in the form of "knowledge at hand" function as a scheme of reference (Schutz, 1963: 306).

The debate between structure and agency addresses the understanding of reality within the arena of human interaction. Within what context do individuals interact? Do actors negotiate boundaries and facts or are they constrained by predetermined rules and facts? The answer to this problem is fundamental to the construction of understanding and is a starting point for social scientists when choosing both methodology and method.[1] Sylvia Hale outlines this problem:

> Proponents of one perspective see people as agents who choose between different courses of action and so consciously create their social world. Advocates of the other approach see people as part of a social system, an existing set of structures that constrains and in many ways determines their actions (Hale, 1995: 14).

There are many perspectives in the social sciences that rely on human agency as the driving factor behind interaction including symbolic, interpretive, and ethnomethodology. Ethnomethodology is a method and theory combined because of its perspective on knowledge creation. Ethnomethodology takes individual accounts of experience to be as valid, if not more authentic than scientific accounts of experience (Weeks, 1995: 02).

The predominant theory of agency in contemporary sociology is ethnomethodology. Ethnomethodology uses a *bottom up approach*, placing emphasis on the moment-to-moment creation of social facts by human agents. Therefore, ethnomethodologists identify human agents as the creators and maintenance persons of what we deem social structure and social fact. Peter Weeks argues,

> Ethnomethodology focuses on how individuals together make sense of and produce what we all come to recognize as social structures in the first place (Weeks, 1995: 02).

Therefore, social actors create "fact" in society through active participation in the construction of knowledge. A "fact" is not a separate principle but inherent in social existence. People are assured of "fact" because they actively consult each other as to what is correct and false. Social structure or "fact" becomes a product of shared human interaction.

Ethnomethodology borrows the natural attitude from phenomenology; the natural attitude treats the world as it appears to actor(s) as the real one. The meanings we place on symbols, conversation, body language, and our social activity is not predetermined but derived from an ongoing process of negotiation. This process of negotiation is not only how we place meaning on interaction but also the way in which we create and maintain common-sense understandings with other social actors (Weeks, 1995).

Ethnomethodologists argue that human interaction begins with stocks of knowledge, acquired by individuals and groups and subsequently shared through culture. The subject acts with the assumption that other people understand their actions based upon inter-subjectivity, that individuals act and experience situations from interchangeable standpoints based upon common-sense knowledge (Weeks, 1995).

The second perspective in the construction of social reality is structure. There are many theories that can be placed in the structural perspective. They include functional, Marxism, and forms of political economy.[2] The structural perspective differs from agency by arguing that *social structures are predetermined and constrain human interaction*, and *social "fact" is an objective truth* (Giddens, 1984).

A "fact" in the structural perspective is not constructed by actors but is an objectified phenomenon that constrains social activity. It exists separately from social actors and is waiting to be discovered or determined by social scientists. An idea is generally considered a "fact" if it has been proven based upon the scientific method.

Structural scientists have been criticized for their lack of an adequate or explicit definition of structure. The traditional measure has been those phenomena that constrain or organize human action; this has become in itself a point for debate. Sylvia Hale notes,

> Structure is a broad macro-sociological term, referring to large-scale and long-term patterns of organization in a society. Roughly equivalent to social institutions. In ethnomethodology, the outcome of practical reasoning processes engaged in by sociologists and others, to account for what seems to be going on (Hale, 1995: 578).

The information individuals receive from culture, religion, and the state constrains action. These constraints are discussed in terms of "appropriate" class interaction, "private" versus "public" action, and "normal" versus "abnormal" behaviour. Giddens notes, "the individual under the structural perspective has been criticized as *homo sociologicus*, a passive receptacle for social structure" (Giddens, 1978: 15).

Social scientists argue the goal of social science is to come to the actualization of truth, or to discover truth within the social paradigm. The process commonly used to come to truth by social scientists is the scientific method or some variation of the scientific method. The structural view predisposes two types of knowledge, a common-sense and a specialized knowledge.

The type of knowledge, which an individual acquires through socialization, is largely referred to as common-sense knowledge, while the knowledge of academics, mechanics, medical persons, etc. is deemed a specialized knowledge. Common-sense knowledge can be distinguished from specialized knowledge based upon its use by individuals in reference to areas in which they have no specialization. Specialized knowledge, in contrast, is characterized by its coherence, concise manner of expression, and consistent explanations of phenomena. Armstrong and Armstrong note,

> Theory is an attempt to organize explanations in a systematic way, to develop a connected and logical understanding of how people and social systems work. . . .theory tells us what to look at, how to look, and what to do about what we find (1990: 11).

"FACT"

This brings us to the debate between the two perspectives concerning fact. Is reality an objective truth or is it created and shared by actors? As previously discussed, ethnomethodologists identify all knowledge as common sense, and structural theorists suggest common sense is distinct from scientific knowledge. Giddens's theory of duality presents a debate for each of these perspectives.

The structure and agency perspectives provide contrasting explanations for social interaction and, what Giddens has termed "empire building endeavours." Scholars such as Giddens and Hale have tried to resolve the debate between human agency and constraining structure by linking the two mediums, forming a conception of duality (Giddens, 1984: 02). Hale links social structure and agency with the following solution:

> . . .human actions are shaped by prior human actions. Structures comprise [the consequences of] actions taken collectively in the past. Actions produce structures for the future. What we choose to do now will shape the circumstances that our children inherit (Hale, 1995: 14).

The agency perspective, in arguing for the creation of social structure through the everyday action of human agents, assumes consciousness and choice on the part of the actor. Human agents, in actively creating structure, must first be conscious they are doing so and have the knowledge to fully realize the implications in their choice. In summation, human agency, with the elements of consciousness and choice, relies upon the actor's already knowing every result of the proposed action.

The effects of human action on a future reality is complex and, thus, unreasonable for any one individual to ascertain. Therefore, total consciousness of what is going on is not a realistic assumption when considering human behaviour. If individuals were to perceive the effects on their future realities, we would have a significant decrease in human misfortune.

However, we know this is not the case. Giddens argues that human action is not consistently linked to intent, suggesting all acts have unintentional consequences that feed back to be the unacknowledged conditions of further acts. Giddens notes,

> The consequences of what actors do, intentionally or unintentionally, are events which would not have happened if the actor had [not] behaved differently, but which are not within the scope of the agents power to have brought about regardless of what the agents' intentions were (Giddens, 1984: 11).

The question, therefore, is not choice in action, but rather the unaccountable result(s) of action and how it affects the structure of human social interaction. Hale and Giddens argue that the effects of human action are linked to time and space. It is, therefore, essential to discuss human action and its effects on structure in terms of a historical distribution. Clow and Machum argue, "how things are organized produce situations to which individuals must respond: Individuals respond in three ways: (1) conform, (2) evade or circumvent, and (3) rebel. These responses feed back *over time* to further affect or have no effect on the way activities are organized" (1999: 21).

Human agents are socialized and acquire a set of common-sense understandings of their social world, and further this knowledge helps them to cope with everyday situations. This common-sense knowledge is, as suggested by ethnomethodologists, biographically determined and humans can, with little difficulty, learn to communicate despite their biographical differences (Weeks, 1995). However, common-sense knowledge is fragmented, incoherent, incomplete, and mostly illogical in nature; this knowledge may be full, part, or of no truth (Clow, 1999). Armstrong and Armstrong note,

> We all carry around in our heads some ideas about how people act and why they act the way they do. These explanations, which are often partial, contradictory and illogical, filter our interpretations of the behaviour and institutions we encounter and influence our interactions with others (1990: 11).

Theory, in contrast, is an attempt to provide an explanation that surpasses that of common-sense knowledge based upon coherence, consistency, and testing. Further, scientific knowledge is falsifiable and can be refuted, as compared to, for example, religious knowledge, which is taken or assumed to be "the truth." Theory, therefore, is not to be taken as an absolute truth but only *a claim to truth*. Armstrong and Armstrong argue,

> Theory is an attempt to organize explanations in a systematic way, to develop a connected and logical understanding of how people and social systems work. To be effective, this search for an overall perspective must be grounded by research that investigates how people actually behave... (1990: 11).

Clow raises the question, what makes the understandings of the academic within his particular area of specialization any better than the individual directly involved in the activity? Clow argues that scholars must, (1) produce systematic, coherent, and comprehensive explanations, which are not incomplete and contradictory, and (2) be committed to checking their explanations against the observation of the phenomena they are studying. Clow further suggests that scientists, like other individuals, rely upon common-sense knowledge outside of their area of speciality:

> Outside their narrow area of professional expertise, where they have devoted their best efforts to making some coherent sense out of a small piece of "the world," the minds of most scientists and scholars are no better organized than the average "man-in-the-street" (1999: 07).

I have identified three forms of knowledge: common sense, specialized or scientific, and absolute truth. *Common sense* is a store of knowledge acquired through biographically determined socialization, which actors use in their day-to-day activities. *Scientific knowledge* is an attempt to provide coherent, concise, and consistent explanations of social interaction, and further is not considered an absolute truth but a claim to truth. *The truth* is an absolute and unattainable state of understanding which we can never achieve because there is no way of accounting for all variables, and being fully conscious of doing so.

These forms of knowledge, and their use by social actors and subsequent effects, can be best understood through historical analysis; human agents have little control over the day-to-day organization of their social lives and do not create their moment-to-moment social reality. The way activities are organized constrains the social actors and they may react through conforming, evading, or rebelling (Clow, 1999); this reaction, however, does not have an effect on how things are organized (social structure) at that particular moment. Further, actors experience, interpret, and react to social phenomena (situations) based upon their assumptions which unknowingly, and knowingly, feed back over time to affect the way in which activities are organized (Clow, 1999; Giddens, 1984).

It is logical, then, to approach the question of social knowledge based upon this rationale with a set of scientific, rather than common-sense assumptions. Common-sense knowledge, our socialization, or our assumptions are inherent in all observers and affects all observation of social phenomena, from what we perceive to what we eventually argue is important.

Clow argues that there can be no observation or subsequent explanation without these assumptions:

> All our observations and our explanations (theories) of events in the world, indeed, all our accounts of the world, are marked and shaped by the presence of implicit or explicit assumptions, perspectives and beliefs which precede our observation and theorizing (Clow, 1996: 08).

PROCESS AND EXCLUSION

To this point we have discussed three types of knowledge and their constitution by social actors. In addition, we have interpreted the social construction of "fact" as the process through which social actors make claims to truth. The objectification of "fact" has been replaced with claims to truth based upon common sense and specialized assumptions.

Thus, a "fact" becomes an unattainable claim that could not be made based upon any set of assumptions, whether specialized or common. Knowledge and knowing then become the best humanity can achieve under the limited consciousness that we employ as social theorists. Social theorists, either academic or non-academic, who suggest they have the "facts," consider knowledge to be a complete truth rather than a constructed truth.

The social construction of knowledge is a process that involves legitimizing the best claim to truth. The construction of "fact" then becomes apparent to all participating in the construction process. The realization that your claim can be falsified allows for emancipation or the empowerment of those individuals participating.

What is the process through which one claim to truth is replaced by another claim to truth as the best representation of "fact"? An adequate answer to this question would involve a complete description too lengthy to complete here. However, characteristics of the process relevant to our discussion can be explored, specifically who is participating and who regulates the construction of "fact."

Academics, grass-root activists, and women's coalitions have undertaken a critical examination of government cuts to our social safety system. This examination represents a critical social inquiry because it challenges the claims to truth made by government in reaction to the concerns of its citizens. In addition, the claims made by grass-root coalitions, academics, and government are all taken, upon first examination, to be derived from a specialized knowledge.

Scholars such as Michael Foucault, Noam Chomsky, and Dorothy Smith have determined that power relations in the discussion of "fact" are unequal. The unequal power relations inherent in their discussions have been explored in relation to social institutions, such as legal, medical, educational, and legislative. The foundation of these inquiries has for the most part been critical, utilizing Marxist, Feminist, Foucauldian, and Political Economic Social Theory.

The formal organizations of our society have traditionally been constructed from the social position of men, the economically privileged, and the Caucasian race (Smith, 1990). This has determined how members of these institutions have interacted with those members of society who were not male, wealthy, and white. The result is the social construction of reality from one position and the subsequent exclusion of all claims to truth that do not agree with that position.

How have formal social organizations processed the claims to truth by those individuals who were not male, wealthy, or white? Macdonald, Noonan, and Beaman (forthcoming in

MacDonald) argue that the legal process, a formal social organization, has reshaped the experiences of marginalized individuals to fit the knowledge categories of those institutions. These authors bring attention to the exclusion of specific claims to truth by the very processes through which individuals are purported to be enabled.

One example of the process through which the legal institution reshapes the experiences of women was brought to my attention at a humans rights conference in the summer of 1998.[3] One individual informed me that she had been denied maternity leave on the basis that she had not given birth to the child. The legal process or organization was defining "mother," in relation to maternity leave, as biological and not social.

The result is the manipulation of claims to truth made by women, minorities, and the poor to support the agenda of the formal institution. Given this point, we can conclude that the empowerment of marginalized groups cannot be achieved through the very formal organizations that oppress them. What course of action can be taken so that the claims to truth made by a marginalized group can be included in the formal creation of truth? How can marginalized groups de-construct the relations of oppression reproduced and enforced by the formal institutions of society?

ANALYSIS

The federal government of Canada wishes to eliminate our sole means of counteracting the poverty inherent in capitalist economic development. The federal government has reduced transfer payments since the 1994–1995 fiscal year by three billion, four hundred and thirty-three million dollars. The provincial governments of Canada were forced, in response to these cuts to reduce the amount of payments to municipal governments, healthcare, and the social welfare system (National Council of Welfare, 1997: 5).

Since 1991, the percentage of Canadian people living in poverty has risen from approximately 16 to 18 percent. In addition, the number of Canadian children living in poverty has risen from approximately 18 to 21 percent. These statistics suggest the reduction of transfer payments to provincial governments is socially unjustified (National Council of Welfare, 1998: 11).

If the reduction of transfer payments is not socially justified then the question arises, is it economically justified? In addition to reducing transfer payments during a time of social crisis in Canada, the federal government has continued to subsidize the business ventures of the economic elite. This would suggest that their cuts are not only socially unjustified but economically unjustified as well. Clarke argues,[4]

> ... corporate tax revenues have dropped from approximately fifteen percent to as low as five percent of overall federal revenues.... More than 80 000 profitable corporations in Canada end up paying no income taxes at all due to numerous tax loopholes and write-offs. (1997: 78).

During a time of social and economic crisis, the federal government has rewarded the tax-paying and working poor of Canada by neglecting them. Instead of addressing the social and economic concerns of the Canadian citizen, the federal government has chosen to subsidize profitable business by reducing transfer payments to our social safety net. In addition, the federal government has failed to provide or plan for the one solution to our problem, the creation of sustainable jobs.

The government has failed to protect the working citizen of Canada by allowing economic policies such as the North American Free Trade Agreement to be protected. The government of Canada has promoted the migration of companies from Canada to Mexico without any sufficient explanation.[5] What interest does the Canadian government have in supporting the exploitation of the Mexican people by multinational corporations?

Given these statistics and subsequent conclusions, how has the federal government responded to opposition leaders, academics, and grass-root protest movements who have voiced their concerns? The federal government has responded in three ways: (1) by ignoring the concerns of their constituents and the statistics, (2) by responding to peaceful protesters through the use of violence, and (3) by making an alternative argument concerning the economy, their actions, and the statistics.

The federal government's first and second response to the concerns of the Canadian public are deplorable and inadequate. However, these responses are consistent with the federal government's policy when dealing with opposition to its interests up to this point. Therefore, these two responses provide no alarming reaction on my part as a Canadian citizen because they have been anticipated.

They have been anticipated especially when the Canadian government deals with the Aboriginal communities of Canada. Some instances of violence inflicted on all Canadians are Oka, Kingsclear, and the student APEC protest. I was present at the Kingsclear tax-protest and witnessed first-hand the violence inflicted on Native children, by the RCMP, when they were gassed. What immediate physical threat do Native children pose to RCMP officers carrying guns?

Further, what threat do student protesters carrying signs pose to RCMP officers carrying guns and wearing bullet-proof vests? The Canadian government clearly fears the international political repercussion of student protesters far more than it does its own citizens. If our government were truly democratic, would they have gassed the student protesters? If the Canadian populace had control over the operation of government, would the Liberal government still be in power?

The third reaction is more interesting than the previous two because the federal government has taken "X" and argued that it is really "Y." For convenience I will restate "X": "X" = instead of addressing the social and economic concerns of the Canadian citizen, the federal government has chosen to subsidize profitable business by reducing transfer payments to our social safety net. As shown, all the evidence to this point suggests that "X" is indeed the correct conclusion.

The federal government has responded with "Y": "Y" = the majority of the individuals who make use of the social safety net (social assistance) are not victims of capitalism and federal mismanagement but are simply lazy. Further, the government argues that these individuals do not want to work, because there are plenty of jobs available for them in the job market. The response of the federal government has been to blame the victim and not the system (Ricciutelli et al., 1998).

The claim to truth made by government officials is grounded in a discussion that excludes those on social assistance and those who are concerned with the deconstruction of our social safety net. Further, this logic is developed after claim "X" is brought to the attention of the government and supports the state agenda. The discussion of claim "X" is framed in terms of normalization, the individual, and economics.

What form has the state's discussion of "X" taken in response to those who protest against the reduction of transfer payments? The form of the state's discussion in the process of constructing knowledge is normative. The state has made a number of claims to truth that presents a normative categorization of the issues and events. The state claims that the norm of the Canadian economy is that there are jobs for those who wish to work.

Therefore, by developing a norm based upon their interests and their evidence, they also create the abnormal. The normal or normative idea that they construct, for example, *there are jobs in Canada for those who wish to work,* becomes the measure by which each additional idea in the process of constructing knowledge is evaluated. Thus, claims to truth that do not agree with *there are jobs in Canada for those who wish to work* become the abnormal.

The reference point in the process of constructing knowledge is predetermined and in the government's favour. Examples such as *there are not enough jobs in Canada for those who wish to work* are seen as deviant and not representing the "truth." Fixing the construction of knowledge as a process allows governments to endorse fabricated truths based upon the normative reference point that they have constructed.

For example, one use of the normative reference could be that the "normal" Canadian citizen has no need for social assistance because they are ambitious and will find work because it exists. In addition, the economy has become increasingly better since the 1991 recession ended and the need for services has decreased. If you need the service then you are not a "normal" Canadian citizen but a lazy and unambitious individual (Hillyard-Little, 1994).

The "normal" Canadian citizen should be concerned with the reduction of the deficit which is fundamental to healthy economic growth. In addition, the "normal" Canadian should embrace the opportunities provided by a more efficient private system of Medicare and government services. Further, the "normal" Canadian should welcome the freedom provided through contract employment and ensure their financial security.

The discussion of social welfare and its validity for those using the system has not been framed in terms of basic human needs and rights but rather in terms of the individual. The Canadian government has framed the discussion of social welfare in terms of deficit reduction and overspending. The validity of the system for the "normal" Canadian is not questioned; indeed one assumes that if the "normal" Canadian needed social welfare then it would be available.

The individuals who use social welfare are deficient in that they do not fit the norm and therefore are not of concern to the functioning of the system. Further, these individuals are left over from an earlier and less efficient era in which the social welfare system created dependents. In addition, social welfare recipients really do not need the support provided to them and will always be on assistance if it is available to them (Banfield, 1970).

As stated earlier, by excluding the voice of marginalized people from the formal discussion of "fact," the state is subjecting and oppressing these individuals to truth claims that do not agree with their social position or their experience of social reality. The result in most instances is horrific because it places undue stress on these individuals and decreases the quality of their lives. However, in the case of welfare recipients it is even worse because they are stripped of their humanity and are subjected to subhuman standards of living.

> Stereotyping permits the conventional member of society to feel justified in strong, even savage condemnation; if an individual is a member of a despised category and shares a host of undesirable characteristics with them, then unambiguous hostility toward him or her should not only be expected, it is demanded. (Goode and Ben-Yehuda, 1994: 72)

The use of the normative frames of discussion by the Canadian government to legitimize their political agenda accomplishes the dehumanization of welfare recipients by segregating them from the average Canadian. This, as Goode and Ben-Yehuda argue, allows and demands that the Canadian population support cuts to the social system — and the implementation of subhuman conditions for welfare recipients.

Some quotations from a government text on the feelings of dehumanization felt by welfare recipients express well the Canadian government's treatment of its own citizens,[6]

> Vouchers are a humiliation that inevitably shakes our already shaken self-esteem and hence our *confidence* without which we *cannot get off* assistance. (Federal-Provincial Study Group, Date unknown; original emphasis).
>
> I'm not human to them and I have to be subservient or they just won't even talk to me. (Hillyard-Little, 1994: 243).
>
> ... I promised that the coming year that I would buy all he needed (school supplies) even if it meant dog-food for supper, after all what's good enough for the injuns is good enough for us. He did not think that was very funny but he did go back to school. (Federal-Provincial Study Group, Date unknown).

Before 1991 and the current cuts to transfer payments, there was sufficient evidence to support the claim that welfare recipients received less than was required for a minimal standard of living. The following quotations have been extracted from a text published by the Canadian government before the cuts were implemented. These quotations define well the state of our welfare system before the government decided to abandon its citizens in favour of corporate interests.

> ... why can't they have apples and oranges like other kids? (Federal-Provincial Study Group, Date unknown).
>
> One dentist told me he didn't take welfare cases anymore. Another dentist told me to get someone else to remove three stitches. I did it myself. (Federal-Provincial Study Group, Date unknown).

Before the cuts, a welfare recipient with three children only received 72.5% of the money needed to feed a family of three, in accordance with the basic food requirements of the Canada food guide (Hillyard-Little, 1994: 239). The social welfare assistance that was received has, according to Hillyard-Little, always been below the subsistence level. This is appalling in a country that excuses 80 000 profitable corporations a year from paying taxes (Clarke, 1997: 78).

The information presented in this section provides a picture of welfare recipients before the cuts and allows some speculation concerning the state of social assistance today. The deconstruction of the system, in the face of rising unemployment and the increase of Canadians living below the poverty line, suggests that the picture of the average Canadian presented by the government is misleading. What interest does the state have in manipulating "X" to appear as "Y"?

The federal government wishes to legitimize their current economic strategy that is geared toward global competition, based upon attracting multinational corporations to Canada. Further, Hillyard-Little (1994) argues that the Canadian government's cuts to the assistance plan is funding this economic strategy and the move toward a privatized state. Further, the state monopoly over formal knowledge-creating institutions allows the Canadian government to facilitate the fabrication of myth; rather than relying on specialized knowledge and statistics.

CONCLUSION

Two perspectives concerning the social construction of knowledge were discussed in this chapter. The first perspective argued that social agents create their social reality from moment to moment. The second perspective argued that social reality is predetermined and constrains social actors.

The discussion of knowledge and "fact" brought attention to common-sense and specialized knowledge types. Common-sense knowledge is based upon biographically determined experience, and specialized knowledge is based upon scientific inquiry. The conclusion of the "fact" section is that there are three forms of knowledge including, common sense, specialized, and true fact.

True fact is not attainable and the discussion of "fact" becomes a forum where claims to truth are made based upon common-sense or specialized knowledge. One claim to truth may be sustained and reproduced or replaced by another claim to truth. This is the process of constructing knowledge that has been pointed out as exclusionary. The shape of the "fact" discussion is exclusionary because it allows the empowerment of few and the marginalization of many.

The state represents a participant in the process through which claims to truth are made, reproduced, and replaced. The role of the state has been traditionally defined as an avenue through which the Canadian citizen's opinion would be heard. As discussed, specific groups are marginalized through the very state institutions that are said to empower them.

The example that we cited was the dehumanization of welfare recipients and their construction as "lazy" by state institutions that wish to legitimize cuts to the Canadian welfare system. By replacing a strong claim to truth with a weaker claim to truth, the government engages in the manufacture of myth to support state agenda. This allows for the reproduction of state control through myth rather than the reproduction of knowledge.

The social construction of welfare recipients as "lazy," thus, represents a process through which the state gains control over the Canadian population through the manipulation of a claim to truth. By dehumanizing the segment of the Canadian population adversely affected by the state agenda, the Canadian government has been able to support the deconstruction of the Canadian welfare state.

ENDNOTES

1. Method is the act of collecting evidence and methodology is the logic that the act of data collection is based upon.

2. For example, Dorothy Smith (1987) has developed a political economy of sorts but relies upon a dual interpretation of reality.

3. The Atlantic Human Rights Conference (summer of 1998) at St. Thomas University in Fredericton, New Brunswick.

4. I first saw a variation of this quotation in O'Neill, E (1997). *From Global Economies to Local Cuts: Globalization and Structural Change in Our Own Backyard.* In Ricciutelli, L. et al. (eds.). (1997). *Confronting The Cuts: A Sourcebook for Women in Ontario.* Toronto: Inanna Publications and Education Inc.

5. Recently, the Volvo plant near Halifax, Nova Scotia, was scheduled to shut down and move to Mexico.

6. I would like to draw attention to the reference to Aboriginal peoples in the third quote. It demonstrates well the state of dehumanization felt by these people, as the Canadian gov-

ernment has for years used the tactic of dehumanization to legitimize the genocide of Canada's Aboriginal population.

REFERENCES

Armstrong, P. and Armstrong, H. (1990). *Theorizing Women's Work*, Toronto: Garamond Press.

Banfield, E (1970). In Finsterbusch, K. and McKenna, G. (eds. Fifth edition). (1988). *Taking Sides: Clashing Views on Controversial Social Issues*. Dushkin Publishing Group, Inc.

Becker, H. (1993). *How I Learned What a Crock Was*. In *The Journal of Contemporary Ethnography*, Vol. 22 No. 1, April 1993, 28–35. Sage Publications, Inc.

Best, S. (1995). *The Politics of Historical Vision: Marx, Foucault, Habermas*. New York: The Guilford Press.

Clow, M. (1997) "The Sociological Approach." A chapter in the draft of *Society and Ecology: A Social Science Approach to The Ecological Crisis* (an unpublished manuscript). Fredericton: Department of Sociology, St. Thomas University.

Durkheim, E. (1938) *What is a Social Fact.* pp. 1–13 in *The Rules of Sociological Method*, 2nd ed. Edited by George Catlin. New York: The Free Press, 1938.

Federal-Provincial Study Group. (unknown), *Welfare Recipients Speak for Themselves*. Canada: Health and Welfare Canada.

Finsterbusch, K. and McKenna, G. (eds. Fifth edition). (1988). *Taking Sides: Clashing Views on Controversial Social Issues*. Dushkin Publishing Group, Inc.

Giddens, A. (1978). *The Class Structure of the Advanced Societies*. London: Hutchinson.

Giddens, A. (1984). *The Constitution of Society: Outline of the Theory of Structuration*. Berkeley: University of California Press.

Goode, E. and Ben-Yehuda, Nachman. (1994) *Moral Panics: The Social Construction of Deviance*. Cambridge: Blackwell.

Hale, S. 1990, 1995 (2nd ed). *Controversies in Sociology: A Canadian Introduction*. Toronto: Copp Clark Pitman Ltd.

Hillyard-Little, M. (1994) *"Manhunts and bingo blabs": The moral regulation of Ontario single mothers.* In *The Canadian Journal of Sociology* 19(2):1994.

National Council of Welfare. (1997). *Another Look at Welfare Reform*. Canada.

National Council of Welfare. (1998). *Profiles of Welfare: Myths and Realities*. Canada.

National Council of Welfare. (1998). *Poverty Profile*. Canada.

Nozick, M (1992). *No Place Like Home: Building Sustainable Communities*. The Canadian Council for Social Development.

O'Neill, E. (1997). *From Global Economies to Local Cuts: Globalization and Structural Change in Our Own Backyard*. In Ricciutelli, L. et al. (eds.). (1997). *Confronting The Cuts: A Sourcebook for Women in Ontario*. Toronto: Inanna Publications and Education Inc.

Pierson, C. (1991). *Beyond The Welfare State?* Pennsylvania: The Pennsylvania State University Press.

Ricciutelli, L. et al. (eds.). (1998) *Confronting The Cuts: A Sourcebook for Women in Ontario.* Toronto: Inanna Publications and Education Inc.

Smith, D. (1987). *The Everyday World as Problematic: A Feminist Sociology.* Toronto: University of Toronto Press.

Smith, D. (1990). *Conceptual Practices of Power: A Feminist Sociology of Knowledge.* Toronto: University of Toronto Press.

Schutz, A. (1963). *Common-Sense and Scientific Interpretation of Human Action.* In Natanson, M. (ed.), *Philosophy of the Social Sciences: A Reader* (pp. 302–346). New York: Random House.

Weeks, P. (1995) *Ethnomethodology.* 5th ed. In Hale, S. 1990, 1995 (2nd ed). *Controversies in Sociology: A Canadian Introduction.* Toronto: Copp Clark Pitman Ltd.

"LEAVING NORMAL" Constructing the Family at the Movies and in Law

C h a p t e r 10

Rebecca Johnson

INTRODUCTION

> Families have long been viewed as among the most essential and universal units of society. This sense of the shared experience of family has led to an often unexamined consensus regarding what exactly constitutes a family. Thus, while we speak of families as though we all know what family [are], we see no need to define the concepts embedded within the term. [footnotes omitted]

(Franklin 1990–91: 1051–52)

Ian Hacking argues that some things, like bacteria, seem to exist independent of description. Other things, particular things that humans do, seem to be intimately connected to our descriptions of those things (Hacking 1986: 230). As Franklin points out in the quotation which opened this section, people often function as if families (like bacteria?) existed independent of description. As she puts it, "the family is often regarded in law as a private social force, the existence of which the law must respect and take into account, rather than as an entity which is defined by the law itself." (Franklin 1995: 1051–52) However, when one is called upon to provide an account of either the content of the family, or of its social significance, the "unexamined consensus" falls apart. One is then forced to confront the ways in which our notions of family are indeed intimately tied to the ways in which we describe the family, and purposes for which we construct our definitions.

In this paper, I explore the ways in which "normal" and "deviant" families are constructed, both in popular culture and in law. From popular culture, I examine the portrayal of normal family life in the movie, *Leaving Normal*. From law, I examine the judgment of the Supreme Court of Canada in *Mossop v. Canada*.[1] In both instances, I explore the ways in which popular and legal discourses participate in shaping societal visions of the normal family. I will suggest that while these discourses often construct a narrow description of the normal family, this description is not monolithic. Indeed, within both popular culture and law, one encounters counter-hegemonic moments, that is, moments where the discourses suggest room for other ways of thinking about how the concepts of normalcy and deviance apply to life within the family.

POPULAR CULTURE AND THE "NORMAL" FAMILY

Our descriptions of the world around us are intimately tied to our beliefs about that world. Indeed, as John Berger argued in the BBC production "Ways of Seeing," the very way we see things is affected by what we know or what we believe. (Berger, 1972). And the way we see things matters because, as Richard Dyer puts it, "How we are seen determines in part how we are treated; how we treat others is based on how we see them; such seeing comes from representation." (Millbank 1996: 452).

All societies construct symbolic boundaries, boundaries that establish the limits of acceptable and unacceptable identity and behaviour. The boundaries are policed and maintained in part through representations of normalcy and deviance. Some of these representations emerge in society's formal mechanisms of control, such as law. So the law, for example, represents certain kinds of families (and family behaviours) as normal, and prescribes a variety of punishments for families whose behaviour deviates from that which is represented within law as normal. In this way, law's representations of the family serve to delineate that which is safe/normal and that which is dangerous/deviant.

But these formal mechanisms of control are not the only ones operational within society. Formal mechanisms always run alongside a series of informal mechanisms of social control, such as norms, standards, beliefs, and expectations (Gavigan, 1986). These informal norms can be just as powerful as the formal mechanisms. Indeed, as Foucault reminds us, power's success is often proportional to its ability to hide its own mechanisms (Foucault, 1990; 1978: 86). Thus, it is useful to examine the ways that informal mechanisms of social control such as popular culture participate in the production and maintenance of certain visions of the family as normal or deviant.

Certainly, the average evening of television viewing confirms that popular culture does indeed reflect a certain range of family forms as "normal." In general, the norm is of a middle-class heterosexual couple with children. While other kinds of families are also present in popular culture (e.g., the single-parent family, the working mother, the poor family), families that do not conform to the standard are often treated as humorous, anomalous, as failures, as unfortunate. In the popular media, such families are all too often vilified, and held responsible for a number of social woes (Rivers, 1996).

However, while popular cultural representations of the family often serve to maintain the current order, culture is never simply order-maintaining. Because culture operates at the level of symbolic representation, it not only constructs and maintains social order, it also bears the seeds of social transformation (Eisenstadt, 1992). Thus, any examination of popular culture should be attentive to the ways in which particular texts maintain or subvert the current order. It is this capacity to change things that makes certain texts (be they books, movies, or legal judgments) so important. As bell hooks says,

> Movies make magic. They change things. ... [G]iving audiences what is real is precisely what movies do not do. They give the reimagined, reinvented version of the real. It may look like something familiar, but in actuality it is a different universe from the world of the real. That's what makes movies so compelling. (hooks, 1996: 1)

Some texts, be they books, movies or judgments, are particularly compelling in this way. As writer Jeanett Winterson puts it, "Strong texts work along the borders of our minds and alter what already exists. They could not do this if they merely reflected what already exists." (hooks, 1996: 2). The movie *Leaving Normal* is one such strong text.

The movie begins with a close-up of Marianne as a small girl, singing and drawing a picture: a mother, a father, and two children, standing happily in front of a house. Her singing gradually is drowned out by other sounds: adults yelling at each other, and a young girl crying. As Marianne continues drawing and singing "Twinkle, Twinkle, Little Star" quietly to herself, we understand that her picture is not a family portrait, but is a wish: the wish for a different kind of family. The picture represents not the family she is part of, but the family of her imagination: a "normal" family — a family with proper roots. As the opening credits begin to roll by, we see the family in a van, on the road at night and on the move again, the young Marianne sitting in the back, looking up at the stars and wishing. Her childhood drawing of the normal family is the ideological background against which the remaining action in the film takes place.

The action moves to the present, where an adult Marianne (played by Meg Tilly) is in a bus and on the road again. Through a series of snapshot conversations she holds with various passengers, we learn that she has just married a man she doesn't really know, and is moving to a town named Normal to start a life with him. Will theirs be the normal family she has been searching for all this time? We next see Marianne happily arranging things in the kitchen of a small house. Her husband enters the room, and within seconds, slaps her across the face for "yapping, and messing with my stuff." A stunned looking Marianne grabs her coat and walks out the door. The action shifts to the local bar, where the hardened and smart-mouthed waitress Darly (Christine Lahti) is bidding farewell to the local drunks, and attempting to apologize to a fellow waitress for having slept with the woman's husband ("twice ... a week ... for two years"). Darly is ecstatic over news that her ship has come in: her ex-husband has died, and she has re-inherited the house in Alaska that the two of them had started building during their short marriage 15 years earlier. Darly is quitting her job, and heading for Alaska.

As Darly leaves the bar she passes Marianne, who is sitting (penniless) at the bus stop weeping. Darly, in high spirits, offers to drop Marianne off a few states away at her older sister's house. They arrive at Marianne's sister's house. At this point in the movie, Marianne's childhood drawing again emerges as a ghostly overlay. Indeed, her sister seems to have found the normal family of Marianne's imagination: a husband, a child, an upper-middle-class home. And yet, as viewers, we do not feel an affinity with this superficially normal family. Darly is invited to spend the night, while the sister and brother-in-law attempt to intervene in Marianne's life, offering to get her a normal job, so she can start a normal life. In the middle of the night, this vision of fearful normalcy becomes too much, and Marianne decides not to stay with her sister and her "normal" family, but rather to follow Darly to Alaska. The two women sneak out of the house in the early morning, and make their escape.

But the road trip takes a catastrophic turn: Darly's car first breaks down, and then is destroyed by vandals. The women hitch a ride with an odd trucker named Leon, and his emotional and sensitive novel-reading nephew Harry. The women sneak off at a truck stop, sticking Harry and Leon (who thinks he is going to get some action) with the bill. They then end up on the road with the truck stop's talkative and rotund waitress "CC." CC, who has a car and mobile home, quits her job and joins the women in their road trip in order to return to her search for true love ("It must exist, because I have spent so much time looking for it!"). And though Darly mocks the concept of true love, it is not long before true love does indeed find CC. The very skinny millionaire Dan Earl Spicy Jones ("the third largest spice and herb farmer in western Canada") falls in love with CC at first sight. CC gives her car and trailer to Darly and Marianne as a parting gift, saying gently, "You are not the best friends I have ever had, but you are certainly the most recent."

And so the two women continue towards Darly's dream home in Alaska. On the way, details of Darly's family life emerge as the two women share stories about each other's pasts. It is clear that Darly's life did not conform to a vision of normal. She met her husband while she was a dancer in a strip club. Worse yet, she finally reveals to a shocked Marianne, "I split on my kid when she was two days old. One thing I'm in the hospital, next thing I know, I'm on the road." The two women finally arrive in Alaska. However, like everything else along the way, it turns out differently than expected. The home Darly expects to see, and that Marianne hopes to share, turns out to be no more than an abandoned shell. Darly's ex-husband abandoned work on it the day she abandoned him 15 years earlier. The house is a mere frame, no walls, only a hint of roof. Further, it is littered with garbage from two homeless illiterate teenaged Inuit boys who are squatting there.

The two women, in shock but tired from their travels, decide to stay there for a short while. They let the two boys (whose father is in jail) continue to live around the house in exchange for their help in cleaning up the site. The two women find jobs in town, Marianne begins teaching the boys to read, Darly confronts the past she has left behind, and Marianne begins confronting the dreams she has been chasing. Harry comes to Alaska to find Marianne, but Marianne decides not to follow love on the road, but to stay in Alaska. Darly fills out forms that might someday enable her abandoned daughter to find her. Having travelled as far from Normal as one can, the women find some kind of peace in Alaska. The movie ends with a scene of the strangely configured foursome (Marianne, Darly, and the two Inuit boys), sitting at the dinner table in the house without walls. We hear Darly saying "get your elbows off the table," and "eat your vegetables." This is the familiar language of the family dinner table. The language brings to memory Marianne's childhood drawing of the family of her dreams. As the camera pulls back and the picture begins to fade away, we hear Darly saying grace: "Please bless this home and family, whatever the hell it is ... and please help us to keep going somehow."

Leaving Normal is a strong text that works along the borders of the mind. The movie creates an eclectic world, a reimagined, reinvented version of the real. One can see order-transforming elements in the movie in the ways that it plays explicitly with the notion of "normal" in the context of family relationships. Indeed, in its very title, the movie announces its challenge to societally held assumptions about normal and deviant families. The title, "Leaving Normal" is both pun and road map. The film is a road movie that starts in the town of Normal. It follows the adventures of Marianne and Darly as they leave Normal, and head for Alaska. But on a more complex level, the movie raises a series of continually emerging questions: What is normal? What does it mean to leave normal behind? What might lie at the end of the road for those who do leave normal behind? The movie asks us to question the meaning of "normal" as it is currently constructed.

To situate its challenge, the movie begins by foregrounding its opponent: the ideological stronghold of the normal family. The movie does not explicitly articulate all the norms that make up the social representation of the normal family. It relies on the "unexamined consensus regarding what exactly constitutes a family," and the norms that make up this consensus are captured and suggested in Marianne's initial drawing. Marianne is driven by the dream of a normal life, with a normal family and normal roots. It is this search that brings her to the town of Normal. Here, the movie is suggestive. What is not normal in the situation? Is it the speed with which Marianne enters her short-lived marriage, or is it the violence she encounters there? Is the violence an aberration, or is it normal? Certainly, Marianne's husband justifies himself by explaining his reaction as the normal one of a husband whose wife has yapped and messed with his stuff. If this is so, in running from the marriage, is Marianne running to or from normalcy? Normal or not, this violence is far from the stuff of Marianne's childhood dreaming. In leaving Normal, she is continuing her searching for the ideal family and home.

Darly, though less idealistic than Marianne, has also lived her life in the shadow of images of normalcy. The difference is that while Marianne has been running towards the ever elusive ideal family and home, Darly has been running away. She chose to abandon husband and child, perhaps attempting to avoid what she saw as the prison of normalcy. But whether running towards or running away from, both Marianne and Darly's lives have unfolded against the ever present (though rarely articulated) vision of the normal family.

The search for normal continually leaves the women coming up short. In the end, it is only once the women have driven as far from Normal as one can go, that an authentic family begins to emerge. It is in Alaska that Marianne and Darly stop searching and running, and start constructing. The family at the end of the movie is not the "mother, father, two children, and house" of Marianne's drawing. Nonetheless, as viewers we see it as a family. Watching Marianne, Darly, and the Inuit boys, the viewer is left with a sense of "rightness," a sense that the women (and the boys) have constructed a family that, for all its oddness, is nonetheless "normal." If anything is flawed, it is the ideology of normalcy, and not the family that has been constructed.

The movie plays with the vast chasm between the unexamined consensus regarding the normal family, and the lives of the main characters. Though the main characters do not conform to the norms, we are drawn to sympathize and identify with them. The movie does not focus on their deviance, but rather serves to destabilize the social consensus that would characterize these people as deviant. The movie offers to the viewers a stream of alternative representations of relationships and families. It characterizes the supposedly normal life of Marianne's sister as nightmarish, and we cheer when the women sneak out and escape to the road. It also decentres notions of romantic love by illustrating them in unexpected and bizarre contexts: the very obese waitress CC and the skinny and strange-looking millionaire Canadian herb farmer fall in love during a single dance. Harry tries to find Marianne by sending form letters to every woman with her name in every state. Very little in the movie manages to replicate traditional views of normalcy. Indeed, the movie is peopled almost entirely with characters and situations that are "deviant." And yet, as viewers we come to see these characters positively: though they do not fit well with the stereotypical norms, there is something about their behaviours that seems fitting, that seems right.

In the end, the movie both assumes and challenges common assumptions about what makes a normal family. Marianne's search for family ends only once she has left Normal behind. And the movie manages to highlight the constructedness of the family. For very clearly, the family Marianne ends up with is a construction: it is less something found, than something achieved. It is something pieced together out of scraps and remnants from the fabric of divergent lives. But the movie does not simply show us that Marianne and Darly's family is a construction. It hints that all families are just such constructions. That a family is a construction does not diminish the value of that family. Marianne had been attempting to construct a family all along. However, her attempts to find something of value were continually subverted by her adherence to a set of ideas about what a normal family was supposed to look like. It was only once she set aside those images that she found herself in the middle of the thing she had been searching for. As she put it, "I didn't choose this, it chose me. We were just making it up as we went along."

One of the interesting things about movies is that they explicitly allow for multiple viewpoints. In a movie like *Leaving Normal*, we can see how informal mechanisms of social control both identify the dominant representations of family, and allow for challenges to those representations. In the section that follows, I turn my attention to one of the more formal mechanisms of social control: the law. I will examine how the law represents the family as normal or deviant. I will argue that legal judgments (just like movies), reveal the presence of multiple and sometimes conflicting representations of normalcy and deviance within the family.

LAW AND THE "NORMAL" FAMILY

> Laws never tell the whole story. Yet they matter. They allow and sometimes even instigate change."
>
> (Eisenstein 1994: 50)

Law matters. And for those interested in the construction of normal and deviant families, the law matters in complex ways. It functions as an instrument both of coercion, and of persuasion. While discussions about the law often focus on the explicitly coercive potential of law, it is important not to underestimate the persuasive power of law. A large measure of law's persuasive power lies in the power of naming. As Pierre Bourdieu tells us, the law, through its judgments, confers identity, status, and powers upon various actors. "Law is the quintessential form of the symbolic power of naming that creates the things named, and creates social groups in particular."(Bourdieu 1987: 838). One of the social groups that law participates in creating is the family.

Of course, as I pointed out in the section above, the law is not alone in this creative venture. There are dialectical relationships between various interpretations existing in popular culture and law. To return to Bourdieu's analysis of the power of law, "[i]t would not be excessive to say that [law] *creates* the social world, but only if we remember that it is this world which first creates the law."(Bourdieu 1987: 839). But while both popular culture and law contain representations of normalcy, it is important to remain attentive to significant differences in the enforcement of those representations. The law can back up its representations with coercive force. It can use this coercive force to compel individuals to act in accordance with law's description of the world. The law's power to define the normal and deviant family matters in important ways because the law can allocate benefits to those whose lives match the law's dictates, while reserving punishments for those who deviate from the law's norms. Indeed, in support of its representations, law has the power to restrain, hurt, render helpless, even kill (Cover 1986).

But the law not only coerces, it also attempts to persuade. Indeed, the legitimacy of law's coercive force depends in some measure on the ability of legal discourse to convince those who hear its pronouncements, that those pronouncements are justified in light of some social reality. As Robert Gordon reminds us,

> The power exerted by a legal regime consists less in the force that it can bring to bear against violators of its rules than in its capacity to persuade people that the world described in its images and categories is the only attainable world in which a sane person would want to live (Gordon, 1984: 109).

How then does the law describe the normal family, and attempt to persuade us of the legitimacy of its description? First, it is important to remain aware that the law does not provide a single monolithic definition of family. Although most people have an image of what constitutes a "traditional" family, neither legislation nor the common law reflects a consistent definition. The legal definition of family changes somewhat from context to context. So, for example, some individuals may be a family for the purposes of income assistance under welfare legislation, but not a family for the purpose of income tax legislation (Freeman, 1994: 58).

But while there is some flexibility in definition, the law has consistently defined some kinds of families as deviant. In particular, the law has revealed its general unwillingness to see same-sex couples as families. Jody Freeman articulates the problem as follows:

> [T]he field of "family" law is implicitly based on a heterosexual norm. Although no statute explicitly defines "family" for all purposes, and despite the fact that one can find inconsistency in the definition if one searches for it, an impressive variety of legislation, legal holdings, rules, and omissions, taken together, nonetheless reinforce the notion that a "normal" family comprises two heterosexual parents and their children (Freeman, 1994: 44–45).

Even where laws have prohibited discrimination based on sexual orientation, law has at the same time continued to represent the same-sex relationships as deviant through definitions of spouse that require the parties to be of the opposite sex. This requirement means that same-sex marriage is definitionally impossible.[2] Through such definitions and exclusions, the law constructs a vision of the normal family that places same-sex couples into the category of deviant. Such a vision is evident in the Supreme Court of Canada decision in *Mossop v. Canada.*

Brian Mossop and his partner, Ken Popert, had known each other since 1974, and had lived together since 1976 in a jointly owned and maintained home. Each was the beneficiary of the other's will, and they were known to their friends, family, and acquaintances as a couple. In 1985, Mossop was employed as a translator for the Secretary of State. In June of that year, Popert's father died, and Mossop took a day off work to attend the funeral. Under the terms of his collective agreement, he was entitled to up to four days of bereavement leave upon the death of a member of his immediate family. The day after the funeral, Mossop applied for bereavement leave. His request was turned down on the basis that a member of his immediate family had not died. The collective agreement defined "immediate family" as:

> ... father, mother, brother, sister, spouse (including common-law spouse resident with the employee), child (including child of common-law spouse), or ward of the employee, father-in-law, mother-in-law, and in addition a relative who permanently resides in the employee's household or with whom the employee permanently resides.

In the definition section of the collective agreement, the term "common-law spouse" was given more precise meaning:

> ... a "common-law spouse" relationship is said to exist when, for a continuous period of at least one year, an employee has lived with a person of the opposite sex, publicly represented that person to be his/her spouse, and lives and intends to continue to live with that person as if that person were his/her spouse.

Mossop and Popert fell squarely within the definition of "common-law spouse" except for the requirement that they be of the opposite sex. Thus, as far as the collective agreement went, Brian Mossop and Ken Popert were not part of each other's immediate family.

As such, the employer argued, Ken's Popert's father was even more surely not a member of Brian Mossop's immediate family.

Brian Mossop then lodged a complaint with the Canadian Human Rights Commission.[3] According to the 1985 *Canadian Human Rights Act*, employers were prohibited from discriminating against employees on the basis of "race, national or ethnic origin, colour, religion, age, sex, marital status, family status, disability and conviction for which a pardon has been granted." Mossop argued that his employer, by adopting a collective agreement which only recognized a spousal relationship where the parties were of the opposite sex, had discriminated against him on the basis of his family status. The Human Rights Tribunal agreed, concluding that the undefined term "family status" in the *Canadian Human Rights Act* could include same-sex couples, and that the opposite sex requirement was a form of discrimination based on family status.

The employer appealed, and the Federal Court of Appeal reversed the decision of the Tribunal. The Court found that family status meant legal status, and that no such status had been recognized for gay or lesbian couples. Further, they were of the opinion that the "real" issue was sexual orientation and not family status. That is, if there was any discrimination, it was discrimination on the basis of sexual orientation, and the *Canadian Human Rights Act* did not at that time prohibit this form of discrimination.[4]

The Supreme Court of Canada then granted leave to appeal, and heard the case.[5] The majority concluded that the term "family status" in the *Canadian Human Rights Act* did not include a homosexual relationship between two individuals, and that the employer had thus not discriminated. Three judges dissented. They concluded that the term "family status" was broad enough to include same-sex couples living together in long-term relationships, and that the employer was guilty of discriminating against Mossop.

The legal system, Gabel tells us, works at many different levels to shape popular consciousness toward accepting the political legitimacy of the status quo. (Gabel and Harris, 1982–83) Through its interpretive power, the law constructs the normal family as the heterosexual family. In this section, I will explore law's persuasive means. Certainly, the coercive power of the law was brought to bear since the law denied a family-based benefit to Mossop and Popert. Turning though to the persuasive power of law, I will explore how the majority judges attempt to persuade the reader that the "normal family" excludes same-sex couples, and how the dissenting judges attempt to persuade the reader of the opposite proposition. What kinds of justifications do the majority judges use to explain why their interpretation of the normal family should have social force? At the same time, what kinds of challenges to the status quo can be seen in the dissenting judgment?

The Majority (Chief Justice Lamer, Justice La Forest, Justice Sopinka, Justice Iacobucci)

Two judges wrote decisions for the majority. Those reasons are slightly different. The first was written by Chief Justice Lamer, who begins by stating that the only issue before the Court was the proper interpretation of the phrase "family status." The Court was to determine who was currently included within the family. The Court was not to decide whether or not the government *should* extend benefits to same-sex couples. Chief Justice Lamer's first technique of persuasion is to evoke a boundary between neutral observation of the world, and political decision-making. Here, he portrays the Court as a neutral decision-maker, called upon to neutrally cast its gaze outwards in order to tell us "what is." Such language tends to imply the existence of some existing reality called "family."

But before telling us what this objective reality is, Chief Justice Lamer introduces a second technique of persuasion: the language of choice and blame. Chief Justice Lamer informs the reader that Mossop had been invited to amend the action to bring an equality claim under s. 15 of the *Canadian Charter of Rights and Freedoms*.[6] He had been asked to argue that the *Canadian Human Rights Act* violated the *Charter* by failing to include protection on the basis of sexual orientation. That is, rather than deciding whether the employer had commited family status discrimination against Mossop under the *Canadian Human Rights Act,* Chief Justice Lamer wanted to discuss whether or not Parliament's failure to prohibit sexual orientation discrimination in the *Canadian Human Rights Act* was a violation of the equality provisions of the *Charter of Rights and Freedoms*.[7] Put simply, Chief Justice Lamer wanted to discuss the case in terms of sexual orientation, and not in terms of family status. Mossop, however, wanted the focus to be on the meaning of family and not the meaning of sexual orientation. He was not asking the court to tell Parliament to amend the *Canadian Human Rights Act* to prohibit sexual orientation discrimination. Rather, he was asking the court to conclude that the actions of his employer already constituted discrimination on the basis of family status. Thus, Mossop declined to amend his claim. Chief Justice Lamer informs the reader of this decision, and takes Mossop to task for insisting that the court focus not on sexual orientation, but on family status. He suggests that Mossop's eventual loss is thus Mossop's own fault. According to Chief Justice Lamer, if the case must be examined using the lens of family rather than the lens of sexual orientation, the Court has no choice but to rule against Mossop.[8]

How does he come to this conclusion that the refusal of the bereavement leave benefit could not constitute discrimination on the basis of family status? First, Chief Justice Lamer finds that the meaning of the phrase "family status" cannot be discerned without considering the relevance of sexual orientation. In 1983, Parliament chose to prohibit discrimination on the basis of "family status." They did not, however, prohibit discrimination on the basis of "sexual orientation." This action, he concludes, shows that Parliament intended that family status protection be reserved exclusively for heterosexual families. An attempt to include same-sex couples within the term "family status" would be a way of indirectly introducing protection based on sexual orientation, and Parliament had specifically chosen not to extend such protection. Further, Chief Justice Lamer commented, such an interpretation would lead to anomalous results: "while homosexuals who are not couples would receive no protection under the Act, those who are would be protected" (Mossop, 673).[9] In short, if discrimination involves sexual orientation, it cannot also involve discrimination on the basis of family status. Family status must somehow be free from the taint of sexual orientation. Given the absence of sexual orientation protection, sexual orientation must be used to interpret the scope of family status. The two categories are, he concludes, mutually exclusive.

The second of the two majority judgments was written by Justice La Forest. He, like Chief Justice Lamer, focuses on the meaning of "family status." He relies on his observation that the dominant conception of the family is what he calls the "traditional family." While he does not provide a definition of the traditional family, it is clear that, as he uses the term, it does not include "relationships dependent on a same-sex living arrangement" (Mossop, 676). Like Chief Justice Lamer, Justice La Forest states that it may well be that Parliament should grant bereavement leave to homosexual couples as it does to heterosexual couples. However, he adds, that is an issue for Parliament to address, not an issue for the courts. On his interpretation of the language, Parliament did not intend that same-sex couples should receive this kind of benefit, and it is not for the courts to overturn this legislative intention. According to Justice La Forest, Parliament has clearly defined the meaning of "family status." The Court's job, according to him, is not to substitute its own vision for that of Parliament, but is only to declare what Parliament's vision is. In short, it is the government, and not the courts, who have determined the meaning of the phrase "family status." The Court's job is not to determine the meaning, but only to enforce the meaning which was given to the term by Parliament.

It is interesting that both majority judgments use language which suggests that the Court is constrained: they don't necessarily think that the phrase "family status" should exclude same-sex couples, but they state that such an interpretation is the one adopted by the government. It is not the place of the courts, they argue, to overturn the clear intention of Parliament. This argument is compelling on one level. Certainly, there is value to a division of powers between the government and the judiciary. One would be concerned if an unelected judiciary were to regularly overrule the decisions of elected decision makers. However, the majority assertion that Parliament expressly chose to exclude same-sex couples begins to seem a bit suspicious when one looks more closely at comments made by various governmental officials. Indeed, the evidence seems to be that, in the face of debate on this very issue, Parliament chose *not* to provide a statutory definition of the phrase "family status." Rather, Parliament determined that the task of giving meaning to the phrase should be left to the human rights tribunals who would be administering the *Canadian Human Rights Act*. Indeed, the Minister of Justice said, "It will be up to the commission, the tribunals it appoints, and in the final cases, the courts, to ascertain in a given case the meaning to be given to these concepts"[10] He added, "These words are being interpreted by the Canadian Human Rights Commission. We trust them to interpret and issue regulations."[11] In light of such comments, it looks suspiciously as though the majority judges are inventing a Parliamentary intent that did not otherwise exist. Indeed, despite their protestations to the contrary, the majority do in fact put forward their own interpretation of the phrase "family status," but do so in a way that suggests that the decision is made by Parliament, and not by themselves. In the end, they tell us, they are bound by an objective reality. Family status cannot be used to extend protection designed for normal families to same-sex couples. Without telling the reader exactly what *is* included in the family, they tell the reader what is *not* included. In effect, this is negative interpretation. A quite different approach is taken by the judges in dissent.

The Dissent: (Madam Justice L'Heureux-Dubé, Justice Cory, Madam Justice McLachlin)

Madam Justice L'Heureux-Dubé begins by stating that the meaning of highly controversial terms (such as "family") cannot be settled by linguistic fiat. Indeed, she argues, if one examines the purpose of the *Canadian Human Rights Act*, the text itself, and the intent of Parliament in extending protection, it is clear that "family status" must mean something more than simply the traditional family. She suggests that any sense of consensus as to the meaning of family may well be illusory. Indeed, the unexamined consensus begins to fall apart as soon as one examines it more closely. To persuade the reader of the ambiguity of the term "family status," she provides a number of differing definitions of the family. It is useful to review these definitions, as they do illustrate the difficulty of finding a working definition.[12]

Census Canada defines family as "a husband and wife (with or without children who have never been married, regardless of age) or a parent with one or more children never married, living in the same dwelling. A family may consist, also, of a man or woman living with a guardianship child or ward under 21 years of age for whom no pay was received."[13]

The American Home Economics Association (AHEA) defines a family as "two or more persons who share resources, share responsibility for decisions, share values and goals, and have commitments to one another over time."[14] Kenneth G. Terkelson defines a family as a "small social system made up of individuals related to each other by reason of strong reciprocal affections and loyalties, and comprising a permanent household (or cluster of households) that persists over years and decades."[15] M. Stuart says there are five critical attributes to the concept of family: 1. The family is a system or unit; 2. Its members may or may not be related and may or may not live together; 3. The unit may or may not contain children; 4. There is commitment and attachment among unit members that include future obligation; 5. The unit care-giving functions consist of protection, nourishment, and socialization of its members.[16] Dr. Margrit Eichler suggests that attempts to define the family invariably result in exclusion and that it is more appropriate to talk about families, or familial interaction. She states that this interaction occurs in several dimensions: the procreative dimension; the socialization dimension; the sexual dimension; the residential dimension; the economic dimension; and the emotional dimension.[17] Lorraine M. Wright and M. Leahey comment:

> Designating a group of people with a term such as "couple," "nuclear family," "single parent family," specifies attributes of membership, but these distinctions of grouping are not more or less "families" by reason of labelling. It is the attributes of affection, strong emotional ties, a sense of belonging and durability of membership that determine family composition. We have found the following definition of family to be most useful in our clinical work: the family is who they say they are.[18]

The variety in the definitions gives one a clear sense of how contested the notion of family really is. By providing this host of definitions, Madam Justice L'Heureux-Dubé illustrates the weakness of the majority's interpretation of family status. It is interesting to recall that the majority judges argued that they were not defining the meaning of family, but were merely articulating the definition intended by Parliament: the court was not "creating" the family — the family was a creation of society (Parliament). Such a position evokes Bourdieu's comment about the relationship between law and society. In the dissent, Madam Justice L'Heureux-Dubé also invokes the relationship between law and society, but this invocation leads her to a different conclusion. She reminds the reader, "the family is not merely a creation of law ... the changing nature of family relationships also has an impact on the law." (Mossop, 706). Rather than asserting a definition allegedly constructed by society (Parliament), she looks at the changing nature of family relationships within society in order to arrive at the most apt legal definition of the family.

In examining the changing nature of family relationships, Madam Justice L'Heureux-Dubé alerts the reader to the distance that sometimes exists between ideological visions and reality. While the "traditional family," captured in reruns of "Ozzie and Harriet," may exert an ideological force on the public imagination, Madam Justice L'Heureux-Dubé relies on current statistics to reveal that a very large number of Canadians do not live within the boundaries of that ideologically rooted traditional family. Indeed, the evidence brought forward in the case established that the traditional family form co-exists with numerous other family forms. The form taken by the family, be it traditional or otherwise, may be a choice for some. But for others, she says, the structure of the family may be part of a natural response to changing social and political pressures. The definition of family, she concludes, must be capable of adapting to the changed family structures which are the result of these pressures.

In order to define the scope of protection for family status, Madam Justice L'Heureux-Dubé argues that it is essential not to look at specific family forms, but rather at the values that lie at the base of societal support for the family. After reviewing a number of these values, she quotes Jane E. Larson, who said, "It is the social utility of families that we all recognize, not any one proper form that 'the family' must assume; it is the responsibility and community that the family creates that is its most important social function and its social value" (Larson, 1992: 1014). Madam Justice L'Heureux-Dubé concludes that, "if there is value in encouraging individuals to form stable and emotionally intimate relationships, such relationships can be forged and maintained in a wide variety of family forms." (Mossop, 710). In her judgment, she suggests that the definition should focus on the functions filled by the grouping, and draws the conclusion that Mossop and Popert were no less a family for being of the same sex than other couples would be for being of the opposite sex. That is, there was no reason to define the same-sex couple or family as anything other than normal.

In the majority and the dissenting judgments, we see quite different techniques of persuasion, techniques designed to garner support for quite different interpretations of the boundaries of the normal family. The majority engage in definition by negative implication: we don't learn what the family "is," but we are told what the family "is not." The majority obscures its own participation in the construction of this definition: making reference to undefined terms like "traditional family," and to the intention of elected representatives, the majority relies on a division between the legal and the political.

The dissenters, who are seeking to displace the above definition, attempt to persuade by emphasizing the relationship between law and society. Making significant reference to societal factors, they seek to establish that a narrow legal definition must give way in the face of a changed social reality. Rather than making reference to a narrow vision of Parliamentary intent, the dissenters rely on a broader vision of social values: values which suggest the necessity of a broader vision of family.

Of course, the dissenters remain just that: dissenters. The majority view prevailed, and the coercive power of law was used to deny benefits to Mossop and Popert. But what are the implications of the case for the question, "what is the normal family?" While Mossop did not win, it is not clear the case should be seen as a loss. First, compared with many other cases of this nature, there was relatively little at stake economically. Indeed, there was really no money at stake. Mossop had taken one day off work and, while his employer did not want to call it bereavement leave, they did offer him a day of "special leave." The issue was not a monetary one as much as a symbolic one: it was about the recognition and acknowledgment of Mossop and Popert's "family." It was an attempt to have the law see that they were there, and that they were "normal" rather than "deviant." The majority was not prepared to give them this symbolic win. However, on another front, there were some gains. Three of the judges used the language of nomalcy rather than deviance. They looked at Mossop and Popert and saw a family, not just a collection of unconnected individuals. Further, the case served to raise questions in the larger community. Why *should* this relationship be treated differently than other common-law relationships? Was bereavement important only to heterosexuals? Should society assume that same-sex couples do not suffer when their loved ones die?

The close split on the court illustrates the increasing weakness of a representation of the family which portrays it as an exclusively two-parent heterosexual union with children. The persuasive power of this representation becomes even weaker as the courts addresss questions about "why"? Why is it important socially that the family assume a certain form? What functions do we expect the family to fill? Is form as important as substance? If a given form fills the functions of family, should we treat it as family? Even within a single legal judgment, the reader is exposed to both order-maintaining and order-transforming representations of the family. At the end of the day, the question is: which representations are more persuasive to the reader?

CONCLUSION

How should one describe the boundary of the normal family? Whatever way one chooses to describe the boundaries, it is clear that not all families will negotiate the boundaries in ways that are satisfactory either to their members, or to the larger society of which they are a part. Nonetheless, whether looking at popular culture or law, a close examination of the family requires us to ask why it is necessary to define the family in the first place. For what purposes do we define families as normal or deviant? The answer to this question depends in part on what we think families are, or what we think they should be. Is the normal family a matter of form or of function? That is, are we concerned with "who" makes up a family, or with "what" a family should do?

What then is the normal family? In both *Leaving Normal* and *Mossop v. Canada,* we see how a focus on deviance takes attention off the hard work of constructing and deconstructing that is continually going on. Indeed, both film and legal judgment suggest that we may participate in maintaining current visions of deviance and normalcy through the simple act of neglecting to critically examine our assumptions about the family. Film and law are two arenas of representation where one cannot only participate in stabilizing a status quo, but can also attempt to re-configure what is. Film does this by encouraging the watcher to create new subject positions, to imagine the subject differently. In *Leaving Normal*, we imagine a different kind of family. Legal discourse functions in a very similar fashion, and encourages the reader to believe that the family is a specific kind of objective reality. In *Mossop v. Canada,* the majority and dissent present us with different visions of the family, one excluding the other including same-sex couples.

Our notions of what is a normal or deviant family are part of a larger symbolic system. And, as Bourdieu reminds us, symbolic systems are not something that, like bacteria, simply exist. They are living and changing social constructions. This is important to acknowledge since, as Bourdieu puts it:

> if we grant that symbolic systems are social products that contribute to making the world, that they do not simply mirror social relations but help constitute them, then one can, within limits, transform the world by transforming its representation (Bourdieu and Wacquant, 1992: 14).

ENDNOTES

1. *Mossop v. Canada* (1993), 100 D.L.R. (4th) 658. All quotations used in this article will refer to the D.LR. version of the case, and will be cited simply as "Mossop" with the page number following.

2. For a classic example, consider the case of *Layland v. Ontario* (1993), 104 D.L.R. (4th) 214. In this Ontario case, two men wanted to get married, and attempted to get a marriage licence. The clerk refused the license. The court upheld a challenge to this refusal, saying that there was a common law prohibition against the marriage of same-sex couples. In this case, the judge said that this requirement did not discriminate on the basis of sexual orientation. The requirement did not prevent gays and lesbians from

marrying — it only prohibited them from marrying someone of the same sex. So, for example, a lesbian would be granted to marriage license as long as she intended to marry a man. Once can't help but raise a quizzical eyebrow at the notion that this requirement does not discriminate. The judge seems to assume that sexual orientation (or rather, sexual orientation for gays and lesbians) is irrelevant to one's choice of life partner. Certainly, one doubts that the judge would have been so sanguine if the legislation had prohibited people of the opposite sex entering into marriage with each other.

3. In Canada, complaints about discrimination in the workforce are dealt with under provincial and federal human rights acts. These acts generally prohibit employers from discriminating against their employees on the basis of things such as race, religion, sex, disability, etc. Where an employee believes that his/her employer's behaviour has been discriminatory, the employee can make a complaint to the relevant human rights commission. Since Mossop was employed by the federal government, his complaint was made to the federal Canadian Human Rights Commission (which deals with the government as an employer). When a person complains to a human rights commission, the commission will first try to resolve the problem through discussion and mediation with the parties. If the matter cannot be resolved, the parties will appear before a human rights tribunal. These tribunals are somewhat like courts, but they deal only with complaints of discrimination under the human rights acts. Each party will present his/her argument to the tribunal, and the tribunal will then make a decision. If one of the parties feels that the tribunal made a mistake in applying the law, an appeal can be made to the Court of Appeal. Similarly, if the Court of Appeal makes an error in the law, then a party can seek leave to appeal to the Supreme Court. If the Supreme Court is of the opinion that the problem is a matter of national concern, they may grant an appeal, and hear the case. That is exactly what happened in Mossop.

4. A bit of history may be in order here. While the various provincial and federal human rights codes are similar in many respects, there are some differences. For example, while each of these pieces of legislation prohibit discrimination on the basis of race, only some of them prohibit discrimination on the basis of political opinion. At the time the Mossop case was brought, only Quebec prohibited discrimination on the basis of sexual orientation. Thus, if Mossop had complained that he was suffering discrimination on the basis of sexual orientation, there would have been no remedy: the *Canadian Human Rights Act* did not prevent employers from discriminating on that basis. Things did change significantly, however, during the 1980s and 1990s. Currently, each of the provincial and federal human rights codes in Canada has been amended (either by legislatures or by courts) to include a prohibition on sexual orientation discrimination. Further, many employers have, on their own initiative, modified their benefits packages to ensure that similar benefits are provided to their employees regardless of sexual orientation.

5. When the Supreme Court hears a case, they sit in a panel with an uneven number of judges (5, 7, or 9, depending on a number of factors including the seriousness of the case). Where the judges all agree about the resolution of the case, they write a single judgement (sometime referred to as a "unanimous judgement"). Of course, the judges do not always agree. In such cases, the side that "wins" is the one that gets the support of a majority of the judges. The winning side is called the majority, and the other side is called the dissent. Sometimes the judges disagree not about the outcome of the case,

but rather about the reasons for the outcome. They then write separate judgements explaining the reasons for their disagreement. These reasons are important, because they explain how the judge would resolve future similar problems where the facts were slightly different. So, in a single case, there may be more than one judgment on the majority side, or more than one dissenting judgement. Indeed, in rare cases, there are nearly as many sets of reasons as there are judges who listened to the case.

6. Section 15(1) of the *Charter* says: "Every individual is equal before and under the law and has the right to the equal protection and equal benefit of the law without discrimination and, in particular, without discrimination based on race, national or ethnic origin, colour, religion, sex, age or mental or physical disability." The section does not contain any explicit reference to sexual orientation. However, in an earlier case called *Andrews v. Law Society of British Columbia*, [1989] 1 S.C.R. 143, the court concluded that the list of enumerated grounds in section 15 was not exhaustive. Because the language of the text says "and, in particular," the Court had concluded that the government would also be prohibited from discriminating against citizens on grounds that were analogous to those that were listed. In the *Andrews* case, the court had concluded that "citizenship" was analogous to the enumerated grounds. At the time the Mossop case was being argued, there were several cases where lower courts had concluded that "sexual orientation" was also an analogous ground of discrimination. However, none of those cases had yet come before the Supreme Court of Canada, so there had been no occasion for a definitive statement confirming or rejecting this conclusion.

7. To clarify the distinction between the case Mossop brought and the case Chief Justice Lamer *wanted* Mossop to bring, it is useful to keep in mind that s. 15(1) of the *Charter* does not apply directly to relationships between individual citizens. It only applies to the relationship between the citizen and the government. Section 15(1) of the *Charter* does not prohibit one citizen from discriminating against another citizen, or an employer from discriminating against an employee. The relationship of citizens to each other is regulated by provincial and federal human rights codes, such as the *Canadian Human Rights Act*. These codes (or acts) do prevent citizens from discriminating against other citizens, but they do so on more limited terms than those set out in the *Charter*. Thus, an employer may be allowed to continue with a discriminatory employment practice if there is a good reason for the practice. For example, consider an employer who requires all employees on a construction site to wear hard hats. People who do not wear these hard hats are fired. This requirement would have the effect of discriminating against Sikh employees, who would be unable to wear a hard hat because of their religious commitment to cover their hair in a turban. However, under a human rights act, the employer could nonetheless insist on the hard hats because of safety issues on construction sites. Even though the hard hat requirement does have an unintended discriminatory effect, it is also a bona fide occupational requirement. For more on this, see *Bhinder v. C.N.R.*, [1985] 2 S.C.R. 561. In this way, human rights codes mediate between various competing interests (ie. equality and safety) in relationships between individual citizens. The *Charter* guarantee of equality is a rather different beast, as it regulates the constitutional status of governmental action. Here, Chief Justice Lamer does not wish to examine the dispute between employer and employee over

the meaning of family. Rather, he is interested in a possible constitutional dispute between the government and the courts involving the scope of the analogous grounds in s. 15 of the *Charter*.

8. At the time the *Mossop* judgement was issued, many activists suggested that this was a postive note in the judgement. It suggested, they argued, that Chief Justice Lamer would have ruled in favour of Mossop had the case been brought as a s. 15 *Charter* challenge. Two years later, in the case, *Egan and Nesbit v. Canada*, [1995] 2 SCR 713, two men brought the very kind of challenge that Chief Justice Lamer had punished Mossop for not bringing. Egan and Nesbit argued that Parliament was discriminating against them on the basis of sexual orientation by restricting certain pension benefits to exclusively opposite-sex couples. On the basis of comments made in *Mossop*, one might have expected Chief Justice Lamer to be sympathetic to this claim. However, in an interesting about face, Chief Justice Lamer concluded that the pension benefit could legitimately be withheld from same-sex couples. With the benefit of hindsight, is it difficult not to see Chief Justice Lamer's comment in *Mossop* as rather disingenous.

9. This is interesting logic. The implication is that, for example, lesbians or gays who are also black should not be able to argue that they have suffered discrimination based on race.

10. "Minutes of Proceedings and Evidence of the Standing Committee on Justice and Legal Affairs," Issue No. 114, December 20, 1982, at p. 17.

11. "Minutes of Proceedings and Evidence of the Standing Committee on Justice and Legal Affairs," Issue No. 115, December 21, 1982, at p. 73.

12. These definitions appear in the Mossop dissent, on pages 704–706.

13. Jean E. Veevers, *The Family in Canada,* 1971 Census of Canada, Vol. 5, Pt. 3, Catalogue 99–725, bulletin 5.3–3 (1977) at p. 3.

14. Irene Diamond, ed., *Families, Politics and Public Policy: A Feminist Dialogue on Women and the State* (New York: Longman, 1983), at p. 8.

15. Kenneth G. Terkelson, "Toward a Theory of the Family Life Cycle," in B. Carter and N. McGoldrick, eds., *The Family Life Cycle: A Framework for Family Therapy* (New York: Gardner Press, 1980), p. 23.

16. M. Stuart, "An Analysis of the Concept of Family" in Ann L. Whall and Jacqueline-Fawcett, eds., *Family Theory Development in Nursing: State of the Science and Art* (Philadelphia: F.A. Davis, 1991), p. 40.

17. Margrit Eichler, *Families in Canada Today: Recent Changes and Their Policy Consequences*, 2nd. 3d. (Toronto: Gage, 1988).

18. Lorraine M. Wright and M. Leahey, *Nurses and Families: A Guide to Family Assessment and Intervention*, 2nd ed. (Philadelphia: F.A. Davis, 1994) at 3–3, 3–4.

REFERENCES

Berger, J. 1972. *Ways of Seeing*. London: British Broadcasting Corporation.

Bourdieu, P. 1987. 'The Force of Law: Toward a Sociology of the Juridical Field'. *Hastings Law Journal* 38: 805–853.

Bourdieu, P. and Wacquant, L.J.D. 1992. *An Invitation to Reflexive Sociology*. Chicago: University of Chicago Press.

Cover, R.M. 1986. 'Violence and the Word'. *Yale Law Journal* 95: 1601.

Eisenstadt, S.N. 1992. 'The Order-Maintaining and Order-Transforming Dimensions of Culture' in Münch, R. and Smelser, N.J. (eds.) *Theory of Culture*. Berkeley: University of California Press.

Eisenstein, Z.R. 1994. *The Color of Gender: Reimagining Democracy*. Berkeley: University of California Press.

Foucault, M. 1990 (1978). *The History of Sexuality, Volume 1: An Introduction*. New York: Vintage Books.

Franklin, K. 1990–1991. 'A Family Like Any Other Family: Alternative Methods of Defining Family in Law' *New York University Review of Law & Social Change 18*: 1027.

Freeman, J. 1994. 'Defining Family in Mossop v. DSS: The Challenge of Anti-Essentialism and Interactive Discrimination for Human Rights Litigation'. *U of T.L.J.* 44: 41–96.

Gabel, P. and Harris, P. 1982–83. 'Building Power and Breaking Images: Critical Legal Theory and the Practice of Law'. *Review of Law and Social Change* 11: 369–411.

Gavigan, S.A.M. 1986. 'Women, Law and Patriarchal Relations: Perspectives within the Sociology of Law' in Boyd, N. (ed.) *The Social Dimensions of Law*. Scarborough, Ont.: Prentice-Hall Canada Inc.

Gordon, R. 1984. 'Critical Legal Histories'. *Stanford Law Review* 36: 57.

Hacking, I. 1986. 'Making Up People' in Heller, T.C. (ed.) *Reconstructing Individualism: Autonomy, Individuality, and the Self in Western Thought*. Stanford, CA: Stanford University Press.

hooks, b. 1996. *Reel to Real: Race, Sex, and Class at the Movies*. New York: Routledge.

Larson, J. 1992. 'Discussion'. *Cornell Law Review* 77: 1012.

Millbank, J. 1996. 'From Butch to Butcher's Knife: Film, Crime and Lesbian Sexuality'. *Sydney Law Review* 18: 431–473.

Rivers, C. 1996. *Slick Spins and Fractured Facts: How Cultural Myths Distort the News*. New York: Columbia University Press.

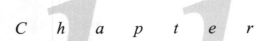

C h a p t e r

THE GOOD
MOTHER

Sandra Wachholz

INTRODUCTION

Over the last two decades in Canada a growing number of feminist scholars have sought to explore and delineate the constellation of ideas and images that constitute what has come to be known as the "ideology of motherhood" (Boyd, 1989; Day, 1990; Findlay, 1997; Kline, 1993; Nelson, 1996). Central to this ideology, as Kline (1993) suggests, are the core assumptions that motherhood is a natural, desired, and ultimate goal for most women, that women should be largely responsible for the care of children,[1] and that motherhood should function within a heterosexual family framework — one that is "... nuclear in form, patriarchal in content" (Gavigan, 1993: 597).

Intersecting with the ideologies of family and womanhood, the ideology of motherhood has done much to shape and limit women's lives and to construct the criteria of "good" and "bad" mothers. Historically, women who have deviated from the ideals set forth by the ideology of motherhood have often been subject to being constructed as deviant, "unfit'"mothers. Within this ideological framework, lesbian mothers are particularly vulnerable to being considered "bad mothers" since they depart, on several accounts, from such ideals (Glenn, et al., 1994; Kline, 1993; Roberts, 1993a; Roberts, 1993b). As Day (1990) notes, "Motherhood for straight women is a fulfillment of a social role expectation, while motherhood for lesbians is seen as an antithesis" (p. 36). Thus, in both "pursuing" and "doing" motherhood in a heterosexual, patriarchal milieu, lesbians are often confronted with a myriad of social and legal difficulties based on their sexuality. These difficulties, in turn, are frequently more complex for those lesbians who also face the additional challenges of, for example, racism and classism. Heterosexism does not function within a vacuum, but rather operates in complex interaction with other forms of oppression (Kline, 1993).

It is important to note, however, that lesbian mothers are not simply passive victims. Through a variety of individual and collective political actions, they have sought to resist and challenge the central assumptions of the ideology of motherhood. Indeed, the very existence of lesbian motherhood can be thought of as an act of resistance to the ideology of motherhood; it is an expanding practice that threatens the hold of this belief system (Fineman, 1991).

With this in mind, this chapter explores the different ways in which the ideology of motherhood constructs lesbian mothers as deviant and the concomitant difficulties that this poses for these women. Some of the actions that have been taken by lesbian mothers to defy this oppression are also discussed. To date, feminists writing in the area of crime and deviance have devoted surprisingly little attention to this subject. This is an unfortunate hiatus given the level of oppression that many lesbians endure pursuant to being constructed as deviant through the ideology of motherhood. Thus, drawing on the narratives of lesbian mothers, this chapter seeks to make visible and confront one of the many social constructions of deviance in our everyday lives that fosters human suffering.

The chapter begins with a succinct review of the nature and core assumptions of the ideology of motherhood. Thereafter, it addresses the ways in which the ideology of motherhood constructs lesbian mothers as deviant and "bad" mothers, and the difficulties that this poses for them in the areas of pursuing, maintaining, sharing, and managing motherhood.

THE IDEOLOGY OF MOTHERHOOD: GOOD AND BAD MOTHERS

Motherhood, as Fineman (1991) suggests, is "... a colonized concept — an event physically practiced and experienced by women, but occupied and defined by the core concepts of patriarchal ideology" (p. 289). Thus, although the experience of having a mother/child relationship can be the source of great happiness for women, motherhood is thought to play an important role in the reinforcement of patriarchy and the other forms of oppression that women experience (Lewin, 1993; Roberts, 1993a; Roberts, 1993b). The institution of motherhood, and its attendant ideals about the proper roles and behaviour for women, is identified as having done much to shape and limit the choices that women make about their lives (Kline, 1993; Glenn, et al., 1994).

Notably, the images and ideas that surround motherhood and which establish ideals about "good" and "bad" mothers and "good" and "bad" mothering constitute what various scholars refer to as the ideology of motherhood. This ideology is complex and is molded not only on the basis of gender, but also on race and other social relations (Findlay, 1997; Roberts, 1993a; Glenn, et al., 1994). As Roberts (1993a) underscores, "Patriarchy does not treat Black and white motherhood identically ... the image of the Black mother has always diverged from and often contradicted the image of white motherhood" (p. 6). As such, the ideology of motherhood is not simply a coherent world view, but rather can be thought of as a constellation of different discourses about motherhood against which women's lives are judged (Boyd, 1989).

However, it is important to indicate that while the ideology of motherhood is complex and dynamic, various scholars suggest that there are several core assumptions that constitute this belief system. As noted earlier, the first of these assumptions is that motherhood is a natural and essential goal for most women. The ideological and structural pressure that society exerts on most women to be mothers is thought to render motherhood compulsory under patriarchy (Fineman, 1991; Roberts, 1993b; Wilson, 1991). Motherhood, as Roberts (1993a) argues, is "... a woman's major social role" (p. 10). As such, the status of childbearer is thought to be intrinsically tied to womanhood.

The second core expectation embedded within the ideology of motherhood is that women should be largely responsible for the well-being and care of children. Childcare has been constructed as an obligation that is both normal and inevitable for most females. This is not to suggest, however, that this assumption has not undergone some alteration over time. The ideology of motherhood, and its attendant components, have experienced shifts pursuant to the feminist movement and changes in the political economy of capitalism. While a complete discussion of the history and evolution of this ideology is beyond the scope of this chapter, it now has, for example, some countenance for the 'working mother' and over the last decade men have been identified as having an important role in child-rearing. Nonetheless, women are still expected to be the primary care-givers to children (Boyd, 1989; Kline, 1993). It is still assumed that females will fulfill what Kline (1993) refers to as the "primary care requirement" (p. 310).

Concomitant with the expectation that women are largely responsible for the welfare of children is the assumption that women will be "good" mothers regardless of the material and social conditions of their lives. It is presumed that women should be able to subordinate their own needs, to act unselfishly regardless of whether they have sufficient support or financial resources to engage in care-giving (Hutchison, 1992). "Good mothering", as Kline argues, is an act that is presented as "... natural, necessary and universal" for most women regardless of the realities of their lives (p. 315).

The third and final core assumption is that motherhood should function within the ideologically dominant model of family which is heterosexual, nuclear, and patriarchal in nature. While the nuclear family is increasingly less typical, it still provides a prism through which to judge women's lives (Gavigan, 1993). As Fineman (1993) laments:

> Patriarchal ideology may have adopted to twentieth-century shifts in expressions of sexuality and redefinitions of gender roles, but the fundamental composition and nature of the core images remain constant. Mother and child are defined by the patriarch (p. 289).

Thus, under the influence of the ideology of motherhood, the nuclear family, with its defined gender roles and prescription for heterosexuality, continues to be the ideologically dominant family form.

With respect to the impact of the ideology of motherhood, it is important to note that the oppression that it yields manifests itself in a multitude of ways. It has meant, for example, that women have not been able to participate on equal terms with men in the paid labour market given the dictate that they should be the primary care-givers to children. Allocating this responsibility to women has done much to structure the sexual division of labour both within the home and in the public workforce (Boyd, 1989).

In turn, the oppressive nature of the ideology of motherhood is clearly evident in its construction of "good" and "bad" mothers. Women who deviate from the ideals of this ideology are often constructed as "unfit" and are thus subject to social and legal regulation. The women who have been most inclined to be considered "bad" mothers and to be judged most harshly against the ideals of motherhood are those who have been devalued on the basis of their social location. Historically, for example, disabled women, Black women, unmarried women, first nations women, and lesbian women have been most likely to be considered deviant mothers. For such women, motherhood has generally been discouraged. Thus, as Kline (1993) suggests, motherhood can be conceptualized as "... a privilege that can be withheld, both ideologically and in more material ways, from women who are not members of the dominant groups in society or who are otherwise considered 'unfit'" (p. 131).

Within this social construction, then, the women who are classified as "bad" or "unfit" mothers often face significant difficulties. Lesbian mothers, as noted earlier, are one of the groups who are confronted with a range of problems that are driven, in significant ways, by the oppressive nature of the ideology of motherhood. While lesbian mothers face many issues that are not fundamentally different from the problems heterosexual mothers endure, e.g., low income, difficulty finding housing and child care, they are burdened with additional challenges which are based on their sexuality (Day, 1990). The following sections explore some of these challenges that are, as various scholars argue, informed and reinforced by the ideology of motherhood (Findlay, 1997; Nelson, 1996).

PURSUING MOTHERHOOD

As noted, the status of childbearer is considered to be a biological destiny for most women. As such, many women are subject to a great deal of ideological pressure to become mothers (Roberts, 1993). The pursuit of motherhood by lesbians, however, has often been devalued and discouraged (Reimann, 1997). At each stage tied to becoming a mother, lesbians face the possibility of being constructed as deviant and "unfit" for motherhood given the heterosexual prescription imbued within the ideology of motherhood.

For example, the decision by lesbians to have a child is generally not surrounded by a great deal of social and familial support or encouragement (Lewin, 1993; Nelson, 1996; Roberts, 1993). As Nelson (1996) states, "not only are ... [pronatal] expectations absent, the opposite is often true; family and friends expect lesbian women not to have children" (p. 5). In this regard, Nelson (1996) reports that in the course of her in-depth interviews with twelve women who had conceived children within a lesbian relationship, virtually all of the participants indicated that they had to justify their decision to have a child to friends and family members. In turn, many of the women stated that when they informed their immediate family members of their pregnancy or of the decision to have a child, the first question posed to them was "Why?" These mothers were put in the precarious position of having to defend their right to motherhood. Reflecting her frustration at having to justify her decision to pursue motherhood, one of the women in Nelson's (1996) study stated:

> ... I have the right. I can do it, it doesn't matter. And I'd be a better parent than a lot of people, and I might not be as good a parent as a lot of people, but just because I'm lesbian doesn't mean I shouldn't have babies (p. 34).

Under the ideology of motherhood, however, lesbianism and motherhood are often constructed as mutually exclusive choices (Nelson, 1996). Thus, although motherhood is generally considered to be compulsory for most women, when considering motherhood lesbians often bear the task of defending their choice.

Lesbian women seeking motherhood also face many obstacles in their efforts to achieve pregnancy. Although currently the majority of children of lesbian mothers were conceived in prior heterosexual relationships, growing numbers of lesbians, either single or in lesbian relationships, are choosing to have children (Day, 1990; Arnup, 1994). However, at infertility clinics, sperm banks, and family-planning centres across Canada, lesbians face the burden of potentially encountering what Gartrell et al. (1996) refer to as "homophobic gatekeepers" (p. 273). Through both official policies and informal practices, lesbians are routinely being denied access to current reproductive technologies and resources. These practices, in accordance with the ideology of motherhood, "... ensure that the institution of motherhood remains safely contained within the confines of heterosexual marriage" (Arnup, 1994: 115).

Historically, lesbians seeking donor insemination within the bounds of established medical practices have frequently had their applications denied under the guise that such services are only available to married, heterosexual women (Arnup, 1994; Day, 1990; Nelson, 1996). Such practices have been the source of great pain and anguish for many women. As one woman stated with respect to her encounters with a family doctor:

> ... [I] said that I was in a long-term lesbian relationship ... and we decided that we wanted to have a child ... He said, "No, sorry I can't help you with that. That's not something I believe should be done." ... I left and cried all the way home (cited in Nelson, 1996: 54).

It is important to note, however, that there are now a few sperm bank companies and a growing number of physicians in Canada who are willing to assist lesbian women with insemination. In Vancouver, as a case in point, a commercial sperm bank now offers services to lesbians (Findlay, 1997). ReproMed, a Toronto-based company which ships sperm across Canada, also does not screen recipients on the basis of sexual orientation (Nelson, 1996). Assisted insemination through the medical industry is, however, a very expensive option since many provincial health care plans do not cover the full cost of such practices (Nelson, 1996). Thus, low-income lesbian women generally do not have the same level of access to alternative insemination as affluent married couples. In this instance, then, heterosexism and classism function together to deter many lesbian women from such services.

Insemination outside of the medical establishment has, nonetheless, been a long-standing practice among lesbians. As Achilles (1990) states, it is probably "... the oldest, least visible, and most widespread" (p. 288) of the reproductive technologies in use today. For many women, self-insemination has proven to be an effective and accessible means through which to achieve pregnancy. Within some lesbian communities, fairly complex support systems have emerged that consist of individuals who procure donors, verify HIV tests, and transport sperm (Nelson, 1996). As Arnup (1994) underscores, members of the medical establishment who have constructed lesbian women as unfit for alternative insemination and, as such, motherhood, have done much to fuel the development of these support networks. Thus, they can be thought of as forms of resistance to the oppression that lesbian mothers encounter in their pursuit of motherhood.

MAINTAINING MOTHERHOOD

In addition to posing a challenge to lesbians who seek to become mothers, the ideology of motherhood frequently makes it difficult for lesbian women to "maintain" motherhood. Given that lesbian mothers deviate from the heterosexual ideals of the ideology of motherhood, they are vulnerable to being identified by the courts as unfit to maintain motherhood in custody battles with former husbands. Thus, although one of the core assumptions of the ideology of motherhood is that women should be largely responsible for the care of children, this tenet has not functioned in a uniformly advantageous manner for women in custody litigation (Arnup, 1994; Boyd, 1989; Lewin, 1993). As Boyd (1989) notes, "While creating a preference for awarding custody to mothers, the preference only operates when the mother demonstrates conduct or a lifestyle which accords with the assumptions of the ideology of motherhood" (p. 119).

Lesbian women are subject to being treated as deviant and unfit parents under the "best interest of the child" standard which is applied in such cases. Although being lesbian itself is deemed to no longer bar custody, the wide judicial discretion that judges wield when considering the interests of children has meant that the sexual orientation of the parent can seep into custody decisions. There are no formal rules for determining what criteria should be used to judge the best interest of children. Thus, factors such as concern about the exposure of children to "stigma" have been used to deny custodial rights to lesbian mothers (Arnup, 1994; Findlay, 1997). For example, in the first reported Canadian custody dispute involving a lesbian mother, *Case v. Case* (1974), the judge noted that the sexual orientation of the mother was not a relevant consideration. He then went on to describe the father's lifestyle as stable and the mother's as irregular. He awarded custody to the father and noted, "I greatly fear that if these children are raised by the mother they will be too much in contact with people of abnormal tastes and proclivities" (p. 138). In this case, and as research on current lesbian custody cases reveals, judges may enunciate that a mother's sexual orientation plays no role in their decisions, but will then go on to employ stereotypes about lesbians in their consideration of factors relevant to an individual's ability to act as a parent (Arnup, 1989; Findlay, 1997).

The homophobic stereotypes about lesbian mothers that present them as deviant and unfit to maintain motherhood stand in sharp contrast to the findings that appear in the myriad of studies that have sought to examine the psychosocial development and functioning of children raised by lesbians (Gartrell, et al. 1996). Studies that have been designed to compare children reared in lesbian and heterosexual households consistently demonstrate that there are few or no differences between the two groups' development of gender identity and gender role behaviour (Gottman, 1990; Huggins, 1989). In turn, studies have shown that these two groups, when carefully matched, show little difference in terms of their relationships with other children, self-concept, intelligence, and moral judgment (Green et al., 1986; Patterson, 1994). Not surprisingly, research also suggests that heterosexual and lesbian mothers are more similar than different (Gartrell, et al., 1996). Through the use of, for example, the Bem Sex Role Inventory (Kweskin and Cook, 1982) and unstructured in-depth interviews (Javaid, 1993), researchers have found only a very limited number of differences between the two groups. Quite understandably, lesbian mothers do express greater concern about homophobia and custody litigation.

Even against the weight of this research, however, a significant number of judges continue to conflate homophobia and the "best interest of the child" (Findlay, 1997). Thus, in recognition of their vulnerability to the views of these judges, lesbian mothers have tended to develop carefully designed strategies to protect themselves against custody litigation. Some women have reduced their claims to marital property and spousal support while others have chosen to conceal their sexual orientation (Lewin, 1993). As a case in point, one lesbian mother employed the following strategies to avoid custody litigation:

> I'm a lesbian and my kids don't even really know about it. To go back to court over child support would give my ex-husband the opportunity to bring in the lesbian issue again ... And I did make it financially. I took in a boarder, rented out the garage (cited in Lewin, 1993: 169).

Such actions can be thought of as ways in which lesbian mothers negotiate to maintain motherhood in the face of the oppression brought to bear upon them by the ideology of motherhood. As Lewin (1993) underscores, "Custody disputes provide a platform for the performance of gender [and power], a platform on which claims to goodness and value are dramatized and in the process reinforced" (p. 179).

SHARING MOTHERHOOD

The oppressive nature of the ideology of motherhood also manifests itself in a myriad of ways in the lives of lesbian couples who choose to share parenting. The idealized nuclear heterosexual family form, which is informed and reinforced by this ideology, is used as a prism through which to examine and judge lesbian families. Within this context, lesbian women who share motherhood face significant levels of social disapproval and legal discrimination. Such couples find themselves in a "... highly policed, gendered arena" (Reimann, 1997).

In this regard, non-biological mothers in co-parenting lesbian families, are frequently rendered deviant and face legal invisibility. With respect to families where the children were conceived within a lesbian relationship, the legal invisibility of the non-biological mother begins at the point of the birth of the child. Unlike heterosexual couples, the non-biological mothers cannot be registered as a child's co-parent on a birth certificate. This form of legal discrimination is one of many that non-biological mothers encounter given that they have no inherent legal authority over the children that they are parenting. Reflecting this concern, many of the non-biological lesbian mothers that Nelson (1996) interviewed in Alberta spoke of difficulties in getting their children admitted to, for example, day cares, schools, and hospitals, given that they could not prove their maternal identity. As one woman in Nelson's study underscored, these legal barriers can have profound emotional repercussions:

> And it is really hard, because I'm the weird one. Elly's the mom so she's not the weird one, but I'm the second one so I'm the one that's the oddball (p. 86).

It is important to note, however, in situations where two women have decided to conceive and raise a child, non-biological mothers can now acquire parental rights that will be recognized by law through the establishment of a co-parent agreement. This confers custody rights and can be registered as a court order under the *Family Relations Act*. In turn, changes in the *Adoption Act* in 1995 now provide non-biological mothers with the opportunity to adopt a child under the status of "co-mother" in a stepparent adoption. However, if the child has come from a heterosexual relationship, the father's consent is generally required (Findlay, 1997). Nonetheless, such adoptions are still quite rare and expensive. Classism and other forms of oppression function to deter stepparent adoptions (Reimann, 1997). Lesbian women in disadvantaged socio-economic positions are clearly less likely to be in a position to afford the legal fees associated with such adoptions.

In addition to facing legal challenges regarding parental rights, non-biological co-mothers indicate that they often suffer from social invisibility. As Nelson (1996) suggests, these mothers are all too often "... conceptually displaced" (p. 61) given that the ideologically dominant family form does not afford a position for two mothers. As one co-mother explained, "There's a tendency to think of the [lesbian family] as the mother-and-child and her partner" (Nelson, 1996: 61). As such, many non-biological mothers experience marginalization — a problem which can vary significantly pursuant to a woman's social location. While very little research has been completed in this area, factors such as class, race, ethnicity, and age are thought to play an important role in the degree of invisibility that co-mothers experience (Collins, 1994; Reimann, 1997).

The marginalization of non-biological mothers has meant that they have had to struggle to define and secure their parental role in both the private and public spheres of their lives.

Reflecting this challenge, studies indicate that family members of biological mothers may hesitate to acknowledge and respect the maternal role of non-biological mothers (Reimann, 1997). Nelson (1996) found that while most of the biological mothers' parents were willing to accept the child as their grandchild, some were reluctant to acknowledge that the co-mother had a relationship with their daughter and grandchild. As she noted, "Very often the grandparents restricted their interests to their grandchild, largely ignoring their daughter's other 'family'" (p. 106). In some instances, however, the birth of a child meant that the parents and siblings of the lesbian couple were more forthright in their acknowledgment and, in turn, acceptance of the lesbian relationship.

The lack of a socially acknowledged parenting role for non-biological mothers can also be seen in the types of questions that are posed to lesbian couples. Driven by ideological assumptions about the nuclear family form, strangers may stop lesbian couples and ask, "Who is the mother?" Such encounters, as one non-biological co-mother lamented, can be emotionally draining:

> I have no trouble when I'm alone with Jack and somebody asks me, "Is he yours?" And I say, "Yes." When I'm with Janet, if somebody asks, I point to her. It's odd (Reimann, 1997: 165).

It is important to note that such encounters may also be quite hurtful for the biological mother. Instead of being viewed as a member of a co-parenting family, birth-mothers are routinely perceived as single mothers by many. Concerned about the lack of recognition as a member of a lesbian co-parent family, one woman stated:

> Well in the [lesbian] community definitely we're perceived as a family. Iris' family perceives us as a family. My family is learning how to perceive us a family. You know, just because we're lesbians they have some difficulty. They can't see us as a heterosexual family, so there's some resistance (cited in Nelson, 1996: 104).

Lesbian co-parents have, however, developed a number of strategies to deal with the social disapproval that they encounter in their effort to share motherhood. At the individual level, some couples engage in what Blaisure and Allen (1995) refer to as "public acts of equality." This entails a display of actions that are designed to demonstrate that they are equal mothers. These actions take the form of, for example, a lesbian couple's conscious decision to take turns carrying their baby in public.

At the collective level, women have formed lesbian mother support groups as a means to honour, share, and acknowledge their mothering experiences (Reimann, 1997). To that end, activities in these groups include such things as networking, problem solving, and sharing information about nonhomophobic service providers. The groups function to reduce the isolation that many lesbian mothers experience in the current non-supportive social milieu where they are generally constructed as deviant. While such groups can be found in many urban areas in Canada, to date few exist in rural communities. Where they do exist, however, they are thought to be an important resource for couples who are working to renegotiate the meaning of motherhood (Gatrell, et al., 1996).

MANAGING MOTHERHOOD: STIGMA MANAGEMENT

The heterosexual prescription embedded within the ideology of motherhood makes the daily practices of mothering more complex and stressful for lesbians, given that they bear the task of guarding their children against homophobic statements and actions (Day, 1990). Although lesbians face many of the same emotional and practical concerns of heterosexual couples, "doing motherhood" entails engaging in activities to protect their children from homophobic stigma. Reflecting such concerns one woman stated:

> Well, you grow up in this culture with this intense homophobia ... I didn't want to damage my children in any way [due to] dominant cultural stereotypes about lesbians ... They do have to deal with those issues in school or whatever. So I just wanted to be really careful [when I revealed my sexual orientation].[2]

As this statement underscores and as studies indicate, an important part of managing motherhood for lesbians involves stigma management — a task which is even more challenging for those families that have to deal with multiple forms of discrimination and oppression (Gartrell, et al., 1996).

Based on a fear that their children will be ridiculed or ostracized for having lesbian mothers, then, a minority of women conceal their sexual orientation from their children, family, and wider community. While it may not be the only reason for being discreet about their lesbianism, it is clearly a very important one. Explaining this posture, one woman stated:

> I could come out if I wish to come out. But the children do not have the defenses yet, are not strong enough emotionally to face the fear of being out, and what that fear means to them ... Nobody's ready to face that yet ... And I don't want them to be ostracized ... (Nelson, 1996: 78).

In such instances, women segregate their lives into arenas where they are mothers and lesbians. This action requires significant attention to information management and boundary maintenance. Time must be devoted to, for example, making sure that nothing can be found in a woman's home that might reveal her sexual orientation, and she must negotiate a limit on her partner's access to her home (Day, 1990; Lewin, 1994). For these women, as Lewin (1994) notes, "segregation may seem the best way to protect children from being stigmatized" (p. 345).

At another level, the desire to protect their children from homophobic attitudes has meant that some women are only partly open about their lesbianism. In a longitudinal study of 84 lesbian families who had recently conceived a child through donor insemination, almost half (48%) indicated that they would be only relatively open about their sexuality given their concerns about the impact of homophobia on their children (Gartrell, 1996). In this regard, Nelson (1996) found that many of the lesbian mothers she interviewed "kept a low profile" about their sexuality as part of a strategy to shield their children from harm. These women indicated that they exercise great caution when deciding who should have knowledge about their sexual orientation. Thus, as one lesbian mother stated, "Even finding a babysitter takes on an added dimension for lesbian mothers" (Day, 1990: 36).

As a means to deal with discrimination toward their children, studies indicate that educating children about prejudice is a high priority for many lesbian mothers (Gartrell et al., 1996; Lewin, 1994). Underscoring the importance of such education, one prospective mother stated:

> ... [I hope to provide my son with] ... a real appreciation for how much we care for each other, a real appreciation for the variety of ways people relate to other people in the world, and an appreciation for the strengths of living in nontraditional relationships (cited in Gatrell, et al., 1996: 278)

The gay and lesbian support groups that have recently been established in schools also serve as an important means to deal with the stigma and ostracism that children of lesbian parents often encounter from their peers. These groups advocate directly on behalf of gay and lesbian students, but also provide an arena where the children of gay and lesbian parents can come together to share information and concerns with each other (Nelson, 1996).

CONCLUSION

As argued throughout this chapter, the constellation of ideas that constitute the ideology of motherhood create conditions that leave lesbian mothers vulnerable to being constructed as unfit for motherhood. As such, lesbian mothers face a significant array of social and legal difficulties. Starting with the decision to have a child, many lesbian mothers find themselves in non-supportive environments where their desire to conceive is called into question. This is but one of the many challenges that lesbian mothers are confronted with in the process of "pursuing and doing" motherhood in a society where they are subject to being identified as deviant pursuant to the ideology of motherhood.

Despite these drawbacks, however, growing numbers of lesbian women are choosing to pursue motherhood to the extent that there now appears to be a lesbian "baby boom" (Reimann, 1997). While all too often these women experience social disapproval and legal discrimination based on their sexuality, they do, in fact, face many of the same emotional and practical concerns as heterosexual women. As one lesbian mother stated, "A mother is a mother. Some things are no different, lesbian or otherwise" (Day, 1990: 46).

Indeed, recognition of the similarities between lesbian and heterosexual mothers and the ways in which their lives coincide is being facilitated by the growing number of lesbian families and their political activism. This movement, as Nelson (1996) notes, will hopefully encourage more people to reassess their views on what it means to be a mother and on the social construction of "good" and "bad" mothers. After all, as one lesbian mother stated, "Whatever the make-up of the family, if there is love and honesty, then it doesn't matter who's in the family."[3]

ENDNOTES

1. Collins (1994) notes that given African American women's work in paid child care outside of their homes for white children, family members from both genders have played an important role in caring for African American children.

2. In-depth interview in Portland, Maine; April, 1998.

3. In-depth interview in Portland, Maine; April, 1998.

REFERENCES

Achilles, R. (1990). Desperately seeking babies. New technologies of hope and despair. In K. Arnup, A. Levesque, & R. Pierson (Eds), *Delivering motherhood: Maternal ideologies and practices in the 19th and 20th centuries* (pp. 288–299). London: Routledge.

Arnup, K. (1989). "Mothers just like others": Lesbians, divorce, and child custody in Canada. *Canadian Journal of Women and the Law,* 318–32.

Arnup, K. (1994). Finding fathers: Artificial insemination, lesbians, and the law. *Canadian Journal of Women and the Law, 7,* 97–115.

Blaisure, K. and Allen, K. (1995). Feminists and the Ideology and Practice of Marital Equality. *Journal of Marriage and the Family,* 57 (February): 5–19.

Boyd, S. (1989). Child custody, ideologies, and employment. *Canadian Journal of Women and the Law, 3,* 111–133.

Case v. Case (1974), 18 R.F.L. 135 (Sask. Queens Bench).

Collins, P. (1994). Shifting the center: Race, class, and feminist theorizing about motherhood. In E. Glenn, G. Chang & L. Forcey (Eds.), *Mothering: Ideology, experience, and agency* (pp.45–65). New York: Routledge.

Day, D. (1990). Lesbian/motherhood. In S. Stone (Ed.), *Lesbians in Canada* (pp. 35–47). Toronto: Between the Lines.

Findlay, B. (1997). All in the family values. *Canadian Journal of Family and the Law, 14,* 129–196.

Fineman, M. (1991). Images of mothers in poverty discourses. *Duke Law Journal,* 274–295.

Gartrell, N., Hamilton, J., Banks, A., Mosbacher, D., Reed, N., Sparks, C., Bishop, H. (1996). The national lesbian family study: Interviews with prospective mothers. *American Journal of Orthopsychiatry, 66* (2), 272–281.

Gavigan, S. (1993). Paradise lost, paradox revisited: The implications of familial ideology for feminist, lesbian and gay engagement to law. *Osgoode Hall Law Journal, 31* (3), 590–624.

Glenn, E., Chang, G. & Forcey, L. (Eds.). (1994). *Mothering: Ideology, experience, and agency.* New York: Routledge.

Gottman, J. (1990). Children of gay and lesbian parents. In F. Bozett & M. Sussman (Eds), *Homosexuality and family relations* (pp. 177–196). New York: Harrington Park Press.

Green, R. Mandel, Hotvedt, M., Gray, J. & Smith, L. (1986). Lesbian mothers and their children: A comparison with solo parent heterosexual mothers and their children. *Archives of Sexual Behavior, 15* (2), 167–183.

Huggins, S. (1989). A comparative study of self-esteem of adolescent children of divorced lesbian mothers and divorced heterosexual mothers. In F. Bozett (Ed.), *Homosexuality and the family* (pp. 123–135). New York: Harrington Park Press.

Hutchison, E. (1992). Child welfare as a woman's issue. *Families in societiy: The journal of contemporary human services 73,* 67–78.

Javaid, G. (1993). The children of homosexual and heterosexual single mothers. *Child Psychiatry and Human Development,* 23 (4), 235–248.

Kline, M. (1993). Complicating the ideology of motherhood: Child welfare law and First Nation women. *Queens Law Journal,* 18, 306–342.

Kweskin, S. & Cook, A. (1982). Heterosexual and homosexual mothers' self-described sex-role behavior and ideal sex-role behavior in children. *Sex Roles,* 8, 967–975.

Lewin, E. (1993). *Lesbian mothers: Accounts of gender in American culture*. Ithaca: Cornell University Press.

Lewin, E. (1994). Negotiating lesbian motherhood: The dialectics of resistance and accommodation. In E. Glenn, G. Chang & L. Forcey (Eds.), *Mothering: Ideology, experience, and agency* (pp. 333–353).New York: Routledge.

Nelson, F. (1996). Lesbian motherhood: An exploration of Canadian lesbian families. Toronto: University of Toronto Press.

Patterson, C. (1994). Children of the lesbian baby boom: Behavioral adjustment, self-concepts and sex role identity. In B. Greene & G. Herek (Eds.), *Lesbian and gay psychology: Theory, research and clinical applications*. Thousand Oaks, CA: Sage.

Reimann, R. (1997). Does biology matter? Lesbian couples' transition to parenthood and their division of labor. *Qualitative Sociology*, 20 (2), 53–185.

Roberts, D. (1993a). Racism and patriarchy in the meaning of motherhood. *Journal of Gender and the Law*, 1 (1), 1–38.

Roberts, D. (1993b). Motherhood and crime. *Iowa Law Review*, 79, 95–141.

"GROWING UP" UNDER SUSPICION The Problematization of "Youth" in Recent Criminologies

C h a p t e r

12

Nob Doran

A generation or so ago, a small number of criminologists, on both sides of the Atlantic, pioneered a radically new approach to the study of delinquency and crime. Inspired by theoretical developments emanating from American sociology, they argued for a bottom-up approach which called into question many of the taken-for-granted assumptions of much prior criminology. In the USA one might point to Becker's (1953, 1963) work as seminal in this regard. Rather than seeing deviance as something performed by (typically pathological) individuals, Becker pointed out the inherently social, "labelling" process which constituted both deviance and crime in contemporary society. On the other side of the Atlantic, Cohen's (1967, 1971, 1972) work displayed similar intellectual foundations. He began his scholarly life by importing Becker's, and other Americans', insights into the relatively arid environment of the existing "British mainstream criminology." Moreover, he, and a small group of other like-minded sociologists, quickly went on to form the influential "National Deviancy conference" and from such developments there emerged both a new approach to crime studies and a strident critique of the prior British criminological tradition.

In one early paper outlining the latter's inadequacies, Cohen (1974) singled out for critique both the early work of Goring (1919) and a then current research project being undertaken at the Cambridge institute of delinquency — D. J. West's longitudinal survey of delinquency development.[1] Like other recent critiques of positivist criminology (Matza, 1964, 1969; Taylor, Walton and Young, 1973), Cohen pointed out how this type of statistical research keeps falling into what Matza calls the "positivist trap." Whereas Goring's positivism might be excused because of the intellectual era in which he lived, the more contemporary work of West (1969) falls back into the positivist trap of simply collecting a

Revised version of a paper presented at the 1998 meetings of the Canadian Sociology and Anthropology Association, University of Ottawa, Ottawa, Ontario, June 1998.

wide range of statistics in order to see "which items or which combination of items would prove to be the clearest determinants of future delinquency" (West, 1969: 2, quoted in Cohen, 1974: 19). In contrast to West's prioritization of "prediction" over understanding, Cohen and others argued for an approach which not only put the experiential understanding of youth at the centre of analysis, but also insisted in line with what was becoming known as the labelling tradition in the USA, that analytic focus should now be brought to bear on the agencies of social control that create crime and delinquency, and not just the criminals and delinquents who were processed through such agencies.

In one sense, they were attempting something of a paradigm shift in the way that criminology understood itself. Against the theoretical paucity of this prior, pragmatic and positivist criminology in which West's prospective longitudinal survey (even though it would continue for many years into the future) would be able to go "no further than the extraordinary jumble of eclectic positivism that rendered the work of the Gluecks such an anachronism" (Cohen 1974: 19), the new interactionist alternative suggested a quite different approach to "criminal careers" — one which sought to pay careful attention to the interaction of individual and state control agents, via detailed, empirical analyses of this sequential process.

Yet, a generation or so later, one might look back in bemusement as to the actual unfolding of criminological discourse(s) since that time. On the one hand, if one traces the success or otherwise of these labelling theorists, one not only sees a strange return to an apparently "positivist" criminology among at least some of these scholars, but also a widespread move away from their original analytic focus on the "labelling process." On the other hand, longitudinal surveys, despite their typical expense, are becoming increasingly central to the criminological endeavour. In fact, this longitudinal approach has not only continued, but is thriving today. In the UK, Farrington (the long-time collaborator with West on the Cambridge project) has been very influential in promoting this type of research (Farrington, 1986, 1992a, 1992b 1994; Farrington et al., 1986; Farrington and West, 1990) in recent years. In the US, there has also been a resurgence of interest in such studies. Although the Gluecks' pioneering work in this area (e.g., 1930, 1934, 1937, 1940, 1943) was largely discredited by the 1960s, Sampson and Laub (1993) have recently reworked the Gluecks' "longitudinal" data to come up with a formal "developmental" theory of crime, while Wolfgang et al.'s (1972) cohort study introduced the concept of the "chronic offender" into criminological discourse. Not surprisingly, this "finding" that about 6% of the sample accounted for over half of all the arrests, prompted successful calls for more longitudinal research into the development of "criminal careers" (Blumstein et al., 1986a, 1986b). For example, Farrington is now participating in a large prospective longitudinal project (of 1500 boys) being undertaken in Pittsburgh, USA (Farrington et al., 1996).

In fact, it might be argued that what we are witnessing today is the emergence of a more general criminological "surveillance" of youth (and childhood). In contrast to the nineteenth century, when it was the working class who came under this "scientific surveillance" through institutions like the prison, and later through discourses like criminology, the last twenty years or so seem to have witnessed a significant mutation in mainstream criminology's understanding of where most criminality is located. Today, it is the discursive category of "youth" which seems to be replacing that of "class" as the primary focus for official understandings of crime.[2] Consequently, any analytic reaction to this mutation needs to reflect both an awareness of this transformation and a means for explaining it. In other words, one needs to begin analysis of this "social change" as a specific, temporally located discursive construction.

Thus the purpose of my returning to Cohen's work is not to show how inaccurate it was as a portent for future "positivist" criminological development, nor to express sadness at the future directions which some of this interactionist-influenced criminology took, but rather to suggest that Cohen's early critique needs to be reworked, with some of his own later work as well as the research of others, if it is to serve as a basis for further development in this loosely defined field of qualitative criminology. Specifically, one might want to begin analysis of these discursive developments of the last 20 years or so; not only the proliferation of these apparently positivistic longitudinal studies, but also the diminution in the strength and vigour of the "alternative" tradition. In part, a central question that animates this paper is why has this mainstream criminology been so resistant to the challenges of the "interactionist," and similar, critiques? And relatedly, how has "mainstream criminology" been able to ignore, disqualify, or incorporate these alternative criminological accounts? To answer these questions, however, will require a shift away from a simple concern with competing "validity" claims about types of criminology, and will necessitate utilizing a framework of analysis that examines not only competing knowledges, but also the power relations within and between these "criminologies."

Of course, Foucault (1977, 1979, 1980, 1985) is the inspiration here for much of the remaining analysis. Specifically, Foucault's work on the emergence of disciplinary surveillance of working-class life in the nineteenth century will serve as a guide for these preliminary investigations into the emerging disciplinary surveillance of "youth." Yet Foucault's account cannot simply be transplanted to explain this mutation of the late twentieth century. Instead, the Foucauldian thesis must also be elaborated and complemented in several ways. First, it will be necessary to show the specific utility of genealogical analysis for an understanding of the "problematization" of "youth" and not just "class." Second, the Foucauldian thesis must also be elaborated to explain not only recent mutations in the "carceral continuum," but also the mutations in its criminologies. Finally, the Foucauldian thesis has little room for acting subjects. Yet the interactionist approach prioritized the "meaningful" nature of youth activity. So a start needs to be made on developing an approach that can link both levels of analysis.

BEYOND POSITIVIST CRIMINOLOGY? LESSONS FROM A GENERATION OF RESEARCH

The purpose of this section is not to attempt a comprehensive review of the research carried out by those loosely affiliated with, or influenced by, the "sociology of deviance" that emerged in the wake of Becker's early work. Nor is it to try and resurrect a dying corpse (Sumner, 1994). Instead, I simply want to put down a few signposts detailing some of the developments within this field, while at the same time situating them within mainstream criminology more generally. Although the notion of the criminal career is important for both these traditions, not only did they tackle this problem quite differently, but the interactionist tradition, for the most part, quickly became marginalized and displaced.

Yet a generation or so ago, the criminological landscape was quite different. Becker's early work not only made the famous claim that

> deviance is *not* a quality of the act the person commits, but rather a consequence of the application by others of rules and sanctions to an "offender" (1963: 9).

It also suggested that in order to understand the sequential process of "becoming" a deviant, one might wish to analyze this process in terms of the concept of "career" (1963: 24).

But it was the emphasis on "labelling" that animated much of the early research in North America. Empirical work on the police as "labellers" (Piliavin and Briar, 1964; Werthman and Piliavin, 1967; Bittner, 1967) was quickly surpassed by theoretically more sophisticated interpretations that typically went in one of two directions. The ethnomethodological variant pursued this research in a phenomenological direction (Cicourel, 1968; Pollner, 1974a; 1974b; Sudnow, 1965; Wieder, 1974), while the Marxist variant attempted to situate this interaction within a macro-theoretical framework of political economy (Chambliss, 1973; 1978; Platt, 1975; Quinney, 1970).

On the other side of the Atlantic, similar intellectual developments were taking place. On the one hand, there was a similar attempt at developing a phenomenological direction. Both Atkinson (1971) and Phillipson (1971) attempted to steer their work in an ethnomethodological or phenomenological direction, but quickly ended up leaving the field of crime and deviance altogether. On the other hand, although Young's early work (1971a, 1971b) was also heavily dependent upon the labelling perspective, this quickly transformed itself into a concern with the "Young Marx" and a "New Criminology" (Taylor, Walton and Young, 1973, 1975). And although this "critical criminology" inspired much theoretical debate about the utility and possibility of using Marx's work for the study of crime, perhaps the most original applications of Marx to the study of deviance came from a somewhat different source. Under the leadership of Stuart Hall and inspired by the recent emergence of "cultural studies" as a quasi-independent discipline, this group took it upon themselves to analyze the formation of the peculiarly British youth subcultures which had emerged since the second world war. This "Birmingham" School's (Hall and Jefferson, 1976; Willis, 1977, Hall et al., 1978; Hebdidge, 1979), influences were initially more Gramscian than interactionist. But there was cross-fertilization between the groups, with Cohen's later work (1980), for example, responding, albeit uneasily, to the insights of these scholars, and Hall et al.'s (1978) work incorporating significant insights from Cohen (1972).

Although the early studies were particularly gender-blind, empirical and theoretical developments within Britain at least, ensured that a feminist articulation of "youth deviance" quickly surfaced. Angela McRobbie's work (McRobbie and Garber, 1976; McRobbie, 1980) is exemplary in this regard, as she not only insisted on finding a space for the voice of women (young, working-class girls in particular), and on identifying commonalities between the subcultural and the feminist projects, but she also went on to critique the romanticization of "male youth subcultures" by the subcultural theorists' inability to see the sexual and racial brutality which often permeated the subcultures that they studied.

At around the same time, Carol Smart (1976) was beginning her critique of mainstream criminology, through a similar theoretical strategy to Cohen. She too identified the "positivist" nature of prior criminology's treatment of women and how it reinforced conventional sexual stereotypes about women's "nature." Moreover, a similar outpouring of research (Clark and Lewis, 1977; Hanmer and Saunders, 1984; Kelly, 1987; Radford, 1987; Stanko, 1988; Gelsthorpe and Morris, 1990), typically beginning from the embodied experiences of women quickly emerged. Although not all of it was qualitative, and much of it was inspired by various macro-theoretical frameworks, this nascent feminist criminology also sought to place the experience of women in a central analytic position.

Yet 20 or so years later, both the interactionist and the feminist critiques seem to have had little impact on mainstream criminology (Cohen, 1985, 1988, 1996; Gelsthorpe and Morris, 1988; Heidensohn, 1995). In fact, it appears that quantification in criminology is flourishing, if not expanding. Longitudinal surveys have become more popular since Cohen's critique, while victim surveys, frequently sensitive to the concerns of women, have also proliferated in recent years. Perhaps more surprisingly, for those academically formed after the original "intellectual critique," was the fact that many of the British labelling theorists who joined with Cohen in articulating a qualitative position vis-à-vis the "positivist trap" of mainstream criminology, now went on to adopt not only a suspiciously "positivist" (Smart, 1990) "left realist" position (Lea and Young, 1984; Young, 1986, 1987, 1988; Lea, 1987; Matthews and Young, 1986, 1992; Young and Matthews, 1992); but also started to reclaim the quantitative methods reminiscent of that approach (Kinsey, 1984; Jones, Maclean and Young, 1986). That is, they may not be currently engaged in longitudinal surveys, but they have turned their empirical and theoretical attention to the production of local victim surveys.

But if we were to examine these quantitative analyses for what they "do" rather than simply what they "say" (Austin 1972), the results are quite instructive. Whereas the alternative criminologies, discussed above, prioritized the fact that women's and youths' voices needed to be heard within criminological discourse, these newer surveys not only recast them as "objects" of analysis but subtly reframe them as oppositional entities. For example, most of the current longitudinal research seeks to identify "risk" factors for the onset of later criminality (cf. Castel, 1991). Thus the mother-child relationship now gets problematized as the family becomes a site for extensive criminological investigation (Farrington, 1997). On the other hand, left realism not only used victim surveys to subtly misinterpret women's concerns (Gelsthorpe and Morris, 1988; Doran 1994a), but also used them to direct attention onto a new "dangerous class, that of youth" (Lea and Young, 1984).

In other words, one result of these longitudinal surveys, along with similar conclusions from other recent "mainstream criminological" theorizing (Gottfriedson and Hirschi, 1990; Wilson and Herrnstein 1985) is to foreground early family life as a major source of later delinquency. Moreover, the delinquent is typically male in character, such that mothers must now fear that if they do not provide appropriate supervision and discipline, a young offender could result. On the other hand, the left realist victimization surveys are not only suggesting that women's fear of crime is perhaps exaggerated, but that the main perpetrators of such victimizations are no longer to be identified as working class but rather as "youth"; especially minority youth or working class youth.

As we can see from this brief overview of a generation or so of criminological developments, these critiques of positivism did not succeed in diminishing the power of this form of discourse. The analytic questions which will be the concern of the rest of this paper can now be more clearly formulated. First, given the generational fortunes of these criminologies, how might one start to understand them in their wider socio-historical context? Second, given the distinctive intellectual "reversal" of some of these "alternative" criminologists, how might one begin examining this as an analytic phenomenon? And, as will be seen, Foucault provides an essential departure point for such considerations.

THE "PROBLEMATIZATION" OF YOUTH: TOWARDS A GENEALOGICAL ANALYSIS

Foucault's criminological work has been tremendously influential since its inception 20 or so years ago. Seeking to go beyond traditional Marxist and Durkheimian analyses of penality, Foucault introduced a critical analysis which challenged most of the "conventional wisdom" in the field, both theoretically and empirically. Beginning from a sharp juxtaposition of two entirely different systems of punishment; the spectacle of scaffolds and hangings of the French *Ancien Regime* to the more familiar prison-centred system, Foucault seeks to question certain of our taken-for-granted assumptions about crime and punishment. Through a combination of historical narrative and structural analysis, he shows how the prison itself was only one of several possibilities for penology's future direction at the beginning of the nineteenth century, but that its successful implementation was based on much more than its simple ability to deprive people of their liberty. Foucault's major claims are that the "panoptic" prison is extremely adept at bringing together previously perfected techniques of discipline and surveillance (these had been developed over the course of the eighteenth century in such diverse institutions as the school, the hospital, the military, and the workshop) in order to produce over the course of the nineteenth century "docile bodies." However, these docile bodies were not prisoners made compliant for economic purposes only, as much of Rusche and Kirchheimer's (1939) analysis of penality suggests. For Foucault, this docility has a political element to it as well. That is, this disciplinary power is able to fabricate "subjects"; disciplined and obedient subjects, despite the nineteenth century's overt rhetoric concerning the equality of all before the law. Moreover, this disciplinary project is targeted at one group in particular, the working class. The revolutionary period in France brings into play a definite class antagonism which, according to Foucault, is subsequently contained in large part due to the machinations of the new panoptic prison system. This containment is possible because the prison fabricates what later criminology has taken for granted, namely the delinquent. The invention of "delinquency" is based on the prison's ability not only to "correct" individuals but also to obtain information on them. By this process, one can start understanding crime in terms of the types of person who might engage in crime. The institution of the prison allows for "scientific" knowledge of the individual to be obtained on these working-class inmates. That is, they become the subject of intense scientific surveillance for the first time in history.

Not surprisingly, "criminology" as a scientific discipline emerged out of this institutional matrix, but took for granted, not only that these "delinquents" were a lower class phenomenon but that they were different from the "normal" individual. And these underlying assumptions remained an essential part of the discipline until the 1960s. At the same time, it was not just a question of the prison producing information on inmates. Delinquency was also fabricated by the relationship which was set up between the prison, the police, and these newly identified individuals. "Police surveillance provides the prison with offenders, which the prison transforms into delinquents, the targets and auxiliaries of police supervisions, which regularly send back a certain number of them to prison" (Foucault 1977: 282). Thus the delinquent class gets created as a sub-species of the working class. But through these processes of discipline and surveillance, this "delinquent" class is much less dangerous and more acceptable than the politically volatile and seditious working class of the early nineteenth century. This discursive imposition was not accepted without resistance however. Foucault, in a curiously neglected section, details the attempts by workers and their media to erect a "counter-discourse" to resist this new articulation of crime and delinquency. Workers' newspapers, like *La Fraternité* and *L'Humanitaire,* as well as radicals like the Fourierists, all attempted to articulate an understanding of crime located in society and the rich rather than the poor (1977: 285–92).

In sum, Foucault's analysis is a thought-provoking and magisterial thesis which has had enormous influence throughout the social sciences. And although it might be argued that this influence has been greater outside of criminology rather than within, it nevertheless has stimulated significant criminological research (Garland, 1985a, 1985b, 1990, 1992; Pasquino, 1991; Cohen,1985; Cohen and Scull, 1983). Yet it seems unable to fully comprehend these criminological developments since the 1960s (cf. Garland, 1992). Thus in order to try and connect Foucault's historical understanding with the more "embodied" understandings prevalent in Cohen's (and Smart's) early work, we will need to develop these Foucauldian insights in a number of directions.

Disciplinary Power and "Juvenile Delinquency"

Despite Foucault's dramatic reversal of many of criminology's foundational tenets, and despite the apparent usefulness which his analysis suggests for any analysis of the carceral continuum, it must be remembered that Foucault said nothing about "juvenile delinquency" itself. So, in order to understand these transformations in how "youth" are understood, we must first examine how this disciplinary power also fabricated the juvenile delinquent as well as the adult criminal.

Donzelot's first book (1979) gave an impressive genealogy of the emergence of juvenile delinquency in France within its broader concern with the "policing of families" (cf. Meyer, 1983). Moreover, Donzelot was at pains to remark upon the usefulness of the accompanying psy-professions for ensuring the stability of family life in the welfare state era. He specifically documents the struggle between a number of competing discourses which could be used to regulate families and how psychoanalysis, because of its ability to "float," was able to accomplish this regulation much more efficaciously than for example, psychiatry, whose tools were too blunt for mundane use with juveniles and their families. Nevertheless, Donzelot's initial foray into this field is lacking with regard to recent transformations in this field of tutelage under the welfare state era. That is, Donzelot does not foresee the massive mutation which transforms the "juvenile delinquent" into the "young offender." Thus, whereas the "juvenile delinquent" was primarily comprehended in terms of a discourse which prioritized guidance and tutelage (Donzelot, 1979), the "young offender" is to be first understood within a framework of "law and rights" (Corrado and Turnbull, 1992; Corrado and Markwart, 1992). In fact, neither Foucault nor Donzelot were able to foresee the rapidity of the transformations which were about to occur in the fields of "crime and delinquency," despite their own familiarity with the history of discontinuities, which is the hallmark of much of their work.

Mutations in the Social, and the Problem of "Resistance"

Cohen (1985), however, provides a nice, easily accessible overview of these transformations and the recent paradigm shift in Western notions of crime and criminology. Where both Foucault and Donzelot provide genealogies of crime and delinquency in the era of the welfare state, Cohen's work details the transformations in the system which have constituted the post-welfare era. Concentrating more on extending Foucault's analysis to take into account these transformations, Cohen's emphasis is on the changes in our social control frameworks — the movements towards decentralization, deprofessionalization, deinstitutionalization and behaviourism (1985: 31) — or what he summarizes, rather inelegantly as "destructuring." Throughout much of this work, he argues that despite its rhetoric, the "destructuring" movement has simultaneously worked to "deinstitutionalize" populations (in prisons, asylums etc.), while at the same time extending the net of "social control" through community programs whose interests lie in the further surveillance, discipline and classification of targeted groups.

Yet, he finishes by reflecting upon his own (and others') adversarial relationship to these changes in criminal justice over the last 20–30 years. He observes that most current adversarial views display a profound pessimism when they self-reflect upon the accomplishments of their own proposals for reform as well as their more general place within the system: or, as Cohen himself puts it; "first, that the cure might be worse than the disease and, second, that most radical and oppositional attacks on the system will end up being absorbed, co-opted and even strengthening it" (1985: 239–40). Cohen himself, acknowledges his personal ambivalence on this matter. Reflecting upon his own move from "social work" into "sociology" so as to better understand the "real causes" (1985: 236) of social problems, Cohen appreciates the intellectual clarity that this move gave him, but he, nevertheless, regrets the practical ineffectiveness of the "adversarial critiques" which were mounted. Yet, he does not want to abandon them completely. Thus he finishes this book arguing, almost half-heartedly, for an approach he calls "moral pragmatism."

Refreshing in its honest acknowledgment of the pitfalls which were confronted by the early "sociologists of deviance," Cohen's reflections, nevertheless, appear to be ones emanating from a tired combatant in the oppositional battle against a too-powerful criminology. Like the Fourierists of the nineteenth century, Cohen and others also attempted to resist (cf. Cohen, 1988) a certain re-articulation of crime and the criminal. Yet, what is lacking in his account is any analysis of this change. Cohen can only give us an apology that things didn't turn out that well for this "adversarial criminology." He cannot give us an analysis of that transformation.

Fortunately, however, Donzelot's still untranslated work on the emergence and demise of the French welfare state, *L'invention du social* (1984, 1994), is useful in this regard. Not only does he give a "genealogy" of the rise of the "social" and its accompanying Durkheimian sociology, but he also analyzes the emergence, in the 1960s, of the "resistances" to this power/knowledge and the "mobilization of society" which resulted. In other words, rather than lamenting the failure of the discourses of resistance, Donzelot seeks to analyze exactly how they might fit within a larger framework of power/knowledge. Moreover, whereas other researchers today understand the new post-welfare state era in terms of the concept of "governmentality,"[3] it is Donzelot who most explicitly connects this current period with the prior era of the "social" and displays the character of the mutation from one to the other. But Donzelot's strength is not just in his analysis of the emergence of this "*social du troisième type*" (Donzelot, 1984), but also in his attention to the corresponding mutations in power/knowledge. That is, he first identifies the usage of the technologies of "insurance," "statistics" and "social rights" as being essential for the creation of the "social," but he then sees a mutation in the 1960s, specifically the introduction of a new "knowledge" framework, significantly different than either the knowledges of normalization which Foucault had identified in the "disciplinary" era, or the technologies of the "social" which Donzelot himself had first recognized.

He goes on to argue that this post-normalization science began from the belated realization of the inadequacies of the normalizing sciences. That is, starting from the 1960s, oppositional discourses emerged. And against the old power of the norm, these critiques prioritized the notion of "rights" (1984: 241). And Donzelot goes on to ask a question similar to that posed by Cohen's pessimistic commentators mentioned above; did this critical discourse challenge state intervention or did it just extend it (1984: 241–2)? But rather than leaving this as an open question, Donzelot suggests that a third way quickly emerged out of this struggle between the old normalizing and functional discourses of the welfare state and this new and oppositional critical discourse (now getting tangled up in its own contradictions). This third way not only owed a lot to the development of "systems analysis" in the 1950s, but it also took as a primary analytic concern, the question of "resistance." That is, unlike the normalizing sciences which saw resistance as simply irrational behaviour, the new "strategic analysis" model (cf. Crozier and Friedberg, 1977) tried to incorporate resistance into the very heart of the model (1984: 242). Now all actors are seen as possessing certain rationalities and power. Instead of power being viewed as something to be held by one group or another (1984: 243), power becomes the very fabric of all social relationships. No longer would it be possible to "grasp" power in the interests of the subordinate. Instead, power is in every social relationship. And it is seductive, because to refuse to play this new game is tantamount to denying the existence of others, the legitimacy of their goals, and the need for selecting with them the realization of one's own plans (1984: 245). In other words, this new strategic analysis seeks to incorporate "resistance" by first accepting its existence and then by "inviting" it to participate in new games of power sharing, even though these power relationships are in no way egalitarian ones.

Although Donzelot's analysis here is suggestive, rather than exhaustive, its great advantage over Cohen's is that it attempts an analysis of the question of "incorporation" rather than simply bemoaning the fact that it has happened. In the final section, we need to pursue further this understanding of "incorporation," but unlike Donzelot, we need to examine this phenomenon from the perspective of those who are subjected to these processes.

Genealogy from Below

The genealogical analyses discussed so far still display what one might call a top-down perspective. That is, the perspective that Foucault, and later Cohen and Donzelot all adopt is one which prioritizes the actions of power/knowledge on bodies, but doesn't begin the analysis from the embodied perspective of the bodies on whom these technologies operate. Thus final consideration must now be given to the limitations of such analysis. Here, of course, one must consult the feminist literature for assistance. In quite explicit terms, they have pointed out not only the usefulness of the Foucaualdian paradigm for understanding how disciplinary power works on bodies, in this case, gendered ones, but they have been equally strident in pointing out its limitations (Diamond and Quinby, 1988; Sawicki, 1991, Ramazanoglu, 1993; McNay, 1993). And although, many different aspects of the Foucauldian oeuvre have been subjected to feminist interpretation, it is again Carol Smart's work which is most appropriate to these "criminological" considerations.

Like Cohen, Smart too has travelled from an initial critique of positivist criminology to an understanding of the usefulness of Foucault. But unlike Cohen, her own embodied position as a woman is always central to her analysis. As a consequence, Smart (1989) suggests that one of the most important contemporary consequences of the operation of power/knowledge, at least in the realm of law, is that it works to "disqualify" women's voices (because of the discursive categories it uses to comprehend the social and criminal world). And although Smart is much less pessimistic than Cohen about the future directions of any oppositional discourse, she acknowledges that the women's movement must come to terms with the recognition that they are trapped within a struggle over "knowledges" and that feminism itself has frequently been marginalized by these older, and more authoritative discourses of criminology and law.

Nevertheless, it is clear from Smart's work that the critical discourses of Foucault, Donzelot, and even Cohen are inadequate in that they fail to deal with the experiential bodies on whom these power/knowledge techniques are applied. Thus it is not enough to engage in top-down genealogical analysis, one must engage in a "genealogy from below." That is, one must engage in a form of analysis which begins from the experiential, albeit discursively constructed (Smart, 1995), bodies of those upon whom this disciplinary power is enacted.

Yet Smart herself is rather unclear as to the specifics of this "disqualification" process. She never really clarifies the mechanisms used to accomplish it. In contrast, Dorothy Smith's work is precisely focused on the mechanisms of this disqualification, or silencing. Although she does not use Foucault or Donzelot, she explicitly identifies how certain contemporary social scientific discourses, such as sociology and psychiatry, silence women's voices (Smith, 1974, 1990). Moreover, she demonstrates how this is typically accomplished through the mundane processes of "scientific" investigation, such as carrying out statistical surveys and collecting the "facts." Against this distortion brought about by such "human sciences," Smith (1987) has pioneered an alternative "sociology," which pays attention to the everyday world of women, rather than dismissing it.

Unfortunately, Smith's strength is in showing the specifics of how these social scientific discourses silence subordinate voices, rather than how such discourses might subsequently incorporate resistant voices. However, other studies have extended these Smithian insights and suggested that the historical emergence of certain state "statistics" in the nineteenth century not only provided information, but they also operated to incorporate an increasingly hostile working class. And they did this by mundanely codifying that antithetical, experiential culture into these new "scientific" state discourses, by such mundane practices as the routine collection of statistics on those hostile bodies (Doran, 1994b; Doran, 1996). One result of such work was that an initial hostile working class actually started to "speak" this discourse once its members saw the "productive" potential of this power/knowledge. On the other hand, their prior cultural experience was destroyed, or more accurately, codified and transformed in this process.

CONCLUSION

This paper began from what appeared to be, at first glance, a very straightforward question: namely, why have longitudinal studies on youth continued to expand and flourish in the last 20 to 30 years, even after they had been subjected to both specific and general critiques of their "positivist" methodologies and assumptions? As has also been suggested, to even begin answering this question has necessitated a wide-ranging examination of a variety of relevant material. Even now the puzzle is far from complete. Nevertheless, some clarity has been obtained. By situating these intellectual "resistances" to mainstream criminology in the wider theoretical context of Foucault's theorizing on power/knowledge, one can begin to ask questions about the possible "disciplinary" power inherent in recent concerns with obtaining statistical (and in this case, longitudinal) information on "youth."

Furthermore, Donzelot's recent work alerted us to the need for examining the specificity of the recent mutations in the power/knowledge model and how one model transforms itself into its successor. As importantly, although there may be some similarities between the disciplinary power operating in the nineteenth century and today, there are significant differences which must also be explained. By following the twisting mutations of power/knowledge from that period until today, Donzelot's work helps enormously in such a task: a task, however, which is only now beginning. Finally, other qualitative research into the effects of imposing "statistics" (and other disciplinary technologies) on bodies has alerted us to the need to study not just issues of silencing and disqualification, but also to examine the specific ways in which resistances might get incorporated by these "disciplinary" discourses.

ENDNOTES

1. This prospective longitudinal study tracked 411 working-class boys from London, England, from the age of about 8 (in the early 1960s) until adulthood, in order to examine their propensities towards later delinquent and criminal behaviour. (For some examples of the work which emanated from this study see West, 1982; West and Farrington, 1973, 1977).

2. If one wanted to trace this development within the American criminological literature, one might consult the following as some of the examples which helped constitute this mutation: Nye, Short and Olsen (1958), Dentler and Monroe (1961), Tittle, Villemez and Smith (1978), Tittle and Meier (1990), Hirschi and Gottfredson (1983), Steffensmeier and Streifel (1991).

3. This is a rapidly growing field, with scholars from around the world contributing to its its proliferation. Nevertheless, Burchell et al. (1991) and Barry et al. (1996) give some sense of its general contours.

REFERENCES

Atkinson, J. M. (1971) 'Societal Reactions to Suicide' in S. Cohen (ed) *Images of Deviance* Harmondsworth: Penguin.

Austin, J. L. (1972) *How to do things with words* Oxford: Clarendon Press.

Barry, A., Osborne, T., and Rose, N. (eds) (1996) *Foucault and Political Reason* London: UCL Press.

Becker, H. S. (1953), 'Becoming a Marihuana user', *American Journal of Sociology, 59*, pp. 235–42.

Becker, H. S. (1963), *Outsiders: Studies in the sociology of deviance,* London: Macmillan.

Bittner, E. (1967), 'The Police on skid row: a study of peacekeeping', *American Sociological Review, 32* (5), pp. 699–715.

Blumstein, A., Cohen, J., Roth, J.A. and Visher, C.A. (eds) (1986a), *Criminal Careers and "Career Criminals",* vol. 1, Washington, D.C.: National Academy Press.

Blumstein, A., Cohen, J., Roth, J.A. and Visher, C.A. (eds) (1986b), *Criminal Careers and "Career Criminals",* vol. 2, Washington, D.C.: National Academy Press.

Burchell, G., Gordon, C., and Miller, P. (eds) (1991) *The Foucault Effect*. Chicago: University of Chicago Press.

Castel, R. (1991) 'From Dangerousness to Risk' in Burchell, G., Gordon, C., and Miller, P. (eds) *The Foucault Effect*. Chicago: University of Chicago Press.

Chambliss, W. (1973) 'The Saints and the Roughnecks' *Society 11*, 24–31.

Chambliss, W. (1978) *On the Take: From Petty Crooks to Presidents* Bloomington: Indiana University Press.

Cicourel, A. V. (1968), *The Social Organization of Juvenile Justice*, New York: Wiley.

Clark, L., and Lewis, D. (1977) *Rape: The Price of Coercive Sexuality*, Toronto: The Women's Press.

Cohen, S. (1967), 'Mods Rockers and the Rest', *The Howard Journal, 12*, pp.121–30.

Cohen, S. (1971), 'Introduction' in S. Cohen (ed), *Images of Deviance*, Harmondsworth: Penguin Books.

Cohen, S. (1972) *Folk Devils and Moral Panics*, London: MacGibbon & Kee.

Cohen, S. (1974), 'Criminology and the sociology of deviance in Britain', in P. Rock and M. McIntosh (eds), *Deviance and Social Control,* London: Tavistock.

Cohen, S. (1980), *Folk Devils and Moral Panics,* 2nd ed.n, Oxford: Martin Robertson.

Cohen, S. (1985) *Visions of Social Control*, Cambridge: Polity Press.

Cohen, S. (1988), *Against Criminology*, New Brunswick, NJ: Transaction Books.

Cohen, S. (1996) 'Crime and Politics: Spot the Difference' *British Journal of Sociology 47* (1) 1–21.

Cohen, S., and Scull, A. (eds) (1983) *Social Control and the State*, Oxford: Robertson.

Corrado, R and Markwart, A. (1992) 'The Evolution and Implementation of a New Era of Juvenile Justice in Canada' in Corrado, R., Bala, N., Linden, R., and Le Blanc, M. (eds) *Juvenile Justice in Canada* Toronto: Butterworths.

Corrado, R., and Turnbull, S. (1992) 'A Comparative Examination of the Modified Justice Model in the United Kingdom and the United States' in Corrado, R., Bala, N., Linden, R., and Le Blanc, M. (eds) *Juvenile Justice in Canada* Toronto: Butterworths.

Crozier, M., and Friedberg, E. (1977) *Actors and Systems* Chicago: University of Chicago Press.

Dentler, R., and Monroe, L. (1961) 'Social Correlates of Early Adolescent Theft' *American Sociological Review 63*, 733–43.

Diamond, I., and Quinby, L. (eds) (1988) *Feminism and Foucault*, Boston: Northeastern University Press.

Donzelot, J. (1979), *The Policing of Families* New York: Pantheon.

Donzelot, J. (1984). *L'invention du Social* Paris: Fayard.

Donzelot, J. (1994). *L'invention du Social* Paris: Seuil.

Doran, C. (1994a) 'Codifying Women's Bodies: Towards a Genealogy of British Victimology' *Women and Criminal Justice 5* (2): 45–70.

Doran, N. (1994b) 'Risky Business: Codifying Embodied Experience in the Manchester Unity of Oddfellows' in *Journal of Historical Sociology 7* (2), 131–154.

Doran, N. (1996) 'From embodied "health" to official "accidents": Class, codification and early British Factory Legislation, 1831–1844' *Social and Legal Studies 5* (4), 523–546.

Farrington, D. P. (1986), 'Age and Crime', in M. Tonry and N. Morris (eds), *Crime and Justice*, vol. 7, Chicago: University of Chicgago Press.

Farrington, D. P. (1992a), 'Explaining the beginning, progress and ending of antisocial behavior from birth to adulthood', in J. Mcord,(ed.), *Advances in Criminology Theory*, vol. 3, *Facts, Frameworks and Forecasts*, New Brunswick, NJ: Transaction Books.

Farrington, D. P. (1992b), 'Juvenile Delinquency', in J. C. Coleman (ed.), *The School Years*, 2nd edn, London: Routledge & Kegan Paul.

Farrington D. P. (1994), ' Human development and criminal careers', in M. Maguire, R. Morgan and R. Reiner (eds), *The Oxford Handbook of Criminology*, Oxford: Clarendon Press.

Farrington D. P. (1997), ' Human development and criminal careers', in M. Maguire, R. Morgan and R. Reiner (eds), *The Oxford Handbook of Criminology*, 2nd edition. Oxford: Clarendon Press.

Farrington, D. P., Ohlin, L. E. and Wilson J. Q. (eds) (1986), *Understanding and Controlling Crime: Toward a New Research Strategy*, New York: Springer-Verlag.

Farrington, D. P. and West, D. J. (1990) 'The Cambridge study in delinquent development: a long-term follow-up of 411 London males', in H. J. Kerner and G. Kaiser (eds), *Criminality: Personality, behavior and life history*, Berlin: Springer-Verlag.

Farrington, D. P., Loeber, R., Stouthamer-Loeber, M., Van Kammen, W., Schmidt, L. (1996) 'Self-reported delinquency and a combined delinquency seriousness scale based on boys, mothers and teachers: concurrent and predictive validity for African-Americans and Caucasians' *Criminology 34* (4), pp 493–517.

Foucault, M. (1977), *Discipline and Punish*, London: Allen Lane.

Foucault, M. (1979), *The History of Sexuality: An introduction*, London: Allen Lane.

Foucault, M. (1980), 'Two Lectures' in C.Gordon (ed.), *Power/Knowledge:Selected Interviews & Other Writings 1972–1977*, New York: Pantheon Books.

Foucault, M. (1985), *The Use of Pleasure: Volume 2 of The History of Sexuality*, New York: Pantheon Books.

Garland, D. (1985a), 'The Criminal and his Science' *British Journal of Criminology 25* (2), 109–37.

Garland, D. (1985b),*Punishment and Welfare*, Aldershot: Gower.

Garland, D. (1990), *Punishment and Modern Society: A study in social theory*, Oxford: Oxford University Press.

Garland, D. (1992), 'Criminological knowledge and its relation to power', *British Journal of Criminology*, *32* (4), pp. 403–22.

Gelsthorpe, L. and Morris, A. (1988),' Feminism and criminology in Britain', *British Journal of Criminology*, *28* (2), Spring, pp. 93–109.

Gelsthorpe, L. and Morris, A. (eds) (1990), *Feminist Perspectives in Criminology*, London: Routledge & Kegan Paul.

Glueck, S. and Glueck, E. (1930), *500 Criminal Careers*, New York: A. A. Knopf.

Glueck, S. and Glueck, E. (1934), *One Thousand Juvenile Delinquents*, Cambridge, Mass.: Harvard University Press.

Glueck, S. and Glueck, E. (1937), *Later Criminal Careers*, New York: The Commonwealth Fund.

Glueck, S. and Glueck, E. (1940) *Juvenile Delinquents Grown Up,* New York: The Commonwealth Fund.

Glueck, S. and Glueck, E. (1943) *Criminal Careers in Retrospect,* New York: The Commonwealth Fund.

Goring, C. (1919), *The English Convict*, London: Methuen.

Gottfredson, M.R. and Hirschi, T. (1990), *A General Theory of Crime*, Stanford: Stanford University Press.

Hall, S., Critcher, C., Jefferson, T., Clarke, J. and Roberts, B. (1978), *Policing the Crisis: Mugging, the state and law and order*, London: Macmillan.

Hall, S. and Jefferson, T. (eds) (1976), *Resistance through Rituals: Youth subcultures in post-war Britain*, London: Hutchinson.

Hanmer, J. and Saunders, S. (1984), *Well Founded Fears: A community study of violence to women*, London: Hutchinson.

Hebdige, D. (1979), *Subculture: The meaning of style*, London: Methuen.

Heidensohn, F. (1995) 'Feminist perspectives and their impact on criminology and criminal justice in Britain' in Rafter, N. H., and Heidensohn, F. (eds) *International Feminist Perspectives in Criminology,* Buckingham: Open University Press.

Hirschi, T., and Gottfredson, M. (1983) 'Age and the Explanation of Crime' *American Journal of Sociology 89*, 552–84.

Jones, T., Maclean, B. and Young, J. (1986), *The Inslington Crime Survey*, Aldershot: Gower.

Kelly, L. (1987), 'The Continuum of Sexual Violence', in J. Hanmer and M. Maynard (eds), *Women, Violence and Social Control*, Atlantic Highlands, NJ: Humanities Press International, Inc.

Kinsey, R. (1984), *The Merseyside Crime Survey: First report*, Liverpool: Merseyside County Council.

Lea, J. (1987), 'Left realism: a defence', *Contemporary Crises, 11*, pp. 357–70.

Lea, J. and Young, J. (1984), *What Is to Be Done About Law and Order?* New York: Penguin.

McNay, L. (1993) *Foucault and Feminism,* Boston: Northeastern University Press.

McRobbie, A. (1980), 'Settling Accounts with Subculture,' *Screen Education, 34*, Spring, pp.

McRobbie, A. and Garber, J. (1976), 'Girls and Subcultures', in S. Hall and T. Jefferson (eds), *Resistance through Rituals*, London: Hutchinson.

Matthews, R. and Young, J. (eds.) (1986) *Confronting Crime* London: Sage.

Matthews, R. and Young, J. (eds.) (1992), *Issues in Realist Criminology*, London: Sage

Matza, D. (1964), *Delinquency and Drift*, New York: Wiley.

Matza, D. (1969), *Becoming Deviant*, Englewood Cliffs, NJ: Prentice Hall.

Meyer, P. (1983) *The Child and the State,* New York: Cambridge University Press.

Nye, I., Short, J., and Olsen, V (1958), 'Socio-economic status and Delinquent Behaviour' *American Journal of Sociology*, *63*, 381–89.

Pasquino, P (1991) 'Criminology: The Birth of a special Knowledge' in Burchelll, G., Gordon, C., and Miller, P. (eds) *The Foucault Effect,* Chicago: University of Chicago Press.

Phillipson, M. (1971) *Sociological Aspects of Crime and Delinquency,* London: Routledge and Kegan Paul.

Piliavin, I and Briar, S. (1964) 'Police Encounters with Juveniles' *American Journal of Sociology 70*, 206–14.

Platt, A. (1975) *The Child Savers: The Invention of Delinquency, 2nd edition*, Chicago: Chicago University Press.

Pollner, M. (1974a), 'Mundane reasoning', *Philosophy of Social Sciences*, *4* (1).

Pollner, M. (1974b) 'Sociological and Common-Sense Models of the Labelling Process' in R. Turner (ed) *Ethnomethodology* Harmondsworth: Penguin.

Quinney, R. (1970) *The Social Reality of Crime*, Boston: Little, Brown.

Radford, J. (1987), 'Policing male violence', in J. Hanmer and M. Maynard (eds), *Women, Violence and Social Control*, London: Macmillan.

Ramazanoglu, C. (ed) (1993) *Up against Foucault*, New York: Routledge.

Rusche, G. and Kirchheimer, O. ([1939] 1968) *Punishment and Social Structure*, New York: Columbia University Press.

Sampson, R., and Laub, J. (1993) *Crime in the Making*, Cambridge: Harvard University Press.

Sawicki, J. (1991) *Disciplining Foucault* New York: Routledge.

Smart, C. (1976), *Women, Crime and Criminology: A feminist critique*, London: Routledge & Kegan Paul.

Smart, C. (1989), *Feminism and the Power of Law*, London: Routledge.

Smart, C. (1990), 'Feminist approaches to criminology, or postmodern woman meets atavistic man', in L. R. Gelsthorpe and A. M. Morris (eds), *Feminist Perspectives in Criminiology*, London: Routledge & Kegan Paul.

Smart, C. (1995) 'Postscript for the 1990's, or "Still Angry After all These Years"' in C. Smart *Law, Crime and Sexuality*, London: Sage.

Smith, D. E. (1974) 'The Ideological Practice of Sociology' *Catalyst 8*, 39–54.

Smith, D. E. (1987) *The Everyday World as Problematic,* Toronto: University of Toronto Press.

Smith, D. E. (1990) *The Conceptual Practices of Power,* Toronto: University of Toronto Press.

Stanko, E. (1988), 'Hidden violence against women', in M. Maguire and J. Pointing (eds), *Victims of Crime: A new deal?*, Milton Keynes: Open University Press.

Steffensmeier, D., and Streifel, C. (1991) 'Age, Gender and Crime across Three Historical Periods: 1935, 1960 and 1985' *Social Forces 69*, 869–94.

Sudnow, D. (1965), 'Normal crimes: sociological features of the penal code in a public defender office', *Social Problems, 12*, Winter.

Sumner, C. S. (1994), *The Sociology of Deviance: An obituary*, Buckingham: Open University Press.

Taylor, I., Walton, P. and Young J. (1973), *The New Criminology: For a social theory of deviance*, London: Routledge & Kegan Paul.

Taylor, I., Walton, P. and Young, J. (eds) (1975), *Critical Criminology*, London: Routledge & Kegan Paul.

Tittle, C., Villemez, W., and Smith, D. (1978) 'The Myth of Social Class and Criminality: An Empirical Assessment of the Empirical Evidence', *American Sociological Review, 43*, 643–56.

Tittle, C and Meier, R. (1990) 'Specifying the SES/Delinquency Relationship' *Criminology 28* 271–301.

Werthman,, C and Piliavin I. (1967) 'Gang Members and the Police' in D. Bordua (ed) *The Police: Six Sociological Essays* New York: John Wiley and Sons.

West, D.J. (1969), *Present Conduct and Future Delinquency: First Report of the Cambridge Study in Delinquent Development*, New York: International Universities Press, Inc.

West, D. J.(1982), *Delinquency: Its roots, careers and prospects*, London: Heinemann.

West, D .J. and Farrington, D. P. (1973), *Who Becomes Delinquent?*, London: Heinemann.

West, D. J. and Farrington, D.P. (1977), *The Delinquent Way of Life*, London: Heinemann.

Wieder, D. L. (1974) *Language and Social Reality,* The Hague: Mouton.

Willis, P. (1977), *Learning to Labour: How working class kids get working class jobs*, Farnborough: Saxon House.

Wilson, J. Q. and Herrnstein, R. (1985), *Crime and Human Nature*, New York: Simon & Schuster.

Wolfgang, M., Figlio, R., and Sellin, T. (1972) *Delinquency in a Birth Cohort*, Chicago: University of Chicago Press.

Young, J. (1971a) 'The Role of the Police as Amplifiers of Deviance' in S. Cohen (ed) *Images of Deviance* Harmondsworth: Penguin.

Young, J. (1971b), *The Drugtakers: The social meaning of drug use*, London: Paladin.

Young, J. (1986), 'The failure of criminology: the need for a radical realism', in R. Matthews and J. Young (eds), *Confronting Crime*, London: Sage.

Young, J. (1987), ' The tasks facing a realist criminology', *Contemporary Crises, 11*, pp. 337–56.

Young, J. (1988), 'Radical criminology in Britain: the emergence of a competing paradigm', in P. Rock (ed.), *A History of British Criminology*, Oxford: Oxford University Press.

Young, J. and Matthews, R. (eds.) (1992), *Rethinking Criminology: The realist debate*, London: Sage.

THE BODY BEAUTIFUL Adolescent Girls and Images of Beauty

Beverly J. Matthews

INTRODUCTION

The tyranny of appearance norms have long been recognized in the lives of women (see Brownmiller, 1984; Greer, 1970; or Freedman, 1986, for example). Both academic literature and the popular media have examined factors which underlie the intense pressure women experience to adhere to a cultural ideal and the price they pay for either attempting to comply or failing to do so (see Chernin, 1981; Shute, 1992; Hesse-Biber, 1996; or Bordo, 1993). While we are aware of the problem among older teenagers and adult women, recent studies indicate that even girls in early adolescence are prone to eating problems and a preoccupation with food (Pipher, 1996; Brumberg, 1997). Some of the literature in this area focuses on media images and unhealthy portrayals of beauty and the ways in which women are influenced by such portrayals (Wolf, 1991). While this has been a fruitful line of inquiry, it is incomplete. It implies that women uncritically, or helplessly, follow a cultural ideal, simply because it is prescribed by society. The findings of this research study into the social world of adolescent girls reveal that straining to conform to the "ideal look" is not always an end in itself, that it is often a purposeful act designed to achieve social goals.

Young women are surrounded by images which define attractiveness as a very particular, thin, "perfect" ideal. While many strive to achieve this goal, they do not all do so out of blind conformity, or simply because they have negative images of themselves. The problem is more complex: many girls use appearance as a means for achieving social status and power; they conform to avoid the costs associated with deviating from the ideal. They experience the gender system in a unique way, because of their stage in life, which compounds the pressures all women experience around appearance; however, these girls are not all misguided individuals passively following a societal definition of beauty. Just like older women, adolescents are working to negotiate and achieve their individual goals within a micro and macro gender structure. They are actively finding their location within the peer arena and their relationships with food and appearance play a key role in this endeavour. In this research, in-depth interviews with adolescent women reveal much about the adolescent world and the importance of appearance norms within it.

EXAMINING THE MULTILEVEL GENDER SYSTEM AND THE SOCIAL WORLD OF ADOLESCENT GIRLS

When studying the social world, it is essential to recognize the interplay between the individual and the social context. Although women have the freedom to make their own choices, these choices are constrained by the socially created structures which surround them. Sociologists have long recognized the existence of social structures and have worked to explain their relation to individuals: "social structures create social persons who (re)create social structures who create social persons who (re)create ... ad infinitum" (Stryker, 1980: 53). They also recognize that such structures operate on two levels. "[W]e inhabit the *micro-world* of our immediate experience with others in face-to-face relations. Beyond that, with varying degrees of significance and continuity, we inhabit a *macro-world* consisting of much larger structures.... Both worlds are essential to our experience of society" (Berger and Berger, 1975: 8). Sociologists and feminists have studied the creation of the social person and the role that gender plays in that development. They have also examined the gendered dimensions of social structures and their impact upon members of the society (see Risman and Schwartz, 1989; Smith,1987; Bem, 1993).

Through my research into gender and social behaviour (Matthews and Beaujot, 1997; Matthews, 1997) it has become clear that the gender system can be more fully understood by acknowledging that it operates on several levels at one time. And that analyses are more complete when three levels are integrated into the explanatory framework. This tri-level model of the gender system includes the individual gender role orientation, a micro structure, and a macro structure. On the most basic level, men and women have individual gender role orientations, which they have developed through socialization and interaction over the course of their lives. These orientations consist of their beliefs about the appropriate roles for women and men and serve as guidelines for choices regarding presentation of self, relationships, and activities, as well as attitudes and values. However, these gender role orientations alone do not determine behaviour. Women's choices about how to behave, and how to present themselves are also influenced by the micro level gender structure, where they encounter others in daily interaction and negotiate their roles. Conforming to expectations is an integral part of interaction; people play roles in order to facilitate communication and joint action. They are also influenced by the macro level gender structure: the societal context which provides a landscape within which people act out their choices. It is my contention that the combination of the three levels and the way in which they interact, sometimes complementary and sometimes contradictory, can advance our understanding of the gender system and of young women's actions concerning weight and appearance.

For women making decisions about weight, food, and dieting, it is apparent that all three levels of the gender system influence their choices and behaviour. The macro structure, which has evolved over time, emphasizes the importance of appearance for women. While women's accomplishments are many, they continue to be judged by their appearance. It provides media images of "perfect bodies" and advertising which constantly criticizes and undermines women with appearance "flaws" (e.g., extra pounds, "problem" skin, gray hair). On the micro level, appearance is also salient. Because slenderness is the norm, there is some pressure in daily interaction to achieve it. Friends and family often encourage, and occasionally coerce, women into dieting and following the cultural ideal. Choosing not to diet, not following the ideal, seems to imply either slovenliness — "she's really let herself go" — or a personal statement about her unwillingness to conform. It is rarely accepted as a woman choosing to be comfortable with herself as she is. Thus interaction with others is influenced by their interpretation of her appearance. At the individual level, women's understanding of themselves is filtered through the existing social structures. Women know that they may be afforded more attention and respect if they follow the ideal;[1] they may also have internalized the societal standards throughout their lives. Thus, not "measuring up" to the ideal may cause personal anguish.

Women's decisions to diet are bound up with several levels of gender and must be considered in this light. The three levels of gender may be complementary or contradictory. That is, while people all live in a social world that appears to appreciate and promote only one body type, individual micro structures or individual gender role orientations may be in agreement or at odds with this standard. Women may be surrounded by people who disregard the cultural ideal and thus feel less pressure to conform in their interactions. They may have developed a critical stance to the societal ideal and experience no internal misgivings about weight and appearance. Or they may experience pressure on all three levels to follow the ideal. Clearly, in order to understand women's relationships to food and diet it is insufficient to focus on only one level. Women's social contexts and their individual gender role orientations are unique and must be considered as such.

Adolescence compounds the imperatives of the gender system. While all people feel the effects of the gender systems in which they operate, adolescents face unique challenges; adolescence is (1) a time of identity construction and (2) a time to find one's own location in the social world. They must navigate their ways through the layers of gender, making their choices and moderating their behaviours based on the context in which they live. And because individuals in this age group do not necessarily have a strong gender role orientation guiding their choices and actions, they are more vulnerable to the influences of the micro and macro gender structures. Also, because they have moved into a new "adolescent world," they can no longer rely on the "borrowed identity" from their childhood or the social status of their families. They must construct a unique self and establish their own position within the social world. This new self will largely be based on measures of status determined by peer groups and the broader youth culture.

Scholars and clinicians have developed a body of literature which discusses adolescent experience in great detail. We can trace study in this area back to Erikson's theory of stages. He argued that adolescence is a time of identity construction (Erikson, 1956). Until adolescence, identity is acquired through the family; individuals are socialized to see themselves much as the family sees them. In childhood, attitudes, values, and definitions are accepted uncritically. During adolescence, the earlier "borrowed" identity is questioned. Individuals ask themselves whether they agree with what they have been told, what they have learned. While reconstructing themselves, adolescents rely less on families (who played an important role in defining their childhood selves) and, in an effort to become independent and autonomous, turn towards their peers and societal standards. Part of this identity construction is, of course, the gender role orientation. Not just "who am I?" but "who am I as a woman?" "What does this involve?" "How should I act? think?" By the time these girls become adults, most have developed a sense of who they are as women. Therefore, when they are confronted with external stressors — for example, pressure from conflicts among individual, micro, and macro levels of the gender system — they have an internal sense of self that provides direction, which is lacking during early adolescence.

During adolescence, peers play a critical role. They are all experiencing similar changes, though at varying paces. By observing each other, they gain a sense of what is considered desirable and appropriate. While they observe, they are painfully aware that they are also being observed. The "imaginary audience" hypothesis suggests that adolescents are so sensitive to the evaluation/judgment of others that they perceive an audience, and behave accordingly, even when they are not being observed (Elkind and Bowen, 1979). As each adolescent is looking at others she is gathering the "raw resources" to shape her "self." Seltzer calls this the "comparative act" (Seltzer, 1989). Through the evaluation and critique and assessment of peers as well as imitation and experimentation, an adolescent gains the materials necessary to construct her "self." The knowledge that one is both judging and being judged makes adolescents highly conscious of their social desirability. Seltzer describes the adolescent world as the "peer arena," the micro structure where identity is constructed.

A further aspect of adolescence is finding one's location; that is, answering the question "where do I fit in?" This clearly is associated with the "social desirability" mentioned above. Just as the adult society is stratified — around class, race, and gender, for example — and one gains social power through position based on resources, the adolescent world is also hierarchical and also involves social power. The young person must find his or her place in this social structure. The social class from which the adolescent has come is still prevalent, but it is not sufficient to define who has power in the peer arena because it is based on the parent's resources and not on the adolescent's own characteristics. So the hierarchy among adolescents is based largely on personal resources. Because a significant part of constructing the self at this point is coming to understand gender role orientation and sexuality, the adolescent hierarchy is based in large part on one's presentation of manhood or womanhood. That is to say, the more "manly" men, displaying evidence of the strength, courage, and competence stereotypically expected of males, are considered more desirable than others. And among women, appearance and desirability are key attributes.

The powerful effect of the peer arena determines where any individual will fit in the social world. And in this arena, status is linked to appearance. Do you look the part? Or, as important, are you "playing" the part by dieting and making appearance a key part of your conversations and social world? Drawing messages from the larger macro gender structure, peers set the rules for "fitting in." And the unstable aspect of individual adolescents' own sense of self and their incomplete individual gender role orientation makes withstanding the pressure to conform difficult. By later adolescence, the tendency to conform is reduced (Berndt, 1979); individuals are more sure of themselves, have established their identities and gender role orientations, and may be, therefore, less vulnerable to the pressures of the micro and macro structures.

THIS STUDY

We undertook a qualitative research project in the summer of 1997 in Southern Alberta entitled "Growing Up Female." Through 25 depth interviews and a focus group with 6 girls, we explored adolescents' own perceptions of the challenges they face and how they navigate through the peer arena. The analysis was based on the principles of grounded theory (Glaser and Strauss, 1967; Strauss, 1987). That is, rather than trying to verify a specific hypothesis, we attempted to see their world as adolescents see it and discover how the three levels of the sex/gender system interact in their lives. From listening to the girls, reviewing the tapes, and examining transcripts, patterns emerged. The patterns were then explored more fully in subsequent interviews. The goal was not to quantify, but rather to get a sense of the importance of conforming to appearance norms within the adolescent social hierarchy.

The study began with a "typical" sample of young women chosen to represent different ages, social classes, and family arrangements. We quickly came to recognize that one's location in the hierarchy — insider, outsider, popular, outcast, etc. — was a critical variable and that the sample needed to reflect this diversity as well. (The girls' location in the hierarchy was also seen to influence them in terms of vulnerability to outside pressure and suggestion, but not in the ways one might predict.) The girls interviewed were from junior high, high school (one of whom attended an all-girl's high school), post-secondary institutions, and "drop outs" (many of whom had moved to alternative schools).

The importance of qualitative studies is that they can answer the question "why?" While quantitative studies can measure patterns to determine how many suffer from eating disorders and/or depression, and can assess the correlation between class, race, family, and behaviour numerically, one must look deeper to understand the underlying causal connection between these behaviours and the social factors in the girls' lives. One must try to understand their social world as they define and live it. It is vital for the researchers to avoid directing the discussions so as not to artificially focus on "constraints." Questions about what boys do to them or what society does to them denies the agency of the young women. Instead, this study asked the girls what they did to get along in their world. What are the rules in their world? Where did the rules come from?

Once we had collected information from all of the respondents, we identified patterns and came to understand how fully social hierarchy, and therefore social power, influenced their lives and how salient appearance is within that hierarchy. The best way to convey these findings is through case studies. In the following section, I will present the cases of women located in each of the various positions in the adolescent hierarchy, allowing each to speak about where they fit and how they came to hold that position. (Obviously, names have been changed but other details are unaltered.)

FINDINGS

Not surprisingly, the study indicates that for adolescent girls, appearance is salient, and notions about what is a desirable appearance are influenced by cultural norms: the macro structure provides powerful images and pressures. However, the girls made it clear that they were not all victims blindly following a goal set by the larger society without thought. And not all were dissatisfied with their appearances — not even all of those who spent a considerable amount of time and energy complaining about themselves and dieting. As they explained, appearance equals status. "Life would be easier if you looked like that [like the women on "Melrose Place" because people give you an easier time if you are pretty. If more guys like you, the girls give you an easier time, ... I don't think it should be that way, but I think society puts a lot of importance on your looks and size." And dieting and "fat" talk are also linked to status. The girls say they hate their bodies, or themselves, but when they discuss it more fully they often acknowledge that these statements are a means of fitting in.[2] They see that being part of the group means "obsessing" about their bodies, and group membership leads to success and social power. Those who fit the appearance criteria belong to the elite group, have power, know they have it, and enjoy wielding it. They reinforce their own position by deliberately making others feel inadequate. In fact, the power that they gain from their elite status is the power to exclude others. Their actions enhance their own positions while making appearance more salient for all girls (that is, making the micro structure extremely appearance-based).

The findings indicate that the most difficult time for young women was during junior high school, sooner than most people would like to believe is the case. Why should twelve year olds be caught up in issues about body and appearance? Are they trying to attract boys or men? Not really. They perceive other girls as both their audience and their harshest critics. Therefore, their preoccupation with weight and body is not about being desirable to the boys so much as gaining acceptance within the hierarchy. Boys can certainly exacerbate the pressure through name-calling and harassment, but this is only one part of the larger issue: finding your place in the social world is based on playing a role and looking the part. Even girls who attended all-girls' schools were subject to appearance pressures.

By later adolescence, women have already begun to develop a stronger sense of self and grown less vulnerable to the group's definition of who they are. By the end of high school, most girls had worked through much of their confusion and vulnerability. While they continued to talk about dieting and eating, about shape and size, this was much less about really planning to change their physical appearance than about "playing the game." Those who wanted to fit into the social hierarchy recognized that playing by these rules was necessary. However, by this stage, many girls had found their own groups of friends and set their own goals and challenges; they felt freer to express their own gender role orientations rather than following the group's definition of "woman."[3]

But in early adolescence, in junior high, most girls are just beginning the process of becoming independent and autonomous. There is a shift from living with the self-image that your parents and family defined for you to finding your "own" self with the assistance of peers. The peers' opinions count for a great deal because they form the social world in which this new self must establish herself. This is for most girls the period of most intense pressure to be autonomous and independent, greatest confusion about self, and therefore greatest vulnerability. And in this setting, young adolescent girls are becoming themselves, adults, and "women."

As indicated, most of the girls had worked through and beyond this understanding that their self-worth and status as women was tied to appearance by the time they reached the end of high school. But some girls did not get past this stage as easily as others. They continued to measure themselves by their appearance.

The Elite Group

The first group of those who had trouble moving beyond the adolescent definitions of desirability is made up of girls who were popular in junior high and high school; they were at the top of the social hierarchy. They seemed to be the winners who enjoyed the power that accompanied their status. They basked in the attention of all: other girls, boys, and most teachers. Two of the respondents talked about their experiences at the top of this hierarchy.

Jillian said that she is so good at being part of the group that she has no very clear sense of who she is. While in high school she knew exactly where she belonged. "I was definitely one of the popular ones." She said bluntly, "I consider myself to be pretty, that might have something to do with it [her popularity]. All my friends were popular." In fact, she revelled in the attention she received. She was teased by the boys about her looks ("I have big boobs") but found this flattering rather than intimidating or threatening. Being a part of the elite group was not a problem while in the insulated world of the high school, but she feels completely lost since leaving school. She found that the attributes that had given her power were no longer as valuable and she had no sense of direction. Jillian had allowed herself to be defined by the micro structure of her peer group and did not develop her own identity. She adopted the norms of the group without truly developing her own gender role orientation. Now that she has moved into a new environment, and without the guidance of her own individual gender role orientation, she feels aimless. "Where I stand now I'm not going anywhere. I'm not moving forward, I'm not moving backward, I'm just not going anywhere."

Reva was also very popular in high school, but recognized even at the time that this popularity had no solid foundation. She tried to hang on to status and popularity via appearance but was constantly concerned about it. "I was insecure but I don't know if other people knew it." She was unsure of her "self" and her true desirability. She recognized that popularity in high school was all about "material things, the way things look, everything on the outside." And she knew that she and her friends maintained their position by belittling others: "I think we were back stabbers and snobby, pretty snobby." But at the time this seemed reasonable. Having a boyfriend was an affirmation of Reva's status and her desirability. When she and her boyfriend broke up, she believed that she need only lose weight to regain her social position. "Actually, there were a couple of us that wanted to like, starve ourselves, try to lose weight so we just wouldn't eat." As a result, she developed an eating disorder. Eventually, she went into counselling and slowly has come to recognize the damage that her bulimia caused. But at the time, being thin made sense and gaining even a little bit of weight "really stressed me out."

Being in the elite group is no guarantee of success or well-being. While it worked for some in the short-term because they really did attain power — the power to exclude others — it did not bring long-term contentment. Upon graduation, the micro structure which had given girls power and a valued position was disbanded, leaving them directionless. Even within high school, all was not well. While this group appeared to dictate what was the appropriate appearance around the school, this was often a reflection of media images. "Popular" respondents mentioned TV shows and magazines that influenced their "style." And maintaining their social position involved a constant effort to keep up with the cultural ideal. For some this seemed easy, but for others like Reva, it was both difficult and undermining.

The "Wannabes"

While this seems like a pejorative term, it's how these girls describe themselves. They believe they will be in the most popular group if they just make a few changes; as a result, they spend their adolescent years struggling to reach the top of the pyramid. Kim is a member of this group. She says she understands the hierarchy and knows how it works: "The pressure increases as you move towards the popular group. You always have to prove yourself — based on how you look." She also knows that she is very close to the top and believes she could get there if she could just play the game right. And despite acknowledging that being popular doesn't always allow you to be a good person — "Popular people are jerks, they don't care about others, are very competitive, and treat people badly" — this doesn't stop her from wanting to be one of them. She works hard to win favour, to accept the rules. She believes that she could be popular if she was just a bit thinner. People in her group tend to diet for real, thinking they are just ten pounds away from having social power. She said the whole group began smoking on the same day when one person found out that it suppressed appetite. "We always talked about weight and how to lose it — drink Slimfast®, take Dexatrim®." Expending so much energy on reaching the top of the social hierarchy means that Kim spends little time trying to find her own direction or "self." She just knows she isn't happy. She feels "insecure, always beating myself up" and says "trying to fit in is limiting." She does not have a strong sense of self and therefore accepts the peer arena as the ultimate arbiter. The unquestioning acceptance of the peer arena and of the validity of the social hierarchy leaves people in this group, like those in the group "above" them on the popularity scale, vulnerable to a gender system which focuses on appearance. Their gender role orientation reflects this desire to achieve the ideal appearance: being a woman means looking the part.

Life in the Middle

The girls on the next level "down" on the hierarchical scale are the least vulnerable. While girls in this group still cope with pressure in the peer arena, they know they will never be at the top. As a result, they tend to examine it more critically, asking whether increased popularity is worth achieving. The answer is usually no. These girls form their own rules, have outside interests, and define "self" by a standard other than that of the hierarchy. One result of this alternate definition of self is that appearance is less salient than ability.

The individuals in this group often have outside interests — music, sports, religion, or the guiding movement, for example — that seem to help them find a self-worth regardless of their status at school. And at school they either are not picked on or don't let it bother them because they know that it isn't real. They construct their "self" based on what they are, not on what someone tells them they should be. Jana is never going to be at the top of the social hierarchy; she knows it and doesn't care. Her parents are of different races and she perceives that being biracial makes her "different." But it isn't a problem for her, she says, she just has to find her own way. When listening to Jana, she convinces you that this makes her stronger. She sees other "kids who try their hardest to be like another person and follow what they do" but distinguishes herself. She says unequivocally, "I am who I am." Racial slurs don't bother her, she makes a joke of it. When her best friend goes on and on about being fat, Jana believes "she does it just for attention." She isn't affected by media images either: "I'm not saying they're not beautiful but I'm saying that you don't know what's under all that make-up, that's four hours of make-up put on. I could look like that too." In essence, Jana isn't caught up in the gender system because she is not trying to prove herself in the peer arena. She has a strong sense of self, and does not accept the salience of appearance. However, she also notes that "I've never gotten fat so it has never been an issue for me." She can be truly comfortable with herself even when others in her world are striving to attain an ideal.

Una is also in this middle group. She is involved in both music and sports and spends much of her time with these activities. She says, "there's no pressure in my group. We don't have to spend time on make-up and hair." They don't want to be skinny partly because "the coach encourages us to stay fit." "I just don't have the time or the money to keep up." But she does acknowledge that it was harder to "be yourself" in junior high: "People were starting to form groups and you were left out if you didn't follow the group." But her close circle of friends didn't value the "popular" behaviours and didn't try to look the part.

Freedom from the tyranny of the gender system — which offers an almost impossible beauty standard — seems much more attainable for these young women. Because they do not have an opportunity to join the elite group, and because they have other qualities which make them strong, they are less vulnerable to its dictates. Not being part of the "in" crowd enables them to critique the hierarchy and its norms. In essence, these girls have developed gender role orientations which conflict with the macro structure and most of them have found a group of peers who also reject the salience of appearance.

On The Fringe

The next group — the "lowest" on the scale I have identified — is that of individuals who define themselves as "outsiders." They believe they are excluded because of their size and shape (though some of them have other characteristics which also contribute to their exclusion). These girls don't have the ability to break out of the outsider role into which they have been cast. For adolescents in this group, not fitting in really hurts; they feel rejected, ridiculed, isolated. Because they are so far from the norm — often very overweight or dealing with severe acne — they feel that they are suffering at the hands of their peers.

Some do come to hate themselves because they are treated so cruelly. Rachel describes one hurtful experience "I was trying to walk through the crowd when one guy said 'R, you don't belong in this crowd.' There was another girl who told me to f___ off. I was watching them I guess. I was pretty shy too. But I think *it* made me shy" The "it" she refers to is being excluded for not looking the "right" way. She feels very alone, even though there are several other girls on the "outside." She now "rejects the image thing" because she knows she doesn't fit ("I'm big boned like my dad") but she tried really hard in junior high. She really hated herself, even though she believed she was good on the inside, because of the way she was treated, because her body was devalued. In fact, Rachel feels pressure from her family to try harder to fit in — her mom would like her to change her appearance but she says she "just gave up trying."

Terry was also on the outside because of her weight. She had a couple of close friends "but the rest just left me out." Unlike Rachel, though, she "successfully" lost weight and reaped the rewards of following the group standard. She wanted to be small no matter what and simply stopped eating. At first everyone was pleased. She got more attention at school. People noticed her and talked to her. Initially, Terry liked being popular. "I felt better for a while but then came to realize that my life still sucked. Even when I was skinny I wasn't happy." She came to hate being popular because she could see more clearly than most how artificial the distinction was. Terry believes being skinny actually made her feel worse because the "popular Terry" wasn't the "real Terry." Her peers only saw her outside and still didn't recognize her true worth. Her family and few close friends became worried and did not support her dieting. And "I got tired of measuring every mouthful, having everyone watching and measuring every mouthful, so I started eating again." She gained the weight back and is now more comfortable with herself. "A whole new world opened up when I left school." Both Terry and Rachel understood how the social hierarchy worked. They knew how to gain power by following the mandate of the peer group. But they both chose not to. They lost status within the micro structure but grew more comfortable with themselves.

Karla was in a similar situation and it was terribly damaging. She started out in the popular group but "I found you had to stoop quite low to become popular. You had to be willing to be rude to all the other people." She wanted to be friendly to everyone and eventually the popular crowd turned their backs on her. They began to harass her and single her out; most of the insults were based on her appearance. "After a while, when so many people tell you something, you know you start to believe it's true, like you get it from enough people it starts to seem true, so I got enough people telling me I was ugly enough times, it kind of makes you believe it." Eventually she quit school because it became unbearable. She'd like to go back but "it's hard to get started up again if you live in the same place and you stay in the same place because everyone knows your past.... I can't start over again because the people who knew me, knew me as a geek, a freak." She feels better about herself now but doesn't want to face that kind of pressure again.

Examining the fringe group in terms of the three levels of gender, the "hell" for these girls was the micro gender structure of the peer arena; however, the values of the microsystem seemed to be reinforced — though not caused — by the larger macro structure. Our society is far more conscious of racism and sexism than of "lookism," especially as it is manifested in the adolescent world. Rachel and Karla internalized the negative messages directed at them by their peers. And they both came to hate themselves. Fortunately, they also both were able to overcome those feelings and recognize that their value was determined neither by their appearance nor by the critics in the peer arena.

IMPLICATIONS

Why is appearance so salient for adolescent girls? This study reinforces the understanding that at this period in her life, a girl has few measuring sticks and no long list of personal accomplishments. She must seek some means of reassuring herself that she is becoming an adult, a woman, an individual separate from her earlier, family-defined self. The larger macro gender structure of fashion magazines and advertisements sends messages that appearance is an important feature of power and desirability. This notion is adopted by adolescent girls in part because it is a field over which many feel they have some control (however illusory such a perception might be). They think that they can change their bodies, their clothing, their hairstyles. And they recognize that a specific kind of beauty is valued by the society at large. Thus appearance becomes a standard. This means that appearance actually does serve as a means of attaining social acceptability and power within the peer arena. As the study revealed, becoming a woman has less to do with the role one might play and more to do with the body. An interesting — perhaps startling — paradox emerged when we asked the respondents to define "woman." On the one hand, being a woman, they said, does not constrain career choices. They believe women can become anything they want. As available "sexual" roles grow, women are not defined by filling a specific role — for example, wife or mother. And as they perceive that more and more options are available in the work world, no particular job defines "woman." On the other hand, something distinguishes women from men. And that something is appearance. It is the girl's body that makes her a woman. Therefore, being a woman means one should be preoccupied with one's body and making one's body fit the part. None of the girls we spoke to was trying to diet to avoid growing up into womanhood; indeed, they were dieting to *achieve* womanhood, which they have come to accept is characterized by a very particular physical stature.

Young women are not all passive recipients of society's messages about the body. They perceive that they are not victims, that they are not trying to achieve certain appearances because men or boys want them to. Instead, they see themselves as actively involved in struggles with other women. Their female peers are the harshest critics. Among these critics, appearance brings social power, even if it is only the power to exclude others. They want the right body in order to attain social power and to prove themselves as women. Having a "boyfriend" is important in part because it sends a message to the peer arena that one has successfully achieved the requisite look. This becomes part of the measuring stick.

When the three levels of the gender system — the individual, micro, and macro levels — all agree that appearance is salient, the girl who experiences this will strive to attain the beauty standard. She believes that achieving this look will bring her social acceptance and membership into the elite group. If she fails to measure up to the standard, she faces the painful realization that she will be devalued by those with power in the peer arena. However, if she also learns that the imperatives of the peer arena are not absolute, and she is able to develop her own gender role orientation, then appearance loses its salience, and the elite group loses its power over her. If the three levels do not all agree, if girls have developed gender role orientations which do not incorporate the societal beauty ideal, or they belong to micro structures (as adolescents, perhaps a group of friends, sports team, or social club apart from the school-based peer arena) which value ability rather than appearance, then they are less subject to the appearance standards.

While adolescent girls face an exaggerated version of the gender system, all women are subject to the same forces. We must find our way within a societal landscape that valorizes beauty often above ability. And frequently we must do so in micro structures (in the work place and in our homes) which adopt this standard and devalue our actions. Like these adolescent girls, we remain strong if we develop gender role orientations which do not centre around appearance. And if we foster relationships and micro structures which value women for their strength and skill rather than their outward appearance. The results of this study are suggestive — not yet detailed enough or broad enough to be conclusive — but give us some insight into girls' own perceptions of their world and perhaps into the roots of gender role uncertainty that continues for some women into adulthood.

ENDNOTES

1. Obviously, this is a generalization. An important point of this argument is that individual women — especially adult women — move in microstructures and have developed "selves" that allow them to function effectively in a way inconsistent with the "body beautiful" standards of the larger society.

2. This is not say that some girls didn't experience genuine pain and self-hatred — their situations will be explored more fully in subsequent sections. It does mean that many girls are not as negative about themselves as it might appear from listening to their conversations among their peers.

3. It is possible that for university women living in dormitories, food, eating, and weight once again become salient as a new social hierarchy must be established. While this was not investigated in this study, we are currently interviewing women in residences to see if the pattern re-emerges.

REFERENCES

Bem, S. 1993. *The Lenses of Gender*. New Haven: Yale University Press.

Berger, P. and B. Berger. 1975. *Sociology: A Biographical Approach*. New York: Basic Books.

Berndt, T. 1979. "Developmental Changes in Conformity to Peers and Parents." *Developmental Psychology*. Vol. 15. p. 606–616.

Bordo, S. 1993. *Unbearable Weight: Feminism, Western Culture and the Body*. Los Angeles: University of California Press.

Brownmiller, S. 1984. *Femininity*. New York: Linden Press.

Brumberg, J. 1997. *The Body Project: An Intimate History of American Girls*. New York: Random House.

Chernin, K. 1981. *The Obsession: Reflections on the Tyranny of Slenderness*. New York: Harper and Row.

Elkind, D. and Bowen. 1979. "Imaginary Audience Behaviour in Children and Adults." *Developmental Psychology*. Vol. 15, p. 33–44.

Erikson, E. 1956. "The Problem of Ego Identity." *Journal of the American Psychoanalytic Association*. Vol. 4. p. 56–121.

Freedman, R. 1986. *Beauty Bound*. Lexington, Massachusetts: D.C. Heath and Company.

Glaser, B. and A. Strauss. 1967. *The Discovery of Grounded Theory*. Chicago: Aldine Publishing Co.

Greer, G. 1970. *The Female Eunuch*. London: MacGibbon & Kee.

Hesse-Biber S. 1996. *Am I Thin Enough Yet?: The Cult of Thinness and the Commercialization of Identity*. New York: Oxford University Press.

Matthews, B. 1997. "The Gender System and Fertility: An Examination of the Hidden Links." Population Studies Centre: Working Paper.

Matthews, B. and R. Beaujot. 1997. "Gender Orientations and Fertility Strategies." *Canadian Review of Sociology and Anthropology* 34(4): 415–428.

Pipher, M. 1996. *Reviving Ophelia: Saving the Selves of Adolescent Girls*. New York: Ballantine Books.

Risman, B. and P. Schwartz. 1989. *Gender in Intimate Relationships*: *A Microstructural Approach*. Belmont: Wadsworth Publishing Co.

Seltzer, V. 1989. *The Psychosocial Worlds of the Adolescent: Public and Private*. New York: John Wiley and Sons.

Shute, J. 1992. *Life Size*. New York: Avon Books.

Smith, D. 1987. *The Everyday World as Problematic: A Feminist Sociology*. Toronto: University of Toronto Press.

Strauss, A. 1987. *Qualitative Analysis for Social Scientists*. New York: Cambridge University Press.

Stryker, S. 1980. *Symbolic Interactionism: A Social Structural Version*. Menlo Park: Benjamin Cummings Publishing.

Wolf, N. 1991. *The Beauty Myth*. New York: Morrow Books.

THE SOCIAL CONSTRUCTION OF WOMEN'S SEXUALITY AS DEVIANT

C h a p t e r

14

Gayle MacDonald

INTRODUCTION

Why is a chapter needed on the social construction of women's sexuality? To begin with, it is not always clear as to what, exactly, constitutes a definition of women's sexuality ... should a definition include cultural expectations, sexual practices, historical stereotypes, or actual behaviours of women and girls? Nor is it clear from where such definitions would come. Should a definition of women's sexuality only come from women? If that is the case, then clearly what we come to know as a definition of sexuality is anything but a definition that comes from women. Some authors talk about "gaze" as a social construction, that is, the ways by which women create, express, and define their sexuality is usually from a vantage point of being looked at, which could be seen as a sexuality for others, rather than themselves. What does this mean? How does a sexuality for "others" get translated into behaviours, attitudes, or social positioning? This paper will explore some of these ideas. In other words, this paper will focus on how definitions of women's sexuality are constructed within the social world, and what the implications are for the use of such definitions.

It is apparent that many actions of women which are sexual in nature are defined by men, and defined in ways that are not conducive to healthy sexuality. For example, it is apparent that when literatures from across the disciplines are examined, certain patterns of repression are revealed around women's sexuality. Social control mechanisms used to limit or control the sexual behaviour of women and girls can include social practices of institutions such as the family, the church, or even the law. What the literature also reveals is that women's sexuality has been mystified, deviantized, vilified, or glorified (particularly in its virgin state) dependent on time, context, social and economic circumstance, sexual orientation, age, race, and physical and mental ability. It is clear that there are experiences all women

With thanks to research assistants Shawna Crozier and Jason Doherty.

share, that are common to definitions of women's sexuality, such as a biological reproductive capacity, and there are experiences that can be common only to a group of women, such as the repression of lesbian sexual identities (Leeks, 1996). However, we will discover that even those aspects of women's sexuality we tend to take for granted, such as the ability to reproduce, are not always shared or even desired by all women; in other words, there can be uncommon practices around reproduction. Further, one might think that prostitutes have very little in common with women who do not work the sex trades, but research shows that there are actually experiences prostitutes have which are common to many working women (Shaver, 1996). What is common and uncommon about many of these categorizations is examined in this chapter.

SEXUALITY AS "SOCIAL PRACTICE"

It is commonly assumed, in the social world, that one's sexuality is biologically determined, we genetically acquire it at birth. I would like to present the argument here, similar to that presented by VanEvery (1996), that sexuality "can be understood as *sexual* practices and as *social* practices" (36). The focus of this work is on the latter, that is, that sexuality is a social act, and that any social act has boundaries that are defined in the social world. These boundaries can be understood as what is permissible or allowable: what is "too far" regarding women's sexual practices and, conversely, what is "not enough." For example, it is usually assumed that when women initiate sex or talk about sexual experiences openly or have more than one partner (all behaviours men do quite acceptably) that these sexual practices are examples of women going "too far" in their sexual practices. Similarly, a women who, by her twenties, has not slept with more than one person, never talks or jokes about sex, and is assumed to never initiate sex (in other words, the logical extension of the behaviour preferred in the above categorization) is considered to have "not enough" sexual practices. These "standards" of female sexuality have one decided aspect in common, that is, they are both socially constructed. It could be argued that these assumptions often carry great social stigma and are very real practices in the lives of girls and women. What is interesting is when and how these behaviours become deviant within social context. Who is determining how much sex is "too far"? How do we know when women have had "not enough" sex? On what assumptions do these ideas rest?

It is clear from the foregoing paragraph that there are at least two categories of women's sexuality that exist in the social world. This chapter will explore the assumptions inherent in varying definitions of women's sexuality, even if those definitions are treated as fixed stable categories. For example, some definitions, such as "pregnant" or "prostitute," for many people constitute a precise category of a woman's sexual practice. What we find upon further examination is anything but a precise category; indeed, we find that categories might shift over time, and the perception of a category in one time and place might differ significantly from another in yet another time and place. A prostitute could be pregnant, for example, and a crack-addicted teen can be pregnant. Pregnancy can also be artificially induced. What, then, is normative practice for women's sexuality? If we can disrupt categories easily by simply giving an example that doesn't fit, then what categories, if any, work to describe women's sexuality?

This chapter will examine these ideas, and argue that regardless of category, definition, or sexual practice, every aspect of women's sexuality, in one context or another, can be considered as deviant.

SOCIAL CONSTRUCTIONISM

The theoretical paradigm that best explains the idea that sexuality is a social act is broadly known within sociology as interpretive sociology. Interpretive sociology looks at micro-relations within social structures, or everyday practices that can become institutional practices, as Dorothy Smith (1995) would argue that interpretive sociology can also be thought of, as Weeks (1995) points out, a "series of everyday practices."

Included within the interpretive tradition are earlier works by theorists such as Max Weber, who examines religion and institutional practices such as bureaucracy in order to explain social structure. Erving Goffman's work in the 1960s focused on roles we play as scripts, based on how we perceive ourselves in particular social contexts, or how we perceive ourselves relative to someone else. For Goffman, the relationship of the body is one with both "self identity and social identity," which he studies through interesting examples such as embarrassment, but as Shilling (1993) points out, he lacks a theoretical understanding of how these concepts of shared meaning (such as a gesture or a body movement) come to be linked with an understanding of the body in the social world (86, 88).

We "act" differently, then, according to our understanding of the relative importance of the person with whom we are interacting. Dorothy Smith, on the other hand, argued that "the local particularities of home and family" are part of where women's lives are constantly embedded not, as other theorists would argue, in the formal organizations of society (Hale, 195: 468). For Smith, women are rooted in the "everyday," in the micro relations and decision making that happens between intimates and family, regardless of whether or not women are in the public sphere playing other roles, such as professors or students. Dr. Smith also argues that it is important to uncover the ways in which women participate in the social world, including the academic one, when the very conversations and practices that make up the world of women are largely ignored, both in policy making and in academic "talk."

For social constructionists generally (Erving Goffman and, later, the more radical Michel Foucault), the argument around socially constructed interaction includes not only "talk," but categories of the body as well. It is these categories of the body that are most interesting to us here, as they will give us a window to talk about sexuality as a social practice, and to discuss women's sexuality as deviant within that context.

In Shilling's work on the social body (1993), he echoes the tracing of naturalistic to social constructionist to feminist analyses of the body. Naturalistic theories, for example, focus on the biological body as determining social, economic, and political power (1993: 41). Shilling traces, for example, how the characterization of women as "weak" and "unstable" led to increased medicalization and management of women's bodies in the 19th century (Shilling, 1993). What this reveals is how easily naturalistic theories led to assumptions of disease around women's sexuality, and the ensuing social control mechanisms that such assumptions create.

Social constructionist theories, on the other hand, are much more concerned with the socially created boundaries around women's bodies and sexuality, and the implications such boundaries had for the expression of women's sexuality. Shilling points out, however, that there are differing meanings for the body within social constructionist work, particularly that of Foucault.

> For Foucault, the body is not only given meaning by discourse, but is wholly constituted by discourse. In effect, the body vanishes as a biological entity and becomes instead a socially constructed product which is infinitely malleable and highly unstable (Shilling, 1993: 74).

Foucault's work talks of both the historicities and the particular "strategies" that inform us about sexuality. For Foucault, "there were four great strategies relating to sexuality ... the hysterisation of women's bodies; a pedagogisation of children's sex; a socialisation of procreative behaviour; and a psychiatrisation of perverse pleasure" (Bell, 1993: 18). Particular bodies became the target of these strategies; the most relevant for this discussion is the "hysterical woman" and the "perverse adult." What Foucault teaches us is that discourse as well as particular strategies for "dealing" with those so labelled as hysterical or perverse, became common language, and were well-evidenced in particular social control mechanisms around the body. For Shilling, the strength of Foucault's analysis rests ultimately on his insistence that the body is controlled through surveillance and stimulation. For example, fertility, health and illness, diet and habitation, all became a focus in the 20th century for surveillance and social control, as well as sexuality as an expression of self-identity and lifestyle (Shilling, 1993: 77).

Where feminist work intersects with Foucault is around the notion of defining concepts around women's bodies as socially, rather than naturally, constructed. Feminists further agree with Foucault that particular "strategies," as he calls them, are frequently employed to socially control women's bodies, as well as their expressions of sexuality. Nowhere is this more apparent than in the field of medicine.[1] What, for example, constitutes "normal" sexual appetite for women? Are there socially prescribed "normal" and "abnormal" sexual practices which define and circumscribe women's sexual expression in the social world? How do these practices influence women's perceptions of their bodies?

What is useful for the current analysis is that sexuality is viewed entirely differently from theories on deviance. That is, theories on deviance tend to focus on two key areas pertaining to women of interest to criminal law, specifically. They are prostitution and sexual assault (McDermid Gomme, 1993). In more recent deviance texts, authors are beginning to address concepts of "femicide," which inverts what we normally think of in killings, "homicide" (Ellis and Dekeseredy, 1996).[2] But none of these works specifically focus on the social construction of women's sexuality as deviant. In other words, deviance is an expression most often used to designate "other," someone different from the norm, someone who doesn't quite fit. It is this premise that needs exploration, as it is nowhere more apparent than in the area of women's sexuality.

SEXUALITY AND TYPOLOGIES

This section will examine the need to explore or rename categorizations of women's sexualities. We might begin by asking the question, what does it mean to think about sexuality and typologies? For the sake of argument, it is useful to see what types of themes, patterns, or common (or uncommon) experiences women have around sexuality which have been explored by researchers already.

Groneman's (1994) work demonstrates a decidedly dominant definition of women's sexuality, a unilateral defining process that attempted to "fix" what was female.

> In the late nineteenth century ... even minor transgressions of the social structures that defined "feminine" modesty could be classified as diseased ... Starting in the late eighteenth century, woman's nature was increasingly defined as inextricably bound up with her reproductive organs. This supposedly objective, scientific "fact" created the new framework within which physicians and other authorities found justifications for the limitations of women's social and economic roles ... (Groneman, 1994: 342).

Groneman demonstrates that many sexual practices, lesbianism, so-called nymphomania, and prostitution were grouped together (356) and deviantized in attempts to socially control such practices. Any attempts to socially control women's sexuality, however, often had horrific consequences, as any historical work on botched abortion attempts demonstrates. The general health and well-being of women, particularly young women, was often used as a rationale by medical authorities in particular, both to subvert women's authority as healers and care-providers, and to control young women.

What Groneman's work stunningly reveals is that clitorectomies, believed over the past decade to exist only in countries with un-Western cultures and religions, was, indeed practised in the 19th century as a "cure" for any disease supposedly associated with female sexuality.

> Lesbians, nymphomaniacs, and prostitutes — and by extension, suffragists, feminists and the modern woman — were not only considered diseased, but dangerous as well. Physicians were particularly upset by the sexual response of very young girls or old women. Too young or too old to reproduce, little girls' and postmenopausal women's sexual desires were considered by some doctors as signs of disease (Groneman, 1994: 356–7).

In field work on women's experience of sexuality (Daniluk, 1993), it was found that women experience a number of common themes connected to the complexity of sexual identity (53). They are structural/institutional sources of oppression, such as medicine, religion, sexual violence and the media, sexual development within patriarchal culture in terms of sexual expression, reproduction, body image, and intimate relationships (58–65). What this means is that social forces themselves can create conditions under which women experience oppression in expressing their sexuality in any form.

To understand Daniluk's work more fully, one need only think of the number of admonitions in most religious doctrine around women's sexuality, which circumscribe sexual relations and reproductive capacities within and outside of marriage (read not encouraged at all, in the latter!) If we examined this example further, we would soon realize that young women who are lesbians, young women who desire to be sexually active, and women who are artificially inseminated, are not included in these definitions of sexuality. If we examined, in addition, the media messages around women's sexuality, that women's sexuality is associated with the sale of everything from toothpaste to automobiles, we would soon come up with the question: just what aspects of female sexuality are valued, celebrated, and nourished, as opposed to which aspects are dominated, exploited, and destroyed?

The news is not altogether negative. Daniluk claims that not all of these experiences were completely alien to women; some were nurturing, uplifting, and actually healthy. In other words, women's sexuality seems to somehow survive intact *despite* the incursions of dominant and patriarchal discourse. To put it another way, if institutional practices and male-centred power relations create specific definitions and social practices common to women's sexuality, it does not subsume those healthier, female-centred expressions of women's sexuality, at least not entirely.

It is very clear to most of us that women's sexuality is not nurtured, celebrated, or revered in western culture. On the other hand, what is clear is that certain definitions of women's sexuality, or archetypes of what women are supposed to be sexually, are quite valued. There is only one problem with this: the vast majority of women do not fit the prescribed image of women's sexuality. In fact, some researchers have actually explored how these prescriptions are actually manifest in a culturally familiar form, such as magazines.

Researchers such as Durham have explored this idea, by examining a sample of women's magazines to illustrate her hypothesis. Durham examines how women's sexuality is "channelled in socially prescribed directions" and she explores how women's magazines contribute to some (Durham, 1996: 19).

What Durham goes on to illustrate is how, exactly, a concept of woman is presented in text and through image as an idealized size and sexual orientation. What this means is that women's magazines continually encourage and sustain certain images of women that are neither representative of the average body type (in fact, they are usually "off the mark" quite substantially in terms of average body size) nor do they represent women who are not heterosexual. The message is simple and clear: look good to catch a man. This concept is encouraged both through a vast consumerism of "beauty" products and great care, time, and attention to the maintenance of this image through diet, surveillance, make-up, and exercise. In other words, it takes a lot of work, money, and energy to become the normative, socially prescribed woman. This idea can again be examined from the point of view of an economically disadvantaged woman, a poor woman or girl, a single mom, a homeless teen ... how much money can they spend on beauty products? Can these beauty products be used on all bodies, including all those non-white or larger or disabled bodies that are rarely seen in such publications?

But let's take our examination of these ideas in another direction. Let's assume that the diet has been scrupulously followed, and the advice on clothing, beauty tips, manners, and behaviour are adhered to by young women. In other words, the state of " normative" sexual expression/identity is achieved. Are young women then happy and comfortable in this role? Are these expressions of women's sexuality rewarded, accepted, are they pleasuring for young women? What the following analysis reveals is that there are many dimensions through which women's sexuality can be fashioned, but all, in the end, can be considered deviant in any given time or context.

CONFORMIST

There are three categories I've developed to analyze social constructions of women's sexuality: conformist, nonconformist, and transcending boundaries. I define these categories three ways, as any categorization (be it wife, lover, or prostitute), can overlap others. For purposes of this paper, then, it is preferable to talk about how sexual practices can be accomplished in a variety of social settings or social contexts.

Conformist conceptions of women's sexuality are those which adhere to status quo perceptions of women's sexuality, such as motherhood or monogamous sexual relations between heterosexuals who are married, for example. Conformity, in this regard, can be defined as a conception of sexuality that is intimately connected to the experience of childbirth as an affirming act of female sexuality. Arguably, this category might also include lesbian families which emulate straight marriages, that is, monogamous sexual relations and the birthing/adoption of children. One could argue that liberal discourse on "rights" including family rights and the demand for reproductive "rights" (the right to experience childbirth) could fit into this category. Closeted lesbian/bisexual women are to be included here as well, as closeting, by definition involves a conforming, hidden life.

Despite the fact that conformist behaviour is treated as the "desirable" one in dominant cultures, it is clear that even young girls do not wish to publicly acclaim their sexuality in any way. In other words, one would think that if young women are conforming to sexual norms, if they are "fitting in," so to speak, to accepted, established scenarios of sexuality and body image, they should feel quite comfortable with their sexuality. Research such as that by Holland et al. (1994) shows that they do not. As Holland et al. illustrate,[3] even the lack of explicit language used by young girls to describe sex reflects a "dominant culture proscription for them to "keep hidden" the secrets of sexuality," including, they add, menstruation.[4] The disembodiment young women exhibited in this study illustrates the difficulty women have in (a) expressing sexual desire, (b) defining good sexual experience, and (c) actualizing their sexual desire, in the form of sexual relations over which they have control. These findings are disturbing, as they indicate that young women generally do not express, name, or initiate sexual desire. How desire is socially constructed is the focus of yet another study.

Conducted by Gigi Durham, a study examining issues of young women's magazines, notably *Cosmopolitan, Glamour,* and *Seventeen* from June 1994–June 1995, for topics of women's sexuality and/or desire revealed a total of 68 articles obtained for analysis (1996: 22). What the author does is to construct the contradictions and paradoxes surrounding desire for young women. For example, although the author points out that many articles "emphasized women's freedoms ... in seeking out sexual partners and expressing sexuality," the way in which that sexuality was described, constructed, and presented in the magazines always involved submission to male desire (23).

What a rendition such as this omits is sexual pleasure for "her" so to speak, or an examination of what pleasures a woman, in terms of presentation of the body and of sexual desire. In other words, the images of desire and of sexuality presented in these magazines are most decidedly unilinear, and more representative of culturally prescribed expectations than they are of actual experiences. Rarely, if at all, for example, do we see accurate portrayals of the level of violence encountered by young women in their sexual experiences with men, nor do we see portrayals of lesbian desire as a legitimate form of sexual expression. Large women are not portrayed in these magazines (except by inference: in other words, to be large is to be undesiring or undesirable, by default) and neither are women with disabilities, who have different sexual requirements. In other words, the experiences are not always reflective of the actual experiences of young women.

Cultural prescriptions, then, such as those found in magazines, reinforce the normativeness of assumptions around sexuality. Durham's study reveals the reinforcement of those normative prescriptions through information on the "management" of the body that female sexuality requires in a conformist culture: the sculpting, maintenance, primping, exercising, dieting, starvation, and body adornments of all types "required" for women to look good, presumably, not for themselves, but for men.

What does this tell us about how this happens? Why is female desire constructed to pleasure men? Janet Holland has an idea here that might help explain how this happens:

> To understand men's power to appropriate female desire, and the part women play in accepting or resisting this power, we need to understand issues of control in relation to the body (Holland, 27).

Issues of control in relation to the body happen in the everyday, mundane experiences that women face in the social world, particularly in the family. This is commonly understood in households organized on heterosexual models of relations that male power is actualized in the everyday, so that even dinner is served when "the man" of the household needs it served. In other words, everyone eats when "daddy" eats. The analogy holds true with sexual relations. The sex act is defined by male coitus, everything is a precursor to ejaculation, which is the defining moment of the sexual act, in fact any other activity up to and after that point is referred to as exactly that: "before" and "after" sex. In other words, caressing, oral sex, shared fantasy, female orgasm, or any other activity does not get defined in the same way(s). What this illustrates is how insidious male sexual power actually is, as male sexual power can construct a definition of sex to which conformist women adhere. What this really means is that initiation of sex, where, when, if, and how sex happens is not negotiated space between the couple, it is defined and determined by the male.

If this is what actually happens in relationships, and these relationships are then further managed by media image, then what does this actually tell us about definitions of female sexuality? What does it mean to young women, in particular, to have the script "written" and rehearsed so well as they come into their awareness of sexual desire? What it means is the reinforcement of conformity in terms of female sexuality — which, by definition, renders alternative sexual expression, both in image and in actuality, other, different, and deviant. Put another way, if a young woman runs away from home, or is poor, or is raped, or is lesbian, or by either desire or design will not have children or be married, or is disabled, has AIDS, or is larger than size 9, she simply doesn't fit the script of conformity outlined for her by her social world.

It appears, then, if the sexual practices involved in any socially constructed definition of women's sexuality are more conformist than not, there may be more tolerance for these behaviours. However, the definition of what is considered deviant is rarely taken from a women's point of view.

NONCONFORMIST

Nonconformist sexuality can be defined as those social practices of female sexuality that are "outside" the normative prescription for female sexuality (read non-reproductive sex), either as a chosen political practice on the part of the participants or as the social prescriptions of this behaviour by conformist definers. Examples of nonconformist sexual practices could include non-monogamous heterosexual or lesbian relationships, prostitutes, radical lesbian separatists, and heterosexuals who choose to remain childless. Nonconformist sexual practices could also include violent sexual practices which do not involve consent, either sex and/or pornography with children, or normative sexual engagements after bouts of violence.

There are sexual practices that are politically chosen, such as radical lesbian separatists or non-monogamous lesbian or heterosexual relationships, and there are nonconformist practices involving erotica and other props, which are nonconformist but do not involve harm. (Legal definitions of harm are not always useful here, as they may outlaw practices which, between consenting adults, are nonconformist but nevertheless pleasurable.) An important distinction should be made here between practices which are consensual and involve partners on an equal footing with each other, and those which are non-consensual, and involve an imbalance of power. Sex acts involving children are usually considered to be non-consensual, for example.[5] To illustrate, in a recent study on sex offenders, it was found that when the victims of sexual assault in legal cases were *children*, the offenders were more likely to receive *shorter* sentences (Byers et al., 1997). This seeming contradiction actually fits with definitions of what is sexually deviant and what is not: when heterosexual men practise deviant behaviour, it is clear that they are protected by sanction of law, rather than punished. However, when women work at what is considered deviant sexual practice, such as the sex trade industry, it is clear, even from many feminist readings of sexual practice, that such work is nonconformist and can garner little sympathy under the law.

This irony is not lost to researchers working in this area (Shaver, 1996; Lowman, 1990). What is even more telling, however, are when sexual practices that are considered deviant in one cultural setting, let's say a Western definition, for example, are imported from another country/culture. Leslie Jeffrey (1998) has explored the economic and political organization around Thai brothels, first initiated after the Vietnam war for "R and R" venues for the American military. Flight "tours" of Canadian clientele have been brought in to patronize said brothels, a relationship that Jeffrey argues has been supported by state apparatus in Thailand and, arguably, in those countries exporting clients (which include England, Germany, and the US, as well as Canada). Practices such as the importation of sex trade workers to Canada have been noticed by organizations which track the movements of sex trafficking. Preliminary work in Canada (Jeffrey, 1998) has indicated that young Thai women, some of whom think they may become au pair workers or nannies in Canada or the US, are actually brought over by pimps, who then take their passports and claim the girls "owe" them the passage fare to Canada, if they ever want to see home again.

What this information offers to the current discussion is an interesting paradox: if we in western culture believe that sex trade work is nonconformist, and have socially structured sanctions at every venue to socialize girls and women to that fact, how is it possible that the sex-trade workers can actually be imported into the country? We know, if we study other literatures on immigrant women, that many services are denied immigrant women, such as language training, job skills, etc. How is it possible that young women can be brought into the country, work, and escape largely undetected by both police and immigration officials? Studies answering these questions have yet to be conducted in Canada. The paradox is interesting, however, as there appears to be a distinction between sexual practices themselves as deviant and the sexual practitioners, depending on the example used. Are the sexual practitioners the young women or the sex traffickers who are really pimps? Is it the sexual practice that is deviant or *where* it occurs?

It is clear, then, that the sexual practice *itself* may not constitute nonconformity. Perhaps the presence or absence of consent might offer a clearer definition. In cases of sexual violence, many feel that the boundaries are clear: those who practice sexual violence are potential offenders, those who receive it are victims. Under most circumstances, that definition holds: rapists, wife-batterers, incest perpetrators, pedophiles, and pedophiles who murder are immediate examples that spring to mind. But are there circumstances in which forms of violence are permissible, even acceptable? This statement seems unthinkable in most feminist circles. Perhaps the last category visited here, that of transcending boundaries, might shed some light on this apparent contradiction.

One might think of nonconformity, then, as the "evidence" of deviant behaviour in women's sexuality. But is the social construction of the virtue or value of women's sexuality, such as that which occurs with the sex trade worker, the true indicator of deviance? Feminists themselves have contradicted their apparent support for the expression of women's sexuality. In a publication of conference proceedings aptly titled "Good Girls, Bad Girls: Feminists and Sex Trade Workers Face to Face," feminists are accused of taking victim stands far too quickly concerning prostitution. Prostitutes rights groups, such as COYOTE (Call Off Your Old Tired Ethics) or others of similar ilk, have long argued that feminists take a simplistic view of sex trade workers, and do not account for situations in which prostitutes act according to their own free will. Such debates are interesting to us here, as they illustrate that ideas of conformity versus nonconformity might hinge on abstract ideas such as consent, rather than actual acts. If that is the case what, then, becomes the deviant sexual practice? Shouldn't the deviant, given that logic, be the client for sex workers, the pimps that make a living off the avails of women and girls in the sex trade, or the pornography industry? These questions get at some of the more problematic, unanswered queries raised by analyses that focus on the sexuality of women as socially constructed, rather than naturally occurring.

TRANSCENDING BOUNDARIES

Transcending boundaries refers to sexual practices which go beyond the conformist (sex for reproduction) and nonconformist (sex for recreation, work, or violent sexual practices) categories. This category involves sexual practices which play with sexual boundaries, both social and physiological, and include sexual practices that many women who would place themselves in the first two categories would not consider sexual at all, but involve real or aesthetic violence. There are both benign and more sinister practices that might fall under this categorization. They may include, under the benign categories, female body builders, transvestites, bisexuals, and out lesbians who choose to marry heterosexual men. The more sinister form might include sado-masochistic (SM) practices, bondage, and violent pornography. What is common to all of these practices is that they cross boundaries, of even what is considered nonconformist sexuality, both in image, such as the body builders (Aoki, 1996:59–74), or what is historically considered "too much" sex, such as nymphomania (Groneman, 1994: 337–361) or the (re)presentation of women's sexuality that occurs with cross-dressing (Tewksbury, 1994: 27–43). What all of these categories also have in common is an idea that social practices around sexuality, definitions of gender, and constructions of the sexual are categories that move along a continuum of acceptability/non-acceptability, rather than a fixed or agreed upon point. As Richard Tewksbury suggests, in his analysis of female impersonators:

> Female impersonators see themselves as impersonators of women, not as women (33). The transformative process by which men construct visual and interactional images of women provide opportunities for examining how negotiated definitions of gender are socially constructed (1994:41).

In his study, Tewksbury demonstrates that even that which is nominally considered to be deviantized sexual practice, in other words, men who dress up as women and perform, has rationale, purpose, even legitimacy within certain contexts. In some of his examples, in which men are confused quite often with women, he illustrates clearly just how "performative" and artificial our notions of gender are. In other words, to be confused for a woman if one is a man impersonating a woman is to achieve a certain sense of satisfaction: the man has "passed" as a woman, the boundary has been successfully crossed.

Other, more recent examples of transcending boundaries include fairly normative sexual desire, but nonconformist practices to achieve same. I place these practices in this categorization as the transcendence of boundaries required are social, rather than physiological. These sexual practices could include those of the elderly, as well as the sexual practices of physically and mentally challenged women. When one thinks of sexual practices, one doesn't often conjure up images of making love with someone after chemotherapy or bowel surgery, or with a burn victim or someone who is crippled or aged. Our socially constructed images of sexuality operate with pristine, polished, perfect bodies, images fed to us with dazzling rapidity through multimedia forums. These images are barely blemished, let alone severely damaged. Where, then, do the sexual practices of the women described above fit? They fit in transcending boundaries, which is exactly what women with mental and physical challenges have to do to have anything approaching normative sexuality. What places these sexual practices here is how women with these challenges are viewed, rather than how these women may construct their own sexualities.

The subject of this section comes from a category of sexual behaviour that is deviantized by a majority of sexual practitioners, however they define themselves, and that is consensual sado-masochistic (SM) sexual activity. The public attention a recent case in Toronto received is a case in point. The case involves charges that were brought against a woman for being the keeper of a common bawdy house, which is being disputed by the defendant. She argues that her definition as a dominatrix should prevail, that what she offers is erotic and actualized fantasy, rather than "sex for sale." This contestation offers some interesting challenges, both to law and to social perception. Law tends to treat any form of sexuality that may contain violence as prohibitive. SM practitioners argue that their sexual practices involve the consensual participation in some type of pain rituals, all sexually connotative to the participants. The literature on these behaviours, as Andrea Beckman points out, is sparse.

> Very much in contrast to the area of sexual behaviours in which sexology, psychiatry, psychology and various media provide discourses and endless specifying categories, the area of "discrete altered states of consciousness" offers a lot of scientific silence (Beckman, 1998: 4).

Beckman's work intersects Foucauldian notions of "transcendental experiences through consensual SM" and "the history of truth" (Beckman, 1998: 2). Beckman cites that in *The History of Sexuality (II)* Foucault "suggested that the only way to go beyond an identification of ourselves with our "sex-drive" or "genital desire" would be a return to "bodies and pleasures." Beckman's analysis of this is that Foucault was arguing that we needed to abolish "the internal supervisor"; that is, everything is possible within a negotiated, consensual attempt to "push limits" of the sexual experience. Foucault, himself a practitioner of SM, connects what he terms "limit experiences" to a revelation of an inner self, an inner truth. This truth, Beckman argues, needs to involve "deliberate exposure of an individual to experiences of mental and/or physical pain [which] allows for possible changes of 'self'." For Foucault, as well as other philosophers she explores, truth has to be "founded on experience and is always uncertain, fragmented and experimental" (Beckman, 1998: 3).

What Beckman explores in her paper, in her interviews with 14 out of 16 practitioners of consensual SM is that their experience with the achievement of transcendence appears to happen most often in the "bottom" position (also known as "subs" or "slaves") rather than those in the "top" (6).What is ironic here is that, contrary to all literature on sexuality, transcendence is achieved when participants push "physical limits" and are essentially in positions of submission. This flies directly in the face of most feminist literature which argues the opposite, in fact, that submission in sexual practices is the most exploitative of women. To assume a literal position of submission, as SM requires, is seemingly antithetical to all that has been argued as beneficial for the sexual emancipation of women's sexual expression. But Beckman does not let her readers rest easily with the concept of submission. She rightly points out that the notion of adherence to ritual, endurance past limits, and submission to greater transcendent or spiritual awakening is at the core of many religious/transcendental experiences, including Christianity. Beckman's work raises many interesting questions around dominance and submission and the questioning of rigid sexual ordering that ignorance of SM might imply.

So what do these examples tell us about the social construction of women's sexuality as deviant? That it appears that many sexual practices, even those considered normative, can be constructed as deviant given specific social, cultural, or economic circumstances. But as even the last example (SM) demonstrates, there is often an internal logic, a place for practices arguably deviantized by a majority of sexual practitioners, within the social world.

All sexual practices, then, have a social context. Not all, especially those of women, are valued, respected, or even tolerated. Prescriptions for the "good mother" abound, but women who practise even this conformist sexual role often get vilified and blamed for every ensuing behaviour of the children, and get very little economic support or even moral support for the complexities of family life in a social world that increasingly devalues it, while proclaiming women's equality at the same time. The irony of a sexuality of women that demands submission to authority (SM being the exception), surveillance of the body and of the self, maintenance of a rigid definition of body form, and forced reproduction will only continue to serve, as it has over the centuries, the needs of straight men. Alternative definitions of women's sexuality, even within conformist categories, are sorely needed. For only these constructions will truly release women's sexuality from the construction of deviant behaviour.

ENDNOTES

1. Bryan Turner examines notions of reproduction and regulation from a theoretical point of view. He argues cogently that the changing nature of disease in the 20th century (the AIDS epidemic, for example), aging populations, the impact of technology, and the failure of hospitals to deal with these issues adequately, leave a great deal of room for sociological analysis (1992: 155–156).

2. What is useful about this distinction is that it begins to focus our attention on the "female" aspect of being a victim of violence, and given that most victims of interpersonal violence *are women*, it is a designation long overdue.

3. In that study, the difficulties of interviewing women in their middle to late teens about sex practices and sexuality posed such difficulties the authors are writing another piece on that!

4. I think it is both interesting and revealing that the spell check on my computer did not recognize the word "menstruation," one of the most common coming-of-age physiological acts of the female body.

5. However, at a conference on Gender, Law and Sexuality at Keele University, UK, in June, 1998, there were a great number of papers discussing at length the differences in the age of consent for sexual practices. This was topical in Britain at that time, as there was a private member's bill before the House of Lords that argued against a two-tiered age level for consenting to sexual activity, the age of consent for heterosexual practices was sixteen, for gay/lesbian sexual practices, eighteen.

REFERENCES

Aoki, Doug. "Sex and Muscle: The Female Bodybuilder meets Lacan," *Body and Society* Vol. 2 (4): 59–74, 1996.

Beckman, Andrea. *The potential for 'transcendence' with the context of consensual 'SM,'* paper presented at the International Conference on *Gender, Sexuality and Law* held at Keele University, Stoke-on-Trent, UK, June, 1998.

Bell, Laurie. *Good Girls, Bad Girls: Sex Trade Workers and Feminists Face to Face* Toronto: The Women's Press, 1987.

Bell, Vikki. *Interrogating Incest: Feminism, Foucault and the law* London: Routledge, 1993.

Byers, S., Roland Crooks, Brian Griffiths, Brian Mackiu, Gayle MacDonald, Greg MacDonald, Raymonde Marcoux-Galarneau, Cheryl Renaud, Brenda Thomas, Brian Thompson, and Pamela Yates. *The extent of Sex offences and the Nature of Sex offenders in New Brunswick: A Research Project.* Report Submitted to the New Brunswick Department of the Solicitor General and Correctional Services Canada by the Sex Offenders Research Team of the Muriel McQueen Fergusson Centre for Family Violence Research, 1997.

Currie, Dawn and Valerie Raoul. "Anatomy of Gender: women's struggle for the body," Ottawa: Carleton University Press, 1992.

Daniluk, Judith C. "The meaning and experience of female sexuality: a phenomenological analysis," *Psychology of Women Quarterly* 17 (1993) 53–69.

Durham, Gigi. "The Taming of the Shrew: women's magazines and the regulation of desire," *Journal of Communication Inquiry* 20:1 (Spring, 1996): 18–31.

Groneman, Sylvia. "Nymphomania: The Historical Construction of Female Sexuality," *Signs: Journal of Women in Culture and Society,* vol. 19, no. 2, 1994: 337–361.

Hale, Sylvia M. *Controversies in Sociology, A Canadian Introduction* (2nd ed.) Toronto: Copp Clark, Ltd., 1995.

Holland, Janet, Caroline Ramazanoglu, Sue Sharpe, and Rachel Thomson. "Power and Desire: the embodiment of female sexuality" in *Feminist Review* 46, (Spring, 1994): 21–38.

Jeffrey, Leslie. "Prostitution in Thailand," Guest speaker, Gender Studies Week, March 1998, St. Thomas University, Fredericton NB, Canada.

Jeffrey, Leslie. *Sex and borders: Gender, national identity and the 'prostitution problem' in Thailand.* PhD Dissertation, York University, Toronto. Forthcoming.

Leeks, Wendy. "Out of the maid's room: Dora, Stratonice and the lesbian analyst" in *Outlooks: Lesbian and Gay Sexualities and Visual Cultures,* Peter Horne and Reina Lewis (eds) London: Routledge, 1996: 48–60.

Lowman. J. "Notions of Formal Equality Before the Law: The Experience of Street Prostitutes and their Customers" in *The Journal of Human Justice,* Spring 1990.

MacDonald, Gayle. "(In)difference: women, sexuality, deviance and law," paper presented to the International Conference on *Gender, Sexuality and Law* held at Keele University, Stoke-on-Trent, UK, June, 1998.

Shaver, F. "The Regulation of Prostitution: Setting the Morality Trap." In Schissel, B. and Mahood, L. (eds). *Social Control in Canada: Issues in the Social Construction of Deviance*, (1996).

Schatzki, Theodore R. and Wolfgang Natter. *The Social and Political Body*, New York: The Guilford Press, 1996.

Shilling, Chris. *The Body and Social Theory,* London: Sage, 1993.

Shildrick, Margrit. *Leaky Bodies and Boundaries: Feminism, postmodernism and (bio) ethics.* London: Routledge, 1997.

Smith, D. *The Everyday World as Problematic: A Feminist Sociology.* Toronto: The University of Toronto Press, 1987.

Tewksbury, Richard. "Gender construction and the female impersonator: the process of transforming 'he' to 'she,' *Deviant Behavior: An interdisciplinary journal,* 15, (1994):27–43.

VanEvery, Jo. "Sinking into his arms ... Arms in his sink: Heterosexuality and Feminism Revisited" in *Sexualizing the Social: Power and the Organization of Sexuality,* Lisa Adkins and Vicki Merchant (eds) London: MacMillan, 1996.

Weeks, Peter. *The Microsociology of Everyday Life in Controversies in Sociology: A Canadian Introduction.* Hale, S. Toronto, Ontario: Copp Clark Ltd, 1995.

Zatz, Noah D. "Sex Work/Sex Act: Law, Labor, and Desire in Constructions of Prostitution," *Signs: Journal of Women in Culture and Society,* vol. 22, no. 2, (1997): 277–308.

ORDERED LIVES AND DISORDERED SOULS
Pathologizing Female Bodies of the Colonial Frontier[1]

C h a p t e r

15

Jo-Anne Fiske

The female deviant is a cultural and historic figure caught in a web of meanings and significations. She is known to us not only by her actions — the thievery of Moll Cutpurse in the seventeenth century, the recent killing spree of Karla Holmolka — but by her corporeality — the fat woman of the circus, the adolescent anorexic of the contemporary post-modern epoch, the flamboyant dress of the prostitute. Situated in opposition to signifiers of prevailing norms, the female deviant is recognized by markers of differences between and within social categories defined by age, class, race, and ethnicity. The female deviant surfaces through images and metaphors that mark bodily differences so that the sexualized/racialized female body functions to ensure masculinity as a universal marker of humanity and to submerge recognition of the specific male sexed body (Grosz 1994: 4, 14).

Enmeshed in cultural and historic webs of social signification, the female deviant lacks constancy over time and place; as cultural norms of the body change through time, so does the meaning of the female figure historically cast as a deviant. Markers of virtue or sin within one epoch can emerge as their opposites in another. While we no longer view the body of the leper as a mark of sinfulness, as was the case in the Middle Ages, so we now contest the emaciated body of AIDS as signification of the licentious pervert or drug addict.

In this chapter I illustrate this broad understanding of history as a reading of the materials of normalcy by looking at how two historical female figures — the Roman Catholic nun and the Aboriginal school student[2] — are now being placed in opposition to each other through inscription of their bodies and consider how they function as signifiers of "Western civilization" (the hierarchy of values through which Western culture defines itself), through the regime of colonial education[3] in the nineteenth and twentieth centuries. I take as my starting point that a reconstruction of past conceptualizations of deviance reveals contemporary public knowledge/power struggles that are configured within a post-colonial political economy. I base my interpretation on Foucault's conception of the role of the body in power/knowledge relations as being encapsulated by power relations that constitute "the political technology of the body." The relations of power render the body useful as a productive and a subjugated body. They

> ... invest it, mark it, train it, torture it, force it to carry out tasks, to perform ceremonies, to emit signs ... there may be a "knowledge" of the body that is not exactly the science of its functioning, and a mastery of its forces, that is more the ability to conquer them (Foucault, 1977: 26).

This allows me to follow Grosz (1994: 116) in her "focus on the body as a social object, as a text to be marked, traced, written upon by various regimes of institutional, (discursive and nondiscursive) power." This metaphor of the body as text draws our attention to the constitution of the body in culturally specific ways that are capable of being "written over, retraced, redefined ... producing the body as a text which is as complicated and indeterminate as any literary manuscript" (Grosz, 1994: 117).

Drawing together Foucault's notion of the political technology of the body and Grosz's metaphor of the body as text illuminates the specific ways in which women function as "all purpose deviants" (Schur, 1984: 7) within the sexual economies of the Western colonial project and its reincarnation in contemporary neo-conservative defence of civilization against multiculturalism and legal pluralism. Within these discourses, the residential school of history and the current struggle to redefine its im/moral regime index a Western (Christian) anxiety about risking the economic and religious borders which Western society shares with its various others. This anxiety is now variously expressed in terms of fear of the decline of Western civilization through multiculturalism, multilinguilism and the rise of crime, addictions, and immorality as measured in the shifting nature of family relations through divorce, institutionalization of common-law marriages, and tolerance of same-sex relations. Interwoven with this dread is a condemnation of the transformation of the legal order to include alternative discourses of Aboriginal healing and spiritual integrity — which underscores the strategies of social redress sought by First Nations on behalf of students who suffered physical, sexual, and cultural abuses at the now long-closed residential schools. These fears arise from an apprehension that such diversity in judicial judgment will have revolutionary ramifications, including further undermining of the rights of the nuclear patriarchal family and the institution of marriage, which are argued to be the constitutive elements of civil society and its order, and which provide an ideology through which female deviance may be designated.[4]

Underpinning the legitimating discourses of colonialism and contemporary civilization are narratives of femininity that act as "a set of disciplinary practices regulating the body, its gestures, appetite, shape, size, movement, appearance and so forth" (Sawicki 1991: 89). Narratives of femininity express a distrust of female sexuality through designations of deviance that are inscribed upon the body. These inscriptions function to discredit individual women or categories of women and "place them in the wrong" and thus bring them into the power domain of experts who would seek to efface the identifying inscriptions which have rendered them deviant.

Bodily inscriptions of the Catholic teaching sister and the female student take their meanings from the prevailing normative discourses of imperialism, which gave rise to the institutionalization of children. Colonial education practices that are signified by the particular regimes of residential or boarding schools arose within an era marked by discourses of modernity and progress and are but one example of an imperial concern with normality and abnormality, with containment and reform, respectability, and deviance. Idealization of the bourgeois class underpinned other rationalizations for forcible removal of children from social milieux viewed as deviant and for their confinement in institutions. Throughout Europe, in the second half of the nineteenth century, reformatories, orphanages, kindergarten, and institutions for children of the indigent were increasingly seen as the appropriate intervention of state and church into family relations for the purposes of "making the masses themselves wiser and better" (John Stuart Mill, cited by Young, 1995: 56; see also Foucault, 1977; Stoler, 1995). Within this political economy of normality it is the institutionalization of the child that marks her/him with the negative sign; the very existence of the residential school signified not only the deviance of the child, but also of the child's family and the extended community in which the family's life took meaning.

Although the prevailing discourses frequently equated the lower classes of Europe with non-Europeans as "savage" and "barbarians" and hence in need of acculturation to middle-class mores, colonial education practices differed in intent and consequence through racialization of sexual desire. Civilization was alleged to rest on the control of desire and to be rendered visible through refined habits of culture, possession of private property, and the exercise of rationality. Civilization took its meaning, as it does now, in contrast with the putative "wild"; savagery and barbarism were read into the practices of the "other" as a threat to the fragile achievements of civilized peoples who felt compelled to maintain constant vigilance over their socio-sexual borders (Patterson, 1997: 13).

Discourses of civilization emerged during the Enlightenment as a complex interweaving of religious precepts and secular faith in industrial technology and human advancement (Eze 1997). Victorian presumptions of civilization carried both confidence in human progress through technology and the control of desire, and fear of miscegenation (Young, 1997). Through association of non-European peoples with the wilderness, Aboriginal women of North America (as was the case for indigenous women elsewhere) came to be marked as deviants through purported demonstration of uncultivated tastes, sentimentality, and the lack of reason and judgment.

The signs of putative deviance that underscored racialization of the Aboriginal body are linked through surface appearances with the wild animals and the wilderness, and thus function to express the social hierarchy of colonial civilization. School accounts are replete with references to "wild" and "untamed" children who were described as having "raven" black hair or eyes, and bodily performances of unbridled creatures. Investment of the wilderness in the Aboriginal female body marked whiteness as synonymous with civilization. Within this "regime of truth," to borrow Foucault's words, civilization necessitated control of all unfettered female sexuality, but most particularly of non-European sexuality which both attracted and repelled the sensibilities of settler society.[5]

For more than three centuries, the presence of the teaching sister on the Canadian colonial frontier positioned the virgin body in opposition to the untamed feminine body of the non-civilized other. The religious sister (and to a lesser extent her spinster Protestant counterpart) established the boundary between the sacred and profane by investing her body with inscripted distinctions to the female body available to male lust. Thus distanced from socio-sexual possibilities of intimacy with the frontier other, the virgin nun could safely cross frontier boundaries without imposing threats to the colonial racial hierarchy.

The historic body of the nun takes its meaning from narratives of domesticated femininity. Symbolic of the highest veneration of womanhood within Catholic narratives of sexuality, discipline of her body is understood in relation to the regulation of the secular female body, which perpetually represents the threat of Eve (Warner, 1976: 73, 225; Leonard, 1995: 40).

Her covered body and head signalled the relationship of body and soul and marked the integrity of the physical body as synonymous with the purity of her faith, her vocation, and her self-determination. Outward markers of the subjugated body index the subordination of womanhood to man, of wife to husband, through her status as Bride of Christ. Her vows of poverty and chastity, ensured through physical separation of her vocational life from secular society, were reminiscent of a past ethos of cloistering and strict avoidance of all male contact save her priest/confessor (Makowski, 1997).

The defining symbols of virtue and civilization inscripted upon her by her clothing and bodily performances function as testaments to inner depths of the secret self and the religious subjects' private practices of self-mortification and corporeal denial, which arise from Christian doctrine of Eve as the "mother of the fall," whose actions "distorted God's original desire that men and women be equal" (Leonard, 1995: 39, 40). These symbols derive their meaning from and grant social significance to the "natural" vocation of womanhood, marriage and motherhood, which are understood to be the essence of the universal feminine subject (Warner, 1976: 289, 336; Leonard, 1995: 17).

Inscription of a natural essence on the universal feminine body encodes the potential deviance on the body of motherhood that stands outside Christian patriarchy and simultaneously casts suspicion upon the socially isolated figure of innocence and virtue that lives beyond the surveillance of the male gaze (McNamara, 1997: 5). Her body resonates with historic texts of the "unnatural" rejection of her sexuality. Variously inscribed by notions of pollution, unbridled sexuality, and temptation that are held as feminine constants, the virgin requires protection from herself in order to safeguard her heart and body in complete chastity (MacNamara, 1997). Historically, this protection could only be found through enclosure, as the twelfth century theologian Peter Abelard incited of the nuns of his day. "Solitude," he instructed, "is indeed all the more necessary for your woman's frailty, inasmuch as for our part we are less attached by the conflicts of carnal temptations and are less likely to stray towards bodily things through the senses." Not trusting the nuns to obey his injunctions, he held the local church authority responsible for enforcing cloister regulations, in order to ensure the nuns would "preserve their bodies from carnal contagion" (*The Letters of Abelard and Heloise*, cited by Makowski, 1997: 31).

Nonetheless, the virgin's seclusion from secular society marked the capacity to exceed cultural expectations and did not (and does not now) protect her from suspicion. That which is marginal is always associated with danger and vulnerability; hence the excess of her piety inculcated social disbelief in her purity, expressed through circulation of apocryphal stories of sexual orgies, abortions, the murder of unwanted babies, and trips away from the mission field to give birth to babies fathered by priests (McNamara, 1997: 4, 569; Burke, 1993: 256). Thus by the very inscriptions of piety and purity upon her body, the religious sister is reinscribed as potential deviant; chastity gives rise to literary speculation as to her sex life (McNamara, 1997: 599).

The church seeks to reconcile her "unnatural" acts through positing them as an alternative expression of the feminine principle of love. "[T]he consecrated religious goes on to be ... mother of many and co-operates with families in witnessing the virtues of fidelity, sacrifice, mortification and self-denial" (Leonard, 1995: 28). Her actions of devotion to others in substitution for her natural inclination toward marriage and motherhood can be read as emulation of the sacrifices of Mary and Christ. The Catholic concept of sacrifice mandates bodily suffering and worldly renunciation, both of which must be written onto the body through self-denial of pleasure and desire.

In her role as universal mother on the colonial frontier, the virgin nun carried out her mission to civilize the school children through inscribing the body of the "other" with the same texts as those she inscribed and had had inscribed by others on her own body. Bodily inscriptions, however, do not invoke constant meaning as they cross the threshold of the frontier. Written upon the body of the female student, these inscriptions were transformed from symbols of desired sanctity into perceptions of deviance and perversion. In the colonial regime of knowledge, the unfettered body of the adolescent female indexed the "untamed" mind and soul and provided symbolic justification for political and ecclesiastical authority over it. The female Aboriginal body indexed the social hierarchy of the frontier; what was wrong the individual body signified was wrong with an entire social category of the "other" and hence, in its "natural" (or untamed) state was pathologized.[6]

Having been conceived as potentially threatening through the racialization/sexualization of their bodies, the female students were compelled to wear unbecoming uniforms, denied bodily decorations that could be interpreted by their keepers as seductive, and confined to recreational activities that marked a feminine docility and modesty (Fiske, 1989: 251). School routines demanded disciplined movements, silence when working and studying, and strict separation from the opposite sex, even from brothers and other close male kin (Fiske, 1989; Knockwood, 1992; Furness, 1992; Jaine, 1993).

Colonial acceptance of designations of inherent feminine deviance bolstered the power of school staff and offered the general public justification for abdicating a social responsibility for Aboriginal students in general, and for the subjugation of females in particular. The notions of extreme virtue invested in the virgin female placed her beyond the male gaze and therefore outside of secular scrutiny, giving school staff unquestioned dominion over the children. Discipline became a coded action inscribed by the intersection of a theology of corporeal sin and a secular faith in charitable reform that affirmed not only the right but the duty of school staff to punish the body as they saw fit (Furness, 1992; Fiske, 1989; Miller, 1996). And although the bodies of all Aboriginal children were imprinted with a variety of messages imbued with the Western anxiety to sustain cultural boundaries through racial purity, within patriarchal society racialization of female sexuality took precedence as abhorred displays of ignorance and wickedness (Fiske, 1989: 250). Fear of the degradation of the white race was a subtext of discipline threaded through the daily habitation of domestic and school routines, and was often incited as a rationale for the schools themselves (Fiske, 1989). Terror of miscegenation arose from religious conventions that understood female sexuality as defilement and in the schools was expressed in the near constant surveillance of girls' bodies, from monitoring their clothing and hair styles through to controlling their access to sanitary supplies during their menstrual cycles. Narratives of feminine deviance prompted school staff, with the approval of federal government officials, to retain adolescent girls in school until a marriage was arranged for them. Their presence in the schools was not predicated on a commitment to education — the federal government only supported their studies to the eighth grade — but to protect them from the presumed immorality of their parents and to prevent them from moving freely into the labour force of colonial society.

Civilization discourses calling for emotional constraint and repression of sentiment legitimated disciplinary practices that simulated the self-mortification and self-denial of the religious sisters. Denial of food and water in consequence of violation of school regulations, harsh physical punishments ranging from slaps to whipping, and enforced solitary isolation were common practices believed to discipline mind and soul through bodily suffering and humiliation. Catholic doctrine of seeking redress from sins and temptations through emulation of Christ's suffering and sacrifices provided legitimating discourses for punishing ordeals that required students to posture themselves with outstretched arms in cruciform positions or to prolonged kneeling in the chapel. This "political technology of the body" was framed as an exemplary imposition of order upon chaos through the subjugation of the female body as representative of the wilderness, the very space of Christian temptation.

It has been argued (Fiske, 1989) that the pedagogy of residential schools rested on psychological assumptions of the young mind as a *tabula rasa,* but in practice it was the body not the mind that was treated as the blank page. The commonplace manner of corporeal discipline underscored the accepted wisdom that the (literary) body was capable of bearing meaning and hence its violent inscriptions were decipherable as a deterrent to the other girls, who were expected to read the messages fearfully. Humiliating punishment and body inscriptions provided spectacles reminiscent of the practice of eighteenth century tortures (Foucault, 1977) wherein ritualized attacks on the body replicated in symbolic ways the alleged crime, as for example, acts of pride punished by shaven heads. In this liturgy of regulations, spectacles of punishment affirmed the power relations of settler society and were experienced as textual confirmation of the corporeal shame invested in the female Aboriginal body.

Transformation of the mind and soul was read from the textual body in myriad ways that were taken for granted by the school staff and authorities and settler society at large. Personal hygiene and domestic order invested in the female body a civility that emulated bourgeois domesticity and envisioned the ultimate formation of a Christian wife/mother. In practical everyday life, normality was inferred directly from the body; the visual text marked larger, invisible meanings. Ceremonial performances in uniformed pipe and drum bands signified the acquisition of culture and the shedding of the "wild" temperament presumed upon Aboriginal women. Thus were visitors often overawed by the semblance of Western deportment, which gave them relief from their sexual phobias, confidence in the power of religious instruction to sustain sexual/social borders, and reassurance in their own essential racialized goodness that needed neither extraordinary surveillance nor bodily marking.

As Foucault has postulated, meanings and intensities in bodily discipline take their shape through the creation of a productive and subjected body, which was realized in the residential schools through the subjugation of scholarship to productive work deemed necessary for discipline of body, mind, and soul, and made essential by the impoverishment of the schools through government practices of underfunding. Girls' productive labour, such as sewing, knitting, cooking, food preservation, farming and gardening, was justified as "domestic science" and as the natural feminine labours of the domesticated housewife. Thus were female students designated deviants twice over, by the need to be domesticated and by the signs they produced through their subjugated labour: the awkward student uniforms, the crafted work sold for the students' keep, and the domestic services rendered to teaching and administrative staff.

Within the political field of the anxious frontier, imperial-wide discourses on childhood institutions not only made confinement legal, they created opportunity and motive for corporeal punishments that often verged on (and sometimes crossed into) torture and rendered these as normative treatment of the undisciplined body. Harsh discipline of body signified the conquered subject of colonial settler society, compliant to the power/knowledge regimes of the state and church. Within this regime of sexual knowledge, inscriptions occurred both violently and in more subtle forms. The prison-like routines of early rising, daily prayer sessions, menial work, limited, rote learning, and harsh discipline[7] were condoned by settler society at large and so readily taken for granted that the school administrators and teaching staff neither felt the need to apologize for their extreme discipline nor to be coy in their records. My reading of hundreds of pages of archival records of several residential schools revealed the routine manner in which young girls were subjected to harsh discipline within the classroom and workroom.[8] Recent disclosures before the Royal Commission on Aboriginal Peoples, the courts, police, and media include allegations of applying electric shocks (by use of an "electric chair"), head shaving, solitary confinement in dank cellars and closets, humiliating ceremonies of ridicule for bed wetting, and piercing the tongue with needles for speaking their own languages.[9]

Former students' current disclosures of physical, sexual, and psychological abuses represent a rebellion against the ways in which Aboriginal peoples were collectively categorized as being outside of civilization and their children were classified as deviant subjects to be reconstituted in the image of the European. They refuse doctrines of civilization to read the inscription of their bodies as texts of colonial brutality that carry with them the threat of cultural annihilation and genocide.[10] Their narratives of normalcy and deviance reverse the official system of symbols so that deviance is now inscribed upon the bodies and performances of the teaching sisters and imputed to a commonsensical knowledge that sexual abstinence rather than sexual activity is deviant. Marginality of the virgin is perceived as an excess of cultural expectations, and thus her body is retraced as a deviant. Oral histories of residential schools are often cast in the genre of gothic horror tales and draw upon apocryphal stories of sexual excess, furtive abortions, disguised pregnancies, or sexual assignations with male students and Aboriginal employees.

In this discourse, as in Catholic doctrines of virginity, it is not the truths about individuals' sexuality that seals their fate but how they are perceived within a particular regime of truth. It is not the facts of the teachers' sexuality (for such cannot be known in any empirical sense) that are at issue but the ways in which their sexuality is invested that displaces a narrative of holiness with an account of deviancy. Thus the former students' quest for justice[11] draws upon counterdiscourses of normality/deviance and reverses the reading of the body from outside/inside to inside/outside through common knowledge interpretations of Freudian psychology and appeals to an Aboriginal spirituality that connects the fractured body of abusive institutions to a wounded soul.

Former students of the Catholic residential schools[12] now read the inscription of their bodies as evidence of mendacious intent to harm and/or as the consequences of a perversion arising from their teachers' repressed sexuality and their renunciation of motherhood. Building on their own suffering as a consequence of corporeal deprivation, regimentation, and sexual repression, former students and their therapists, lawyers, and political leaders inscribe messages of pathology over the texts of Christian forbearance, sacrifice, and self-discipline.

The virgin body draped in modest vestments no longer functions as a symbol of psychic or religious integrity but as evidence of a fractured subject torn asunder by renunciation of the corporeal relations enjoyed universally. In this text, the traditionally garbed nun of the frontier school is recalled as being "unnatural" and a pale spectre of death whose humanity was masked in blackness (Knockwood, 1994). She is no longer viewed as "mother to all" because of her renunciation of worldly life, but as a figure forever denied maternal compassion.

Disciplinary regimentation of the constrained and disavowed body constitutes a malevolent technology of power, a technological intervention that breaks the psyche and gives rise to a shared traumatized state known as the "residential (mission) school syndrome," a psychological syndrome that functions symbolically in the political sphere as a general category to attack the pervasive consequences of colonial education. Prison-like facilities that sequestered children from their families and settler society are exposed as places of terror and often evil; no longer a sanctuary from immorality of home community or depraved frontiersmen, they are revealed as the space of perversion as countless disclosures of abuse of female and male children by their presumed guardians are made public. Innocence and vulnerability are retraced over texts of unfettered female sexuality to redeem the female student who suffered sexual predations of the male authorities around her.[13]

Aboriginal discourses of abuse counter the Christian narratives of sin and temptation used to justify the harsh nature of the schools with the concept of the "wounded soul." The etiology of a now-suffering populace beset by tragic rates of social dysfunction and individual reliance on alcohol and/or other addictive substances is placed within the concept of spiritual abuses, the foundation of which is the Christian mission of conversion (Assembly of First Nations, 1994).

Refusal to accept Christian notions of sin and soul incite resistance from the neoconservative political position so that condemnation of the schools and the judicial testimonies and convictions that have followed now exist in a new maelstrom of socio-sexual anxieties. Fear of the decline of western civilization has become the most recent discourse of racialized sexuality that disavows difference within and demands a homogenization of an Anglo-centric civilization. In the counter-discourses that seek to refute conceptions of the colonial body as abused, traumatized, and victimized, the charitable virgin of settler society resignifies the continuing anxiety of Western Christian civilization to bring into civil society the untamed "other." This counter-discourse upholds the "strict discipline" of the residential school and the commitment to Christianity, while seeking to reconstitute age-old conceptions of the feminine body as corrupting and passionate.

The discursive tactics deployed by church supporters to contest tales of abuse and trauma at the hands of missionary staff are varied. They range from denial, to calls for "the other side of the residential school story," through to repositioning Christian missionaries as "handy scapegoats" of "radical native politicians." "Native militants" are accused of "ideological rants" loaded with unsubstantiated "lurid" tales for the "pretext" of using taxpayers' monies for investigations and compensation practices.[14]

Violence and suffering are minimized by locating the abuse within narratives of benevolent service that provided "virtually the only education available to Canada's Aboriginal peoples in the white culture that was engulfing them." Nuns are constructed as voluntary exiles on an isolated frontier "who gave their lives to Indian children with love in their hearts and at enormous sacrifice, when the rest of white society cared nothing about them." Texts extolling virtuous sacrifice deny the coercive brutality endured by the children by placing it within an understanding of the "harsh" discipline, which was "true in schools generally." Complaints of abusive discipline practices, including hours of enforced kneeling or holding other painful postures, and denial of daily food and water, are dismissed as "innocuous recollections" (despite the archival records of these punishments, such as the Kuper Island School Conduct Books, which were kept by the teaching staff).

Denial leads to anger at the judicial responses to the grief and injuries now validated by the rising number of criminal convictions of clerics for rape, sexual assaults, and, most commonly, pedophilia. Church authorities have reacted in fear to the level of compensation awarded to former students and present their financial obligations as a consequence of vicarious liability as a "major threat to every church in Canada." They are supported in their claim by those civil rights lawyers who invoke prophesies of the demise of social agencies that arose as colonizing forces. "The implications are enormous. There might never be girls' soccer in your neighbourhood again. The Boy Scouts could fold" (9 June 1998, *Globe and Mail*, A1, A5).

Denial of abusive torment expresses nostalgia for a past colonial era and a Christian fundamentalist neo-conservative anxiety over the supposed decline of western civilization. Within the pessimistic discourse that marks the end of the millennium with fears of Revelations, the bodies of the female adolescent student and the virgin nun emerge as anomalous sites within a conflicted contemporary morality. Neo-conservative agendas for a less socialistic democracy in favour of a return to a charitable regime dominated by Christian authorities requires the recuperation of the pious nun motivated by a universal maternal longing and sacrificial benevolence; a recuperation of the historic nun in the image of the "saintly" Mother Teresa.

Recuperation of the virtuous religious sister, however, is impossible without disavowal of the other within our midst. Disavowal goes beyond denial of history to the reconstruction of the native "heathen," who in embracing native spirituality as a foundation of healing and justice can be positioned as threatening to Christian order. Whether the Aboriginal woman is denigrated as ungrateful recipient of Christian charity, as an unfit mother, or as immoral unmarried mother and pagan, she re-emerges within the imperial precepts as deviant to Christian patriarchal normalcy.

ENDNOTES

1. This research was funded by a grant from the Social Science Research and Humanities Council. I would like to thank Patty Ginn and Denise McDonald for their able assistance in drawing together the research materials for this study.

2. Residential schools were equally stressful for boys and girls. However, differences did prevail (and continue to do so) in the ways in which they were subjected to constructs of deviance, and I have chosen to limit this discussion to the femininity narratives from which female deviance has been constructed and resisted.

3. My focus is on the current revelations of the moral crises that existed within the nineteenth and twentieth century institutions known to us as the Indian residential school. The Canadian government favoured a legally enforced schooling system that separated children from their communities in order to assimilate the children into the Canadian body politic through the destruction of their native languages, religions, and political economies. Much has been written about the nature of the schools and the abuse suffered within them, and I do not detail these issues here. A list of relevant personal accounts and historical and anthropological studies is included in the bibliography.

4. The Reform party is currently the most vocal national voice in this regard. Neo-conservative news magazines such as *British Columbia Report* and *Alberta Report* provide weekly commentary on these issues. Thomas Patterson offers an interesting review of the American neo-conservative position on Western Civilization and the role of conservative politics and scholarship, which strongly influence Canadian sentiments.

5. The fantasy of European desire was addressed in numerous texts of social criticism and literature of the day. Alfred Lord Tennyson's *Locksley Hall*, has been described as having an "influence on the young minds of Tennyson's day [that] was immense" (in Houghton & Stange, 1959: 33). Its hero, rejected in love, ponders fleeing to a colonial paradise; "There the passions cramp'd no longer shall have scope and breathing space; I will take some savage woman, she shall rear my dusky race." But he reconsiders and cries out with revulsion, "But I count the gray barbarian lower than the Christian child" and rejects being "Mated with a squalid savage," who he fears will be steeped in monstrous crime.

6. Descriptions of the school life and treatment and interpretation of the female students' bodies are drawn from my earlier work on Lejac Residential school (Fiske, 1989; 1991; 1996).

7. The penal comparison is often rejected in current defence of the charitable intents of the school; however the similarities are clear. In *Discipline and Punishment*, Foucault describes a similar routine from the rules of a "House of young prisoners in Paris, circa 1832" (1977: 6).

8. Interested readers can locate the relevant files in the National Archives RG10 series and in the Ottawa and Vancouver archives of the Oblates of Mary Immaculate, a Catholic congregation of brothers and priests, and in the archives of various teaching congregations.

9. While insistence on English as a superior language had its counterpart in England, where Irish and Welsh were forbidden in schools, the rationale for violently destroying Aboriginal languages has a racial peculiarity in the Catholic schools. Violent prohibition has often been justified on the grounds that this was the only way the children would gain English proficiency, yet the French sisters and priests learned English at the same time, without violent restrictions on their capacity to write and speak in their mother tongue.

10. Chrisjohn and Young (1997) criticize narratives which pathologize the bodies of former students and teaching staff as an unfortunate political ploy that will once again reinscribe students as needing professional intervention and thereby placing them yet again within the biopower of outside authorities and experts, an important consideration not only in this instance but for critical understandings of the social consequences of discourses of deviance and normality. Their concerns are exemplified by the creation of a "healing fund" that will hire and administer professionals through an Ottawa based bureaucracy.

11. At the time of writing, August 1997, approximately 1000 cases of alleged abuse at the residential schools (Protestant and Catholic) were either pending or already before the courts.

12. Similar readings of the punitive regimes of the Protestant residential schools are also made. Richard King's *The School at Mopass* was the first scholarly work to link the marginality of the school staff to a disturbing regime of sexuality.

13. The most publicized case of this nature was the trial of Bishop Hubert O'Connor, former principal of Saint Joseph's Residential School at Williams Lake. This case, in which he was initially convicted and then acquitted in higher court in 1997, received wide attention when issues of evidence went to the Supreme Court of Canada. In a precedent-setting decision, the Supreme Court ruled that a plaintiff alleging sexual abuse, rape, etc. must, when commanded by a judge to do so, release her medical, counselling, and psychological records to the defendant. This ruling places female victims in legal jeopardy, for such "evidence" provides knowledge that can be used to constitute her as an unstable/fractured subject and hence an unreliable witness.

14. These and the following citations are from *British Columbia Report*, 3 December, 1990, and 5 September, 1994.

REFERENCES

Assembly of First Nations, (1994) *Breaking the Silence: An Interpretive Study of Residential School Impact and Healing as Illustrated by the Stories of First Nations Individuals*. Ottawa: Assembly of First Nations.

Burke, Joan F. (1993) These Catholic Sisters are all Mamas! Celibacy and the Metaphor of Maternity. *Women and Missions: Past and Present*. Fiona Bowie, Deborah Kirkwood and Shirley Ardener, eds., Providence/Oxford: Berg Publishers.

Chrisjohn, Roland and Sherri Young (1997) *The Circle Game: Shadows and Substance in the Indian Residential School Experience in Canada*. Penticton, B.C.: Theytus Books Ltd.

Eze, Emannuel Chukwudi (1997) *Race and the Enlightenment: A Reader*. London: Cambridge, Mass.

Fiske, Jo-Anne (1989) *Life at Lejac. Sa Ts'E: Historical Perspectives on Northern British Columbia*. Thomas Thorner, ed., Prince George: College of New Caledonia Press.

_____ (1991) Gender and the Paradox of Residential Education in Carrier Society. *Women and Education: A Canadian Perspective*, 2nd edition. Jane Gaskell and Arlene McLaren, eds., Edmonton: Detsilig Enterprises Ltd.

_____ (1996) Pocahontas's Granddaughters: Spiritual Tradition and Transition of Carrier Women of British Columbia. *Ethnohistory*, 43(4): 663–681.

Foucault, Michel, (1977) *Discipline and Punish: The Birth of the Prison*. (Robert Hurley, trans.) London: Allen Lane.

Furness, Elizabeth (1992) *Victims of Benevolence: The Dark Legacy of Williams Lake Residential School*. Vancouver: Arsenal Press.

Grant, Agnes (1996) *No End of Grief: Indian Residential Schools in Canada*. Winnipeg: Pemmican Publications Ltd.

Grosz, Elizabeth (1994) *Volatile Bodies: Toward a Corporeal Feminism*. Bloomington: Indiana University Press.

Jaine, Linda (1993) *Residential Schools: The Stolen Years*. Saskatoon: University Extension Press.

Knockwood, Isabelle (1992) *Out of the Depths: The Experiences of Mi'kmaw Children at the Indian Residential School in Shubenacadie*. Nova Scotia. Lockeport, NS: Roseway Publishing.

King, Richard, (1967) *The School at Mopass: A Problem of Identity.* New York: Holt Rinehart and Winston.

Leonard, Richard, SJ (1995) *Beloved Daughters: 100 Years of Papal Teaching on Women.* Ottawa: Novalis.

Makowski, Elizabeth (1997) *Canon Law and Cloistered Women: Periculoso and Its Commentators 1298–1545.* Washington, D.C: The Catholic University of America Press.

McNamara Jo Ann Kay (1996) *Sisters in Arms: Catholic Nuns through Two Millenia.* Cambridge, Mass.: Harvard University Press.

Miller, J.R. (1996) *Shingwauk's Vision: A History of Native Residential Schools.* Toronto: University of Toronto Press.

Patterson, Thomas (1997) *Inventing Civilization.* New York: Monthly Review Press.

Sawicki, Jana (1991) *Disciplining Foucault: Feminism, Power and the Body.* London: Routledge.

Schur, Edwin M. (1984) *Labeling Women Deviant: Gender, Stigma, and Social Control.* Philadelphia: Temple University Press.

Stoler, Ann Laura (1995) *Race and the Education of Desire: Foucault's History of Sexuality and the Colonial Order of Things.* Durham: Duke University Press.

Sutherland, Agnes, s.g.m. (1996) *Northerners Say: "Thanks, Sisters."* Ottawa: Tri-graphic Printing.

Tennyson, Alfred Lord, (1959) Locksley Hall. *Victorian Poetry and Poetics.* Walter E. Hughton, and G. Robert Stange, eds., Boston: Houghton Mifflin Company.

Warner, Marina (1976) *Alone of All Her Sex: The Myth and the Cult of the Virgin Mary.* London: Picador.

Young, Robert J. C. (1995) *Colonial Desire: Hybridity in Theory, Culture and Race.* London: Routledge.

VIOLENCE IN THE MILITARY COMMUNITY

Deborah Harrison

INTRODUCTION

"Violence" comes from the word "violate," to which the *Oxford Dictionary* attributes at least three meanings that are relevant: (1) to treat irreverently; to desecrate, dishonour, profane, or defile; (2) to interfere with by appropriation; (3) to treat without proper respect or regard. One meaning of "violence" itself is "undue constraint applied to some natural process, habit, etc., so as to prevent its free development or exercise." While it is based on empirical work, this paper is mainly a conceptual effort which links the above definitions of violence with the socially constructed genderedness of the military community, and the consequences for military wives of military combat readiness. It argues that capturing the essence of the situation of military wives necessitates using a conceptualization of violence which is broad enough to incorporate physical abuse, psychological abuse, *and* extreme economic vulnerability.

I begin with a description of our empirical research, including its underlying feminist epistemology. From there I move to an analysis of the ways military combat readiness organizes the gendered work experiences of military wives, a description of some of Canadian military wives' recent acts of resistance, and some provisional conclusions.

METHODOLOGY

Between 1990 and 1993, Lucie Laliberté[1] and I conducted a national study of Canadian military wives (Harrison and Laliberté, 1993, 1994, 1997).[2] The first stage of our research consisted of travelling to Canadian military communities in Ontario, Québec, New Brunswick, Nova Scotia, Alberta, and Germany, interviewing in an oral historical open-ended way (confidentially and anonymously) 112 English- and French-speaking wives and former wives, representing all ranks and service elements.[3] These interviews provided us with a wealth of detail about military wives' lives, which enabled us to frame their routine activities as *work* and supplement existing sociological knowledge of domestic labour, corporate wives, family violence, and older women, pensions, and poverty.

These interviews also gave us a solid sense of the standpoint of the military wife, insofar as this standpoint could be theorized as a unitary entity. By "standpoint of the military wife" I mean the situation of the woman who marries a man, and by so doing simultaneously subjects herself to the control of the military institution. We assumed that the military wife's personal and economic well-being — her health, safety, and ability to exercise some control over her life — was distinct from the well-being of the military institution. And, indeed, our interviews showed us how the Canadian military, in asserting its necessary control over its members, asserts analogous control over their wives.

Our research was informed by the feminist sociological methodology of *institutional ethnography*, as developed by Dorothy E. Smith (1986, 1987). Institutional ethnography methodology builds on Karl Marx's theory of alienation — his understanding that those who have been excluded from "the making of ideology, knowledge, and culture" find themselves caught up in systems that define, without reflecting, their own lived experiences. An institutional ethnography's first task is to discover disempowered persons' lived experiences in order to fashion these experiences into its intellectual starting point. Its second task is to attempt to understand how these experiences reflect social relations which, although not superficially visible, comprise an important segment of the social formation's "relations of ruling" (Smith, 1992). One among many of these relations of ruling is constituted by the social formation's military apparatus (cf. Mills, 1956).

Like many feminist methods, institutional ethnography rejects positivism's assertion that there is a detached position, uncontaminated by experience, from which social phenomena can be scrutinized. Institutional ethnographers follow the critique of positivism in asserting that since human beings are a part of what they observe, every observation is inevitably rooted in the observer's (or some other human being's) limited experience. Every investigation begins with particular assumptions, and these assumptions shape the investigation's results. Every investigation thus begins from a determinate place. No observer can avoid the responsibility of making a human choice about where this place shall be. The institutional ethnographer's human choice is to begin his/her research from the standpoints of the actualities of his/her subjects' lives. Needless to say, this epistemological stance is relativistic. From it, one might be tempted to conclude that what the institutional ethnographer discovers is neither more nor less "true" than what is found by a researcher using traditional methods: each perspective is equally valid. On the other hand, until recently women's perspectives have been so excluded from sociological research that institutional ethnographies should be valued for the enormous significance of the knowledge vacuums they fill.

Our quest to determine how the military asserts its control over wives was not confined to our interviews with the 112 wives. In order to understand the relationship of wives' work to the military organization, we needed to understand how wives' work contributes to the military, how the military makes sure that wives' work gets done, and the overall place of wives' work within the military's structures and goals. Hence, after carrying out our interviews with wives, we reformulated their accounts as issues that we problematized during our subsequent interviews with 48 Canadian military members and civilian staff of military facilities. In the second stage of our research, we interviewed military members in the same confidential, anonymous, open-ended, oral historical way in which we had interviewed the wives. We obtained members' perspectives on the problems identified by the wives. We also learned what members' work means to them. We then continued to ascend the military hierarchy, interviewing, in a more focused and policy-oriented way, military supervisors, social workers, padres, doctors, family support personnel, program administrators, high-ranking generals and, finally, the Deputy Chief of Defence Staff. During this third set of interviews, we learned about the Canadian military's priorities and forms of organization, and about how the military's priorities and forms of organization structure the way the military treats wives, tries to control wives, and benefits from wives' unpaid work. By the end of our research, we had made some specific discoveries about how military relations of ruling are embedded in the everyday work experiences of Canada's military wives. The aspects of military organization that are highlighted in this paper are therefore selective, in the sense that they are the aspects of military organization that we found to be most relevant to the experiences of Canadian military wives.

MILITARY COMBAT READINESS

Accordingly, let us consider military organization. We begin with the imperative of *combat readiness*, which is the military's organizational job. While components of combat readiness include equipment and skills, we will confine ourselves to its motivational side. To achieve and maintain combat readiness, the military must turn ordinary human beings into the kind of people who at any time can be mobilized to make war (cf. Grossman, 1995: 13). It must also motivate the wives of these people (the Canadian military is 90 percent male) to provide the necessary backup support.

The military's most important method of achieving these objectives is *control*. Human beings are not born to be combat-ready and, despite being to varying degrees "pro-military," the civilian environment is not equipped to create combat readiness. Combat readiness must be nurtured in a *total institution*[4] environment, where military recruits are segregated from civilians. During the eight weeks of basic training (seven weeks for officers), recruits exchange their old identities for the military uniform, haircut, and daily routines. They are humiliated, derogated, and emptied of the achievements of their previous lives by being told repeatedly that nothing they did prior to coming to boot camp was important. The vacuum created in recruits' self-esteem by this harassment is then filled with the new "combat-ready" identity that the military wishes to provide. Gradually, drill instructors replace verbal abuse with morsels of positive feedback until, at graduation, the recruits have learned to be proud of themselves in a whole new way. They have acquired a new set of skills and a new support system. They have also embarked on a distinctive new life which has begun to capture their most deeply rooted personal loyalties.

After basic and trades training, the total institution environment continues in more diluted form, as single members merge home with work by living in barracks on the base, and many married members live on the base in Permanent Married Quarters (PMQs). Most Canadian members are also posted to a new location every several years to ensure that they will not establish strong civilian roots. Members participate in the military's distinctive rituals and traditions, such as parades and initiation rites. They wear a distinctive uniform. They consult *military* priests, doctors, lawyers, and social workers, rather than their civilian counterparts. They are taught to believe that civilians are incapable of understanding the military life, and they are encouraged to become more or less insular within the military world.

Encouraging military members to fraternize exclusively with one another relates to perhaps the most important mechanism of military control — *combat bonding* or *combat unit solidarity.* From the point of view of combat, if a member deserted his unit when it was under fire, everyone else in the unit might die. Combat unit bonding exists to make sure that such a catastrophe could not happen, to make each military unit so solidary that, under the stress of combat, its members would be psychologically prepared literally to die to save one another's lives (cf. Grossman, 1995: 148–55).

Bonding is crucial to the military culture and ethos. It is constructed and maintained by the military's separateness from civilians, its member-only social functions, its member-only absences for weeks or months on end (on courses, exercises, peacekeeping missions, or real combat), its rigid hierarchy, its insistence on blind obedience to superiors, its denial of such civic rights as union membership or political participation, and its general antipathy toward the civilian way of life. It is cemented by the expectation that unit members will drink together, by initiation rituals, and by celebrations of the characteristics that unite the members of the unit (and converse denigrations of categories of persons who are different) in preparation for the combat exigency of needing to denigrate and dehumanize the enemy. Cultural pluralism is considered hostile to the objectives of the combat unit. In the words of one member:

> We had such a hassle over the Sikh coming in, because uniformity is the key.... If you are not part of the team, you are not part of the team. It's nothing directed personally at you, it's just the way the unit operates — you are a part of us or you don't exist.... And when you go to boot camp — same uniform, same haircut, same routine, same style — you are part of it. The best is having the same colour, the same haircut, the same religion, the same colour of eyes, the same height, the same weight. Because everybody outside of that — we don't like difference. (Interview #86)

The principle of exclusivity unites the members of a combat unit by dehumanizing members of so-called socially subordinate groups in preparation for dehumanizing the enemy. This dehumanization tendency accounts for the racist dehumanization rituals that "get out of hand" (such as the Somalia murder of Shidane Arone in 1993 by members of the Canadian Airborne Regiment). The exclusivity culture of the combat unit condones vicious treatment of certain categories of people, because of the perceived contribution of in-group solidarity to bonding and combat readiness (cf. Grossman, 1995: 156–70).

One of these categories of people is women. Like other gendered organizations, the military community takes for granted the naturalness of the patriarchal notion of a masculine-feminine polarity, or the idea that men and women are fundamentally different. Relatively few members of this community question the patriarchal dichotomy between "tough warrior" men and supportive "dependent" women. The military uses its socially constructed polarity between masculine and feminine in order to use masculinity as the cementing principle which unites "real" military men in order to distinguish them from non-masculine men and women (cf. Enloe, 1983; 1993). During basic training, male recruits are challenged to become "real men" by proving that they are not women. Instructors encourage stereotypically mas-culine behaviours from recruits by using female-associated words to derogate them. Male re-cruits who perform well gradually earn the right to be addressed as "men," and it is the relief of having earned this right that often crystallizes their organizational loyalty. Excluding and derogating women are important aspects of combat unit bonding. The members of es-pecially "macho" units celebrate their shared maleness by objectifying women, viewing pornography films, and joking about making women the targets of violence. Some of these "macho" unit members report deriving a similar pleasure from raping women to the pleasure they derive from killing (cf. Grossman, 1995: 136–7).

Bonding unites the members of a unit. In a looser way, bonding links present military members with the military members of the past, especially those who died in combat.[5] In the military's view, the risk of dying in combat is the major life circumstance that separates military members from civilians, and bonds military members — past and present — tightly together. As one member puts it:

> We are a society unto ourselves, and we do what we want. I don't have to go to a civilian doctor, dentist, lawyer or — and that's to make you look inward. You know what I am saying? Everything I need is in the Armed Forces, therefore I think of nothing outside. I mean, your thinking is nothing else.... It's the way we do things, it's parades, it's the Mess. It's all done that way to make the bonding this closely. The higher the risk job, the greater the call for the bonding. (Interview #86)

Although military authorities state otherwise when describing official policy, almost any practice is unofficially considered acceptable whose likely outcome is the solidification of bonds among combat unit members, the enhancement of their collective motivation to annihilate a foe, and the increased likelihood that under combat conditions they would stick together sufficiently to survive. Militaries all over the world have resisted integrating gays and women into their combat units because they have been afraid of the destabilizing effect that such integrations might have on the exclusivity that is the essence of combat bonding.[6]

Military organization is partially predicated on the derogation of women. The military nevertheless extends its principle of combat unit bonding to wives and children, to extend its control to the members of military families and to condition these family members to co-operate and co-ordinate with the bonding amongst the men. The well-bonded military unit takes the form of a patriarchal family, in which the commanding officer is called "The Old Man," his wife is called "The Mother Hen," and junior unit members are called "The Kids." Well-bonded units socialize together frequently, their wives and children become friends, and the families support one another during difficult times. Few civilians have experienced the speed and efficiency with which military units take up collections, provide home-cooked food, re-route planes, send flowers, visit hospitals, or get limousines mobilized during an illness or other family crisis.

Wives are drawn into their husbands' units through the social life, the hard times togetherness, the military's various family support programs, and the military rank structure which encourages wives to participate in a parallel social system in which every wife's place relative to the other wives mirrors her husband's place in the ranked world of the men. Wives are also drawn into military bonding by default since they too have been posted every several years, they too have not put down meaningful civilian roots, and they too have been encouraged to depend on the military community for their identities, and often their paying jobs.

Wives are drawn into the military social world so that they themselves can be controlled by the military, and can indirectly contribute to combat discipline among the men (Enloe, 1983: 40). Military philosophy and three decades of military-sponsored social scientific research (especially in the US) indicate that wives who are well integrated into the military community are less likely to complain, less likely to be a burden when their husbands are away on deployments, and more likely to contribute their efforts to the efficient functioning of the military system.[7] A Canadian general uses the example of a regimental wives' function to explain how wives are mobilized to facilitate the integration of other wives, and to manage other wives' anxieties when their husbands are deployed. He summarizes:

The corporals' wives are there. And if they're doing their job properly and they get to know each other, there isn't too much turbulence. And you get to know them on a first name basis by these little groups and associations that these good units and stations and bases are running. When she has a problem she won't be afraid to phone Mary whatever-her-name-is, who's the Master Warrant Officer['s wife] ... And she'll get all kinds of tips and counselling from them. That is a very important contribution. (Interview #145)

Wives are primarily drawn in to the military by their labour. An important part of the military community's genderedness is the community's appropriation of the patriarchal ideology that the gendered division of labour is natural. Gendered labour is a cornerstone of the Canadian military community, in which it is taken for granted that every military wife will: (a) assume 100 percent of the couple's domestic work and childcare responsibilities during the several months of the year her husband is away on deployments; (b) counteract the domestic destabilizing effects of her husband's absences by not seeking, or awarding high priority to, her own paid employment; (c) relinquish her own paid employment every time her husband is posted to a new place; (d) do most of the unpaid work associated with each new posting, such as packing, unpacking, house-hunting, and helping each of her children adjust to a new neighbourhood, school, and peer group; (e) fill the vacuum created by her weak affiliation with the labour market by performing cheap — and often volunteer — work on military bases; and (f) [in the case of senior officers' wives] devote a significant amount of time to entertaining, mentoring other wives, and representing the military in civilian charity work. The same general summarizes the vicarious dedication to the military effort that the Canadian military expects of wives:

> Oh, spouses are in the military! If a person in the military marries somebody that doesn't understand that they are part of the military in the sense that they're going to have to move, and they're going to have to do a whole bunch of things that they normally wouldn't have to do if they married somebody who wasn't in a uniform, either the marriage breaks up or they're going to have to change their views. Because you're marrying an institution here! (Interview #145)

Most military wives are unable to develop a "career" in the middle-class sense, or even a job which they hold long enough to have their pension contributions vested. They also have a much lower rate of participation in the labour market than comparable women who are married to civilians.[8] However, the military regards much more favourably wives who contribute their volunteer efforts to military family support programs than it regards wives who secure good paying jobs off the base and raise a ruckus when their husbands are transferred. The military heartily approves of wives who forego opportunities for good-paying jobs off the base in order to donate their labour to the base community. As a Canadian army officer puts it:

> I often say that there are several types of wives. There are those wives that can't cope, never will be able to cope. There are those wives who couldn't cope and came up with a way to cope, which usually was to go out and remove themselves, start another career, move out of PMQs or whatever, and they generally learned how to cope and do not offer anything as a solution to the problem. And there are those women who have learned how to cope, who offer the solutions to the problems. (Interview #96)

From the military's perspective, many military wives do "offer the solutions to the problems." At enormous cost to themselves, they become and remain loyal to the military, they become well-bonded members of the military community, and they cede to the military's demands for their unpaid and cheap work.

OTHER ASPECTS OF MILITARY CONTROL

Combat bonding is not the only form of control exercised by the military over its members which has implications for civilian wives. Two other relevant forms of military control are *the zero sum nature of combat* and *the significance of combat morale.*

Combat is predicated on a zero-sum model of control according to which success means assuming control over others, in order to kill them or save their lives. The effectiveness of a military unit is often measured by its commander's ability to "take control." In the military's eyes, an order provided by a person in authority is often exactly what it takes to pull a whole unit out of life-threatening jeopardy. As a Canadian navy member explains:

> In the Falklands, a ship got hit — got whacked. And the shock was so great, even though the guys weren't killed. I mean, you are talking maybe 600 or 900 pounds of explosives hit the ship — just picked the ship out of the water. And what they immediately did — they found later on — they took an executive officer — an engineer — and flew him over from the other ship, 'cause the guys were just in a daze. And then as soon as somebody got on there, started issuing orders, everybody immediately came back. And that's where the drill comes by, okay? "Somebody is in charge — I am going to be all right." (Interview #86)

Most persons who are abused by their intimate partners describe these abusers as obsessed with control. While many abusers who are obsessed with control are not members of the military, clearly the military is one of the organizational sites where controlling behaviour is notably valued. The military community is also a place where a member who is perceived to be unable to "control his wife" is threatened with loss of face. Obsession with control supplements the misogynist character of military bonding in helping to account for the relatively high frequency of woman abuse within the military community (cf. Neidig, 1985; MacLeod, 1987; Canadian Panel on Violence Against Women, 1993; Thompson, 1994; Cronin, 1995).

Additionally, in the units that are operationally closest to combat, a shared cavalier attitude toward violence is considered necessary, in order to convince each unit member that the others would be trustworthy enough not to flinch during the real thing (cf. Starr, 1982). A ganglike violent act is the occasional horrific outcome. In Canada, we need only think of the murder of Shidane Arone or, in the United States, the collective sexual assault of women members at the American Tailhook military convention in 1991. Family violence is another frequent situational spillover. A recent issue of *The New York Times* reports that in the United States one spouse or child dies each week at the hands of a military member relative. It cites data from a survey which indicate that one out of every three American army families has experienced domestic violence.[9] A recent American study, which compared 30 army couples with 30 civilian couples, found that 23 percent of the military wives reported being battered, as opposed to only 3.0 percent of the civilian wives in the control group (Griffin et al., 1988). Other American studies indicate that the rate of wife battering is especially high amongst military members in the combat-related trades (Baron and Strauss, 1987; Cook, 1990; Starr, 1982; Neidig, 1985; Solomon, 1988; Maloney, 1988; Gondolf et al., 1991; Shupe et al., 1987; Brown et al., 1981). During our interviews, we heard so many shocking stories from women survivors of violent military marriages that we have every reason to believe that the Canadian situation is similar.

Morale is considered important in the military; military morale is believed to vary positively with the degree to which the persons who give orders are perceived to merit the trust of the persons who obey. Consequently, covering up superiors' mistakes is often considered operationally justifiable. Military culture is rife with anecdotes about covering up: covering up for your buddy's mistakes (which recruits learn to do during basic training), covering up for your superior's mistakes, covering up for the military's mistakes, not letting the side down, appearing — to the external world — to be flawless. Like most other aspects of military culture, the flawless appearance imperative is linked with the military's preoccupation with control. As Mary Edwards Wertsch (1991) observes in her book, *Military Brats*:

> A good military outfit is one that is prepared to control any situation, no matter what the variables. And of course a good military outfit should look and act at all times as if it is in tune with that mission. It's as though, in their polished appearances and rehearsed behavior, the warriors were saying, "Observe how we control ourselves, and you'll know we can control the enemy." (p. 34)

Some of the most important aspects of military warfare (we were told by members we interviewed) are psychological. In this context, the perfect appearance is crucial. The uniform which is perfectly creased, the shoes which are perfectly shined, the tiny parts of the perfectly coordinated brigade which march in the parade square in perfect rhythm, assembling soundlessly to confront and intimidate the foe. This perfect appearance, the coordination of 5000 people raising their guns in unison, is choreographed to destroy the enemy's will. In military discipline, whatever needs to be concealed to create that perfect appearance usually *will* be concealed because, like the solidary combat unit, the perfect appearance is believed to be largely responsible for saving combatants' lives. A navy member uses the example of the Canadian Oka offensive to explain how a formidable appearance is targeted at the enemy's self-confidence:

> Oka, okay? You show up with 5000 troops — a brigade. Okay? What are you doing? You are destroying their determination, their will to fight... That's what you're doing. That's sort of the reverse of self-esteem. That's what we are talking about. You show up — overwhelming force."You haven't got a chance." You just destroy their will. (Interview #86)

Covering up to create this perfect appearance begins at boot camp where, if one person in the squadron makes a mistake, *everyone* is punished, such that it rapidly becomes clear to each squadron member that it is in his interests to cover up for the mistakes of his peers. Recruits subsequently learn to cover up for the mistakes of their superiors. They have no choice in any case, because in a dispute between two versions of the same story it is the superior's version which is believed. On one occasion we encountered during our interviews, a non-commissioned member learned that his own child had been sexually abused, and was forced to cover up for the officer who had done it. On another occasion an air captain was commanded to do whatever it took to get members to attend an unpopular dance, so that his colonel would not lose face for having planned it. On another, a navy member who received a brain injury from a superior during a brawl was told to keep quiet about the matter or face discharge. According to Canadian military philosophy, persons who give orders must appear infallible so that their orders will be followed. This socially constructed infallibility is considered essential to the maintenance of unit morale and to the prevention of outbreaks of mutiny. A senior officer explains:

> It's very important that you have confidence in your superiors, because one day they may ask you to do something very dangerous. And we train for war, we don't train for peace. And

so the whole thing, if you carry it far enough, it's all done because one day you're going to need to call on that trust and confidence in your people. (Interview #26)

It is secrecy which largely preserves this constructed infallibility. This consideration helps to account for the military's organizational tendency to close ranks after abuses have occurred. Analogously, each military member learns that any problem with his personal life, if disclosed, might reflect negatively on the external appearance and/or the internal morale of his unit. Despite the military's official stance that it "needs to know," members are discouraged from coming clean about their personal problems unless they are perceived to be falling down on the performance of their jobs. Hence, the member who is an alcoholic or who batters his wife has every incentive to make sure that his wife keeps quiet.

Shame, fear of worse beatings, or her (often accurate) perception that no one in the community wants to listen, gives the alcoholic's or batterer's wife her own motivations not to tell. Such a wife is often a person who has moved every several years with the military member, has lost touch with her old civilian friends, and has come to believe that the military community and her husband's paycheque represent the only security she has. Such a wife may also realistically fear for her life. The wife who overcomes these fears and is courageous enough to seek help on the base is frequently not believed by the military padre or social worker. These personnel have their own career motivations for keeping military bonding strong and continuing to support the member. Many of them also lack knowledge of woman abuse dynamics. If the wife calls an off-base civilian professional, that person often refers her back to the military. Certainly one of the highest quality-of-life costs of combat readiness is the psychological isolation and physical vulnerability of the military wives who are abuse survivors.

ECONOMIC VULNERABILITY

Not all military wives are targets of woman abuse. However, almost all military wives are made economically vulnerable by the vicissitudes of the military lifestyle. The military's often-successful efforts to encircle wives within combat bonding (described above) lull wives into the false sense of security of believing that the military will always look after them and that they will always belong to the military family. While married, the wife is encouraged to relax and settle into the predictable comforts afforded by the military community: fellowship, housing, built-in social life, and the sharing of a common world. She reckons that the risks involved in following her husband will be minimal, because at every stop the military will provide continuity, familiarity, and a pre-selected circle of new friends. She feels that she can "go with the flow" because, as a result of being free to do his job, her husband will be promoted, the family will benefit, she will be regarded as a career "asset," and the military will supply the rest. She is lulled into believing that what she is doing is not work or sacrifice, but merely her bit for a community that is also doing its bit for her.

Within this mythical construction of "military as family," the military man is one of the country's heroic protectors, whose job of "keeping Canada safe" is the most important job there is. His wife is his cherished consort who is honoured to do her part, to put up with his six-month absences, put her own life on hold, follow him from posting to posting, and cope with the academic and emotional fallout of her children continually changing schools and parting with friends. She is encouraged by the military to be proud of herself for not complaining and to find her own identity in the military community, rather than in the civilian world. She is encouraged to believe that her commitment to playing a military support role should be as boundless as her husband's commitment to sustaining Canada's defence.

The Canadian wife whose marriage ends experiences a rude shock. Relative to civilian wives in the same predicament, she experiences phenomenal downward economic mobility, especially since during her marriage she is unlikely to have kept up her marketable skills or acquired any of her own assets or superannuation. Although she has made numerous sacrifices for the military, the separated wife is treated as if she had never worked for the military at all, as if she had been rendering a mere personal service to some ordinary inconsequential man (cf. Smith, 1985; Burke and Spector, 1991). At the moment of separation, military bonding reaches out to re-encircle the member, at the same time as it conversely slams the door on his wife. A non-commissioned navy officer summarizes the military's attitude toward separated and divorcing wives:

> We will actually try — if we know. We'll bend over backwards for you — for the wife. A guy's wife comes up and she's got a problem — her husband has to go to the Middle East — okay! We'll go out and shovel her sidewalks. We'll go and do all sorts of things — at least at my base. But if she was to be divorced, or separated, or leave, then she's left the mob. She's left the family. Boom! Bingo! That's the way it works. Because we look inward. I told you, we look inward. (Interview #86)

All militaries have been slow to recognize that the unpaid support work wives provide to the military is indeed *work*, that separated and divorced military wives deserve to be compensated for the military work they have done (and the opportunities for civilian work they have lost), and that a pension is deferred remuneration for both partners' work rather than property that belongs exclusively to the member.[10] Militaries have also been slow to recognize that a wife whose social anchor for years was the military community is, at the moment of her separation, a person who has been cruelly cut adrift. A former Canadian army wife summarizes how she felt when her marriage ended:

> I had no identity. I wasn't me. I was somebody's something. Mrs. Chief Warrant Officer. You know? And didn't realize. I thought that was what I was supposed to do. I really thought that was what I was supposed to do. Then suddenly I wasn't required any more. And I was wrapped up in the newspaper and put out like fish bones. (Interview #14)

The situation of the separated or divorced military wife vividly exemplifies the military's exploitative appropriation of wives' work.

MILITARY WIVES' RESISTANCE

Needless to say, there is a profound conflict between the imperative of combat readiness and the well-being of military wives. So unsurprisingly, despite the social isolation of the military community, the impact on husbands' careers, and the military's sophisticated methods of intimidation and control, some Canadian wives have found ways to mobilize and resist.

Wives' methods of resistance have included challenging postings, privileging their own education and job prospects, persuading their husbands to request release from the military, opting out of military socializing, and mustering the courage to leave a husband who is an alcoholic or batterer. At a more public level, the wives of some of the members deployed to the Persian Gulf tried to get their husbands' extra wartime pay allotted to them, to help them keep their families functioning during a period of heightened stress. Canadian wives working at military family resource centres have tried (usually unsuccessfully) to prioritize the actual needs of families over the military's desire to retain tight control over its family support programs.

Organized resistance amongst military wives has been rare. After all, wives are moved so often that strategic affiliations amongst them have little time to develop. The competitive structures of rank also incorporate wives, and inhibit their potential alliances. Finally, most wives are so exhausted from the work of coping with the military lifestyle that they lack the energy that is required to become activists. Despite these obstacles, two recent rebellions of Canadian wives can be considered social movements, in the sense of being collective, organized, public, and sophisticated in their use of communications media.

The first such movement, at CFB [Canadian Forces Base] Calgary in 1979, was prompted by the military's decision to stop charging members a flat rate for PMQ occupancy, and tie PMQ rents to local economies. PMQ occupants in Calgary were hit especially hard, because the city's oil boom was producing inflated prices. Wages did not keep up with the rent hikes. A number of Calgary military members were pushed below the poverty line, which at the time was defined as needing to spend more than 61 percent of one's income on basic necessities.[11] Some members became eligible for welfare.

Despite fear of reprisals from the military, many wives mustered enough courage to complain to the media, and over 95 percent of the wives living in PMQs signed a petition that was sent to the Minister of National Defence. As a result of the well-publicized protests against the Calgary rents, the military instituted an Accommodation Assistance Allowance in areas of Canada which had a high cost of living. But the military took care to post the wives who had spoken out (and their husbands) away from Calgary almost immediately, and did not send any two of them to the same place. The military also took full credit for the Accommodation Assistance Allowance.

The most sustained instance of Canadian wives' organized resistance has been the Organization of Spouses of Military Members (OSOMM). OSOMM originated in 1984 at CFB Penhold, where a group of wives began meeting informally to discuss how they might lobby for a family dental plan (until then, only members were covered), day care, pensions, and a safer traffic intersection. The wives believed that these improvements would help every family on the base, and assumed that the military would agree. But, after the wives had distributed their first newsletter about dental care, traffic intersections, and school lunchrooms, the Base Commander invoked the "political activity" regulation[12] and prohibited them from meeting on the base. His action was corroborated by a letter from the Minister of National Defence. The wives were amazed, especially when they realized that base facilities were being used for a retired members group lobbying for Ronald Reagan's Star Wars. These conservative women, who had always considered themselves part of the military "family," suddenly found themselves transformed into an Enemy. When they threatened to continue distributing their newsletter without permission, military officials threatened to arrest them and evict them from their homes.

Contrary to its original intentions, the wives' group became a movement. Calling itself OSOMM, it responded to the letter from the Minister of Defence by obtaining a Secretary of State Women's Program grant to establish off-base headquarters. OSOMM subsequently mushroomed into a national organization, received considerable notoriety in Parliament and the national media and, sponsored by LEAF (Women's Legal Education and Action Fund), sued the Department of National Defence under the Freedom of Association and

Equality sections of the Charter of Rights and Freedoms. As part of their suit, the wives claimed that their inability to make decisions on issues that affected their daily lives amounted to discrimination on the basis of sex and marital status.

Many wives resigned from OSOMM because of the pressure the military put on their husbands. Nevertheless, the civilian publicity OSOMM received brought results. The wives eventually obtained a dental plan for dependents, a safer traffic intersection near Penhold, and a slightly relaxed definition of political activity on bases (Advisory Group to the Minister of National Defence, 1987).[13] Considering the tremendous insularity of the military community, and the wives' then isolation from civilian feminists, the Penhold wives' accomplishment was immense.

In 1987 OSOMM established a special new chapter, comprising ex-wives who had lost, or were in danger of losing, their earned share of pension benefits. In 1990 OSOMM and four of the members of this chapter filed a second Charter of Rights and Freedoms suit against the Department of National Defence, alleging that certain provisions of the Canadian Forces pension plans discriminated against spouses on the basis of sex and marital status. OSOMM's first lawsuit was dropped in 1991, when the military implemented a national Military Family Support program. But OSOMM's pension lawsuit is still going forward. OSOMM has continued to be a viable organization, which meets regularly, publishes pamphlets, raises funds, and maintains a national network of information and emotional support.

CONCLUSION

The military members we interviewed informed us that combat readiness is the ultimate reason for most of the policies that the Canadian military implements and practises. Combat readiness requires the military to exercise control over its members, and to take organizational steps to ensure that it has secured its members' obedience and loyalty. We were guided to extract this information from the military members by the experiences that had been related to us by their wives.

The military's control over its members is deemed to rely on a combination of military hierarchy, members' military organizational loyalty and, finally, on the deep personal bonding that happens within military units, especially the units that are devoted to combat. An important prerequisite of strong military bonding is believed to be cultural homogeneity; hence the fulfillment of this requirement often devolves into racism and sexism. An important characteristic of military community genderedness is combat units' celebration of masculinity and their converse denigration of women.

Control represents the military's main approach to its members; control is also the essence of what the military does. The zero-sum model of control practised by the military provides positive rewards to military members who successfully exercise control *over* difficult situations; one such situation is an "uppity wife." Hence, in units devoted to combat, violence against women is specifically tolerated and fostered.

Despite its misogynistic tendencies, the Canadian military also expects organizational loyalty and bonding behaviour from wives. The results of this expectation include the loyalty of many wives to the military, the enjoyment by many wives of the camaraderie of the military community, and the consequently greater difficulty experienced by abused wives who attempt to solicit military community support. In the military, obsession with unit morale often translates into the cover-up of problems; this consideration makes it hard for survivors of violence to approach military human services personnel.

By "violence" we usually mean physical or psychological abuse. However, the inclusion of "appropriation" and "constraint" in the definition of violence which opened this paper reminds us that our conceptualization of military family violence must be broader. The economic vulnerability of military wives, and the economic plight of most separated and divorced military wives, also qualify as violence, in the sense of appropriation, or of constraints being "applied to some natural process" in order to "prevent its free development or exercise." The military lifestyle prevents most wives from earning a living in a manner which is commensurate with their abilities. While the same economic vulnerability is true of many married women, the combination of the geographical mobility of the military and the high quantity of unpaid services that the military extracts from wives makes the vulnerability of military wives extreme.

The recent resistances of Canadian military wives provide hope. However, unless the military is forced to take responsibility for its violence toward members' wives, the organizational secrecy around this problem will prevail and abused military wives will continue to suffer in intolerable isolation. The interest shown in the present Somalia Inquiry demonstrates that the public finds unacceptable the Canadian military's view that its failings are no one else's business. The aftermath of Somalia has the potential to subject the actions of the Canadian military to renewed public scrutiny. If an opportune time ever existed to find out more about woman abuse and other forms of violence inflicted on civilians in the Canadian military community, that opportune time exists right now.

ENDNOTES

1. Lucie Laliberté, co-founder of the Organization of Spouses of Military Members (OSOMM), is a partner in the Ottawa law firm Gahrns & Laliberté, which practises in the areas of pensions and family law. Laliberté and I jointly collected all the data for this project, and she was the co-author of our book.

2. Our research was funded by the Social Sciences and Humanities Research Council Women and Work Strategic Grants Program (No. 882-91-0004). The former Minister of National Defence, Hon. Kim Campbell, gave us permission to interview certain high-ranking members of the Military. The former Associate Minister of National Defence, Hon. Mary Collins, and her assistant Deborah MacCulloch, also provided advice and support. This article reworks some of the data we collected.

3. Approximately 60 percent of the spouses we interviewed were (or had been) married to non-commissioned members; 40 percent were (or had been) married to officers. Approximately 40 percent of the members to whom our interviewees were (or had been) married were (or had been) in the army; 40 percent were (or had been) air element members; and 20 percent were (or had been) members of the navy.

4. Erving Goffman (1961) defines a "total institution" as "a place of residence and work where a large number of like-situated individuals, cut off from the wider society for an appreciable period of time, together lead an enclosed, formally administered round of life."

5. For example, according to the Department of National Defence 1994 *Defence White Paper,* Canada's refusal to continue to provide a combat-ready force to NATO would

comprise a betrayal of the "more than 100 000 Canadians [who] have died [over the past 80 years], fighting alongside our allies for common values" (p. 13).

6. The military has always resisted changes in the composition of military personnel, or in military family structure, that would move toward greater liberalism. The recognition of women in combat roles (1989), common-law marriages (1991), and gays and lesbians (1992) have all occurred as a result of successful legal challenges under the Canadian Human Rights Act (combat) or the Charter of Rights and Freedoms (common law, gays/lesbians).

7. See, for example, Spellman, 1976; Montalvo, 1976; McKain, 1976; Stanton, 1976; McCubbin et al., 1978; Orthner, 1980; Szoc, 1982; Kohen, 1984; Segal, 1986; Orthner et al., 1986; Pittman et al., 1988; Bowen et al., 1989; Orthner et al., 1990; Bell et al., 1991; and Campbell et al., 1991.

8. While the work of 53 percent of Canadian military wives is confined to their homes, the same is true of only 23 percent of Canadian women generally. See Organization of Spouses of Military Members, 1992.

9. See "Military Struggling to Stem an Increase in Family Violence," *New York Times,* May 23, 1994.

10. For a detailed discussion of the usual pension entitlement of the separated or divorced military wife, see Harrison/Laliberté, 1994, Chapter 7. After the book went to press, the regulations accompanying the new Pension Benefits Division Act were made public. They were subsequently modified to make the situation slightly more favourable for separated and divorced military spouses, as a result of lobbying on the part of the Organization of Spouses of Military Members.

11. See "Troops on March to Welfare," *Calgary Herald,* October 19, 1979.

12. According to Queen's Regulations and Orders, Article 19:44, military members are not permitted to engage in "political activities," which include campaigning for political parties, displaying political signs during election campaigns, or signing political petitions. The definition of political activity is largely left to individual base commanders.

13. Under the new rules, meetings that the base considers "political" may now be held inside individual PMQs, but not anywhere else on the base.

REFERENCES

Advisory Group to the Minister of National Defence (1987) *The Regulation of Political Activities in Canadian Forces Establishments.* Unpublished report.

Baron, L. and Straus, M.A. (1987) "Four Theories of Rape: A Macrosociological Analysis," *Social Problems* 34: 467–89.

Bell, D.B. et al. (1991) *The Army Family Research Program: Origin, Purpose and Accomplishments.* Army Project Number 2Q263731A792; Alexandria, VA: United States Army Research Institute for the Behavioral and Social Sciences.

Bowen, G. at al. (1989) "Organizational Attitude Toward Families and Satisfaction With the Military as a Way of Life: Perceptions of Civilian Spouses of U.S. Army Members," *Family Perspective* 23:1, pp. 3–13.

Brown, M.M. et al. (1981) "Abusers of Clients of Women's Shelter: Their Socialization and Resources," *Journal of Sociology and Social Welfare* 8:3 (September): 462–70.

Burke, M.A. and Spector, A. (1991) "Falling Through The Cracks: Women Aged 55–64 Living on Their Own," *Canadian Social Trends* 23 (Winter): 14–17.

Calgary Herald (1979) "Troops on March to Welfare." October 19.

Campbell, C.H. et al. (1991) *A Model of Family Factors and Individual and Unit Readiness: Literature Review*. Research Note 91-30; Alexandria, VA: United States Army Research Institute for the Behavioral and Social Sciences.

Canadian Panel on Violence Against Women (1993) *Changing the Landscape: Ending Violence — Achieving Equality*. Ottawa: Supply and Services Canada.

Cook, K.J. (1990) "Cultural Spillover Theory and Violence in the Family: The Case of the Military," paper presented at the American Society of Criminology meetings.

Cronin, C. (1995) "Adolescent Reports of Parental Spousal Violence in Military and Civilian Familes," *Journal of Interpersonal Violence* 10:1 (March): 117–122.

Department of National Defence (1994) *1994 Defence White Paper*. Canada: Minister of Supply and Services.

Enloe, C. (1983) *Does Khaki Become You? The Militarization of Women's Lives*. Boston: South End Press.

Enloe, C. (1993) *The Morning After: Sexual Politics at the End of the Cold War*. Berkeley: University of California Press.

Goffman, E. (1961) *Asylums: Essays on the Social Situation of Mental Patients and Other Inmates*. New York: Doubleday.

Gondolf, E.W. et al. (1991) "Wife Assault Among VA Alcohol Rehabilitation Patients," *Hospital and Community Psychiatry* 42:1 (January): 74–79.

Griffin, W.A. and Morgan, A.R. (1988) "Conflict in Maritally Distressed Military Couples," *American Journal of Family Therapy* 16:1, pp. 14–22.

Grossman, Lt-Col D. (1995) *On Killing: The Psychological Cost of Learning to Kill in War and Society*. Boston: Little, Brown and Company.

Harrison, D. and Laliberté, L. (1993) "How Combat Ideology Structures Military Wives' Domestic Labour," *Studies in Political Economy* 42 (Autumn): 45–80.

Harrison, D. and Laliberté, L. (1994) *No Life Like It: Military Wives in Canada*. Toronto: James Lorimer and Company.

Harrison, D. and Laliberté, L. (1997) "Gender, the Military, and Military Family Support," in Laurie Weinstein and Christine White (eds.), *Wives and Warriors: Women and the Military in the United States and Canada*. Westport, CT: Greenwood.

Kohen, J.A. (1984) "The Military Career is a Family Affair," Journal of Family Issues 5:3 (September): 401–418.

MacLeod, L. (1987) *Battered But Not Beaten ... Preventing Wife Battering in Canada*. Ottawa: Canadian Advisory Council on the Status of Women.

Maloney, L.J. (1988) "Post Traumatic Stresses on Women Partners of Vietnam Veterans," *Smith College Studies in Social Work* 58:2 (March): 122–43.

McCubbin H.I. et al. (1978) "Family Policy in the Armed Forces: An Assessment," *Air University Review* 29:6 (September–October): 46–57.

McKain, J.L. (1976) "Alienation: A Function of Geographical Mobility Among Families," in H.I. McCubbin et al. (eds.), *Families in the Military System*. Beverly Hills: Sage, pp. 69–91.

Mills, C. W. (1956) *The Power Elite*. New York: Oxford University Press.

Montalvo, F.F. (1976) "Family Separation in the Army: A Study of the Problems Encountered and the Caretaking Resources Used by Career Army Families," in H.I. McCubbin et al. (eds.), *Families in the Military System*. Beverly Hills: Sage, pp. 147–173.

Neidig, P.H. (1985) "Domestic Violence in the Military Part II: The Impact of High Levels of Work-Related Stress on Family Functioning," *Military Family* (July–August): 3–5.

New York Times (1994) "Military Struggling to Stem an Increase in Family Violence." May 23.

Organization of Spouses of Military Members (1992) *Brief to the Senate Finance Committee on Bill C-55*, Respecting the Pension Benefits Division Act. Ottawa: September.

Orthner, D.K. (1980) *Families in Blue: A Study of Married and Single Parent Families in the Air Force*. Washington: Department of the Air Force.

Orthner, D.K. et al. (1986) "Family Contributions to Work Commitment," *Journal of Marriage and the Family* 48 (August): 573–81.

Orthner, D.K. et al. (1990) *Building Strong Army Communities*. Research Note 90-110; Alexandria, VA: United States Army Research Institute for the Behavioral and Social Sciences.

Pittman, J. et al. (1988) "Predictors of Spousal Support for the Work Commitments of Husbands," *Journal of Marriage and the Family* 50 (May): 335–48.

Segal, M.W. (1986) "The Military and the Family as Greedy Institutions," *Armed Forces and Society* 13:1 (Fall): 9–38.

Shupe, A. et al. (1987) *Violent Men, Violent Couples: The Dynamics of Domestic Violence*. Lexington, MA: Lexington Books.

Smith, D.E. (1985) "Women, Class and Family," in Varda Burstyn et al., *Women, Class, Family and the State*. Toronto: Garamond, pp. 1–44.

Smith, D.E. (1986) "Institutional Ethnography: A Feminist Method," *Resources for Feminist Research* 15:1, pp. 6–13.

Smith, D.E. (1987) *The Everyday World as Problematic: A Feminist Sociology*. Toronto: University of Toronto Press.

Smith, D.E. (1992) "Feminist Reflections on Political Economy," in M. Patricia Connelly et al. (eds.), *Feminism in Action: Studies in Political Economy*. Toronto: Canadian Scholars' Press, pp. 1–21.

Solomon, Z. (1988) "The Effect of Combat-Related Posttraumatic Stress Disorder on the Family," *Psychiatry* 51 (August): 323–29.

Spellman, S. (1976) "Utilization of Problem-Solving Resources Among Military Families," in H.I. McCubbin et al. (eds.), *Families in the Military System*. Beverly Hills: Sage, pp. 174–206.

Stanton, H.D. (1976) "The Military Family: Its Future in the All-Volunteer Context," in Nancy Goldman et al. (eds.), *The Social Psychology of Military Service*. Beverly Hills: Sage, pp. 135–49.

Starr, P.D. (1982) "Military Socialization in the University: The Role of Subcultures in Navy-Marine ROTC," *Human Organization* 41:1 (Spring): 64–9.

Szoc, R. (1982) *Family Factors Critical to Retention*. San Diego: Naval Personnel Research and Development Center.

Thompson, M. (1994) "Armed Forces: The Living Room War," *Time* 143:21 (May 23): 48–51.

Wertsch, M.E. (1991) *Military Brats: Legacies of Childhood Inside the Fortress*. New York: Random House.

ATTENTION-DEFICIT/ HYPERACTIVITY DISORDER

Constructing Deviance, Constructing Order

Chapter 17

Leonard Green

INTRODUCTION

In *Erewhon,* Samuel Butler describes a fictional country where, if a man commits a crime, he is hospitalized, but " ... if a man falls into ill health, or catches any disorder, or fails bodily in any way before he is seventy years old, he is tried before a jury of his countrymen, and if convicted is held up to public scorn and sentenced more or less severely as the case may be" (1985, p. 102). First published in 1872, *Erewhon* was intended as a satirical response to Darwin's *On the Origin of Species*. We need only consider how the phenomenon of socially disruptive behaviour is portrayed on prime-time television, however, to see that Butler's comments are as relevant to our own time as they were to his.

In the first instance, *King of the Hill*, an animated cartoon which depicts the life of the conservative Hill family, recently devoted an entire episode to socially-disruptive behaviour. When Bobby, an otherwise lethargic adolescent, begins to misbehave at school, he is sent to the guidance counsellor. With the help of the latest medical pamphlets, Bobby is quickly diagnosed with Attention-Deficit/Hyperactivity Disorder or, as she explains to the Hills, ADHD: a mental disorder that can be easily treated with medication. Bobby is soon prescribed the proper dosage, the adults note a substantial improvement, and life goes on. Unbeknownst to the adults, however, Bobby stops taking the pills when he discovers he can no longer concentrate.

The *Simpsons*, also an animated cartoon, revolves around the Simpsons' ten-year-old son, Bart, one of television's more "exuberant" children. Interestingly, his teachers have never suggested that he might be more compliant if similarly medicated. In one episode, however, having signed his name to another student's achievement test, Bart is sent to the Principal's Office. The guidance counsellor decides that Bart is a genius, and his well-documented behavioural problems are discounted as nothing more than evidence that Bart is frustrated at being forced to learn at such a slow pace. Ignoring the possibility that Bart may

263

have cheated, he is enrolled in a school for exceptionally gifted children. At the end of the story, unable to function in his new environment, he engineers his transfer back to his old school.

Presented with the same problem, one child is diagnosed with ADHD, and the other with a superior intellect. In the world of the situation-comedy, this may simply have been the result of comedic licence. At the same time, the results parallel what is occurring in the real world, where there exists much confusion about how to best explain and deal with problem behaviour. When ADHD is suspected, the problem is compounded by the absence of any concise list of symptoms, which may include widely shifting levels of attention, abnormally high levels of activity, and thoughtless or impulsive behaviour. In addition, symptoms are not always present in every individual; are often context-specific, so they may be more obvious in some situations or to particular individuals; may differ in level of severity; and, decrease, disappear, or become more manageable over time. Although they may know little about the complexities of the disorder, parents, teachers, guidance counsellors — individuals with a vested interested in maintaining compliance — are being recognized as "experts" at recognizing the symptoms of and making informal medical prognoses for ADHD.

In this politically correct age, ADHD is the catchword of the day. The generic term, "hyperactive," is used to explain the behaviour of any person considered incapable of exhibiting socially appropriate behaviour. No longer blameworthy, individuals with ADHD are encouraged to embrace their "non-serious," treatable mental disorder. Neither criminal nor immoral, the disorder has resulted in a variety of informal and quasi-formal mechanisms of social control. ADHD is a form of social control masquerading as a disorder. In an age where everyone is looking for the "quick fix," no matter how complex or interconnected the issue, the solution to practically every social problem comes in the shape of a pill. As a result, central nervous system stimulant-medication is *de rigueur* for almost every child, especially male, and many adults considered problematic to their social worlds. Individuals are no longer interested in looking for the underlying causes of social problems.

Focusing on individuals with ADHD rather than social structures, scant attention is paid to maladaptive families, chaotic classrooms, and disorganized workplaces. With an emphasis on definitions, theories, and methodologies, there is little interest in the social characteristics of the disorder. ADHD as a form of social control is almost nonexistent. Issues which may be problematic to individuals are given short shrift. For example, children regarded as self-centred and thoughtless may have increased difficulty making and maintaining friendships; adolescents unable to appreciate the consequences of their actions are more likely to get into trouble; and, adults lacking the ability to remain focused may move from job to job, becoming depressed about their apparent inability to conform.

In the following discussion, we will use social control theories to assess the way the focus on disruptive behaviour has shifted from troubled to troublesome — from private, individual concerns to public, social problems. This will require that we briefly examine the classification systems which organize the disorder, the diagnostic criteria which identify the symptoms and the medical language of *treatment* used to create a perception of humane care rather than coercive control. We will then examine how a variety of unrelated symptoms have been combined to create a single, identifiable disorder. This will help us better understand how informal, personal observations intersect with expert, medical opinions. Rather than examine *what* becomes a social problem, however, the present focus is on *how* social problems are created and *why* disruptive behaviour has been transformed into pathologized deviance. The discussion will conclude with a critique of the informal and formal social control processes which affect individuals, and recommendations for future research.

THEORY

Theories help us understand and make sense of our world. They provide a framework for comparing and contrasting events. In the social world, we use theories to organize and interpret facts. According to social control theories, the medical language of *treatment* is used to control social problems like ADHD. On a micro level, social control theories find the cause of deviance within the individual; on a macro level, within social structures. Simply put, social control theories do not focus on why individuals commit deviant acts, but on why some individuals and not others conform to societal expectations. Control theories are a combination of internal and external control mechanisms. Our values, morals, and beliefs are created through a socialization process, wherein normative behaviour is internalized. In addition to internal processes, our behaviour is reinforced through external forces such as family members and friends, or agents working within control organizations such as the systems of education (teachers) and criminal justice (police). Thus, while some individuals readily adopt appropriate pro-social values, others must be coerced or "shamed" into conformity (Braithwaite, 1989).

Using the singular phrase, "system," to identify complex social institutions such as the education system or the criminal justice system is, in fact, somewhat misleading and wholly inaccurate. Moreover, describing such bureaucracies as "systems," in the first place, is also a form of social control. In reality, they are comprised of a multiplicity of individuals with diverse interests, competing goals, and different needs. Systems incorporate a variety of contradictory mechanisms and different processes — some more and others less connected to state-sponsored and controlled initiatives. For the purposes of informal social control, the term implies a single, systematized locus of power otherwise lacking. As a discourse, the system's power lies in its ability to call itself a single procedure which, properly accessed, will respond to conflict. As a result, systems are often regarded as a rational process which unfolds in an orderly manner, distributing information logically, consistently, and objectively. When the singular term, "system," is used or appears without parentheses, the concept becomes an unintended irony.

The main goal of social control is increased compliance. While theorists may disagree on the degree of force necessary to ensure this compliance, they agree that the implicit or explicit use of force is necessary. Given the opportunity, however, human beings tend toward disruptive, disorderly conduct rather than socially compliant behaviour. As a result, individuals who are considered impulsive, inattentive, or overactive — traits commonly associated with ADHD — would appear to reflect the true nature of human beings. Nonconformity, however, is socially disruptive, and must be contained at all costs. Initially, compliance may be achieved through the use of overt coercion, although this is not the ultimate goal of social control. There are a number of disadvantages with the use of force, however. It is time-consuming, costly, requires constant supervision, and is only partly successful. Over time, an increased dependence on external mechanisms of social control will result in decreased levels of inner control. Rather than creating a heightened level of self-control, the result is the need for increasingly intrusive forms of social control. Hirschi (1969) argues that this is particularly true for children and adolescents, especially those who lack a strong bond to society.

More recently, Gottfredson and Hirschi (1990) expanded their social control theory to account for both delinquent and criminal conduct. In the process, the emphasis has moved from social to self-control. According to Gottfredson and Hirschi, the family is the institution with the greatest responsibility for self-control, although individuals who have been inadequately socialized in the family may still learn self-control from the school. While they do not specifically identify ADHD as a cause of decreased self-control, Gottfredson and Hirschi suggest that individuals who exhibit symptoms which would be diagnosed as ADHD, such as socially unacceptable levels of overactivity, inattentiveness, impulsivity, and a lack of empathy, will also act in socially unacceptable ways. And because this group comprises a relatively heterogeneous population, it is reasonable to assume that such behaviour is an appropriate explanation for both delinquent and criminal behaviour.

THE DISCOVERY/CREATION DICHOTOMY OF DEVIANT BEHAVIOUR

Although used interchangeably, *mental illness* implies a physical, and *mental disorder* a psychological condition. Szasz, one of the most outspoken critics of psychiatry, denies the existence of *mental illness*. According to Szasz, the label is a category which benefits the psychiatric profession rather than the individual. Often misinterpreted and much maligned, Szasz has never denied the reality of the problems called mental illness. Rather than "suffering" from a mental illness, at best, such individuals are experiencing problems in living. The "discovery" that central nervous system stimulant-medications can lead to more socially compliant behaviour would appear to discredit Szasz. See, however, the section on the uncertainty surrounding this discovery.

In the case of ADHD, both the disorder and the treatment have become mechanisms of social control. Conrad and Schneider (1980) suggest that, in part, this is the result of the discovery of childhood and the increased attention placed on children; the net result of which was a greater awareness of potentially problematic behaviours. To study ADHD as pathologized deviance, this apparent discovery/creation dichotomy must be reconciled. The discovery of ADHD implies the existence of an immutable status; previously unrecognized, the focus is on the interpretation of the problem. Conversely, the creation of ADHD assumes the decision to transform unconnected ideas into a single, identifiable theory; previously nonexistent or, at the very least, unrecognizable in their present form, the emphasis is on the architect rather than the architecture.

According to Parsons, the sick role exempts patients from their traditional social responsibilities. Patients must learn the new rules that go along with their new identity. Unable to "get well" on their own, such individuals are not responsible for their condition. Because sickness is undesirable, nobody would want to intentionally get or stay sick. At the same time, patients who are sick have an obligation to seek professional help and cooperate fully in the process of trying to get well. Conrad (1975) extends the concept of the sick role to include individuals with ADHD, and uses Parsons's model to explain how deviant behaviour became a medical problem. From this perspective, individuals with ADHD are not to be blamed for their disorder, but must accept the medical diagnosis, accept professional help, and actively participate in their recovery.

In subsequent work, Conrad and Schneider (1978, 1980) have begun to use the term *medicalization of deviant behaviour* to describe socially disruptive behaviour such as ADHD. The process shares many similarities with Parsons's sick role, particularly the emphasis on discouraging personal responsibility. At the same time, there are notable differences, especially in the area of increased social control, and the greater flexibility which is extended to the medical profession, a flexibility which for the most part, is lacking in the legal realm. This control/treatment dichotomy presupposes the existence of a clearly defined medical condition that will favourably benefit from medical intervention. From this perspective, a social problem such as ADHD is better understood in terms of a medical condition rather than evidence of any conscious decision to engage in deviant behaviour. Neither parents nor teachers are blamed for having failed to control problem children. Not only is the school not considered part of the problem, it is the solution. Teachers, guidance counsellors, nurses and other school personnel are being included in case management plans, behaviour modification programs, and the distribution of stimulant-medications. Instead of looking for more effective ways to teach all children, the solution is to look for better ways to control some children.

Within ADHD, we encounter a *new* form of deviance. Viewed separately, inattention and hyperactivity-impulsivity are neither a modern phenomenon nor evidence of a distinct, mental disorder; together, they provide the basis for pathologized deviance. What is new, however, is not the behaviour, but the way the focus has shifted from a private, individual condition to a public, social problem. This phenomenon emphasizes the importance of definitions and the exclusivity of language. More important, we witness the power to characterize these individuals as lacking in self-control. Rather than helping or encouraging the development of more self-control, the disorder has led to more pervasive forms of social and psychological control. This process denies any level of self-control which may previously have been present. The power to define and diagnose individuals as troublesome is the power to control, and the shift from troubled to troublesome inexorably leads to the development of a variety of social control mechanisms.

Sociology has long struggled with the challenge of interpreting social problems. In recent years, the emphasis has been on the social construction of reality. In this process, patterns of behaviour are subjectively interpreted. Over time, however, the behaviour is objectified as problematic, and is imagined to exist independent of the interpreters. Although this resolves some questions, others are raised. Social problems are ideas constructed through social relations. More important, social problems are realities which threaten to undermine the orderly functioning of society. As a result, deviance is an integral part of the definition. The essence of what is being defined as deviant is incorporated into the final definition. This becomes a somewhat circular process — deviant behaviour is abnormal, and abnormal behaviour is deviant. What is missing is the way deviance is socially situated — the important role social relationships play in defining, regulating, and controlling behaviour.

According to Goode (1978), deviance is external to the individual, and subject to shifting meanings and different interpretations. Deviance is part of one's status, with people becoming rather than being born deviant. Thus, to consider ADHD as pathology or disease, is to question the way deviant behaviour has been created as a medical problem requiring medical treatment. By focusing on the *social* element, social control theorists contend that human beings are inclined to engage in deviant behaviour and will so do unless they are subject to a variety of informal and formal mechanisms of social control. In the process, however, they ignore those who interpret behaviour as deviant, and the power to decide what definition is considered correct. For example, in the case of ADHD, the same behaviour may result in different interpretations — where one individual sees an inability to sustain attention, another may see an active imagination.

What is deviant behaviour and how is it recognized and defined? Why are some behaviours considered normal, while others are considered abnormal, problematic, and deviant? Why are some deviant behaviours considered social problems, subject to social control, while others are considered political problems, liable for legal control? Although criminal acts are considered deviant, not all deviant acts are criminal. Most definitions separate the ideas according to how they are controlled. Deviant acts are behaviours that violate social norms and are informally controlled by parents, teachers, etc.; criminal acts violate legal norms and are subject to informal control by agents of the state, such as police officers and judges.

This creates a number of problems. First, while this approach explains how deviance is controlled, it does not explain where deviance comes from. Second, the process of defining deviance assumes that normative behaviour is the result of a debate between individuals with equal levels of social and political power. Third, the definition does not explain how deviant labels gain legitimacy, or how they function as and lend support to mechanisms of social control. Finally, the narrow focus of describing deviance in social or political forms of control ignores the political control which is exerted on social institutions. The overwhelming success of the medicalization of social problems is precisely because the lines between deviance and sickness have been "blurred."

At times, researchers have traced the historical reasons for these changes, but this is not an essential element for identifying problem populations. Locating the *discovery* of childhood in the post-medieval period, Conrad and Schneider (1980) conclude parental commitment to offspring increased with the likelihood that their children would survive infancy. When many children died during childbirth or shortly afterwards, parents could not afford, either financially or psychologically, to become attached. As the survival rate of children increased, so did the interest in and attachment to children. At the same time, the increased rate of survival led to more attention being paid to problems which were considered unique to children. Although some children undoubtedly engaged in such behaviours, the small numbers made the problems insignificant. As well, behaviours which might now be considered deviant — swearing, sexual promiscuity, underage drinking, truancy from school — although not always condoned, were often tolerated. Thus, concluding that children are more deviant today is incorrect. Instead, modern notions of what is considered acceptable childhood behaviour are closely linked to interests in child welfare. The problems have always existed, only our response has changed. Having recognized a growth in the nature of the behaviour, we have tempered our approach to those individuals whom we identify as deviant.

If the disorder is to be considered a distinct deviant behaviour, the shifting terminology will have to ultimately be related to the significance attached to the symptoms rather than the nature of the problem. The way the problems, and our responses to them, have changed so rapidly makes it difficult to find concrete examples of the disorder in case studies; a clear discussion within the systems of criminal justice is almost wholly absent. At the same time, the absence of a permanent definition makes it easier informally to control individuals with a broad range of deviant behaviours, some more and others less contained within the ADHD rubric.

In 1902, Stills reported on the work he had been conducting on the moral control of defective children. Stills's research is commonly considered the first serious work on ADHD. In 1937, Bradley reported what he called the "paradoxical" discovery that central nervous system stimulant-medication had a calming effect on children with disruptive behaviours. Bradley's nonrandom experiment was conducted on 9 girls and 21 boys, ranging from 5 to 14 years of age, patients at the Emma Pendleton Bradley Home for behaviour-disturbed children. Although the drug therapy lasted only one week, 15 of the patients showed dramatic increases in more socially acceptable behaviour, decreased mood swings, and increased school performance.

Bradley's discovery that stimulant-medication could control overactive behaviour appears to suggest that the behaviour is the result of a chemical imbalance in the brain, although this has yet to be shown. Despite the lack of any scientific proof for such a claim, the belief persists that ADHD is biologically, genetically and/or neurologically based. There are several problems with this conclusion. As well as not knowing exactly why stimulant-medication produces more compliant behaviour in some individuals, there is little research on why the medication is successful (that is, increases compliance) in some cases and not others. In Bradley's case, he noted improvements in only about 50% of the children. Such medications, when used in concert with other treatment regimens such as behaviour modification therapy, may reduce or control hyperactivity in social settings, but they do cut cure it. Rather than consider medication as a last resort, to be used only after all other options have been attempted and failed, however, it is often considered the treatment of choice. In addition, the reliance on medication ignores any underlying social, academic, or psychological difficulties.

While accepting the diagnosis, some parents reject the recommended treatment (particularly the use of stimulant-medication). Instead, they may feel that behaviour modification programs, closer contact between home and school, or educating their child about her or his disorder is more appropriate than experimenting with stimulant-medication. In recent years, naturopathic and homeopathic approaches have become more common. Rather than using synthesized drugs, advocates of naturopathy achieve holistic healing through meditation. Homeopaths treat the child rather than the problem, sometimes using natural derivatives found in animals, plants, and minerals. In an interesting turn of events, at least one major Canadian pharmacy, Shoppers Drug Mart®, has started to market an over-the-counter medication, which it claims may alleviate some of the symptoms associated with ADHD. Available without a medical prescription (or, presumably, even a formal diagnosis), the drug costs a fraction of the price of brand-name or generic stimulant-medications. Regardless of the process, the focus is still on the individual rather than the social setting. More important, alternatives to formal medical diagnoses perpetuate the belief that social control is necessary, albeit through the use of (seemingly) less-intrusive forms, thereby legitimizing both the diagnosis and the role of the observers.

MEDICAL CLASSIFICATION "SYSTEMS"

Classification systems create problems and recommend the appropriate recourse. They also help to increase the public's awareness of problems and how to solve them. Although problems exist without or independently of medical intervention, classification systems organize the way problems are understood. They create increased public awareness of what are publicly owned, social problems, and how they should be treated/controlled. Systems organize the way the problem is interpreted, and establish the language necessary for communication. In particular, therapeutic categories normalize deviance.

Emil Kraepelin (1856–1926) was one of the first individuals to perfect a technique for categorizing and interpreting diseases. His model is based on the belief that an accurate classification can isolate patients with the same diseases, from which similar diagnostic criteria can be determined. Kraepelin's model is still popular today, and is the basis of many of the classification systems currently in use including, e.g., those developed by the American Psychiatric Association, APA, and the World Health Organization, WHO.

Diagnostic and statistical manual of mental disorders, Fourth Edition, *DSM*-IV (APA, 1994) and *International statistical classification of diseases and related health problems,* Tenth Edition, *ICD*-10 (WHO, 1993) are both the most current and common classification systems presently in use. To increase the validity of scientific research, the *ICD*-10 separates theoretical research from methodological constructs. To make the results more applicable to clinical settings, the *DSM*-IV presents a single set of diagnostic criteria for both clinical and research purposes. As a result, diagnoses following *ICD*-10 rather than *DSM*-IV tend to result in a lower overall rate of ADHD. Toone and van der Linden (1997) suggest that this may be one reason rates for attentional-deficits in adults differ between North America and Europe. Although the APA's diagnostic criteria for ADHD is used in the present discussion, we will briefly consider both the *DSM*-IV and *ICD*-10 approaches.

While is less apparent in *DSM*-IV than *ICD*-10, both systems separate the diagnostic criteria for attentional-deficits. In the *DSM*-IV, the symptoms are divided into inattention and hyperactivity-impulsivity; *ICD*-10 lists the symptoms as inattention, hyperactivity, and impulsivity. Because the APA uses the WHO nosology, the diagnostic criteria are almost identical. Each system lists 18 symptoms: nine each under hyperactive and affective headings. In addition, *DSM*-IV requires symptoms to be present in at least two social settings (e.g., school, home, work). Conversely, *ICD*-10 permits a diagnosis for children who present site-specific symptoms (e.g., disturbances which occur only at home or in the classroom).

Depending on the range, severity, history, and continuity of the symptoms, *DSM*-IV provides five possible subtypes: ADHD, Combined Type is diagnosed when the criteria for inattention and hyperactivity-impulsivity are met for the past six months; ADHD, Predominantly Inattentive Type if inattention is present but not hyperactivity-impulsivity; ADHD, Predominantly Hyperactive-Impulsive Type if hyperactivity-impulsivity is present but not inattention; ADHD, In Partial Remission describes individuals who have some symptoms but not enough to substantiate a complete diagnosis; and, ADHD, Not Otherwise Specified should be diagnosed when prominent symptoms of inattention or hyperactivity-impulsivity are present, but are insufficient for a diagnosis of ADHD. An ability to differentiate between such a disorganized group lends credibility to the category, and the diversity of categories implies an ability to delineate between and within the disorder. As a result, one is left with the impression that the diagnostic criteria enable trained professionals to identify not only a general mental disorder but also a specific division within the category.

Depending on their point of view, the *DSM* has been variously described as the "official" diagnostic classification system, *the* "bible" for diagnosing mental disorders, or the world's most powerful manual for diagnosing "alleged" mental disorders. Ironic or otherwise, the range of opinions point to the manual's overwhelming influence. Regardless, there are several obvious limitations, not the least of which the APA itself admits. For our purposes, we will address four of the most significant concerns: how to decide what is a mental disorder, how to differentiate between mental disorders, how to diagnose ADHD, and the multiple purposes of the manual.

First, the APA acknowledges the importance of clearly defined terms for making a valid clinical diagnosis. The editors themselves are the first to admit, however, that they never actually explain what a "mental disorder" is. Regardless, the APA continues to use the term; in fact, it is incorporated in the title of the APA's manual. At most, the decision to adopt an undefined (and, according to the editors, undefinable), highly subjective concept is questionable. Using the definition which appeared in both the *DSM-III* and *DSM-III-R*, the editors imply that a mental disorder is a quantitative, observable fact, and conclude that " ... it is as useful as any other available definition and has helped to guide decisions regarding which conditions on the boundary between normality and pathology should be included in *DSM*-IV" (APA, 1994, p. xxi).

By concluding that the existing definition "is as useful as any other," the APA effectively distances itself from the attendant controversy surrounding the concept and, at the same time, benefits from the uncertainty. The implication is that the decision to adopt a completely untenable definition is a valid, scientific practice. Notwithstanding the inherent limitation of such a definition, the phrase has the advantage of organizing an otherwise chaotic range of symptoms. Accepting the reality that a mental disorder is a label doctors use to categorize a social problem raise the question: How are doctors made aware of social problems? If the behaviours are part of a syndrome, who determines what is normative behaviour?

Second, the APA notes that there are no clinical tests which establish the existence of ADHD. They discount this as a possible limitation by pointing out that research has shown differences between "abnormal" individuals (those who present ADHD-ogenic symptoms) and control subjects, although they do not elaborate on the significance of the results. In many ways, this is a self-referential power. Medical professionals have the power to both name a problem and recommend the strategy which will be used to combat it. In the case of ADHD, the disorder is diagnosed through the subjective observation of a confluence of physical symptoms. The behaviours are interpreted by a variety of agents of social control, including, e.g., parents and teachers, rather than the individual so identified.

Third, rather than diagnosing ADHD through clinical tests (which are difficult to substantiate), physicians conduct interviews with parents and patients. In recent years, research has begun to suggest that quantitative measurement tools are not an appropriate measure of developmental behaviours. ADHD might be better described in terms of a variety of separate symptoms which are identified primarily through physically disruptive behaviour rather than a disorder which can be objectively diagnosed with quantifiable measurements. Rather than considering ADHD in terms of its separate components, Barkley (1994) suggests that clinicians should consider the symptoms as evidence of three separate mental disorders. Sometimes (particularly when the school has recommended the appointment), the physician may wish to examine the patient's school records. In other cases, the patient may be asked to complete a variety of timed games, puzzles, etc., with the results compared to "typical" response rates. Because individuals with ADHD are often unable to consider the severity of their disorder, parents (or, for adults, spouses) are frequently asked to rate presenting symptoms according to the diagnostic criteria. Although psychological examinations are the result of a referral, the APA recommends that physicians should only make a formal diagnosis if there is clinical evidence of the symptoms in two or more social settings (e.g., home, school, work).

The symptoms of ADHD tend to be less problematic in settings where the individual is highly motivated. As well, individuals who meet the criteria for ADHD are, by definition, better able to focus their attention in unique, interesting situations. Thus, evidence of the disorder may be absent in clinical settings. Unable to observe, first-hand, the behaviours which are considered disruptive to social settings, the APA suggests that physicians objectively evaluate behaviours which have been subjectively considered problematic to those who see the individual in a variety of different social settings.

Finally, besides their usefulness for researching and diagnosing mental disorders, diagnostic codes serve many, often contradictory, purposes. Some third parties such as private insurance companies and government departments require *DSM*-IV codes for reimbursement purposes. As well, many schools and some universities have started to use the codes to decide which students are eligible for special assistance. As a result, some parents have even pressured their family doctors to diagnose their children with ADHD, so they will be given greater flexibility in writing timed admissions tests.

FREQUENCY AND PREVALENCE

Over the years, ADHD has undergone many changes. In *DSM*-IV, ADHD is listed in the section "Disorders Usually First Evident in Infancy, Childhood, or Adolescence." *DSM*-IV presents the following diagnostic criteria: levels of inattention and/or hyperactivity-impulsivity that have persisted for at least six months and that are both more persistent and severe than compared to those at a similar developmental level; at least some symptoms must have been present before seven years of age; impairment must be present in two or more settings (e.g., school, work, home); evidence of clinically significant impairment in social, academic, or occupational functioning. The symptoms may not occur exclusively during or be better accounted for by another mental disorder.

Often considered a "male problem," more males than females are diagnosed and treated for ADHD. As a result, males have been the subject of both more intensive and intrusive research. *DSM*-IV suggests the typical male-to-female ratio may range from 4:1 to 9:1. However, the results depend on the population studied, the social setting observed, and the diagnostic criteria used. Rates as high as 10:1 for diagnoses in clinical settings, and as low as 2.5:1 in epidemiological studies, are quite common. At best, behaviours considered inappropriate to one's gender may be considered abnormal, with ADHD more likely to be diagnosed for behaviours that disrupt social settings.

One possible reason why ADHD is considered more frequent in males than females is that the focus is on how disruptive behaviour negatively affects social settings rather than the individuals so labelled. Males are socially conditioned to be more active, assertive, and independent than females. Excessive levels of these traits (which may be redefined as hyperactivity, aggression, and obstinance) are more likely to be present in males. Less attention is paid to issues such as a failure to interact with others and nonverbal refusals to comply, traits which may be more apparent in females. No less personally debilitating, anxiety and depression are not nearly as problematic to social settings as is physically disruptive behaviour.

Compared to the number of elementary school-aged children diagnosed and treated, teachers tend to overestimate the prevalence of ADHD, with estimates ranging from 5% to 15%. However, ratings by medical practitioners range from 1% to 6%. The choice of diagnostic criteria influences the rate of hyperactivity and the population studied. Cultural differences and ethnicity may also be a factor. The diagnosis is also dependent on the severity attached to presenting symptomatology, and the choice of rating scales used.

When *DSM*-IV diagnostic criteria are used, ADHD is estimated at between 3% and 5% of all school-aged children; yet, ratings from 1.7% and 16% are not uncommon. The number of American children diagnosed and treated has almost doubled in the last five years. In 1996, 3.25 million American children (mostly boys), aged 6 to 12, were prescribed psychoactive drugs. Citing Health Canada statistics, Séguin (1998) writes " ... that the amount of Ritalin consumed in Canada in 1996 was 4.6 times more than in 1990." Other diagnostic criteria (e.g., *ICD*) show similar findings.

In addition, most studies examine male children and adolescents, especially those who are already thought to have academic deficits. Those studies which consider both males and females typically include few females. Regardless, the results are often extrapolated to explain the behaviour of both genders. As well, a number of studies focus on youth in remedial education programs. Little research has been compiled on secondary-school youths, even less on adults. Studies on adults with criminal records are almost nonexistent.

In part, the emphasis on youth is due to an assumption that symptoms disappear or subside with age. Where they persist, they are considered secondary to other neurological and physiological difficulties. This ignores the possibility that only the presenting symptoms have changed. The behaviour may also no longer be problematic to social settings, and thus no longer subject to frequent intervention by quasi-professional observers. Another possibility, however, is that adults may have developed better coping strategies to mask their overactivity. For example, cordless telephones allow you to walk around or work at the computer while you talk, and cellular telephones let you carry on a conversation while you are running errands or driving. Considered "hyperactive" at school, they may simply have found jobs where they are no longer required to remain seated, or they may have found a job where their energy level is an advantage.

Projected abnormalities are not only gender-biased, but also result in a differentiated rate of response between and within male and female samples. Barkley (1996) found that mothers of children with ADHD (especially boys) tended to experience more problems than fathers. In part, this may be because mothers may have more frequent contact with children, while fathers only see their children at the end of the day. As well, children may believe that their fathers are more likely to physically punish them. However, a retrospective study of male childhood experiences found no direct link between punitive parenting and ADHD.

The degree to which conduct is considered disruptive will depend on the location where the behaviour occurs and the individual who evaluates it. At home, for example, parents may place few restrictions on their child's behaviour. At school, teachers, who expect students to perform specific tasks in an allotted period of time, may consider any evidence of noncompliance unacceptable. Children and adolescents, living on their own, may have limited contact with individuals interested in assessing their behaviour. Consequently, where the disruptive behaviour may have precipitated the departure from home, there is a much smaller chance that the conduct will be identified as such. Although disruptive behaviour may increase the likelihood that they will be in contact with the police, there is no reason to believe that police will recommend a behavioural assessment rather than a charge.

Social expectations about how males and females should behave with respect to their gender influences how disruptive behaviour is interpreted. Because the meaning attached to behaviour is influenced by social expectations about gender-related behaviour, males and females who present the same symptoms may receive different diagnoses. Females, for example, may be considered unstable rather than hyperactive. As well, one would expect the level of ADHD diagnoses would be higher for males and females considered more hyperactive than their female peers (but less than their male peers) and lower for males and females considered less hyperactive than their male counterparts (but more than their female peers).

As the focus shifts from socially disruptive symptoms to personal distractions, more adolescents, teenagers, and females are being diagnosed and treated for ADHD. Previously considered a childhood disorder which disappeared over time, ADHD is now being diagnosed in adults. As well, recent studies suggest that as many as 80% of those diagnosed with ADHD as children may continue to display sufficient symptoms warranting a diagnosis in adulthood; children of adults diagnosed with ADHD are also more likely to present symptoms for the disorder. Unclear, however, is the question of whether this latter group actually has the disorder, or whether their behaviour is just being more carefully observed.

Some parents are diagnosed after they admit that they have tried their child's medication and discovered they can concentrate better. In part, this may explain the dramatic increase in the production and sale of stimulant-medications. If correct, doctors are either ignoring the evidence, or writing prescriptions which the patient and the parent are sharing. There is little evidence to suggest parents administer the drug to the siblings of children who receive pharmacological treatment for ADHD.

CONCLUSION

There is no question that ADHD has potentially debilitating consequences for the individual. ADHD is not, however, a negative form of deviance, although many forms of deviance are negative only to those who find themselves in a deviant condition. The trend toward "collapsing" deviant and criminal behaviours into a single category is being matched with the "blurring" of formal and informal mechanisms of social control. The symptoms are often considered present, and the debate shifts to *how* rather than *whether* they are related. Having accepted the link, the solution is more control. The lack of a standardized definition, and the way the definitions shift through space and time make it difficult to evaluate the success of social-control policies. Little attention is paid to the impact these policies are having at the personal level. The medical diagnoses, diagnostic criteria, and response to treatment rely on physical symptomatology. Underlying psychological and emotional characteristics are not subject to nearly the same level of attention. This phenomenon makes any attempt to differentiate between and within the various definitions of deviance particularly problematic. One of the greatest difficulties is that the symptoms are frequently used interchangeably to identify a variety of different disorders and conditions.

Most of the symptoms relate to physically noticeable behaviours. Although equally debilitating to the individual, inward turmoil is not disruptive to social institutions. While the level to which the behaviours are disruptive may vary across social contexts, ADHD is disruptive within a variety of social settings, but what is perceived to be a problem in one location may not be considered a problem in another. Thus, problems at school may not be considered problems at home. For example, continually interrupting conversations may be less troubling at home (or in some contexts at home) than at school. This may be because home-settings typically provide more occasions for unstructured activities. Individuals who meet the criteria for ADHD, however, are frequently unable to make appropriate connections between their behaviours and the consequences of their actions. Thus, the failure to establish consistent behavioural expectations between sites may result in increased problems in other locations.

To add to the problem, claims-making organizations such as Learning Disability Associations have begun to speak on behalf of individuals with ADHD. While the symptoms may affect the child's ability to learn, they do not necessarily predict a learning disorder. Cultural factors, lack of opportunity, and inadequate or inconsistent teaching must be ruled out before an individual can be considered for a learning disorder. Regardless, Learning Disability Associations often claim "ownership" of school-aged children considered to have a variety of undefined (frequently undiagnosed) "learning disabilities." This has made it increasingly difficult to differentiate between a wide range of disorders, of which ADHD may exhibit only a fraction of the criteria. As well, a variety of different disruptive behaviours have been "collapsed" into the learning disability category. Academic underachievement is considered so prevalent in children with attentional-deficits that learning disorders and ADHD are often considered the same. Although ADHD includes social and behavioural factors, the learning disorder nosology focuses primarily on learning deficits and, as a result, the problem is situated in the social structure rather than the individual.

The rate of ADHD-diagnoses is connected to school "careers," with diagnoses rising with the onset of school and decreasing as children exit school. This is largely related to the observation of problem behaviours. At best, parents are typically able to compare the behaviour of their child with her or his sibling(s), cousins, and, children in the community. Teachers, on the other hand, can compare an individual child with entire classes or grades; longitudinally, they can make comparisons across several years. Teachers are also required to systematically control, organize, collate, and record information relating to a variety of different issues, such as individual test scores; the number of absences from school, including both legitimate excuses and unauthorized truancies; possible evidence of malnutrition, abuse, and neglect; and medical problems. Teachers are also being trained to detect possible disorders including, e.g., learning disorders and ADHD, which may adversely affect both the learning environment and the individual student.

The lack of a consistent definition of ADHD has led to a number of conflicting court rulings. For example, in the *Deyell Case* (1987), the Alberta Court of Appeal denied the defendant's application to have the Canadian Human Rights Commission hear a case of possible discrimination because of a learning disability. In that case, they had asked the Alberta Court of Queen's Bench to decide if the state was obligated to pay tuition for students with learning disabilities. Finding the concept restrictive, the Court ruled the Province's definition for "physical disabilities" excluded students with obvious learning disabilities. At the same time, however, they concluded that separate schools which accept students with learning disabilities are not customarily available to the public. Despite having been the victim of discrimination, the youth, described as hyperactive, was deemed ineligible for discretionary funding to assist in his education. More recently, the Nova Scotia Department of Education ruled ADHD was a "learning disability." As a result, the Annapolis Valley regional school board was held liable for the 1997–1998 tuition costs of a 14-year-old boy, enrolled in a private school, because his disability meant that he was unable to learn in a public school.

Previously considered a private problem, the creation of a disorder has led to increased social control. Individuals who lack attention and are perceived as overactive and careless are no longer isolated cases. The increased pressure to conform, along with fewer parents at home to "control" children, has resulted in a demand that control be institutionalized. With decreased resources, fewer teachers, and reduced budgets, schools (and parents) have turned to the medical system for assistance.

A focus on systems, mechanisms of social control, and shifting definitions of what ADHD is, is only the beginning. Future research on the way disruptive behaviour has become pathologized deviance must also examine the way unrelated behaviours have become a syndrome with one obvious solution — treatment/control (primarily, the use of stimulant-medications to reduce disobedience and increase compliance). As well, research needs to explore the reasons why the focus is on social settings rather than individual distress. In part, this belief has meant that males tend to be diagnosed and treated for ADHD more often than females. If ADHD is a legitimate syndrome, however, the focus must be on how the disorder affects the self rather than the social structure. Rather than simply discussing ADHD, or the percentages of individuals being diagnosed and treated, the focus must be on the way the treatment of disruptive behaviour is, in reality, the control (through informal social institutions) of individuals who are considered to have ADHD.

REFERENCES

Crime and Delinquency

Bohm, R.B. (1997). *A primer on crime and delinquency*. Toronto: Wadsworth Publishing Company.

Braithwaite, J. (1989). *Crime, shame and reintegration*. New York: Cambridge University Press.

Campbell, D.S., and Davis, R.B. (1981). *Understanding impulsivity and related cognitive styles in inmate students*. Ottawa: Ministry of the Solicitor General of Canada.

Cellini, H.R., and Snowman, J. (1982). Learning disabilities and juvenile delinquents. *Federal Probation, 46*(3), 26–32.

Coons, W.H. (1982). Learning disabilities and criminality. *Canadian Journal of Criminology, 24*(3), 251–265.

Denno, D.W. (1985). Sociological and human developmental explanations of crime: conflict or consensus? *Criminology, 23*(4), 114–119.

Doob, A.N., Marinos, V., and Varma, K. (1995). *Working document. Youth crime and the youth justice system in Canada: A research perspective*. Ottawa: Department of Justice Canada, Research Section.

Dowling, W.D. (1991). Learning disabilities among incarcerated males. *Journal of Correctional Education, 42,* 180–185.

Ellis, D., and DeKeseredy, W. (1996). *The wrong stuff: An introduction to the sociological study of deviance* (2nd ed.). Scarborough: Allyn & Bacon.

Garland, D. (1985). *Punishment and welfare: a history of penal strategies*. Brookfield, VT: Gower Publishing Company.

Goode, E. (1978). *Deviant behavior: An interactionist approach*. Englewood Cliffs, NJ: Prentice-Hall, Inc.

Gottfredson, M.R., and Hirschi, T. (1990). *A general theory of crime*. Stanford, CA: Stanford University Press.

Hilton, N.Z., Jackson, M.A., and Webster, C.D. (1990). *Clinical criminology: Theory, research, and practice*. Toronto: Canadian Scholars' Press Inc.

Hirschi, T. (1969). *Causes of delinquency*. Berkeley: University of California Press.

Jenkins, R.L., and Glickman, S. (1946). Common syndromes in psychiatry: I. Deviant behavior traits. *American Journal of Orthopsychiatry, 16*(2), 244–254.

Maguin, E., and Loeber, R. (1998). Academic performance and delinquency. In M. Tonry (Ed.), *Criminal Justice: A Review of research, 20*, 145–264. Chicago: The University of Chicago Press.

Moser, F., and Doreleijers, T.A.H. (1998). An explorative study of juvenile delinquents with attention-deficit/hyperactivity disorder. *European Journal on Criminal Policy and Research, 5*(2), 67–81.

Pena, D.R. (1986). *Learning disabilities and juvenile delinquency: An exploration of causal processes.* Unpublished doctoral dissertation. Newark, NJ: Sam Houston State University, Faculty of the College of Criminal Justice.

Perlmutter, B.F. (1987). Delinquency and learning disabilities: Evidence for compensatory behaviors and adaptation. *Journal of Youth and Adolescence, 16*(2), 89–95.

Rosenberg, M., and Lewis, A. (1993). *Social deviance: An integrated approach.* Scarborough: Prentice-Hall Canada Inc.

Satterfield, J.H., Hoppe, C.M., and Schell, A.M. (1982). A prospective study of delinquency in 110 adolescent boys with attention deficit disorder and 88 normal adolescent boys. *American Journal of Psychiatry, 139*(9), 795–798.

Schwendinger, H., and Schwendinger, J. (1979). Delinquency and social reform: a radical perspective. In L.T. Empey (Ed.), *Juvenile justice: the progressive legacy and current reforms* (pp. 245–287). Charlottesville: The University Press of Virginia.

Sikorsky, J.B., and McGee, T.P. (1986). Understanding learning disabilities. *Juvenile & Family Court Journal, 3.*

Tittle, C.R. (1995). *Control balance: Toward a general theory of deviance.* Boulder: Westview Press, Inc.

Vitelli, R. (1996). Prevalence of childhood conduct and Attention-Deficit Hyperactivity Disorders in adult maximum-security inmates. *International Journal of Offender Therapy and Comparative Criminology, 40*(4), 263–271.

Whitmore, E.A.W., Kramer, J.R., and Knutson, J.F. (1993). The association between punitive childhood experiences and hyperactivity. *Child Abuse & Neglect, 17,* 357–366.

Zagar, R., Arbit, J., Hughes, J.R., Busell, R.E., & Busch, K. (1989). Developmental and disruptive behavior disorders among delinquents. *Journal of the American Academy of Child and Adolescent Psychiatry, 28*(3), 437–440.

Diagnostics

Achenbach, T.M. (1985). *Assessment and taxonomy of child and adolescent psychopathology.* In A.E. Kazdin (Series Ed.), *Developmental clinical psychology and psychiatry series* (Vol. 3). Beverly Hills: SAGE Publications, Inc.

Amen, D.G. (1997). General adult ADD symptoms checklist. *One A.D.D. Place* [On-line], *Children and adults with Attention Deficit Disorder.* Available: http://www.greatconnect.com/oneaddplace/addcheck.htm

American Psychiatric Association (APA). (1994). *Diagnostic and statistical manual of mental disorders* (4th ed.). Washington, DC: Author.

American Psychiatric Association. (1996). *DSM-IV™ coding update, 1996 edition: includes ICD-9-CM codes. Effective October 1, 1996.* Washington, DC: Author.

Baker, H.J., and Traphagen, V. (1937). *The diagnosis and treatment of behavior-problem children.* In M.V. O'Shea and H.E. O'Shea (Eds.), *Experimental education series.* New York: The Macmillan Company.

Barkley, R.A. (1994). Impaired delayed responding: a unified theory of Attention-Deficit Hyperactivity Disorder. In D.K. Routh (Ed.), *Disruptive behavior disorders in childhood* (pp. 63–112). New York: Plenum Press.

Barkley, R.A. (1996). Attention-Deficit/Hyperactivity Disorder. In J.E. Mash and R.A. Barkley (Eds.), *Child Psychopathology* (pp. 63–112). New York: The Guilford Press.

Bernstein, D.A., Clarke-Stewart, A., Roy, E.J., Srull, T.K., & Wickens, C.D. (1994). *Psychology* (3rd ed.). Toronto: Houghton Mifflin Company.

Biederman, J., Faraone, S.V., Mick, E., Spencer, T., Wilens, T., Kiely, K., Guite, J., Ablon, J.S., Reed, E., and Warbuton, E. (1995). High risk for Attention Deficit Hyperactivity Disorder among children of parents with child onset of the disorder: a pilot study. *American Journal of Psychiatry, 152*(3), 431–435.

Bradley, C. (1937). The behavior of children receiving benzedrine. *American Journal of Psychiatry, 94,* 577–585.

Caplan, P.J. (1995). *They say you're crazy: How the world's most powerful psychiatrists decide who's normal.* Don Mills, ON: Addison-Wesley Publishing Company.

Denckla, M.B. (1996). Biological correlates of learning and attention: what is relevant to learning disability and Attention-Deficit Hyperactivity Disorder? *Child Development, 17*(2), 114–119.

Deutsch, C.K., and Kinsbourne, M. (1990). Genetics and biochemistry in Attention Deficit Disorder. In M. Lewis and S.M. Millers (Eds.), *Handbook of developmental psychopathology* (93–107). New York: Plenum Press.

Edelbrock, C., and Rancurello, M.D. (1985). Childhood hyperactivity: an overview of rating scales and their applications. *Clinical Psychology Review, 5,* 429–445.

Faraone, S.V., Biederman, J., Lehman, B.K., Keenan, K., Norman, D., Seidman, L.J., Kolodny, R., Kraus, I., Perrin, J., and Chen, W.J. (1993). Evidence for the independent familial transmission of Attention Deficit Hyperactivity Disorder and learning disabilities: results from a family genetic study. *American Journal of Psychiatry, 150*(6), 891–895.

Frances, A., First, M.B., and Pincus, H.A. (1995). *DSM-IV guidebook.* Washington, DC: American Psychiatric Press, Inc.

Gallico, R.P., Burns, T.J., and Grob, C.S. (1988). *Emotional and behavioral problems in children with learning disabilities.* Toronto: College-Hill Press.

Goldman, L.S., Genel, M., Bezman, R.J., and Slanetz, P.J. (1998). Diagnosis and treatment of Attention-Deficit/Hyperactivity Disorder in children and adolescents. *Journal of the American Medical Association, 279*(14), 1100–1107.

Goodman, R., and Stevenson, J. (1989a). A twin study of hyperactivity: I. an examination of hyperactivity scores and categories derived from Rutter Teacher and Parent Questionnaires. *Journal of Child Psychology and Psychiatry, 30*(5), 671–689.

Goodman, R., and Stevenson, J. (1989b). A twin study of hyperactivity: II. the aetiological role of genes, family relationships and perinatal adversity. *Journal of Child Psychology and Psychiatry, 30*(5), 691–709.

Grizenko, N., and Pawliuk, N. (1994). Risk and protective factors for disruptive behavior disorders in children. *American Journal of Orthopsychiatry, 64*(4), 534–544.

Hallowell, E.M., and Ratey, J.J. (1994). *Driven to distraction: recognizing and coping with Attention Deficit Disorder from childhood through adulthood.* Toronto: Simon & Schuster, Inc.

Hechtman, L., and Weiss, G. (1983). Long-term outcome of hyperactive children. *American Journal of Orthopsychiatry, 53*(3), 532–541.

Hill, J.C., and Schoener, E.P. (1996). Age-dependent decline of attention deficit hyperactivity disorder. *American Journal of Psychiatry, 153*(9), 1143–1146.

Holborow, P., and Berry, P. (1986). A multi-national, cross-cultural perspective on hyperactivity. *American Journal of Orthopsychiatry, 56*(2), 320–322.

Kendall, P.C., and Braswell, L. (1993). *Cognitive-behavioral therapy for impulsive children* (2nd ed.). New York: The Guilford Press.

Krajicek, M.J., and Tomlinson, A.I.T. (1983). *Detection of developmental problems in children: Birth to adolescence* (2nd ed.). Baltimore: University Park Press.

Kundu, S., and Tufnell, G. (1998). Hyperactive children [On-line], *Family Medicine.* Available: http://www.docnet.org.uk/fammed/Mar98/leadingl.htm

Leung, P.W.L., Luk, S.L., Ho, T.P., Taylor, E., Mak, F.L., and Bacon-Shone, J. (1996). The diagnosis and prevalence of Hyperactivity in Chinese schoolboys. *British Journal of Psychiatry, 168,* 486–496.

Miller, D.K., and Blum, M. (1996). *Overload: attention Deficit Disorder and the addictive brain.* Kansas City, MI: Andrews and McMeel.

Nieves, N. (1991). Childhood psychopathology and learning disabilities: Neuropsychological relationships. In J.E. Obruzt and G.W. Hynd (Eds.), *Neuropsychological foundations of learning disabilities: A handbook of issues, methods, and practice* (pp. 113–145). Toronto: Academic Press, Inc.

Rapp, C.A. (1998). *The strengths model: Case management with people suffering from severe and persistent mental illnesses.* Toronto: Oxford University Press, Inc.

Reichenberg-Ullman, J., and Ullman, R. (1996). *Ritalin-free kids: Safe and effective homeopathic medicine for ADD and other behavioral and learning problems.* Rockin, CT: Prima Publishing.

Sandberg, S. (1996). Hyperkinetic or attention deficit disorder. *American Journal of Psychiatry, 169,* 10–17.

Shoppers Drug Mart®. (1998, August 1). Attention deficit hyperactivity disorder. *Healthwatch® Report,* p. 3.

Stills, G.F. (1902). The Coulstonian lectures on some abnormal psychical conditions in children. *Lancet, 1,* 1008–1012, 1077–1082, 1163–1168.

Ward, M.F., Wender, P.H., and Reimherr, F.W. (1993). The Wender Utah Rating Scale: an aid in the retrospective diagnosis of childhood Attention Deficit/Hyperactivity Disorder. *American Journal of Psychiatry, 150*(6), 885–890.

Wolraich, M.L., Hannah, J.N., Pinnock, T.Y., Baumgaertel, and Brown, J. (1996). Comparison of diagnostic criteria for Attention-Deficit Hyperactivity Disorder in a country-wide sample. *Journal of the American Academy of Child & Adolescent Psychiatry, 35,* 319–324.

World Health Organization (WHO). (1993). *International statistical classification of diseases and related health problems* (10ᵗʰ rev.) (Vols. 1–2). Geneva: Author.

Education

DuPaul, G.J. and Stoner, G. (1994). *ADHD in the schools: Assessment and intervention strategies*, New York: Guilford Press.

Erskine, B. (1998, May 11). Board ordered to pay private school tuition. *The Halifax Chronicle-Herald*, p. A1.

Fachin, K. (1996). Teaching Tommy: A second-grader with Attention Deficit Hyperactivity Disorder. *Phi Delta Kappan, 77*(6), 437–441.

Her Majesty the Queen in Right of Alberta (The Department of Education) and the Calgary Board of Education v. Roy Deyell (1987), *Canadian Human Rights Reporter* 8, D/3688.

Kolata, G. (1996, May 17). Surge in Ritalin use poses ethical dilemma: well-known treatment for attention-deficit disorder is now being given to boost mental performance. *The Globe and Mail* (Atlantic ed.), p. A6.

Séguin, R. (1998, May 27). Ritalin raises alarm in Quebec: schools promote behavioural drug. *The Globe and Mail* (Atlantic Edition), p. A1.

Sockett, H. (1997). Chemistry or character? In A. Molnar (Ed.), *Ninety-sixth yearbook of the National Society for the Study of Education: Part II. The construction of children's character* (pp. 110–119). Chicago: Author.

Toone, B.K., and van der Linden, G.J.H. (1997). Editorial: attention deficit hyperactivity disorder or hyperkinetic disorder in adults. *British Journal of Psychiatry, 170*, 489–491.

Weiss, L. (1992). *Attention Deficit Disorder in adults*. Dallas: Taylor Publishing Company.

Wender, P.H. (1995). *Attention-Deficit Hyperactivity Disorder in adults*. New York: Oxford University Press, Inc.

Social Control

Al-Issa, I. (1982). *Gender and Child Psychopathology*. Toronto: Academic Press, Inc.

Back, K.W. (1983). Compliance and security in an age of sincerity. In M. Rosenbaum (Ed.), *Compliant behavior: Beyond obedience and authority* (pp. 50–76). New York: Human Sciences Press.

Battegay, R. (1983). Compliance? Between freedom and compulsion. In M. Rosenbaum (Ed.), *Compliant behavior: Beyond obedience and authority* (pp. 11–57). New York: Human Sciences Press, Inc.

Becker, H. (1973). *Outsiders: Studies in the sociology of deviance*. New York: Free Press

Ben-Yehuda, N. (1987). *Deviance and moral boundaries: Witchcraft, the occult, science fiction, deviant sciences, and scientists*. Chicago: The University of Chicago Press.

Berger, P.L., & Luckmann, T. (1989). *The social construction of reality: a treatise in the sociology of knowledge*. Toronto: Doubleday.

Butler, S. (1985). *Erewhon*. Toronto: Penguin Books Canada Ltd. (Original work published 1872)

Campbell, S.B. (1990). The socialization and social development of hyperactive children. In M. Lewis and S.M. Miller (Eds.), *Handbook of developmental psychopathology* (pp. 77–91). New York: Plenum Press.

Comte, A. (1974). *The positive philosophy* (H. Martineau, Trans.). New York: AMS Press, Inc. (Original work published 1855)

Conrad, P. (1975). The discovery of hyperkinesis: notes on the medicalization of deviant behavior. *Social Problems, 23*, 12–21.

Conrad, P. (1997). Public eyes and private genes: Historical frames, news constructions, and social problems. *Social Problems, 44*(2), 139–154.

Conrad, P., and Schneider, J.W. (1978). Medicine. In D. Martindale (Series Ed.), *Contributions in Sociology, Number 31*. J.S. Roucek (Ed.), *Social control for the 1980s: a handbook for a democratic society* (346–358). Connecticut: Greenwood Press, Inc.

Conrad, P., and Schneider, J.W. (1980). *Deviance and medicalization: from badness to sickness*. Toronto: The C.V. Mosby Company.

Conte, R.A. (1983). *A behavioral and psychophysiological analysis of hyperactive children*. Unpublished doctoral dissertation. Toronto: University of Toronto, Department of Psychology.

Dain, N. (1994). Psychiatry and anti-psychiatry in the United States. In M.S. Micale and R. Porter (Eds.), *Discovering the history of psychiatry* (pp. 415–444). Toronto: Oxford University Press, Inc.

Gibbs, J.P. (1989). *Control: sociology's central notion*. Chicago: University of Illinois Press.

Gusfield, J.R. (1981). *The culture of public problems: Drinking-driving and the symbolic order*. Chicago: The University of Chicago Press.

Hancock, L. (1996, 18 March). Mother's little helper. *Newsweek*, 176–180.

Hobbes, T. (1985). *Leviathan*. New York: Penguin Books. (Original work published 1651)

Janowitz, M. (1978). The intellectual history of 'social control.' In D. Martindale (Series Ed.), *Contributions in sociology, Number 31*, J.S. Roucek (Ed.), *Social control for the 1980s: A handbook for a democratic society* (pp. 20–45). Connecticut: Greenwood Press, Inc.

Kirk, S.A., and Kutchins, H. (1992). *The selling of DSM: the rhetoric of science in psychiatry*. In J. Best (Series Ed.), *Social problems and social issues* (pp. i–x, 1–270). New York: Aldine de Gruyter.

Machan, D. (1996, August 12). Staying healthy: An agreeable affliction/Only in America: A supposed medical problem gets turned into a tactical career move. *Forbes, 158*(4), pp. 148–151.

Parsons, T. (1951). *The social system*. New York: Free Press.

Pfohl, S. (1994). *Images of deviance and social control: A sociological history* (2nd ed.). Toronto: McGraw-Hill, Inc.

Schacht, T.E. (1985). DSM-III and the politics of truth. *American Psychologist, 40*(5), 513–521.

Schissel, B. (1997). Psychiatric expansionism and social control: The intersection of community care and state policy. *Social Science Research, 26*, 399–418.

Schrag, P., and Divorky, D. (1975). *The myth of the hyperactive child, and other means of child control*. Toronto: Random House of Canada Limited.

Szasz, T. (1961). *The myth of mental illness: foundations of a theory of personal conduct*. New York: Hoeber-Harper.

Vatz, R.E. (1994, July 27). Attention deficit delirium. *The Wall Street Journal* (Eastern Edition), p. A10.

Vatz, R.E., and Weinberg, L.S. (1994). The rhetorical paradigm in psychiatric history: Thomas Szasz and the myth of mental illness. In M.S. Micale and R. Porter (Eds.), *Discovering the history of psychiatry* (pp. 311–330). Toronto: Oxford University Press, Inc.

Weber, T. (1998, May 19). California foster children routinely drugged: medication makes job easier for overburdened caretakers. *New Brunswick Telegraph Journal,* p. A7.

Zachary, G.P. (1997, May 2). Male order: Boys used to be boys, but do some now see boyhood as a malady? *The Wall Street Journal* (Eastern Edition), p. A1.

Contributors

Lori G. Beaman is an assistant professor in the Department of Sociology at the University of Lethbridge. Her past career as a lawyer and her passion for social activism, particularly around the issues of woman abuse and legal aid, have imported a grounded quality in her teaching and her research. She is currently working on legal conceptualizations of religion in Canada, as well as the ways in which law reconstructs notions of the "normal."

Jennifer Butters received her Masters in Sociology from the University of Western Ontario and is currently a Ph.D. candidate in Sociology at the University of Toronto. She has been working at the Addiction Research Foundation division of the Centre for Addiction and Mental Health since 1995 as a Research Assistant and holds a Pre-Doctoral fellowship in the collaborative program: Alcohol, Tobacco, and Other Psychoactive Substances. Her research has focused on crack cocaine and drug market violence and her other research interests include adolescent drug use, issues pertaining to women and drugs, and the sociology of health. She has co-authored three book chapters, has presented and collaborated on several conference papers and recently completed a research report entitled *Poor Women and Crack Use in Downtown Toronto.*

Jason Doherty completed a Bachelor of Arts degree in Sociology at St. Thomas University in 1997. Jason's undergraduate thesis focused on the social organization of labour in urban waste disposal. He is currently working on a Master of Arts degree in Sociology at Acadia University. The focus of Jason's study is the relationship between labour, management, and consumer members in the Atlantic Canadian consumer co-operative movement. The purpose of this study is to bring attention to the role of labour in the Atlantic co-operative movement and to contribute to the viability of the co-operative economic strategy.

"Nob" (after Nobby Stiles—England midfielder in the 1966 World Cup Finals) Doran was born in Luton, Bedfordshire, England. Came to Canada in the "Thatcher years" to pursue a higher degree while waiting for the economy to pick up. Obtained an M.A. and a Ph.D. from the University of Calgary, then taught on the sessional circuit at universities in Saskatchewan, Newfoundland, and Ontario, but is now associated with the Deparment of Social Science at the University of New Brunswick, Saint John. Is still trying to work out exactly what happened with the economy.

Patricia Erickson is a Senior Scientist with the Addiction Research Foundation Division of the recently formed Centre for Addiction and Mental Health. She is also Adjunct Professor and member of the Graduate Faculty in the Department of Sociology at the University of Toronto, and just completed a term as Director of the Collaborative Graduate Program in Alcohol, Tobacco and Other Psychoactive Substances there. She received her doctorate from the University of Glasgow, Scotland.

Her books include *The Steel Drug: Cocaine and Crack in Perspective* (1994) and *Cannabis Criminals: The Social Effects of Punishment on Drug Users* (1980), and she is also co- editor of *Illicit Drugs in Canada: A Risky Business* (1988) and *Windows on Science* (1992). Her most recent book is an edited collection, *Harm Reduction: A New Direction for Drug Policies and Programs* (1997) published by the University of Toronto Press . She is author or co-author of nearly 60 articles for scientific books or journals, and has been invited to speak at many professional and community meetings.

In 1996, she received the Alfred R. Lindesmith Award for achievement in scholarship and writing from the Drug Policy Foundation of Washington, DC.

Jo-Anne Fiske is Associate Professor of Anthropology and Women's Studies at the University of Northern British Columbia. She has published numerous articles in the areas of ethnohistory and cultural relations of the First Nations of central British Columbia, legal pluralism, and on the cultural impact of colonial education. She is co-editor of *New Faces of the Fur Trade*, and is currently engaged in research on issues of constructions of deviance and the institutionalization of children.

Leonard Green currently teaches criminology at St. Thomas University. He received his B.A. (History) from the University of New Brunswick (1986), and M.A. (Criminology) from the University of Toronto (1997), and is preparing to do his Ph.D. in Education. His focus is on the systemic response to ADHD; how the criminal justice system deals with these phenomena, and what role the education system plays in socializing those so-disordered.

Leonard's research interests developed from his own work as a Youth Care Worker, a position he held for a number of years following the completion of his B.A. In this capacity, he experienced first-hand the way systems dealt with ADHD. In the past several years, he has watched as some youth progressed to the adult correctional system and others were able to lead more socially-acceptable lives.

Deborah Harrison is Professor of Sociology and Director of the Muriel McQueen Fergusson Centre for Family Violence Research at the University of New Brunswick. She is author of *The Limits of Liberalism: The Making of Canadian Sociology* (Montréal: Black Rose, 1982), co-editor of *Fragile Truths: 25 Years of Sociology and Anthropology in Canada* (Ottawa: Carleton University Press, 1992), co-author of *No Life Like It: Military Wives in Canada* (Toronto: James Lorimer and Company, 1994), and has published numerous articles. She is presently national coordinator of a study on The Canadian Forces' Response to Woman Abuse which is being conducted jointly by the Muriel McQueen Fergusson Centre and the RESOLVE Research and Education Centre on Violence and Abuse in Manitoba.

Rebecca Johnson is an assistant professor in the Faculty of Law at the University of New Brunswick, where she teaches consitutional law, criminal law, and feminist advocacy. Currently completing an S.J.D. through the University of Michigan, her dissertation explores the ways that women's lives are marked by different combinations of privilege and disadvantage through the intersection of gender with race, class, and sexual orientation. In her life before law, she studied music, then management. She is looking forward to integrating these diverse interests in a course she is preparing to teach representations of women and law in popular culture narratives.

Sandra Kirby is Chair of the Sociology Department at the University of Winnipeg, a former Olympic rower and co-author of the first national survey dealing with high performance athletes and sexual harassment. She is a past president of the Canadian Research Institute for the Advancement of Women (CRIAW) and is a member of the Advisory Council to the Canadian Centre for Ethics and Sport (CCES). Her current research areas include sexual harassment and abuse in sport, lesbian struggles for human rights, and research methods and ethics.

Danielle Laberge is a professor in the Department of Sociology, University of Quebec in Montreal where she teaches methodology, epistemology and sociology of marginality and social control. She is also the scientific coordinator of a research team on homelessness and extreme poverty. Her areas of expertise relate to the use of the penal system in regard to various situations (mental illness, poverty, homelesness, drug abuse).

Pierre Landreville is a professor at the School of Criminology and researcher at the International Centre for Comparative Criminology, University of Montréal. He specializes in questions related to penology, the functioning of the criminal justice system, and more genarally to the sociology of social control.

Nick Larsen is the Criminal Justice Coordinator in the Department of Sociology at Chapman University in Orange County, California. His research interests encompass several areas in law and society, including prostitution control policies, comparative criminal justice, and Native American law/Aboriginal justice. He has published numerous articles on prostitution control in refereed journals. In addition, he has edited a reader, *The Canadian Criminal Justice System: An Issues Approach to the Administration of Justice in Canada* (Canadian Scholars Press, 1995). He is currently engaged in comparative research into Native American justice in Canada and the United States.

Gayle MacDonald is an Associate Professor of Sociology and Criminology at St. Thomas University in Fredericton, New Brunswick. Her areas of research include feminist jurisprudence, sociology of law, and critical criminological theory.

Beverly Matthews completed her Ph.D. in Social Demography at the University of Western Ontario. Her dissertation examined gender structures and fertility strategies. She has taught for both the University of Western Ontario and Memorial University of Newfoundland.

Bev has been at the University of Lethbridge since 1996. In addition to studying the connections between gender and family patterns (cohabitation, marriage, child-bearing, and divorce), she has also undertaken qualitative research into gender and adolescence.

Daphné Morin is a reseach officer in the the the Department of Sociology, University of Quebec in Montreal. She specializes in the study of marginality and social control. She has done extensive research on mental illness and homelessness in a gendered perspective.

Kristine Peace currently studies at the University of Lethbridge. Her research interests include the sociological and psychological study of crime, particularly violent crime, as well as decisions made within the judicial and correctional systems. She has also conducted research on religion, the custody rights of mothers, and legal discourse. Her e-mail address is: kpeace@telusplanet.net.

William Ramp is Assistant Professor of Sociology at the University of Lethbridge, Alberta, Canada. His interests include sociological theories of identity, narrative and embodiment (especially as applied to concepts of citizenship), models of personhood, and forms of community. He is involved in research into the moral and civic ideals of agrarian and co-operative movements in the early 20th century, and into the religious roots of modern concepts of personhood and identity. He has written on contemporary applications of the sociology of Emile Durkheim, and on the relation between Durkheimian sociology and the work of Michel Foucault.

Ted Schrecker (tschrecker@compuserve.com), a political scientist by training, makes his living as a consultant in policy analysis and evaluation, addressing issues as diverse as biotechnology patenting and ethics in the mental health field. He is also an Adjunct Assistant Professor in the Faculty of Environmental Studies, University of Waterloo. He is the author of numerous articles and book chapters, and the editor of *Surviving Globalism: The Social and Environmental Challenges* (London: Macmillan, 1997). In 1998, he was one of just two private scholars to receive an award under the "Trends" program sponsored jointly by the Social Sciences and Humanities Research Council and the Government of Canada's Policy Research Secretariat.

Krista Sneddon worked towards a B.A. in English at the University of Lethbridge, with a parallel passion for study into the roots of societal deviance, the imbalance of power evident in the sociology of law, and the diminishment of the individual through societal and personal surveillance. She has conducted research into the evolution of crime and punishment, the role of the heretic in the formation of a definitive framework for deviance and Foucauldian theory—knowledge is power. On the literary side of the coin, Sneddon has researched the influence of postmodern theory on the development of literary criticism. Krista Sneddon works as a military officer, a journalist, and a freelance writer.

Sandra Wachholz received her Ph.D. in criminology from the Criminal Justice Center at Sam Houston State University in Huntsville, Texas. Her research interests focus on the relationship between female victimization and structural oppression. She is currently teaching in the Criminology Department at the University of Southern Maine in Portland, Maine. She was a Fulbright Scholar at the University of Stockholm during the 1987–88 academic year.

Index